New Directions in Regional Economic Development

New Directions in Regional Economic Development

The Role of Entrepreneurship Theory and Methods, Practice and Policy

Edited by

Sameeksha Desai

Indiana University, USA

Peter Nijkamp

Free University of Amsterdam, the Netherlands

Roger R. Stough

George Mason University, USA

Edward Elgar

Cheltenham, UK • Northampton, MA, USA

Published by
Edward Elgar Publishing Limited
The Lypiatts
15 Lansdown Road
Cheltenham
Glos GL50 2JA
UK

Edward Elgar Publishing, Inc.
William Pratt House
9 Dewey Court
Northampton
Massachusetts 01060
USA

A catalogue record for this book
is available from the British Library

Library of Congress Control Number: 2011924165

MIX
Paper from responsible sources
FSC® C018575

ISBN 978 1 84844 421 8

Typeset by Servis Filmsetting Ltd, Stockport, Cheshire
Printed and bound by MPG Books Group, UK

Contents

Contributors

David Audretsch, Director, Institute for Development Strategies; Ameritech Chair of Economic Development, Indiana University, Bloomington, IN, USA.

Tüzin Baycan-Levent, Associate Professor, Istanbul Technical University, Istanbul, Turkey.

Werner Bönte, Schumpeter School of Business and Economics, Bergische Universität, Wuppertal, Germany.

Terrence E. Brown, Associate Professor in Entrepreneurship and Innovation, Royal Institute of Technology, Stockholm, Sweden.

Shaoming Cheng, Department of Public Administration, Florida International University, Miami, FL, USA.

Tobias Dalhammar, Rural Development Associate, Länsstyrelsen, Skåne län, Sweden.

Sameeksha Desai, Assistant Professor, Indiana University School of Public and Environmental Affairs Bloomington, IN, USA.

Peter M. Frank, Assistant Professor of Economics, Wingate University, Wingate, NC, USA.

Marina van Geenhuizen, Professor of Innovation and Innovation Policy in the Urban Economy, Delft University of Technology, the Netherlands.

Börje Johansson, Jönköping International Business School and Centre of Excellence for Science and Innovation Studies (CESIS), Department for Transport and Economics, Royal Institute of Technology, Stockholm, Sweden.

Charlie Karlsson, Professor of the Economics of Technological Change, Jönköping International Business School and Centre of Excellence for Science and Innovation Studies (CESIS), Department for Transport and Economics, Royal Institute of Technology, Stockholm, Sweden.

Max Keilbach, Max Plank Institute of Economics, Jena, Germany.

Hans Lööf, Jönköping International Business School and Centre of Excellence for Science and Innovation Studies (CESIS), Department for Transport and Economics, Royal Institute of Technology, Stockholm, Sweden.

Ronald W. McQuaid, Director Employment Research Institute (ERI), Business School, Edinburgh Napier University, UK.

Peter Nijkamp, Department of Spatial Economics, Free University, Amsterdam, the Netherlands.

Kristina Nyström, Ratio Institute, Stockholm, Sweden.

Brigitte Preissl, Editor-in-Chief, *Intereconomics*, Wirtschaftsdienst, German National Library of Economics, Hamburg, Germany.

John Sacco, Associate Professor, Department of Public and International Affairs, George Mason University, Fairfax, VA, USA.

Danny P. Soetanto, Institute for Entrepreneurship and Enterprise Development, Lancaster University Management School, Lancaster, UK.

Odd J. Stalebrink, Associate Professor of Public Administration, School of Public Affairs, Pennsylvania State University, USA.

Robert J. Stimson, University of Queensland, Australia.

Roger R. Stough, School of Public Policy, George Mason University, Fairfax, VA, USA.

Maria Teresa de Noronha Vaz, Research Centre for Spatial and Organizational Dynamics, Faculty of Economics, Universidade do Algarve, Campus de Gambelas, Faro, Portugal.

Junbo Yu, Associate Professor, School of Administration, Jilin University, Changchun, China.

Acknowledgements

The editors thank all of the contributors to this book for their multiple efforts to respond to the reviewers' concerns and in finalizing a variety of issues with the format, references, tables and figures required to bring the book to a full professional and publishable level. Also, several persons worked on compiling, editing and revising the material. These included Dabasree Das Gupta and Ghazia Aslam, both from the School of Public Policy at George Mason University, and Julianne Baum who has worked with the team at George Mason to finalize other books. Without their committed and diligent effort the book could not have been developed to a publishable level. Finally we thank Donna Sherrard at George Mason University for managing the diverse and extensive communication required to manage the development of a volume with many different contributors.

PART I

Theory and methods in entrepreneurship and development

1. New directions in regional economic development: an introduction

Roger R. Stough, Sameeksha Desai and Peter Nijkamp

1.1 INTRODUCTION

The field of regional economic development has been transformed by the emergence of endogenous economic growth theory (Romer, 1986, 1990). It has unleashed a flurry of new hypotheses and related inquiries that have in turn created an exciting dynamic in the conceptual, theoretical and empirical foundations of the field. The central feature of the endogenous perspective at the local regional level is the recognition that local initiative matters in how a region grows, adapts to change and adjusts to disequilibrating physical and societal shocks. These include but are not limited to climate change and weather phenomena such as hurricanes, tsunamis and droughts, as well as other non-physical events including wars, cyclical change, new technology and paradigmatic political change. While macro-level resource and development adjustments as always are important for adapting to such shocks, local regions make positive growth-inducing adjustments when they marshal local leadership (Stimson et al., 2009) and use local resources to plan for and drive toward a fruitful adjustment or transformative course for growth and development. It is against this contextual background that we examine some of the new directions in regional economic development.

A major tenet of endogenous growth thinking is that technical change in the first place occurs at the local regional level, thereby focusing and in fact revolutionizing the Solow (1956) seminal conclusion that technological change was the variable that accounted for the discovery that classical factors of production barely explained half of the variance in national economic growth. Because the unit of analysis for this research was at the macro level there remained an unanswered question of exactly how such change occurred. Recent theoretical and empirical research (Acs et al., 2009; Audretsch and Lehmann, 2005) has focused on the creation and transmission of knowledge as the front end of the technical change process and, more generally, the full commercialization of knowledge (Chesbrough et al., 2006). It seems a reasonable conclusion from this work that knowledge and its transformation into economically useful knowledge is a basic element contributing to new research in the field as it provides the key to the origins of the technical change process. We see this to be the case and thus have interpreted the significance of the contribution in terms of this accordingly.

Knowledge is produced in many ways. Universities, research centers and large corporate (public and private) organizations are primary knowledge creation centers. But these are not the only sources of new knowledge as it arises from all sorts of human contemplation and interaction including even the seemingly mundane musings of the fisherman, hiker, commuter and so on. The current time is often referred to as the knowledge age because it is a period of high knowledge creation due to recent innovations in information and communications technology (ICT) that amplify society's ability to produce it and to share it with others, regardless of the source. At the same time, knowledge in its pure form is nothing more than that, and without extensive amplification it usually fails to become economically useful. It is the amplification of knowledge that is critical for the technical change process to produce fruit. How does this amplification occur? Theory has it that it is via the entrepreneur (Acs et al., 2009). The role of the entrepreneur is to see opportunity in knowledge (Schumpeter, 1934), and good ones see opportunity where others do not (Kirzner, 1994 [1985]). The role of the entrepreneur in the technical change process is a major reason why entrepreneurship has become an intense focus of research not only in the technical change literature, but also in the field of regional science as the world of the entrepreneur exists most fully at the local regional level – the level where knowledge is created. This is yet another reason why this book holds entrepreneurship as a primary focus.

But it is not enough to recognize the leadership role of the entrepreneur in knowledge commercialization and the technical change process because there are barriers to entrepreneurial performance that vary from one region to another (and from one nation to another). So the context within which technical change and knowledge commercialization occur is not homogeneous. Acs et al. (2004) have proposed the concept of a 'knowledge filter' that, in their view, offers an explanation for the variation in the rate at which knowledge and knowledge conversion can occur, and likewise variation in the level of entrepreneurial success. The knowledge filter is that which facilitates or detracts from the ease with which both entrepreneurship and knowledge commercialization occur. If the filter is highly restrictive, it is difficult for knowledge to move from its raw form to that which is economically useful. A highly restrictive knowledge filter (for example where the regulatory environment is excessive, capital availability constrained, and the time to form a business is long) creates many barriers for entrepreneurship, thus inhibiting it. At the same time, if the filter is insufficient to prevent chaotic behavior or destructive entrepreneurship (Baumol, 1990), the same inhibiting or inefficient outcome is expected. The knowledge filter then is similar if not analogous to the effect of the social construct of institutional capital (Williamson, 1994): when extremely strong (or extremely weak) it creates many barriers to the process of producing economically useful knowledge and thus supporting entrepreneurial behavior. In short, the relationship between the quality of the technical change environment and the knowledge filter (also institutional quality or capital) is ∩ shaped. The best conditions for technical change and the entrepreneur to create economically valuable knowledge are when the knowledge filter is neither too restrictive nor too relaxed or limited.

One of the most important insights arising from endogenous growth thinking is that technical change is primarily a phenomenon of the local regional context. Viewing technical change as a local motivating phenomenon of economic development, that is in turn driven by knowledge and its transformation into economic useful knowledge (or commercial goods and services) by the entrepreneur, has created a new and enlightening dynamic in the study of regional economic development. It has elevated study of the entrepreneur from almost a non-existent status in the field to a central one in little more than a decade. Today there are a number of important questions about the role of the entrepreneur and entrepreneurship in regional economic development. A number of these are considered in the contributions to this volume. These can be grouped under several major topical areas that relate to the rise of the knowledge age as described above, and in turn to the rise of the entrepreneur in regional economic development. These are:

- The entrepreneur and their place in regional economic development.
- The role and significance of entrepreneurship in regional economic growth.
- The relationship between innovation and entrepreneurship and public policy.
- The nature and importance of knowledge and economically useful knowledge.
- Knowledge commercialization and related barriers – the knowledge filter.

There are both theoretical and conceptual, and empirical questions embedded in each of these general topics. The entrepreneur has been conceptualized as an agent of both general social development and as an agent of the firm or business establishment. Only recently has the entrepreneur been envisioned as an agent of regional economic growth, thus the sorting out what if any overlap with the traditional factors of production exists calls for further theoretical discourse and empirical research. Entrepreneurship has a strong and sometimes confounding relation to other constructs such as leadership and innovation. It is important for the formation of public policy to understand more clearly the difference between entrepreneurship and other constructs that may have a longer lineage in the scholarly realm and may offer competing avenues for policy. Another area where some ambiguity exists is with the knowledge construct itself. For example, critical questions remain regarding how knowledge is created: by a single agent or in a more social context. However, the classical notion of proximity appears to continue to play an important role. Consequently there are questions about accessibility to knowledge (socially and physically). Accessibility is a beginning requirement for the transformation of knowledge into an economically useful form. One question in this context that has occupied the thinking of regional economic scholars is whether knowledge access is enhanced among organizations that form an industrial cluster relative to those that are not clustered. Finally, there are a large number of questions about the barriers to knowledge commercialization, that is, the process whereby raw knowledge is transformed into useful goods and services or commercialized. These focus specifically on the knowledge filter and its components that serve to constrain or accelerate its transformation and entrepreneurial success. Potential barriers of importance are: regulatory burden; availability of capital; industrial structure; special populations (advantaged or disadvantaged) such as migrants and ethnic minorities; availability of business incubation; and the role of high-intensity knowledge production environments like universities and research complexes. Various aspects of these topics and questions are addressed in the contributions to this book. At the same time, while the contributions fit into these general topical areas, they of course are not definitive. Rather, the book should be viewed as contributing to the scholarly debate that has been unfolding around the impacts of endogenous growth theory at the local regional level, and the rise of importance of knowledge and its conversion into useful goods and services.

The book is organized in two parts: theory and methods; and a set of case studies that contribute to the empirical literature and to issues of a public policy nature.

1.2 SUMMARY PRESENTATIONS OF THE CONTRIBUTIONS: THEORY AND METHODS

The theory and methods contributions begin with Chapter 2 by Ronald McQuaid entitled 'The entrepreneur in economic theory'. This chapter, which observes the vast and rich literature on the entrepreneur and entrepreneurship, offers perspectives on starting a business, on being the agent owner of a venture or enterprise, and on the role of personal and/or societal characteristics. While the richness of the construct illustrates its scope and reach, this also means that it has multiple meanings, which in turn has confused theoretical and policy debate, especially in a spatial or local regional context. McQuaid's chapter examines these different perspectives on entrepreneurship and the entrepreneur, concluding that the multiple meanings create considerable opportunity for ambiguity and contradiction when applied in a regional or spatial context. He concludes his analysis with an argument that a synthesis is needed, and proposes a 2 × 2 matrix model whereby the 'different' entrepreneurs are arrayed in relationship to different regional and spatial environments.

Professors John Sacco and Odd Stalebrink in Chapter 3 theoretically examine the nature of what they call 'public sector venture capitalism', or the provision by the public sector of capital for the promotion of private ventures. They identify two major sources of capital for supporting venture formation and growth: the private sector (public investment in firms and private capital); and the public sector. Market imperfection is viewed as the primary class of arguments for public sector investment in private ventures. The European Union Regional Policy and associated fund provides one illustration of a government-supplied venture fund and the problems that arise when government takes on the role of providing capital for private sector ventures. The concluding recommendation is to adopt third-party governance for public venturing projects – this may offer a partial solution to the inefficiencies that arise in such venturing, and in the extreme case where it was operated in a totally 'hands-off' or 'invisible' manner.

In Chapter 4, entitled 'Determinants and impact of entrepreneurship capital: the spatial dimension and a comparison of different econometric approaches', David Audretsch, Werner Bönte and Max Keilbach introduce the concept of entrepreneurship capital, and examine its determinants and impact. They empirically examine the construct of entrepreneurship capital using a production function analysis approach applied to regions in Germany and, while controlling for spatial effects, find that entrepreneurship contributes significantly (was statistically significant) to regional growth along with the traditional factors of production. They also find, and again significantly, that there is an indirect effect of 'technical knowledge' on economic growth, but through entrepreneurship. This is important because it provides some empirical supporting evidence to the claim that entrepreneurship contributes to technical knowledge conversion into growth-producing outcomes, as discussed above. The authors go on to examine these effects with respect to other growth-explaining variables and then interpret the policy implications.

In Chapter 5 Maria Teresa de Noronha Vaz examines the relationship between cooperation, innovation and location, and related policy issues. First she examines determinants of firm location and embeddedness, and relates them to innovative firm activity. Then she considers patterns of industrialization and firm governance models which are used to create a topology for coordination models. Both of these exercises are used to create a conceptual framework for the trajectory that firms follow to achieve innovation in the postmodern era. This trajectory frame begins with spatial embeddedness that in turn leads to technological learning, interfirm coordination models, and on to entrepreneurial strategies. The attributes of the different stages are explained. The trajectory frame is applied in a case study of the agro-food industry as a means to illustrate the interpretive value of this approach. The rest of the chapter explores the policy implications of the analysis and interpretive model.

Chapter 6, entitled 'Differentials in industrial structure and human capital performance across Australia's regions and the settlement system', is written by Robert Stimson. His study of recent regional trends and patterns in industrial structure and human capital, and education and occupation levels, provides a number of insights into the changing conditions in Australia's regions. This is useful in the present context in that it shows that education level – that is, quality of human capital – is rising across the country but more rapidly in metropolitan regions; that industrial structure is trending more toward technology-intensive industries; and that high-income employment is concentrating in metropolitan areas and in 'symbolic analyst' or knowledge-intensive sectors associated with the 'new economy'. Major growth dynamics tend to be concentrated in urban as opposed to more remote locations. This provides a summary of empirically grounded trends that are seen to be emerging in most of the advanced economies. Important for this book is that the stronger regional growth and development dynamics are located in urban areas, which is also the case for knowledge production, knowledge commercialization and especially technology- (knowledge-) intensive entrepreneurship.

Chapter 7 authored by Brigitte Preissl is entitled 'Innovation clusters linking regions'. Preissl examines the well-appreciated thesis that innovation-intensive firms benefit from spatial clustering, due to the ease of knowledge sharing that occurs in a proximal environment where firms have similar or related industrial agendas. Her analysis of knowledge transfer chains in the German automotive industry reveals that timing and quality knowledge inputs are critical for innovation, while the transfer of this knowledge into economically useful knowledge (goods and services) occurs best in environments where relations are based on trust and tacit exchange of information or knowledge. In this sense this chapter complements Chapter 5 by Maria Teresa de Noronha Vaz. A conclusion is then that access to the inputs to innovative performance is easier in a cluster than in market transactions. However, affiliated conclusions are that other non-agglomerative attributes of clusters also are important. One of these is previous or historical interaction among participating organizations, like that which occurs in industrial cluster environments.

1.3 SUMMARIES OF THE CONTRIBUTIONS: CASE STUDIES

Part II of the book focuses on specific issues related to facilitation of the knowledge commercialization or transfer process that are mostly empirical in nature. In each case the analysis is geographically contained in one or more regions and subregions. In short, the cases are region-specific. The importance of this is that spatially disaggregated analyses are possible, which in turn enable, in most cases, the investigator to generate specific empirically based research results.

The first chapter in Part II, Chapter 8, entitled 'Explaining China's economic growth: does entrepreneurship matter?' is by Junbo Yu, Shaoming Cheng and Roger Stough. This chapter examines two research questions: 'How does the interaction between entrepreneurship and entrepreneurship policy contribute to the form, resilience and sustainability of regional economies?' and 'What is the contribution of entrepreneurship to economic growth in transitional economies?' The contribution of entrepreneurship to economic growth among regions in China is examined, using an aggregate production function approach. The findings of this study are compatible with the work of Audretsch and Lehmann (2005). Yu, Cheng and Stough conclude from the policy perspective that: 'under certain conditions, policies focusing on enhancing entrepreneurship capital can prove to be more effective than those targeting the more traditional factors, such as labor'.

Charlie Karlsson and Kristina Nyström, using data from Swedish regions, examine 'Knowledge accessibility and new firm formation' in Chapter 9. They observe that knowledge is often concentrated in a few regions, much as noted in Chapter 6 by Robert Stimson with the Australia case. The huge spatial differences in knowledge in turn lead to large differences in accessibility, partly because the differences in knowledge stock are large and partly because flows of knowledge are in part spatially bounded. In short, accessing and internalizing knowledge is costly, and proximity of the source and the use of knowledge reduce the cost of technically motivated economic change. This leads to a hypothesis that there will be greater new firm formation activities in the regions with more accessibility to knowledge. The empirical investigation confirms the hypothesis along with a series of nuances and caveats.

Tüzin Baycan-Levent and Peter Nijkamp in Chapter 10 examine the driving forces, motivation and performance of migrant female entrepreneurship. The topic is examined via interpretive analysis of a serious review of the literature, and then complemented with an empirical analysis using a rough set analysis methodology of Turkish female entrepreneurs in Amsterdam, the Netherlands. Rough set analysis is useful for extracting information including decision rules from a complex multivariate data set. Because the assumptions are minimal it is also possible to work with their small but diverse sample data set. Critical success variables (rules) for producing profit and sustained development uncovered using rough set analysis include Dutch language ability, initial conditions, other entrepreneurs in the family, employment size and gender. This initial investigation produces a series of working hypotheses in the form of the rule structure of success, and concludes that further research is necessary for further testing.

Tobias Dalhammar and Terrence Brown undertake another investigation of immigrant-created enterprises in Stockholm, Sweden. This contribution, Chapter 11, examines hypotheses about the industrial effects on resource acquisition in immigrant enterprises. There has been a rapid rise of ethnic minority entrepreneurs in Sweden over the past ten or so years. As such it provokes questions not only as to why, but even more importantly about how cultural pull factors are or are not operating and, on the other hand, also structural push factors. The cultural variable operates as a pull factor in that migrants to a new country often first arrive and locate in ethnic enclaves. At the same time immigrants are usually discriminated against in the labor market, a major factor pushing them toward entrepreneurship. The authors observe that despite these generally known factors that influence or push ethnic minorities toward entrepreneurship, these do not explain the great variation found in their involvement in entrepreneurship and business activities in general. The authors recognize a third approach, called the interactive theory, which considers relationships between these and the conditions of migrant entrepreneurs' initial settlement upon arrival. These and other hypotheses are examined through a series of case studies ranging from involvement in ethnic services such as restaurants, to science- and technology-intensive involvement.

In Chapter 12, Peter Frank examines the question of how regions establish growth via entrepreneurship. His chapter, entitled 'The entrepreneurial environment: business incubation in the Charlotte metropolitan region' reports on this by first examining the entrepreneurial environment and then the role that business incubation provides. His examination of the environment or context in Charlotte for entrepreneurship concludes that the preconditions for entrepreneurship are minimal, that is, one would conclude that the knowledge filter in Charlotte is rather tightly meshed. He goes on to examine various incubation models that exist in the study region. A conclusion of this contribution is that a development policy to attract high-quality human capital, that is, innovative and creative workers, is an essential adjunct along with any other investments such as incubation facilities designed to attract and/or support start-up ventures.

Marina van Geenhuizen and Danny Soetanto have contributed Chapter 13, entitled 'University spin-offs: an exploration of age-patterns of obstacles to growth'. The Bayh–Dole Act in the US in the mid-1980s spurred universities to develop technology transfer programs that often involved technology- or knowledge-specialized business start-ups that were spin-offs of university research. The trend to form such programs did not end in the US, but in the 2000s spread to other continents. In this chapter Geenhuizen and Soetanto examine the factors that influence the success of such university-based ventures at different stages of development. Their analysis is based on a sample of some 43 spin-offs at the Delft University of Technology. The empirical analysis finds that early-stage university-based ventures have better ability to solve and prevent problems than those in later stages of development (three or four years on). Based on these findings, the authors offer alternative models for preventing and solving such problems, especially for highly innovative and often technology-intensive ventures. Quantitative and interpretive analysis provide design guidance for transforming existing incubation policies for university spin-offs.

The final contribution, Chapter 14 by Börje Johansson and Hans Lööf, examines the inflows of foreign direct investment (FDI) to Sweden and its consequences for innovation and renewal at the local regional level. This research is empirical and uses a firm-specific data set (2086 firms) to examine innovativeness and the ability to renew firm-level competitiveness. Four classes of firms are created out of the data set, with one end of this classification spectrum being uninational and the other transnational firms. The research, using a variety of descriptive statistical data and regression modeling, finds that uninational firms are less integrated than all the other more open firm classes in a variety of forms of innovative collaboration, and that uninationals have fewer product and process innovations and exhibit lower levels of non-imitation innovations. In short, FDI coming from the transnational context promotes greater innovativeness in the case of Sweden. The policy implications are reasonably obvious for Sweden's economic development and growth, and it is not unreasonable to assume *ceteris paribus* that the findings for Sweden are similar to what one would find in other countries. However a caveat may exist in that the small size of Sweden's home market, and rules governing industry structure, may counter, in part, generalizing the findings obtained for Sweden.

REFERENCES

Acs, A., D. Audretsch, P. Braunerhjelm and B. Carlsson (2004), 'The missing link: the knowledge filter and entrepreneurship in endogenous growth', Discussion Paper no. 4783, London: Centre for Economic Policy Research.

Acs, Z., P. Braunerhjelm, D. Audretsch and B. Carlsson (2009), 'The knowledge spillover theory of entrepreneurship', *Small Business Economics*, **32**, 15–30.

Audretsch, D. and E. Lehmann (2005), 'Does the knowledge spillover theory of entrepreneurship hold for regions?' *Research Policy*, **34**, 1191–1202.

Baumol, W.J. (1990), 'Entrepreneurship: productivity, unproductive, and destructive', *Journal of Political Economy*, **98**(5), 893–921.

Chesbrough, H., W. Vanhaverbeke and J. West (eds) (2006), *Open Innovation: Researching a New Paradigm*, Oxford: Oxford University Press.

Kirzner, J. (1994), 'The entrepreneur in economic theory', in E. Dahmen, L. Hannah and I.M. Kirzner (eds), *The Dynamics of Entrepreneurship*, Lund: Lund University Press, pp. 146–74. First published 1985, Crafoord Lectures No. 5.

Romer, P. (1986), 'Increasing returns and long run growth', *Journal of Political Economy*, **94**, 1002–37.

Romer, P.M. (1990), 'Endogenous technological change', *Journal of Political Economy*, **98**, S71–S102.

Schumpeter, J.A. (1934), *The Theory of Economic Development*, Cambridge, MA: Harvard University Press.

Solow, R.M. (1956), 'A contribution to the theory of economic growth', *Quarterly Journal of Economics*, **70**, 65–94.

Stimson, R., R. Stough and M. Salazar (2009), *Leadership and Institutions in Regional Endogenous Development*, Cheltenham, UK and Northampton, MA, USA: Edward Elgar Publishing.

Williamson, O.E. (1994), *Institutions and Economic Organization: The Governance Perspective*, Washington, DC: World Bank.

2. The entrepreneur in economic theory

Ronald W. McQuaid

2.1 INTRODUCTION

Entrepreneurship has been seen as key to economic development in many countries across the globe for many years (OECD, 1998, 2003; UN, 2004). For instance, in the European Union's Employment Strategies entrepreneurship has been given a major role in increasing the dynamism of economies and helping employment creation and improvement (CEC, 1999, 2005).

However, there are a variety of meanings of the term 'entrepreneurship', which permeate and confuse the policy and theoretical debates. Indeed entrepreneurship is an elusive concept associated with a number of overlapping but distinct perspectives and meanings (Ahmed and McQuaid, 2005; Glancey and McQuaid, 2000). Sometimes the concept of entrepreneurship has been taken to mean: a new business start-up; an owner-manager of a small, micro or medium-sized enterprise (SMME); a function in the economy (such as resource allocation, risk-taking, 'middleman' or innovation); a form of behavior (with an entrepreneur being someone who purposefully and systematically searches and analyses change to identify and take the opportunities such changes might offer for economic or social innovation); a set of social or personal characteristics (such as being a great leader).

Each of these perspectives has different implications for policies and for theory, yet the precise meaning or perspective on entrepreneurship is often not made explicit, as many writers implicitly combine more than one of these perspectives. Indeed, a more general theory of entrepreneurship might contain elements from all these perspectives, and regional economic development theory might include an explicit role for entrepreneurship grounded more in entrepreneurship theory.

Much theory has neglected the role of the individual and of entrepreneurship in the regional or national economy and in the competitiveness of organizations, for example in much of traditional neoclassical economics

(Baumol, 1987). However, earlier classical economists, such as Adam Smith, recognized the role of entrepreneurship and since the 1980s its role has begun to be incorporated, to a greater extent at least, in theoretical and applied analysis and synthesis at local, regional and national levels. At a regional level de Groot et al. (2004) argue that while the endogenous growth revolution has helped put risk-taking individuals in the center of economic analysis, Schumpeter's thoughts on innovation are also emphasized (so combining at least two perspectives on the meaning of entrepreneurship). They suggest that space still has a limited role in the dynamic endogenous growth theory, while innovation and economic growth are largely missing in more static new economic geography. Hence there remains a need to bring together space, innovation and economic growth linked together with entrepreneurship.

This chapter considers different perspectives of entrepreneurship and argues that there is a need to bring these into the main theoretical developments linking space and the dynamism, development and adaptability of an economy and society over time (including its response to concerns about the natural environment). However, it argues that we should be explicit as to what we mean when using the term 'entrepreneurship'. These different perspectives are not mutually exclusive. Audretsch (1995) and Cunningham and Lischeron (1991) argue that the term 'entrepreneurship' in itself has three levels of meaning. At the first level entrepreneurship refers to small firms or enterprises. At the second level it refers to new firm formation; and at the third (highest) level it entails innovation and a system-wide coordination of complex production (see also Audretsch and Thurik, 2004). Malechi (1997, p. 157) overlaps this view in arguing that entrepreneurship embraces small businesses and also wider innovation and regional and local development policy. Another form of analysis has been to consider new firm failure (and success) at three levels: micro (individual), meso (market opportunity – which may vary spatially) and macro (national economic, social and cultural factors) (Verheul et al., 2002).

This chapter does not argue that one perspective or definition of entrepreneurship is correct or necessarily better than the others. Rather, it seeks to clarify some of its different meanings, so we can be clear about the differing underlying assumptions and concepts being used, and to draw out some implications for theory and regional development. These five perspectives are now considered in the next sections:

- Entrepreneurship as creating a new business.
- Owner-managers and small, micro and medium-sized enterprise.
- Entrepreneurship as an economic function.

- Entrepreneurship as a form of behaviour.
- Entrepreneurship as a set of personal characteristics.

This is followed by a discussion of issues and synthesis and conclusions.

2.2 ENTREPRENEURSHIP AS CREATING A NEW BUSINESS

The first perspective on entrepreneurship concerns the act or event of setting up a new business (Gartner, 1988). This focuses upon the process of creating a new organization, rather than on who owns or manages it. It suggests that the entrepreneurial role ends once a new organization has been created. The organization itself may continue (perhaps to growth, maturity and decline), but the original entrepreneur takes on different roles in each stage, moving from being an innovator to the non-entrepreneurial roles of being a small business owner, or senior manager of the firm if it becomes large.

This view has been an important component of theories and policies concerning economic development policies at the local, regional and national levels, where encouragement of business start-ups often plays a major role. For example, in Scotland the economic development agency, Scottish Enterprise, had an explicit policy to increase the number of new businesses being formed through its Business Birth Rate Strategy (Scottish Enterprise, 1993). This policy appeared to be partly based upon the argument that it is not possible to 'pick winners' in terms of a priori identifying high-growth firms, and so policies should be aimed at encouraging a large number of start-ups, of whom some will be fast growth. However the success of the policy was limited (Fraser of Allander Institute, 2001), leading to a new strategy focusing on: (1) encouraging innovative high-growth new starts increasing the number and value of high-growth start-ups, including start-ups in technology-based sectors; (2) encouraging more people to start businesses, by providing high-quality business support services to large numbers of people interested in starting up, mainly through the Small Business Gateway, a chain of publicly funded local business support agencies (this includes specific support for more start-ups by women, the young and individuals from social inclusion groups); and (3) increasing the contribution of education to the development of entrepreneurship, developing enterprise among young people, school and university students, and socially excluded groups (Scottish Enterprise, 2002).

Binks and Vale (1990, p. 19) argue that such business start-up-oriented policies, if used as the exclusive means to increase employment growth, need not be synonymous with per capita income growth and may be counterproductive to wider economic development. The emphasis by Scottish Enterprise upon high-growth start-ups would appear to try to address this issue. However, if there are large numbers of start-up firms, particularly in more advanced technological sectors and in non-subsistence types of employment (taking an innovation perspective – see below), then it can be argued that some of them are likely to grow into large and high-productivity employers. Hence, new business creation is only one aspect of a sustainable economic development policy.

2.3 OWNER-MANAGERS AND SMALL, MICRO AND MEDIUM-SIZED ENTERPRISE

Entrepreneurship has often been considered as encompassing the role of the owner-manager of a small, micro or medium-sized enterprise (SMME). Some of this type of entrepreneurship can be termed 'routine entrepreneurship' (Leibenstein, 1968, p. 72) which involves the routine coordination and management of an existing business that operates in well-established and clearly defined markets. Hence there may be little innovation in such businesses, and the growth of one business may largely displace similar activity elsewhere in the local economy.

Not all SMMEs are involved in routine activities, and successful small owner-managed firms may grow rapidly and change their management and ownership structures. This perspective of entrepreneurship can sometimes fail to distinguish the 'ordinary' or routine owner-manager from one who transforms the business. However, an economy that can respond to technological, social and economic opportunities is likely also to incorporate the crucial dynamism and job and wealth creation of medium-sized and large firms, and those small firms that grow to become larger organizations. Reassessments of the history of macroeconomic performance during the twentieth century have given greater significance to the role of new and small firms (Acs et al., 1999). However, some argue that a divergence from some 'optimum' level of SMMEs in an economy (through either relatively too many or too few SMMEs) may hinder growth (see Audretsch et al., 2002).

New SMMEs are not synonymous with self-employment; some authors argue (OECD, 2003, p. 58) that self-employment and entrepreneurs(hip) are not fully interchangeable, as conditions for many of the self-employed 'differ little from those experienced by employees', and similarly many entrepreneurship researchers argue that entrepreneurship is different from small business (see Birley and Muzyka, 2000).

2.4 ENTREPRENEURSHIP AS AN ECONOMIC FUNCTION

Entrepreneurship has often been considered as having an important economic function, particularly in the use and allocation of resources to take opportunities presented by changes in the external environment and in driving innovation.

2.4.1 Resource Allocation and Risk-taking

In the eighteenth century the French writer Richard Cantillon first used the term 'entrepreneur' to describe a 'go-between' whereby the person bought goods at certain prices but sold at uncertain prices (as they could not be sure what price they would eventually sell them for). So he or she bore the risk and uncertainty of a venture but kept the surplus after the contractual payments had been made. Later, the French philosopher Jean-Baptiste Say and others widened the concept to include not only the bearing of risks, but also planning, supervising, organizing and even owning the factors of production.

Casson (1999) argues that part of the entrepreneur's role is identifying persistent shocks to the environment that will offer long-term opportunities, and then synthesizing the information and making judgmental decisions based upon it. Kirzner (1973, 1997) further emphasizes this resource allocation function of entrepreneurs as that of being a 'middleman', who is alert to and sees opportunities in the economy and uses this knowledge to gain a profit. Nelson and Winter (1982) take an evolutionary and organization approach and identify a key role for entrepreneurs in the process of economic evolution. Here the organization is a coalition of different interest groups, each with their own agenda.

Inter- and intra-regional links, infrastructure and institutions are also important in resource allocation, although an explicit role for entrepreneurship is often missing. Krugman (1991) argues that the concentration of economic activity in space is due to the increasing returns to scale in production. These are because of 'spillovers' from the pooled labor market, relating to inputs from supplier industries and so on, and information and technological factors within industries. Dynamic inter-industry clusters may also lead to agglomeration economies.

Endogenous growth theory and its application to regional economic development (Nijkamp and Poot, 1998) stresses the endogeneity to the growth process of those factors traditionally treated as exogenous in neoclassical models (such as entrepreneurship, human capital and technology), underlining the way in which some regions create an internal mechanism for promoting or perpetuating their growth. Endogenous growth, driven partly by high levels of entrepreneurship, can thus be a self-reinforcing process whereby knowledge and skills are continuously embellished and the region's competitive base is enhanced. Lucas (1988) argued that public investment in human capital generates spillover effects that increase the productivity of the general labor force and of the regional physical capital stock, and that this could be developed through greater entrepreneurship in the economy. Policies to promote entrepreneurship, improve the regional knowledge infrastructure and upgrade the level of local human capital may therefore be likely to help set in motion those forces that result in regional growth.

2.4.2 Innovation

Another important perspective on entrepreneurship is its economic function in generating innovation and change rather than responding to them, and so causing economic development (Baumol, 1993). Schumpeter (1942) stated that entrepreneurship leads to the implementation of new combinations of means of productions through: introducing new products and methods of production; opening new markets; gaining new sources inputs; or changing the structure of an organization or an industry. Schumpeter views entrepreneurship as a disequilibriating force that causes economic development and leads to the 'creative destruction' of capitalism where some large firms, new firms and industries destroy older ones. This is further discussed in the concluding section.

Many researchers consider innovation as a key component of entrepreneurship, often combining it with other perspectives. For instance, McCann and Arita (2004) consider the relationship between clusters and regional development (and what factors lead local individuals and firms to be entrepreneurial), where entrepreneurship and innovation represent 'something of a continuum which relates the development of the new product or service to the size of the firm in which it originates', hence combining the innovation and SMMEs' perspectives on entrepreneurship.

Acs and Audretsch (1988) argue that small and new firms are the main engines of innovation, due to the greater incentives for the people involved (including property rights) than for those in larger firms. However, others argue that most new businesses are not particularly innovative (Bhide, 2000), so indicating a contrast between entrepreneurship as purely starting an organization and the type of organization started. A focus on innovation does not necessarily imply a focus on new or small firms, since the relationships between a firm's age or size and innovation are not clear, as the literature on intrapreneurship implies. For instance, Harrison (1997) argued that larger firms dominate innovations, as they have resource and market entry advantages and are able to receive immediate benefits from innovations due to their scale and scope. Acs et al. (1999) found that industries where market share is more concentrated among larger firms have higher productivity growth. They suggested a Schumpeterian transition hypothesis where certain small firms may introduce radical innovations, but their impact is magnified by large firms (some of these large firms may have recently been small or new ones that grew or large ones that are particularly agile).

The social characteristics of a region are also important for innovation. Cooke and Clifton (2004) analyze the impact of small and medium-sized enterprises (SMEs) on economic development, primarily in the UK, highlighting the role of trust and social capital in a region (in terms of local links or networks, although different definitions of social capital may alter the analysis and conclusions). Formal and informal collaboration between SMEs in certain functions (such as non-confidential knowledge) can help them overcome the potential economies of scale and scope enjoyed by larger firms. They conclude that the use of social capital by SMEs is ubiquitous, although it rarely takes a non-monetary form. Storper (1995) also emphasizes the importance of social links that exist beyond the boundaries of formally stated and binding contractual relationships within production chains, with the regional as the locus of 'untraded interdependencies' such as labor markets, public institutions and locally or nationally derived rules of action, customs, understanding and values (p. 205). Hence policies which support regional institutions may be important.

2.5 ENTREPRENEURSHIP AS A FORM OF BEHAVIOR

Drucker (1985) argues that entrepreneurship is a form of behavior. He suggests that an entrepreneur is someone who 'always searches for change, responds to it, and exploits it as an opportunity' (p. 25), and that entrepreneurship is 'the purposeful and organized search for changes, and in the systematic analysis of the opportunities such changes might offer for economic or social innovation' (p. 49).

This perspective suggests that entrepreneurs can be defined by their behavior, that is, what they do, rather than who they are (or their personal characteristics). Stevenson and Sahlman (1989) argue: 'entrepreneurship is most fruitfully defined as the relentless pursuit of opportunity without regard to resources currently controlled' (p. 107). They also argue that the process of entrepreneurship starts with identifying opportunity and ends with the achievement of one's goals and gaining the rewards from one's endeavor.

Further, Stevenson (2000) links these forms of behavior to management more generally in terms of critical dimensions of business practice: strategic orientation; commitment to opportunity; commitment of resources; control of resources; management structure; and reward philosophy.

From a policy perspective this points to the need for a 'holistic' or comprehensive view of entrepreneurship incorporating the individual(s) involved, the organization they create or recreate and the external environment within which they operate. An Organisation for Economic Co-operation and Development (OECD, 2003, p. 115) report argues that support for existing social enterprise should essentially be the same as for profit-oriented firms. This may be broadly correct, although one needs to recognize the different motivation, operation and expertise on the board of directors, and the fundamentally different patterns of setting up such social enterprises.

2.6 ENTREPRENEURSHIP AS A SET OF PERSONAL CHARACTERISTICS

The fifth set of perspectives on entrepreneurship focuses upon the personal characteristics, cognitive styles and personality of the entrepreneur, and the social and institutional context in which they operate (Chell et al., 1991; Mitchell et al., 2002). This view has a long history, with Samuel Smiles writing in 1859 about famous nineteenth-century entrepreneurs in the UK. He wrote that Josiah Wedgwood 'by his energy, skill and genius, established the [porcelain and pottery] trade upon a new and solid foundation' (Smiles, 1859, p. 59) and hence employed thousands of families at good wages. According to Smiles, the key psychological traits of an entrepreneur were integrity, self-learning, courage, conscientiousness, patience, perseverance, self-discipline and self-respect. More recent psychological and sociological approaches to entrepreneurship concentrate upon: particular qualities or attitude, there being a 'great leader'; social forces (Reynolds, 1991); or motivations or the effect of personality traits in the classic work by McClelland (1961). There are also links between entrepreneurs' cognitive styles and how they learn or use knowledge and information and their behavior.

Tidd et al. (2005, p. 532) apply this focus on social and personal characteristics to help identify those factors that influence the likelihood of setting up a venture (these include family background, religion, formal education and early work experience, and psychological profile). Wider social networks are also important in the start-up process of firms (McQuaid, 1996), where non-monetary links are arguably more common, and wider, and deeper social networks may make the probability of start-up greater.

Other demographic and social characteristics that affect starting up an organization, or how it is started and managed, may include gender or ethnicity. These approaches to the characteristics of entrepreneurs have been criticized for sometimes providing long lists of traits that when taken together would result in the description of a sort of generic 'Everyman' (Storey, 1994), and they sometimes ignore the circumstances, including financial and social capital or resources and other supply and demand factors, in which the entrepreneurship takes place.

However, the study of characteristics can be useful in helping identify important policy questions. Why are certain groups or types of people over- or under-represented among entrepreneurs, and how is this changing? It has been argued, for instance, that some groups such as women or some minorities have in the past been held back by institutional forces including not being able to access appropriate finance or information so easily.

2.7 SYNTHESIS AND CONCLUSIONS

The concept of entrepreneurship is multidimensional and often unclear. There are various implicit or explicit perspectives on what entrepreneurship means, with many writers combining one or more perspectives either explicitly or implicitly. While no one perspective is necessarily more valid than the others, the questions remain: how do different perspectives of entrepreneurship influence our understanding of the different aspects of regional economic development; and what are the implications and commonalities of the different perspectives? The relationships between entrepreneurship, innovation, knowledge and information need to be more fully explored: to what degree do they represent components of the same or similar processes? The various theories of entrepreneurship have different methodologies, basic assumptions and different objectives. However, most regard entrepreneurship as a specific and vital economic function, and a key force within economies allowing them to develop and function efficiently.

The entrepreneur has an important role in helping the economy to deal with the effective diffusion and use of knowledge, innovation and change, and the associated risks and uncertainty. The question of whether entrepreneurs cause or just respond to these changes is strongly disputed but is fundamental to understanding their role in regional development and in theory.

It may be possible to develop a synthesis of the models showing that in different spatial, industrial and regional circumstances, the different perspectives on entrepreneurship may each offer insights. As discussed earlier, entrepreneurship is seen by Schumpeter (1942) as a disequilibriating force causing economic development through 'creative destruction', where entrepreneurial new or existing firms and industries destroy older ones. This view contrasts with that of Kirzner (1997), who suggests that entrepreneurship is an equilibrating force restoring markets to equilibrium through the process of price adjustment. This may be reconciled through the synthesis of a simple stylized three-staged process (see McQuaid, 2002). This starts with an innovative change, such as through entrepreneurial behaviour in certain existing or new firms or organizations (for example, through technological or organizational innovation) that creates the catalytic Schumperterian event or process (such as a new technological development). In the second stage the entrepreneurial activities of identifying resulting opportunities, deciding on actions and allocating resources to take advantage of them (for example improving competitiveness through adopting or adapting new products or process innovations). This might lead to a Kirzner (1997) type move towards equilibrium and regional convergence. However, Lachmann (1991) argues that there is no certainty of equilibrating forces outweighing disequilibriating forces and so market economies need not necessarily tend towards equilibrium at any time. Later, in the third stage, the opportunities presented by the innovations reduce or are exhausted and firms focus on improving efficiency and price competition, perhaps through 'routine' entrepreneurship (see above).

At each stage different perspectives and branches of theory would have greater explanatory power and there would be different policy requirements. Each stage may also be more likely to occur in different types of regions. In the first stage a range of theoretical perspectives may be useful in explaining change and the roles of some regions as generators and conduits for innovation – for instance with the 'innovative milieux' (Campagni, 1995) and cultural creativity (for example Florida, 2005) being important in some regions together with learning and innovation (for example Cooke and Simmie, 2005). From a policy view, support for innovative start-up or more general firms, or commercializing basic research and supportive 'entrepreneurial culture', including teaching entrepreneurial behavior, may be important. Social and psychological perspectives may be useful in identifying where support may be most needed or most effective. In the second stage the role of policies may be to ensure universal access to the technological or other 'hard' or 'soft' infrastructure, or to help to create markets and other micro-level support infrastructure. Opportunity identification and related entrepreneurial behavior may be important (although it will also be important in the first stage), see for instance Kirzner (1997). In the final stage the policy role may be to ensure a stable macroeconomic environment and effective market operation, where cost competition and more traditional neoclassical approaches take more prominence with greater regional convergence as production moves to lower-cost areas, and technologies (widely defined to include organization and so on) become ubiquitous. Clearly, at any time a region may be at different stages in different technologies or market areas, or for a given industry different regions may be at different stages. In each stage the types of theories and policies overlap but there needs to be integration between policies and policy actors, and a long-term perspective on theoretical developments.

Entrepreneurship, in its various perspectives, results from a combination of: the socio-economic environment such as the opportunities in the economy and the social context entrepreneurs live in (for example, are entrepreneurs encouraged or frowned upon in our society); the personality of the entrepreneur; the learning and use of necessary skills and attitudes; and actually using purposeful insights to do something about the opportunities identified. So the two-way interaction between the entrepreneur and the environment within which they operate is significant and needs to be built into the theory and models of regional development.

It is important that research and policy development fully take account of the differing perspectives of entrepreneurship and make explicit the particular perspective(s) that they are using. No single definition necessarily fully captures the concept, but by being clear about our meaning of the concept and the underlying assumptions we can progress our understanding of entrepreneurship and its relationships to development. There remains no standard theoretical approach to the study of entrepreneurship, but its role in the economy and society is too important for it to be relegated to a footnote.

REFERENCES

Acs, Z.J. and D.B. Audretsch (1988), 'Innovation in large and small firms: an empirical analysis', *American Economic Review*, **78**, 687–90.

Acs, Z.J., R. Morck and B. Yeung (1999), 'Productivity growth and firm size distribution', in Z.J. Acs, B. Carlsson and C. Larlsson (eds), *Entrepreneurship, Small and Medium-Sized Enterprises and the Macroeconomy*, Cambridge: Cambridge University Press, 367–96.

Ahmed, A. and R.W. McQuaid (2005), 'Entrepreneurship, management and sustainable development', *World Review of Entrepreneurship, Management and Sustainable Development*, **1**, 6–30.

Audretsch, D.B. (1995), *Innovation and industry evolution*. Cambridge, MA: MIT Press.

Audretsch, D.B. and R. Thurik (2004), 'A model of the entrepreneurial economy', *International Journal of Entrepreneurship Education*, **2**, 143–66.

Audretsch, D.B., R. Thurik and I. Verheul (2002), *Entrepreneurship: Determinants and Policy in a European–US Comparison*, Amsterdam: Kluwers.
Baumol, W.J. (1987), 'Entrepreneurship in economic theory', *American Economic Review*, Papers and Proceedings, **58**, 64–71.
Baumol, W.J. (1993), 'Formal entrepreneurship theory in economics: existence and bounds', *Journal of Business Venturing*, **3**, 197–210.
Bhide, A. (2000), *The Origin and Evolution of New Businesses*, Oxford: Oxford University Press.
Binks, M. and P. Vale (1990), *Entrepreneurship and Economic Change*, New York: McGraw-Hill.
Birley, S. and D. Muzyka (2000), *Mastering Entrepreneurship: Complete MBA Companion in Entrepreneurship*, London: Pearson Education.
Campagni, R.P. (1995), 'The concept of innovative milieu and its relevance for public policies in European lagging regions', *Papers in Regional Science*, **74**(4), 317–40.
Casson, M. (1999), 'Entrepreneurship and the theory of the firm', in Z.J. Acs, B. Carlsson and C. Larlsson (eds), *Entrepreneurship, Small and Medium-Sized Enterprises and the Macroeconomy*, Cambridge: Cambridge University Press, pp. 45–78.
Chell, E., J.M. Haworth and S.A. Brearley (1991), *The Entrepreneurial Personality: Concepts, Cases and Categories*, London: Routledge.
Commission of the European Communities (CEC) (1999), *The European Employment Strategy: Investing in People; Investing in More and Better Jobs*, Luxembourg: Office for Official Publications of the European Communities.
Commission of the Economic Communities (CEC) (2005), *The Future of the European Employment Strategy: A Strategy for Full Employment and Better Jobs for All*, Luxembourg: Office for Official Publications of the European Communities.
Cooke, P. and N. Clifton (2004), 'Spatial variation in social capital among UK small and medium enterprises', in H.L.F. de Groot, P. Nijkamp and R.R. Stough (eds), *Entrepreneurship and Regional Economic Development: A Spatial Perspective*, Cheltenham, UK and Northampton, MA, USA: Edward Elgar Publishing, pp. 107–37.
Cooke, P. and J. Simmie (2005), 'Knowledge, innovation and the competitiveness of cities', in N. Buck, I. Gordon, A. Harding and I. Turok (eds), *Changing Cities: Rethinking Urban Competitiveness, Cohesion and Governance*, London: Palgrave Macmillan, pp. 97–111.
Cunningham, J.B. and J. Lischeron (1991), 'Defining entrepreneurship', *Journal of Small Business Management*, **29**, 45–61.
Drucker, P.F. (1985), *Innovation and Entrepreneurship*, London: Heinemann.
Florida, R. (2005), *Cities and the Creative Class*, London: Routledge.
Fraser of Allander Institute (2001), *Promoting Business Start-ups: A New Strategic Formula Stage 1: Progress Review*, Glasgow: University of Strathclyde.
Gartner, W.B. (1988), 'Who is an entrepreneur? is the wrong question', *Entrepreneurship Theory and Practice*, **12**, 47–67.
Glancey, K.S. and R.W. McQuaid (2000), *Entrepreneurial Economics*, Basingstoke, UK: Macmillan and New York: St Martin's Press.
de Groot, H.L.F., P. Nijkamp and Roger R. Stough (2004), *Entrepreneurship and Regional Economic Development: A Spatial Perspective*, Cheltenham, UK and Northampton, MA, USA: Edward Elgar.

Harrison, B. (1997), *Lean and Mean: Why Large Corporations will Continue to Dominate the Global Economy*, New York: Guildford Press.
Kirzner, I.M. (1973), *Competition and Entrepreneurship*, Chicago, IL: University of Chicago Press.
Kirzner, I.M. (1997), 'Entrepreneurial discovery and the competitive market process: an Austrian approach', *Journal of Economic Literature*, **35**, 60–85.
Krugman, P. (1991), 'Increasing returns and economic geography', *Journal of Political Economy*, **99**, 483–99.
Lachmann, L.M. (1991), 'Austrian economics as an hermeneutic approach', in D. Lavoie (ed.), *Economics and Hermeneutics*, London: Routledge, pp. 134–46.
Leibenstein, H. (1968), 'Entrepreneurship and development', *American Economic Review*, **58**, 72–83.
Lucas, R.E. (1988), 'On the mechanics of economic development', *Journal of Monetary Economics*, **22**, 3–42.
Malechi, E.J. (1997), *Technology and Economic Development: The Dynamics of Local, Regional and National Competitiveness*, 2nd edition, London: Addison Wesley Longman.
McCann, P. and T. Arita (2004), 'Clusters, entrepreneurship and regional development: a transactions cost perspective on the semiconductor industry', in H.L.F. de Groot, P. Nijkamp and R.R. Stough (eds), *Entrepreneurship and Regional Economic Development: A Spatial Perspective*, Cheltenham, UK and Northampton, MA, USA: Edward Elgar, pp. 225–51.
McClelland, D.C. (1961), *The Achieving Society*, Princeton, NJ: Van Nostrand.
McQuaid, R.W. (1996), 'Social networks, entrepreneurship and regional development', in M. Danson (ed.), *Small Firm Formation and Regional Economic Development*, London: Routledge, pp. 118–31.
McQuaid, R.W. (2002), 'Entrepreneurship and ICT industries: support from regional and local policies', *Regional Studies*, **36**(8), 909–19.
Mitchell, R.K., J.B. Smith, E.A. Morse, K. Seawright, A.M. Peredo and B. McKenzie (2002), 'Are entrepreneurial cognitions universal? Assessing entrepreneurial cognitions cultures', *Entrepreneurship Theory & Practice*, **26**(4), 9–32.
Nelson, R.R. and S.G. Winter (1982), *An Evolutionary Theory of Economic Change*, Cambridge, MA: Harvard University Press.
Nijkamp, P. and J. Poot (1998), 'Spatial perspectives on new theories of economic growth', *Annals of Regional Science*, **32**, 7–38.
Organisation for Economic Co-operation and Development (OECD) (1998), *Fostering Entrepreneurship: A Thematic Review*, Paris: OECD.
Organisation for Economic Co-operation and Development (OECD) (2003), *Entrepreneurship and Local Economic Development: Programme and Policy Recommendations*, Paris: OECD.
Reynolds, P.D. (1991), 'Sociology and entrepreneurship: concepts and contributions', *Entrepreneurship Theory and Practice*, **14**, 47–70.
Schumpeter, J.A. (1942), *Capitalism, Socialism and Democracy*, London: Allen & Unwin.
Scottish Enterprise (1993), *Improving the Business Birth Rate: A Strategy for Scotland*, Glasgow: Scottish Enterprise.
Scottish Enterprise (2002), *Generating Entrepreneurial Dynamism: A New Approach for the Scottish Enterprise Network, The Strategy Explained*, Glasgow: Scottish Enterprise.

Smiles, S. (1859), *Self Help, with Illustrations of Character and Conduct*, London: John Murray; republished (1996), London: IEA.
Stevenson, H. (2000), 'The six dimensions of entrepreneurship', in S. Birley and D. Muzyka (eds), *Mastering Entrepreneurship*, London: Pearson Education, pp. 8–13.
Stevenson, H.H. and W.A. Sahlman (1989), 'The entrepreneurial process', in P. Burns and J. Dewhurst (eds), *Small Business and Entrepreneurship*, Basingstoke: Macmillan, pp. 94–157.
Storey, D.J. (1994), *Understanding the Small Business Sector*, London: Routledge.
Storper, M. (1995), 'The resurgence of regional economies, ten years later', *European Urban and Regional Studies*, **2**, 191–221.
Tidd, J., J. Bessant and K. Pavitt (2005), *Managing Innovation: Integrating Technological, Market and Organizational Change*, 3rd edition, London: John Wiley & Sons.
UN (2004), 'Unleashing entrepreneurship: making business work for the poor', report of the Commission of the Private Sector and Development to the UN, New York: UN.
Verheul, I., N. Bosma, F. Van Der Nol and T. Wong (2002), 'Determinants of entrepreneurship in the United States of America', in D.B. Audretsch, R. Thurik and I. Verheul (eds), *Entrepreneurship: Determinants and Policy in a European–US Comparison*, Boston, MA: Academic Publishers, pp. 209–45.

3. A contemporary perspective on public sector venture capitalism

John Sacco and Odd J. Stalebrink

3.1 INTRODUCTION

Supplying venture capital services in the form of provision of investment capital or credit guarantees has become an increasingly popular policy approach among governments worldwide to facilitate regional enterprise, especially among regions lagging in economic growth. The provision of these services is intended to provide a variety of economic, social and political functions and is often seen as a way to increase economic growth via so-called 'smart targeting'. The funds set aside for these purposes are commonly – and hereinafter – referred to as regional enterprise funds.

The goal of this chapter is to explore contemporary theories for purposes of conceptualizing issues related to the need for regional enterprise funds and the capacity of the public sector to allocate these funds successfully. Particular emphasis is placed on exploring the latter of these issues. Several theoretical perspectives are introduced to shed light on these questions, including theories on market failure, neoclassical and contemporary economic theory and third-party governance. The insight generated in this chapter will be useful not only for purposes of providing a review of the current state of the literature on entrepreneurship and economic development, but also in identifying important research hypotheses.

The chapter is organized into five main sections. Sections 3.2 and 3.3 provide an introduction to regional enterprise funds and a discussion of the problem that these seek to address. Sections 3.4 and 3.5 introduce the above-mentioned theories for purposes of exploring the capacity of government to allocate regional enterprise funds effectively. A final section summarizes and offers concluding remarks.

3.2 BACKGROUND

The primary objective of regional enterprise funds is to promote the development of the private and non-profit sectors by offering assistance to businesses (for example, low-interest loans, loan guarantees and long pay-off periods) in which financial institutions are reluctant to invest. These funding efforts may be described as venture capital programs, put in place by governments to ensure that regional enterprise is not stifled by difficulties in obtaining private finance to fund expansion. Thus, in terms of economics, the assumption underlying these programs is that the lack or dearth of finance to fund business expansion constitutes a market failure that warrants government intervention.

In the US, regional enterprise funds are common at all levels of government. A noteworthy example at the federal level is the United States Small Business Administration (SBA), which provides loans to small business in amounts ranging from $35 000 to $250 000. The stated objective is to: 'help qualified small businesses obtain financing when they might not be eligible for business loans through normal lending channels'.[1] The loans are administered through the SBA's primary business loan program. At the state level, most state governments set aside regional enterprise funds to finance commercial expansion within state borders. One of many examples is the Virginia Capital Access Program, which is administered by the Virginia Small Business Finance Authority. Its stated purpose is to provide: 'access to capital for Virginia businesses by encouraging banks in Virginia to make loans that they would otherwise not make due to a borrower's riskier profile'.[2] Municipal governments have similar programs, sometimes based on municipal industrial bonds or tax relief.

It should be noted that the above programs most often target small and medium-sized enterprises (SMEs). However, similar programs have also been established to provide regional enterprise funds to fund non-profit activities. For example, the Virginia Enterprise Initiative (VEI) provides selected community-based non-profits with up to $50 000 in grant funding to use towards administrative or credit enhancement activities.[3]

From a public policy perspective, the success of enterprise funds is often measured by the extent to which they trigger and lead to sustained economic growth in a particular geographic area. Public policy that makes enterprise funds available to a particular region is therefore often referred to as 'smart targeting'. The underlying presumption is that policy-makers and program administrators have the ability and the necessary information to make 'smart' allocation decisions or, at a minimum, that the results of those decisions would be better than those resulting without government intervention. Efficiency of these programs therefore implies several things. Most importantly, it implies that:

- the political process is capable of assessing the need for enterprise funds to fund business expansion (the extent of the market failure); and
- the political process is capable of allocating these funds to those enterprises that are economically viable, but unable to access funds to support expansion.

This review chapter is centered on offering insight to both of these questions, with particular emphasis placed on the latter.

3.3 PUBLIC SECTOR VENTURE CAPITALISM

Enterprises that seek capital have two general venues to acquire funds. They can acquire such capital in either public or private capital markets; note that the terminology 'public capital' markets does not mean that they are government run, but rather that they are open to the public (Seidman, 2005). The development finance literature has shown that small businesses and start-ups are often excluded from these markets. This exclusion is particularly evident in the case of public capital markets. Seidman (2005) outlines two principal reasons for this. First, small and new firms typically do not have access to public capital markets, due to high transaction costs that make it infeasible to issue small amounts of debt. Seidman reports that an underwriter or investment bank would charge about $720 000 (14.4 percent of proceeds) for a $5 million offering and $920 000 (9.4 percent of proceeds) for a $10 million offering. An initial public offering (IPO) without an investment bank typically runs between $200 000 and $400 000, but is generally not recommended. Seidman also points out that investment banks tend to be biased against small and medium-sized companies. Their preference is for large offerings (above $10 million) and firms that exhibit high growth rates. High growth rates make it easier to sell debt. In addition, small and medium-sized businesses tend to be hit particularly hard by cyclical swings, due to their lack of a track record. As such, they are perceived as being riskier investments.

Similar exclusion problems exist in private capital markets, where high transaction costs tend to prevent small businesses from accessing capital. Loans to these businesses often fall in the range between $50 000 and $100 000. A large portion of these transaction costs are fixed in nature. The costs generally include costs associated with limited information and illiquid contracts, where the fixed component tends to be more substantial. Based on a theory of market failure, these costs are therefore substantial enough to crowd out an entrepreneurial opportunity at the margin. This may take the form of an additional interest rate premium that renders the calculus of opportunities at the margin unprofitable. Alternatively, the entity seeking the capital may be excluded altogether from opportunities to access capital.

Another factor that contributes to the difficulty of small businesses to access capital to support start-ups or expansion is a reduced willingness to take risks during economic downturns. As noted already, this unwillingness tends particularly to affect small businesses and start-ups, due to their often limited track record. A final factor, unique to rural regions, is that rural areas tend to be plagued by monopoly and oligopoly problems (Seidman, 2005). Such a market structure often makes it more expensive to borrow, which may crowd out on the margin small business and potential start-ups.

Given these market failures, small businesses are often forced to rely on angel investors and family members to start or expand business ventures. Such funds, however, are not always readily available. In conclusion, therefore, the economic development finance literature tends to emphasize the importance of closing the alleged shortage of capital to fill the market gap in small business finance. The proposition of the existence of an 'equity gap' has been part of the economic literature for over 60 years (see Macmillan Committee, 1931).

In this chapter, we use the term 'venture capitalism' to capture public sector efforts to close the alleged capital gap. The use of this term in the private sector is associated with investors that invest monies in risky and innovative ventures where the potential for profits are large. Given that the risks tend to be large, the venture capitalist expects to receive a high yield on these types of investments. The application of the term in a public sector setting differs in one important way from this traditional use of the term. The motivation underlying the public sector venture capital investments is driven by the potential of the investment to benefit the targeted community, in terms of creating economic growth and employment opportunities.

3.4 PUBLIC SECTOR VENTURE CAPITALISM THROUGH THE LENS OF ENTREPRENEURSHIP THEORY

To gain insight into the extent to which public officials are capable of allocating regional enterprise funds in an economically efficient manner (that is, is capable of allocating fund to those enterprises that are economically viable, but unable to access funds to support expansion), this chapter draws in part from different theories of entrepreneurship. Theories of entrepreneurship are interesting for this purpose because they emphasize processes associated with the identification and exploitation of previously unrecognized (that is, unexploited) opportunities. As noted above, a critical component that determines the success of government enterprise programs is the ability of public officials to identify unfunded and viable businesses opportunities to fund. Hence, public officials need to be entrepreneurial in the process of allocating enterprise funds. This section provides a theoretical overview of the possibility of entrepreneurial action within government. Several different theoretical frameworks that addresses entrepreneurship directly or indirectly are considered, beginning with traditional neoclassical and contemporary economic theories, followed by discussions of third-party governance.

3.4.1 Entrepreneurship and Economic Theory

Traditional neoclassical economic theory suggests that public officials would always select and pick winners, as long as they are public utility maximizers. This follows from the strong assumptions that it makes about decision-making including access to free and perfect information, and instant decision and rationality (that is, 'economic man'). These effectively assume away all those aspects of decision-making that explain entrepreneurship. In essence, decision-making is viewed as being mechanical. While transaction cost and information economics have partly relaxed these assumptions, one of the most fundamental assumptions remains: that of one-period decision-making. As such, neither of the frameworks allows for processes of discovery and learning, both of which are essential to the understanding of entrepreneurship.

However, there are contemporary frameworks within the realm of economics that emphasize processes of discovery and learning. Perhaps the most well known of these is the Austrian economic tradition. This tradition encompasses theories that are rooted in the works of a handful of Austrian economists, including but not limited to Hayek, Mises and Carl Menger. Since the 1970s there has been resurgence in the interest in the works of these scholars (Vaughn, 2000). This interest has given rise to what has become known as the Austrian economic tradition, or alternatively the Austrian School of economics. The Austrian School places the entrepreneur at the center of economic analysis. Entrepreneurship is viewed as the force that ultimately moves the economy toward a state of equilibrium, rather than accepting that the market is at equilibrium.

Market disequilibrium, thus, is viewed as a positive force that gives rise to a need for entrepreneurs. It spurs searches, discovery, learning and some solutions that move the economy closer toward equilibrium.

The Austrian School defines the term 'entrepreneurship' broadly. It is viewed as a function applying to all those that deal with decision-making under uncertainty. Von Mises writes (1996, p. 253): 'The term entrepreneur as used by catallactic theory means: Acting man exclusively seen from the aspect of uncertainty inherent in every action.'

The Austrian School is helpful for purposes of offering insight into the possibility of entrepreneurship in a public sector context, due to its emphasis on identifying and describing conditions that it views to be necessary for entrepreneurial action. These include the presence in institutions of private property rights, freedom of association and a price system. Based on an analysis of the relative presence of these institutions, the Austrian framework allows for assessment of the capabilities of public policy-makers and government administrators to make 'smarter' venture capitalist decisions (that is, allocation decisions) than those that would have emerged from the market process (that is, without intervention). An overview of the role of these conditions is offered next.

Private property rights

The presence of private property rights is viewed to influence economic decisions by way of providing people with incentives to carry out the entrepreneurial function. Von Mises (1935) explains: 'Private property is viewed to facilitate entrepreneurial action by assuring the existence of market conditions where entrepreneurial actions are directly connected to the individual entrepreneur's economic well-being. In addition, they facilitate economic behavior, by giving people a reason to act responsibly and to take on initiatives (p. 97).'

For purposes of evaluating the merits of regional enterprise funds, the private property argument suggests that a suboptimal supply of talent may result, compared to that discovered through action under incentives in free markets. In other words, if the government provider is operating in an institutional setting that does not allow for proper incentives (price, for instance), one might expect that administrators will elect to err on the side of safety, or simply err because of an inability to collect information from dispersed sources (creditors, vendors and potential vendors). They would rely on internal procedures and guidelines that could be used to 'indemnify' government recipients from personal liability, thus limiting the failure necessary to the market process in Austrian economics. Hence, suboptimal allocation decisions due to improper incentives are implied by the Austrian framework.

The price system

The second institutional condition is the presence of a price system. According to the Austrian School of thought, the price system is a necessary means for assessing the risk and rewards associated with decisions (economic calculation). Prices are therefore essential to the entrepreneurial quest to obtain advantages, perhaps in deciding on preferable location, choice of communication method, coordination of know-how or labor specialization. Mises also proposes that the availability of a process allowing for the development of market prices is a prerequisite for an economy to deal with 'change'. According to von Mises, prices incorporate such change by means of entrepreneurial foresight. That is, entrepreneurs anticipate and calculate profit and loss scenarios, based on individual subjective judgments and past prices. Without monetary values, it is, according to von Mises, 'impossible' for the human mind to calculate or process relatively complex 'profit or loss' scenarios of production. Von Mises writes that such calculation 'requires more exact estimates and some judgment of the economic issues actually involved' (von Mises, 1935, p. 96). Thus, in von Mises' view, monetary values provide guidance critical for individual decision-making. Without prices the entrepreneur is forced to make resource allocation decisions about production processes 'that are relatively short and the expense and income entailed can be easily gauged' (von Mises, 1935).

Hayek's view on prices adds nuance to von Mises' view. According to Hayek, the price system is a mechanism for communicating knowledge and information on both primary and secondary-order goods (that is, 'prices as carriers of knowledge'). Hayek placed particular emphasis on illustrating that market-generated prices were able to incorporate not only 'scientific' knowledge but also knowledge of particular circumstances such as the price of labor versus capital in making business decisions.

Freedom of association

Freedom of association allows people to organize themselves to carry out the entrepreneurial function. The Austrian School implies support for policies allowing for different forms of organization and that reduce barriers to change from one organizational form to another (that is, flexible organizations). Such flexibility may open paths for discovery even in the face of failure. In the case of government as a venture capitalist, the benefits of freedom of association therefore may not be sufficiently realized without distributive participation. Perhaps most importantly, the benefits that would arise from exploring 'partnerships' to test entrepreneurial ideas might not be realized in a traditional hierarchical government context, thus suggesting added inefficiency in the provision of regional enterprise funds from centralized policy.

Changes in corporate life over the past few decades reveal the importance of freedom of association. The battle since 1980 between Alfred Chandler (1977) (large, vertically integrated firms), and his challengers (small firms as the way to growth) has shown that large firms can no longer offer security (pensions, post-retirement benefits, and so on). Thus, many people have become more entrepreneurial, or entrepreneurial outside the integrated firm. With freedom of association, they can form partnerships (non-profits such as s-corporations and Limited Liability Corporations (LLCs), and so on) to test their entrepreneurial ideas. The shape may be large firms, regional dominance by particular industries or small firms: the 'right size' is unknown. It is not the large firm of Chandler (1977) but the fundamentals of Austrian economics that are important to understand. In the mind of Simon and Etzioni (see, for example, Etzioni, 1986 – mixed scanning) it is the search that is important.

Extensions and caveats

The Austrian School of thought is clearly critical in terms of the capacity of governments to distribute regional enterprise funds. According to the Austrian School of thought, shortage of funds does not constitute a market failure. Shortage of funds for entrepreneurs could mean that government borrowing is crowding out private capital, or allowing the private sector to wait until enterprise funding eliminates the failures or near failures. Shortages might also be a signal that entrepreneurs have made mistakes in the past and that creditors are not interested in that particular region. Another implication that follows from Austrian economics is that entrepreneurs can operate successfully without capital. They can start with no capital, sell an idea and realize a return on an idea.

Another problem, taking an Austrian perspective, with allowing for government to act as a venture capitalist vis-à-vis its ability to make allocation decisions, lies in the sovereign not being a 'rejectable' or a losing player. In essence, the sovereign has no test of failure equal to that of the entrepreneur in the market process. Based on this, one could conclude that government would have an inferior learning curve (that is, fall behind), resulting in inferior allocation decisions.

However, public sector entities are seldom purely public or private, but rather hybrid organizations. For example, most public entities participate and compete in the buying and selling of goods and services, experiment with different and more flexible organizational structures, and utilize economic rewards. Hence, it may be argued that if one or more of the institutions are partly available the prospect of successful entrepreneurial actions is enhanced.

It is also possible to argue that regional enterprise funds may help with clustering, which in turn might help to address the problem of knowledge dispersion. If clustering does take place to the advantage of economic growth, it may be clustering of competence (Desrochers, 1998). Clustering may be a function of what Austrians call mutual understanding gained in the search for knowledge. One policy question related to clustering is about the role of these regional enterprise subsidies and industrial bonds for clustering phenomena such as industrial parks. A policy answer would likely say yes to such subsidies and bonds. An Austrian question might be whether government subsidies quench nascent entrepreneurship. If entrepreneurship is part of human behavior, is it possible for government to see advantages and go through trial and error in providing subsidies?

Finally, public policy that targets spatial arrangements, such as regional enterprise funds, may be endowed with a high level of uncertainty because of the multiple targeting involved. A major reason for this is the complexity involved in policies that target spatial arrangements. Such policies often ameliorate problems or induce growth in ways that are difficult to predict. For example, a policy may divert a problem elsewhere or have a negative effect on growth rather than a positive one. It is possible that the unintended consequences of public policy are greater than the intended ones. Hence, the limited ability of policy-makers and administrators to acquire the necessary knowledge and capability to make 'smart' allocation decisions may be of particular importance in this context.

3.4.2 Third-party Governance

Another perspective that fits in part with the Austrian notion of a need for freedom of association and prices is the idea of third-party governance. Third-party governance, as construed by Salamon (2002), allows and encourages parties outside the government (when the government tends to be hierarchical) to participate in all dimensions of policy including making policy, usually within some government constraints or rules. Third-party governance may be viewed in terms of efficiency, under the assumption that governments need to think about markets as powerful ways of reducing the inefficiency of hierarchical government. If structured and supported by an environment that infuses competitive pressures, the third-party governance approach has the potential to be more efficient, in terms of Austrian demands, because of the availability of price as a carrier of information and competition as a way to reduce costs. Third-party governance thus offers a potential route to government use of private venture capital and enterprise funds for a variety of issues, including regional economic development. It would carry Hayek's notion (1944, 1948) of local knowledge as opposed to relying on central knowledge (as in central governmental planning). Because information is so dispersed (that is, private knowledge) in the Austrian view, utilization of local knowledge is one of the keys to economic order.

One difficulty is that third-party governance (Salamon, 2002) has developed as a traditional public policy and public administration tool in the sense that it does not look to economic theory or models as well as democratic parameters. For example, Kelman's chapter (Kelman, 2002, in Salamon, 2002, p. 282) on contracting, or contracting out as it is commonly called, is an example of third-party governance and is thus close to government as venture capital or public–private partnerships. Contracting is a reasonable substitute for government venture capitalism because neither venture capital nor public–private partnerships are covered in Salamon (2002). Contracting, as with government acting as a venture capitalist, does involve choosing 'winners'. These 'winners' are usually the ones which will perform best in terms of efficiency. However, contracting out can include social goals of encouraging minority participation, participation by women and involvement of non-profit entities. While all these can be efficient, the focus on one group is a non-market approach in that the scope of competition may be narrowed.

For now, the Kelman chapter provides a way to see whether third-party governance, as presented in Salamon (2002), can reach beyond Austrian economics toward a public policy 'hands-off' method where 'hands off' implies that price can partly replace government directives. Kelman, while he defines contracting as a business arrangement (Kelman, 2002, p. 282), devotes the bulk of the chapter to a non-economic, traditional public administration reform approach. In his view, contracting has three stages: (1) structuring the business arrangement; (2) source selection; and (3) contract administration (Kelman, 2002, p. 289). The bulk of structuring the business arrangement is a discussion of increasing competition. Kelman (2002, p. 290) examines task contracts (a one-time purchase, for example the purchase of 100 000 gallons of fuel) and delivery order contracts (establishment by the government of a price range for a list of items from one vendor) with respect to which one provides more competition. The huge challenge of complete and enforceable contracts is barely touched on (see his short, two-page discussion of principal–agent theory, Kelman, 2002, p. 305) except in terms of legal sanctions.

3.5 ILLUSTRATION: NEW TECHNOLOGY BASED-FIRMS IN THE EUROPEAN UNION

Murray (1998) provides an illustration of governmental intervention, in the case of lagging regions, in the European Union (EU). Murray traces efforts by the EU to work through its Directorates-General to address poor private investment in new technology-based firms (NTBF). His article exemplifies both public policy intervention and success. The EU solution to imperfections in capital markets is low-interest loans to enterprise funds operated by a large bureaucratic mix. Murray explains:

> Each of the supported funds in the scheme received a reimbursable, interest-free advance of up to 50% of the annual operating costs of the fund over a three to five year period. This loan is due for repayment after ten years when it was deemed that sufficient investment realizations would have been made to enable the return of the advance. (p. 410)

Murray's words suggest the range of bureaucratic involvement required to implement the program. The Directorate-General (DG) in Murray's article is DG XXIII Enterprise Policy, Distributive Trades, Tourism and Cooperatives. The preceding 22 DGs are also part of the EU delivery system for support of industry. According to Murray, two DGs, DG XXIII (Enterprise) and DGXVI (Regional Development), were involved in ensuring a regional dimension to the pilot scheme and the specific inclusion of new funds.

While Murray sees general success for this seed project, his data turn up some disquieting findings about these enterprise funds. His view of the overall success is: 'Thus, the Scheme had met initially one of its objectives of stimulating private sector financial transfers' (ibid). He does concede that the private sector may have seen the government money coming and, as a result, held back on investment. On this issue of the possibility of the private sector holding back, he opines: 'However, the effectiveness of the Commission's intervention, more pessimistically, may conversely be seen as an indication of private investors' circumspection as to the economic viability of regional seed capital investment in the absence of significant EU subsidy' (ibid).

Murray also assumes that estimates made by the funds for capital needs are another indication of success. He writes:

> The effectiveness of the imprimatur of the EU in assisting the process of fund raising was significant, particularly for the regional funds. Fund managers were asked to estimate the amount of finance they believed they would have been able to raise from private investors without the existence of the Scheme. *Only two of the thirteen regional funds reported that they would have been able to raise any finance.* (ibid)

He provides no indication that some of these findings may have been self-serving to the funds under the DGs.

Finally, Murray's finding on measurement by the enterprise funds gives pause for thought about the bureaucracies' ability to monitor results. Murray's findings on performance measures may speak to the reluctance among EU fund managers to provide quantitative data, which is another indication of possible poor or self-serving bureaucratic behavior:

> The regional fund managers appeared to give little priority to quantitative performance variables in their own individual benchmarks for their fund's performance . . . The absence of formal monitoring/evaluation criteria for nearly half the funds in the Scheme was potentially alarming given the managers' fiduciary accountability to their public and private investors. Particularly for regional fund managers, the interim results of substantial investment activity appeared to have received little explicit analysis. (p. 411)

3.6 SUMMARY AND FINAL REMARKS

The main purpose of this chapter was to explore contemporary theories that help to conceptualize issues related to the need for regional enterprise funds and the capacity of the public sector to allocate these funds successfully. Particular emphasis was placed on theorizing about the need for public sector enterprise funds and the extent to which the public sector is capable of making successful allocation decisions. Theoretical perspectives explored included theories on market failure, neoclassical and contemporary economic theory and third-party governance.

The contemporary frameworks were used to offer insights into the prospect of efficient resource allocation decision-making outside the marketplace. The frameworks suggest that the absence of price signals, private property rights and freedom of association greatly inhibit the ability of government units to make efficient economic decisions, and even integrate democratic theory into public policy. Hence, the notion of government as a venture capitalist is fundamentally challenged, in terms of economic efficiency.

In an attempt to offer a remedy, the chapter has also drawn attention to a middle-ground approach to go beyond the challenges raised and still find economic and democratic ways for government to get involved in venture capital programs. The suggestion is to consider reliance on third-party governance and search for means to implement it in what is called a 'hands-off' approach (Williamson, 1991). Third-party governance (also referred to as spontaneous or invisible governance) borrows from Adam Smith's famous dictum (as expressed in Williamson, 1991, p. 159): 'the invisible hand', according to which each businessman . . . 'by pursuing his own interest . . . frequently promotes that of society more effectively than when he intends to promote it'. Third-party governance, as described in the chapter, promises a partial remedy in that it addresses the knowledge issue to which the Austrian framework draws attention. Unfortunately, third-party governance, as developed in its traditional public policy and public administration (non-economics) mode, is far more on the intentional (hands-on) than spontaneous (market or hands-off) side. If the public policy and public administration third-party government literature borrowed more from major questions in economics and sociological economics, it could be perceived as a hands-off or invisible approach. As such it might be able to emulate markets and prices that carry information for entrepreneurial decisions.

NOTES

1. http://www.sbaonline.sba.gov/aboutsba/index.html.
2. http://www.dba.state.va.us/financing/programs/virginia.asp.
3. http://www.dhcd.virginia.gov/CD/VEI/default.htm.

REFERENCES

Chandler, A. (1977), *The Visible Hand: The Managerial Revolution in American Business*, New Haven, CT: Harvard University Press.

Desrochers, P. (1998), 'A geographical perspective on Austrian economics', *Quarterly Journal of Austrian Economics*, **1**(2), 63–83.

Etzioni, A. (1986), 'Mixed scanning revisited', *Public Administration Review*, **46**(1), 8–14.

Hayek, F.A. (1944), *The Road to Serfdom*, Chicago, IL: University of Chicago Press.

Hayek, F.A. (1948), *Individualism and Economic Order*, Chicago, IL: University of Chicago Press.

Kelman, S. (2002), 'Contracting', in L. Salamon (ed.), *Tools of Government: A Guide to the New Governance*, New York: Oxford University Press

Macmillan Committee (1931), *Committee on Finance and Industry*, Cmd. 3897, July 1931, London.

von Mises, L. (1935), 'Economic calculation in the socialist commonwealth', in F.A. Hayek (ed.), *Collectivist Economic Planning*, London: George Routledge & Kegan Paul, pp. 87–130.

von Mises, L. (1944), *Bureaucracy*, Glasgow: W. Hodge & Co.

von Mises, L. (1996), *Human Action: A Treatise on Economics*, 4th edition, San Francisco, CA: Fox & Wilkes.

Murray, G.C. (1998), 'A policy response to regional disparities in the supply of risk capital to new technology-based firms in the European Union: the European Seed Capital Fund Scheme', *Regional Studies*, **32**, 405–9.

Salamon, L. (ed.) (2002), *Tools of Government: A Guide to the New Governance*, New York: Oxford University Press.
Seidman, K.F. (2005), *Economic Development Finance*, London: Sage Publications.
Vaughn, Karen I. (2000), 'The rebirth of Austrian economics: 1974–99', *Journal of the Institute of Economic Affairs*, **20**(1), http://ssrn.com/abstract=233473.
Williamson, O. (1991), 'The new institutional economics: taking stock, looking ahead', *Journal of Economics Literature*, **38**(3), 595–613.

4. Determinants and impact of entrepreneurship capital: the spatial dimension and a comparison of different econometric approaches

David Audretsch, Werner Bönte and Max Keilbach

4.1 INTRODUCTION

Entrepreneurship in new technological fields is often knowledge- or research and development (R&D)-intensive, therefore it is often referred to as 'knowledge-based entrepreneurship'. Arrow (1962b) states that knowledge as an input to production is inherently different to the more traditional inputs such as labor and capital. This is for two reasons: (1) knowledge has a public goods characteristic; and (2) the economic value of new knowledge is intrinsically uncertain and its potential value is asymmetric across economic agents.

While the first aspect has been addressed and formalized within the endogenous growth theory (Arrow, 1962a; Lucas, 1988; Romer, 1990), the second one has not. Rather, endogenous growth theory implicitly assumes that knowledge, once it has been generated, spills over more or less 'automatically' to other firms.[1] However, transforming generally available new economic knowledge into viable new products or technologies – the essence of knowledge spillovers – requires investment with uncertain outcomes and therefore bears risks.

Often, this investment is made by entrepreneurs. By starting up a business, an entrepreneur literally bets on the product he offers (or will be offering) and thus is willing to shoulder the risk that this process bears. By taking on the risk of developing this uncertain knowledge, entrepreneurs increase the amount of utilized knowledge spillovers. Hence this function of risk-taking is an important one in the innovation process.

However the idea that entrepreneurs play an important economic function by taking on risks is certainly not new. In the fourth book of his

Principles, Marshall (1920 [1994]) considered four 'agents of production': land, labor, capital and organization. He understood 'organization' in a structural sense (that is, in the sense that the notion 'industrial organization' reflects) but also in the sense of an activity. Referring to entrepreneurs as 'business men' or 'undertakers' he states that: 'They [that is, the entrepreneurs] "adventure" or "undertake" its risks [that is, the risks of production]; they bring together the capital and the labour required for the work; they arrange or "engineer" its general plan, and superintend its minor details' (Marshall, 1920 [1994], 244).

By commercializing ideas that otherwise would not be pursued and commercialized, entrepreneurship serves as one mechanism facilitating the spillover of knowledge. Thus, entrepreneurship promotes economic performance by serving as a conduit of knowledge spillovers. Baumol (2002b) distinguishes this entrepreneurial function explicitly from the role of larger incumbent corporations who are rather engaged into routinized processes of large-scale innovation. While these processes are quantitatively more important in that R&D expenditure and the number of patents generated are greater, a number of systematic studies have provided evidence that breakthroughs and new products are, rather, introduced by small and young firms, that is, by entrepreneurs.[2] In that sense Baumol (2002b) refers to innovation as an integrated process based on a division of labor between small firms, which launch new products and introduce new technologies, and large firms, which take on these ideas and develop them. Hence entrepreneurial firms and large firms coexist in what Baumol (2002a) calls a 'David–Goliath symbiosis'. In that respect, entrepreneurship plays an important role for the economic dynamics and for the growth process of an economy.

To summarize, in the above discussion two aspects are implicit. One is that contexts (regions or industries) with stronger knowledge intensity are connected with higher levels of technological opportunities and therefore higher opportunities to follow up on these by starting up a new venture. The second aspect concerns the economic function that this process implies. By starting up a new venture and by introducing a new product or technology in the market, the new firm not only serves as a conduit for knowledge spillovers but also creates new knowledge for the economy on the viability of the new product. Hence, following the argumentation given by endogenous growth theory, entrepreneurship will have a positive impact on regional economic performance. The aim of this chapter is to investigate the hypotheses empirically. Of course, entrepreneurship is a concept that is not straightforward to measure. We will therefore use different empirical approaches to investigate our hypothesis.

In the following section we discuss the concept of 'entrepreneurship capital'. Section 4.3 suggests two different approaches to estimate empirically the determinants of entrepreneurship capital and its impact on regional economic performance. Section 4.4 concludes the chapter.

4.2 ENTREPRENEURSHIP CAPITAL: AN EMPIRICAL ASSESSMENT

We follow Audretsch and Keilbach (2004a, 2004b) and define the capacity of a region to generate entrepreneurship as the region's 'entrepreneurship capital'. It is the regional milieu of agents and institutions of an economy, a region or a society that is conducive to the creation of new firms. This involves a number of aspects such as social acceptance of entrepreneurial behavior, but of course also individuals who are willing to deal with the risk of creating new firms, and the activity of bankers and venture capital agents who are willing to share the risks and benefits involved. Hence entrepreneurship capital reflects a number of different legal, institutional and social factors and forces.[3] Regions with a high degree of entrepreneurship capital facilitate the start-up of new firms based on uncertain and asymmetric ideas. On the other hand, regions with a low degree of entrepreneurship capital impede the ability of individuals to start new firms.

While entrepreneurship capital is a concept with a large number of facets, it is certainly evidenced by the creation of new firms. Using data for German regions, we measure entrepreneurship capital of a region as the number of start-ups in that region relative to its population. This is an intensity measure that corrects for the size of the region. We employ two measures for knowledge-based entrepreneurship capital. One is based on high-tech start-ups, that is, start-ups in industries with an average R&D intensity of more than 2.5 percent; the second one is based on start-ups in information and communication technology (ICT) industries, that is, in both manufacturing and service industries that are related to information and communication industries. We use a 'counterfactual' measure that includes start-ups in all of the remaining industries. Start-ups in knowledge-based industries are small in number relative to the others. We therefore group the average number of start-ups of the years 1998 to 2000.

In examining the spatial distribution of entrepreneurship capital in the high-tech industries, three things become evident. First, entrepreneurship capital in the high-tech industries is strongly concentrated in agglomerated regions.[4] Second, entrepreneurship capital in these industries is mainly located in Western Germany. Finally, the spatial distribution of this variable appears to be strongly spatially correlated, indicating that if a region

Table 4.1 Measures of spatial autocorrelation in the variables

	Moran's *I*	Geary's *c*	Getis & Ord's G
Output (GDP)	0.243	0.809	0.018
	(0.000)	(0.043)	(0.000)
Labor	0.350	0.730	0.019
	(0.000)	(0.001)	(0.000)
R&D intensity	0.107	0.718	0.024
	(0.000)	(0.091)	(0.000)
High-tech entrepreneurship	0.452	0.528	0.020
	(0.000)	(0.000)	(0.000)
ICT entrepreneurship	0.522	0.426	0.020
	(0.000)	(0.000)	(0.000)
Low-tech entrepreneurship	0.384	0.564	0.018
	(0.000)	(0.000)	(0.000)
			[$E(G)$ = 0.012]

has a high intensity of entrepreneurship capital, the probability of the neighboring region also to have a high intensity is positive and vice versa for low intensities.

A similar pattern is evident for entrepreneurship capital in the ICT industries. Here, however, entrepreneurship capital in these regions is even more of a Western German phenomenon and the spatial concentration of this variable seems to be even stronger. Table 4.1 shows different measures of spatial autocorrelation. The first column shows a test of spatial autocorrelation based on the standardized measure of Moran's *I* (Moran, 1948). This approach tests whether the correlation of a variable with an unweighted sum of the realization of the same variable in the respective neighboring regions is significant. This approach does not distinguish between positive and negative spatial autocorrelation. Based on this measure, all three measures of entrepreneurship capital have positive and significant spatial autocorrelation, with ICT entrepreneurship showing the strongest correlation.

Another approach to measure spatial autocorrelation has been suggested by Geary (1954), computing the test statistic on the basis of the squared difference of the realization of the variable in a region with the realization of that variable in the respective neighboring regions. Under the null hypothesis of no autocorrelation, the expected value of this test statistic is $c = 1$. The test statistic is smaller than one if the variable is positively autocorrelated and it is larger than one in the case of negative spatial autocorrelation. Thus, the second column of Table 4.1 provides evidence that our measures of entrepreneurship capital are significantly positively correlated.

Finally Getis and Ord (1992) suggest a test statistic that allows us to test whether the spatial autocorrelation is mainly driven by clusters with high-value realizations of the variable or rather by low-value realizations. If the test statistic is above the expected value, the variable is characterized by positive autocorrelation in association with high-valued clusters; if it is below, autocorrelation is positive but driven by low-level realizations. This test statistic gives evidence that the positive spatial autocorrelation in our data is driven by high-level realizations.

Hence the variables in the data set show significant positive autocorrelation that is driven by the regions with a high concentration of entrepreneurship capital. In the empirical approaches suggested in the following section, we will take this autocorrelation into account.

4.3 TWO EMPIRICAL APPROACHES TO MODELING DETERMINANTS: AN IMPACT OF ENTREPRENEURSHIP CAPITAL

The theoretical discussion of section 4.1 suggests a nested cause–effect structure. This nested cause–effect structure suggests an assumed direct effect from 'technical knowledge' on 'economic performance' as it is developed in the literature on endogenous growth (again, see discussion in section 4.1) and examined in a number of empirical studies (for example Griliches, 1995). Here, our interest is more in explicitly analyzing the indirect effect of 'technical knowledge' through entrepreneurship. This suggests the (assumed) positive impact of 'technical knowledge' on entrepreneurship capital, which in turn is assumed to affect economic performance positively. The subsequent two subsections describe different approaches to modeling these relationships.

4.3.1 Measuring Determinants of Entrepreneurship Capital

Variables

In a first step, we estimate the determinants of entrepreneurship capital. We do so using a linear additive structure. We assume the following set of variables to drive entrepreneurship capital.

Economic Output. A high level of economic output implies a large market size, hence a high intensity in economic exchange and therefore a high level of entrepreneurial opportunities. Including the region's level of gross value added of the manufacturing industries, we proxy the level of these opportunities in a very general sense.

Strong economic *GDP Growth* of a region implies increasing wealth, increasing market size, increasing intensity in economic exchange and consequently increasing general opportunities for new businesses. Since it measures the increase in the general economic activity, this variable again proxies general entrepreneurial opportunities. We compute this variable for each region as their average growth rate between 1992 and 2000. Rather than the stock measure of gross domestic product – *GDP*, *GDP Growth* is a measure of the region's past economic performance. We assume that nascent entrepreneurs derive their expectations about the future regional evolution from this past performance.

With *R&D Intensity*, we describe the region's potential of creating new knowledge. We assume that a high regional R&D activity increases regional opportunities to start up new knowledge-based businesses by the mechanisms described in section 4.1. This variable is more specific with respect to opportunity creation as compared to mere GDP growth, and we therefore expect a positive impact of this variable on a region's level of knowledge-based entrepreneurship capital.

Population Density. Glaeser et al. (1992) and Ciccone and Hall (1996) argue that spatial density, hence proximity, increases labor productivity. Similarly, we expect that in densely populated regions, ideas and knowledge flow faster and the provision of ancillary services and inputs is also greater; therefore entrepreneurial opportunities are generated faster and can be appropriated more easily by economic agents. Hence, entrepreneurship capital should be higher in more densely populated regions than in less densely populated regions.

Investment in Manufacturing Industry. This variable measures the investment in physical capital in the producing sector, without the mining industry, of firms with more than 20 employees (measured in 1999). There are three mechanisms to be expected in relation to this variable. The first is that, just as for GDP growth, investment reflects trust in the economic future of the region. Hence we would expect a positive correlation between a region's level of investment and its entrepreneurship capital. The second effect is a 'crowding-out' effect: investment as measured here represents pursuing economic opportunities within incumbent firms rather than in start-ups. If this effect dominates, we would expect a negative correlation between a region's level of investment and its entrepreneurship capital. The third effect is a structural effect: investments in the manufacturing industry are strong where the manufacturing industry is strong. If there is a spatial path-dependent process in the sense that start-ups in these industries are stronger where incumbents of the same firm are located, we would expect a positive sign for the high-tech manufacturing start-ups.

Regional and national authorities use different subsidy schemes as instruments to achieve economic policy goals. Our variable *Subsidies* per person measures the sum of all subsidies that were spent in the respective region, relative to the region's population. Start-up funding is only one among a large number of schemes. With this variable, we aim to describe the economic situation of each region and not to investigate the effectiveness of start-up funding; this would require other methodologies.[5]

Unemployment Rate. That unemployment is linked to entrepreneurship dates back at least to Oxenfeldt (1943), who pointed out that individuals confronted with unemployment and low prospects for wage employment turn to self-employment as a viable alternative. This was an extension of Knight's (1921) view that individuals make a decision among three states: unemployment, self-employment and employment. The actual decision is shaped by the relative prices of these three activities, but there was a clear prediction that entrepreneurship would be positively related to unemployment. However, as Storey (1991) documents, the empirical evidence linking unemployment to entrepreneurship is fraught with ambiguities. While some studies find that greater unemployment serves as a catalyst for start-up activity (Evans and Jovanovic, 1989; Yamawaki, 1990; Evans and Leighton, 1990; Reynolds et al., 1994; Reynolds, et al., 1995), still others have found that unemployment reduces the amount of entrepreneurial activity (Audretsch and Fritsch, 1994; Audretsch, 1995). We test this relationship for our data including the regional unemployment rate in our regressions.

We also aim to investigate whether a high tax burden reduces the propensity to start up a new business, hence the region's entrepreneurship capital. Generally, the German tax system does not make regional distinctions with the exception of business tax, whose multiplier, hence level, is fixed by regional authorities. With these taxes, regional authorities finance their local budget. Consequently, there are two points in relation to the regional business tax. While one side argues that a high business tax prevents firms from settling in the high tax multiplier, rather settling in other regions, the other side argues that the corresponding services attract the firms. We test these arguments by including the regional *Business Tax Multiplier* in the regressions.

Florida (2002) has argued that *Social Diversity* in a society is a proxy for the openness of this society with respect to new ideas. Such openness is important in an environment where new ideas are transformed into business ideas and ultimately to new firm start-ups. Thus, openness contributes to the entrepreneurship capital of that society by enhancing new ideas and the spillover of knowledge. We measure social diversity with an entropy index of the voting behavior on the occasion of the last parliament vote (1998). The measure takes into account all major political parties but also smaller ones. We transform the entropy index to [0,1] such that 0 indicates maximum and 1 indicates no variety.

Industrial Diversity. In the 1990s there was a debate on what type of spatial industry concentration serves as the stronger 'engine to growth': strong concentration of industries (leading to 'Marshall–Arrow–Romer' type of externalities) or strong variety of industries (leading to 'Jacobs' type of externalities).[6] The empirical literature[7] did not come to an unanimous conclusion, suggesting that both effects are important, depending for example on the life cycle of the industry. These two types of externalities describe two different concepts on how generally available new economic knowledge is transformed into viable products.

Both concepts are then important in the entrepreneurial process described above. We test which one of both effects dominates by including a Herfindahl index of industrial diversity in the regressions.

Let us finally consider the impact of *Locational Attractiveness.* It has often been argued (for example Saxenian, 1994) that one of the factors that made Silicon Valley happen was the attractiveness of the place. We investigate whether a similar process can be observed for our measures of entrepreneurship, by including a proxy for locational attractiveness: the number of a county's hotel beds relative to its surface.

Results

Table 4.2 shows the results of a linear regression of these variables against our three measures of entrepreneurship capital. The GDP measures show different behavior. While the contemporary stock measure of *GDP* does not show any significant influence on the agents' propensity to start up a new firm (hence on the region's entrepreneurship capital) *GDP Growth* does so. This is especially for the high-tech-oriented measure. Here, an increase of GDP growth by one percentage point will increase the region's start-up rate by roughly 50 percent. For low-tech entrepreneurship capital, the effect is roughly half as large. On the other hand, GDP growth apparently does not have an impact on the region's ICT start-ups. We assume that this is due to the fact that ICT start-ups were especially strong in the late 1990s and probably decoupled from macroeconomic trends.

The impact of our more specific measure of economic opportunity, *R&D Intensity*, is positive and significant for the knowledge-based measures of entrepreneurship capital, while it is insignificant for low-tech entrepreneurship capital. Hence R&D creates localized generally available knowledge and thus opportunities for knowledge-based entrepreneurship. We see this as evidence for our arguments given in section 4.1.

Entrepreneurship capital is stronger in regions with high *Population Density.* Apparently, the propensity to start up a new firm is greater in

Table 4.2 Determinants of entrepreneurial capital

	Dependent variable: *Entrepreneurship Capital*		
	High-tech	ICT	Low-tech
GDP (Economic output)	0.043	0.0073	0.005
	(0.136)	(0.785)	(0.806)
GDP Growth	0.5003***	0.0896	0.2643
	(0.000)	(0.494)	(0.008)
R&D Intensity	4.4939***	4.1798***	−1.2971
	(0.001)	(0.001)	(0.165)
Population Density	2.0162***	1.8182***	0.8214**
	(0.000)	(0.000)	(0.014)
Investment in Manufacturing Ind.	0.0001	0.001	0.0001
	(0.910)	(0.181)	(0.985)
Subsidies	−0.0031	−0.0135***	0.0023
	(0.476)	(0.001)	(0.454)
Unemployment Rate	−0.0479***	−0.0539***	0.0070**
	(0.000)	(0.000)	(0.042)
Business Tax Multiplier	−0.0257	−0.0791	−0.0657*
	(0.642)	(0.123)	(0.093)
Social Diversity Index	−1.2814***	−0.3058*	−0.0402
	(0.000)	(0.072)	(0.757)
Industry Diversity Index	1.0071***	1.1273***	0.8738***
	(0.000)	(0.000)	(0.000)
Locational Attractiveness	−0.1374	0.094	0.1284
	(0.417)	(0.548)	(0.282)
Constant	−7.609***	−7.708***	−6.023***
	(0.000)	(0.000)	(0.000)
P	0.0033***	0.0048***	0.0032***
(p-value of *LM:* ρ = 0)	(0.000)	(0.007)	(0.006)
Pseudo R^2	0.551	0.652	0.252
Number of observations	435	435	435

cities and surrounding areas. This effect is roughly twice as large for the knowledge-based measures of entrepreneurship capital. Along with the arguments given in section 4.1, we take this as evidence that spatial proximity increases the dissemination of publicly available knowledge and thus increases the opportunities for entrepreneurship.

While dynamic economic growth stimulates the regions' entrepreneurship capital, *Investment in the Manufacturing Industry* does not show a significant impact on entrepreneurship capital regardless of the measure used. This implies either that none of the effects discussed above plays a significant role, or that the effects discussed above are all in effect, but neutralize each other. We cannot solve this ambiguity on the basis of our data set. We therefore leave this for further research.

The level of *Subsidies* per person does not have a significant impact on the region's entrepreneurship capital; for ICT start-ups the impact is even negative. Investigating the statistical basis for this finding we noted that subsidies are negatively correlated with region's gross value added, positively correlated with regional GDP growth and investment, and at the same time negatively correlated with population density (that is, they are relatively larger in weakly populated areas). We therefore assume that the insignificance is due to statistical effects through multicollinearity. Hence we should be careful in interpreting this result as evidence against a positive impact of subsidy schemes. Nevertheless, the fact that subsidies do not show a strong positive impact on start-ups should be investigated further, using for example microeconometric evaluation methods (for example Arvanitis and Keilbach, 2002). Again, we leave this for further research.

An interesting effect occurs when considering the effect of the local *Unemployment Rate*. The impact of regional unemployment is significantly negative for the high-tech-oriented measures and significantly positive for the 'low-tech' measure. We conclude from this finding that the relationship between unemployment and entrepreneurship actually has two faces: start-ups in the 'low-tech' industries have been generated out of unemployment. Apparently this has been chosen as a strategy for self-employment out of a state of unemployment. High-tech start-ups, however, do not follow this strategy. The high qualification that is necessary to start up a firm in a high-tech industry simply does not match the knowledge structure of regions with high unemployment. Rather, high regional unemployment reflects a lack of opportunities for knowledge-based start-ups. Therefore a policy measure that aims to encourage knowledge-based start-ups out of unemployment will probably not generate the expected impact.

The regression results for the regional *Business Tax Multiplier* show a significant negative impact on the start-up intensity (the regional entrepreneurship capital) for our measure of 'low-tech' entrepreneurship capital. High-tech and ICT start-up activities are insensitive with respect to this tax burden. Obviously, the decision to start up or where to locate a high-tech firm is not influenced by the regional tax burden. It is, rather, influenced by other factors (such as the regional R&D intensity that has been discussed above). If these factors are present, an entrepreneur will accept a higher tax burden.

Considering the two diversity measures, *Social Diversity* shows a significant impact on the knowledge-based measures of entrepreneurship capital. The negative sign implies that with decreasing concentration (that is, increasing diversity) the level of knowledge-based entrepreneurship capital increases. Hence increasing social diversity has a positive and significant impact. We take this as confirmation of the arguments of Florida (2002): that is, a high level of social tolerance is positively correlated with the acceptance of new ideas and thus increases a region's entrepreneurship capital. The positive and significant sign of *Industry Diversity* implies that strong industry concentration has a positive impact on the region's propensity to start up new businesses. Hence we find external effects of the Marshall–Arrow–Romer type as having a positive impact on the region's entrepreneurship capital.

Let us finally consider the impact of *Locational Attractiveness*. We do not find significant impact for this variable on the region's entrepreneurship capital, hence on the decision to start up a new business. The results are insignificant for all but the ICT-oriented measure of entrepreneurship capital.

4.3.2 Modeling the Impact of Entrepreneurship Capital

To investigate the impact of entrepreneurship capital empirically we set up an augmented production function that includes entrepreneurship capital explicitly. On this basis we are able to test the impact of entrepreneurship on one hand, and what drives the level of entrepreneurship on the other hand. The first equation is a Cobb–Douglas function of the form:

$$Y_i = K_i^{\alpha} L_i^{\beta} R_i^{\gamma} E_i^{\delta} \tilde{E}_i^{\xi}, \qquad (4.1)$$

where Y_i is economic performance of region i, measured as GDP, K_i is region i's capital endowment, L_i is labor, R_i is region i's R&D intensity, E_i represents the region's endowment with entrepreneurship capital and $\tilde{E}_i$ is the sum of the endowment with entrepreneurship capital of region i's neighbors. A similar equation has been estimated by Audretsch and Keilbach (2004b). Here, however, we augment the equation with the spatial lag of entrepreneurship capital.[8]

The regression results of Table 4.3 provide evidence that entrepreneurship capital has a positive impact on the region's economic performance measured as the region's GDP. Equally the entrepreneurship capital of the respective neighbors exerts a positive impact on the region's economic performance.

We see this as evidence for the fact that some of the aspects of entrepreneurship capital are not limited to the administrative boundaries given by the county's borders. Indeed, some of the aspects captured by our measure of entrepreneurship capital seem to spill over to neighboring regions – such as the risk attitude of people or the social acceptance of entrepreneurship.

The other estimations given in Table 4.3 correspond to the usually

Table 4.3 Estimation of the impact of entrepreneurship capital on regional economic performance

	Dependent variable: *GDP of German Counties*		
Constant	−0.0199	−0.0156	−0.0423
	(0.354)	(0.422)	(0.169)
Capital	0.0735***	0.0869***	0.0655***
	(0.001)	(0.000)	(0.004)
Labor	0.8229***	0.7942***	0.8465***
	(0.000)	(0.000)	(0.000)
R&D Intensity	0.0343***	0.0413***	0.0374***
	(0.000)	(0.000)	(0.000)
High-Tech Entrepreneurship	0.1018***		
	(0.000)		
ICT Entrepreneurship		0.0788***	
		(0.000)	
'Low-Tech' Entrepreneurship			0.1855***
			(0.000)
Lagged High-Tech E	0.0682***		
	(0.001)		
Lagged ICT E	0.0681***		
	(0.001)		
Lagged 'Low-Tech' E			0.0949***
			(0.000)
λ	0.1322***	0.1367***	0.1246***
(p-value of Wald $\lambda = 0$)	(0.000)	(0.000)	(0.000)
Pseudo $R2$	0.940	0.934	0.941

obtained levels (for example Mankiw et al., 1992; Audretsch and Keilbach, 2004a, 2004b). We therefore will not discuss them further.

4.3.3 A Structural Equation Model of Entrepreneurship Capital

In an alternative specification we use a structural equation model (SEM). This section is rather an appetizer than an in-depth analysis of the potential of this approach. This is to keep the size of the chapter tractable. For a more detailed analysis, see Audretsch et al. (2006). SEM is an approach that has two advantages. First, it allows us to treat our variables under investigation – technical knowledge, entrepreneurship capital and economic performance – as 'latent variables' which cannot be perfectly measured by one indicator but can be measured imperfectly by multiple indicators. Hence, we take measurement errors into account. Second,

SEM allows for a flexible specification of the assumed cause–effect structure. In addition to the flexibility that SEM provides, the statistical package LISREL allows us to estimate parameters of the equation system and to present statistical tests for the direct and indirect effects of technical knowledge.[9]

To estimate the model, we use data on the manufacturing industry from 310 West German counties or *Kreise*. Counties are the smallest geographical units in Germany for which relevant data can be obtained. We now measure economic performance as output productivity, that is, economic output relative to two input factors, capital and labor. Hence, we express performance on the basis of an intensity measure that standardizes for input levels. 'Knowledge' (or technical knowledge) is proxied by the level of patents in years 1995 and 1996 in the respective regions.

However, the variables do also have indirect effects which can be computed from the direct effects and thus the total effects. Let us discuss these in turn.

The estimated direct effect of the latent variable 'knowledge' (or technical knowledge) on the latent variable 'productivity' is 0.01 (significant at $\alpha = 0.01$ as the t-value of 2.63 suggests). Entrepreneurship capital increases productivity by 0.03 (significant at $\alpha = 0.01$). Moreover, 'knowledge' exerts a positive and significant impact on entrepreneurship capital by 0.3. The combined indirect effect of 'knowledge' on 'productivity' via 'entrepreneurship capital' is $0.3 \times 0.03 = 0.009$ and therefore the overall effect of knowledge on productivity is $0.01 + 0.009 = 0.019$. This implies that the indirect effect of knowledge via entrepreneurship nearly doubles the direct effect. Hence this model predicts that an increase of technical knowledge in a region by 1 percent will increase entrepreneurship by 0.3 percent and in turn will increase the region's productivity by nearly 0.2 percent.[10]

The effect of entrepreneurship capital of the neighboring regions (that is, the spatial lag of entrepreneurship capital) on the entrepreneurship capital is positive and significant. The indirect effect of the neighboring entrepreneurship capital on output productivity is $0.61 \times 0.03 = 0.0183$. Hence a rise in the level of entrepreneurship capital in the neighboring regions by 1 percent increases the region's output productivity by roughly 0.2 percent. We believe that these findings confirm our discussion of spillover effects of entrepreneurship capital given in the previous section.

4.4 SUMMARY AND CONCLUSION

In this chapter, we investigate two aspects of knowledge-based entrepreneurship: (1) the contribution of entrepreneurship to the dissemination and utilization of new technical knowledge; and (2) the impact of this process on regional economic performance. While endogenous growth theory assumes knowledge to spill over automatically to all existing firms, we argue that this is actually not the case since new economic knowledge is intrinsically uncertain. Therefore, developing new knowledge is risky, and new knowledge is not fully transformed into new products by incumbent firms. This creates opportunities for newly created firms to develop new products on the basis of this 'unused' new knowledge. Entrepreneurs are agents who shoulder this risk and by this process increase the yield of new knowledge; hence entrepreneurship is one mechanism in the process of knowledge spillovers.

Seen through the lens of endogenous growth theory, these arguments define several mechanisms. First, while new knowledge will increase the economic performance of an economy or a region, it will do so to a modest extent. Parts of the new knowledge will be taken on by entrepreneurs, hence new knowledge will increase the level of entrepreneurship in an economy or a region. Second, by this very process, entrepreneurship will increase the exploitation of new knowledge and as such have a positive impact on regional economic performance. Thus, we suppose that new knowledge has a direct positive effect on regional economic performance and an indirect positive effect via entrepreneurial behavior.

In a first step of our analysis, we define the regions' entrepreneurship capital as their capacity for generating entrepreneurship. We then use different modeling approaches to investigate the determinants and impact of entrepreneurship capital. In a first step, we find evidence that the regional level of technological knowledge indeed drives knowledge-based entrepreneurship capital, but not low-tech entrepreneurship capital. We see this as evidence in favor of our argument that contexts with higher levels of knowledge drive knowledge-based entrepreneurship. In a second step, we investigate the impact of entrepreneurship capital on regional economic performance, measured as the level of GDP. We find that all measures of entrepreneurship capital exert a significant positive impact.

In a third step, we merge both argumentations using a structural equation model. Beyond the mere merging, this model allows for a very flexible specification of the assumed interaction of the implied variables. Based on this model, we obtain the following results. First, new knowledge has a positive and significant impact on economic performance. Moreover, new knowledge has a significant positive impact on the regions' level of entrepreneurship capital, which in turn has a significant positive impact on economic performance. Hence we can indeed identify knowledge as contributing to an increase in a region's entrepreneurship capital and, moreover, that entrepreneurship capital acts to increase a region's economic performance. Thus we find evidence for the hypotheses developed in section 4.1.

Both modeling approaches have been done considering the spatial interaction and spatial autocorrelation of entrepreneurship capital. This variable is significantly spatially autocorrelated, as we were able to show in section 4.2. We see this as evidence in favor of the argument that entrepreneurship capital has strong cultural aspects that are indeed locally embedded and locally transmitted and communicated. This would imply that this communication crosses local administrative borders. Hence the cultural aspects of entrepreneurship capital can spill over locally.

A straightforward policy implication of the findings of this chapter would be that in a knowledge-based economy it is not sufficient to focus public policies on the generation of new knowledge in order to generate stronger economic growth. The exploration and use of new knowledge by new firms is also important. Hence, if the EU Commission states that 'while Europe is strong in its innovation process, it is comparatively weak in exploring that new knowledge and transforming it into economic growth',[11] our findings suggest that a strengthening of knowledge-based entrepreneurship will help to resolve this 'European Paradox'.

NOTES

1. This view has been challenged by the literature on absorptive capacity (Cohen and Levinthal, 1990). The knowledge spillover theory of entrepreneurship challenges this view from another angle.
2. For example, Scherer (1980) or CHI Research Inc. (2002). The US Small Business Administration (1995, p. 114) enumerates some 70 important innovations by small firms in the twentieth century, ranging from low-tech innovation such as the Zipper and Bakelite to high-tech ones such as the Nuclear Magnetic Resonance Scanner or the Microprocessor.
3. In that respect the notion of entrepreneurial capital is close to that of social capital (for example Putnam, 1993), though not identical. See Audretsch and Keilbach (2004a) for an in-depth discussion of this issue.
4. We observe a concentration in the region of Munich, Stuttgart, Frankfurt, Hamburg and Berlin.
5. The impact of funding schemes can for example be measured using microeconometric evaluation procedures, for example Arvanitis and Keilbach (2002).
6. The description is very simplified. See for example the literature in the following footnote for more detailed description of the underlying processes. Keilbach (2000) gives a summary of this discussion.
7. See for example Glaeser et al. (1992), Henderson et al. (1995), Henderson (1997) or Ellison and Glaeser (1997).
8. Keilbach (2000) shows that this extension can be done without loss of efficiency in the estimation.
9. For a detailed description of LISREL, see for example Jöreskog and Sörbom (2001).
10. This interpretation as elasticities is possible since the data has been transformed to logarithms.
11. This has been stated in the Commission's December 1995 Green Paper on Innovation.

REFERENCES

Arrow, K.J. (1962a), 'The economic implications of learning by doing', *Review of Economic Studies*, **29**(June), 155–73.
Arrow, K.J. (1962b), 'Economic welfare and the allocation of resources for invention', in R.R. Nelson (ed.), *The Rate and Direction of Inventive Activity: Economic and Social Factors* Vol. 13, Princeton, NJ: Princeton University Press, pp. 609–25.
Arvanitis, S. and M. Keilbach (2002), 'Evaluation methodologies, econometric models I: Microeconometric models', in *Socio-Economic Evaluation of Public RTD Policies (EPUB)*. Vienna: Joanneum Research, Vienna, pp. 101–12.
Audretsch, D. (1995), *Innovation and Industry Evolution*, Cambridge, MA: MIT Press.
Audretsch, D., W. Bönte and M. Keilbach (2006), '*Regional entrepreneurship capital and its impact on knowledge diffusion and economic performance*', mimeo MPI, Jena, June.
Audretsch, D. and M. Fritsch (1994), 'The geography of firm births in Germany', *Regional Studies*, **28**, 359–65.
Audretsch, D. and M. Keilbach (2004a), 'Does entrepreneurship capital matter?' *Entrepreneurship Theory and Practice*, **28**, 419–29.
Audretsch, D. and M. Keilbach (2004b), 'Entrepreneurship capital and economic performance', *Regional Studies*, **38**, 949–59.
Baumol, W.J. (2002a), 'Entrepreneurship, innovation and growth: the David–Goliath symbiosis', *Journal of Entrepreneurial Finance and Business Ventures*, **7**(2), 1–10.
Baumol, W.J. (2002b), *Free Market Innovation Machine: Analyzing the Growth Miracle of Capitalism.* Princeton, NJ: Princeton University Press.
CHI Research Inc. (2002), 'Small serial innovators: the small firm contribution to technical change Working Paper, Haddon Heights, NJ.
Ciccone, A. and R. Hall (1996), 'Productivity and the density of economic activity', *American Economic Review*, **86**, 54–70.
Cohen, W. and D. Levinthal (1990), 'Absorptive capacity: a new perspective on learning and innovation', *Administrative Science Quarterly*, **35**, 128–52.
Ellison, G. and E. Glaeser (1997), 'Geographic concentration in the US manufacturing industries: a dartboard approach', *Journal of Political Economy*, **105**, 889–927.
European Commission (1995), *Green Paper on Innovation, COM (95) 688 final*, Brussels.
Evans, D. and B. Jovanovic (1989), 'Estimates of a model of entrepreneurial choice under liquidity constraints', *Journal of Political Economy*, **97**(2), 657–74.
Evans, D. and L. Leighton (1990), 'Small business formation by unemployed and employed workers', *Small Business Economics*, **2**, 313–30.
Florida, R. (2002), *The Rise of the Creative Class*, New York: Basic Books.
Geary, R. (1954), 'The contiguity ratio and statistical mapping', *Incorporated Statistician*, **5**, 115–45.
Getis, A. and J. Ord (1992), 'The analysis of spatial association by use of distance statistics', *Geographical Analysis*, **24**, 189–206.
Glaeser, E., H. Kallal, J. Scheinkmann and A. Shleifer (1992), 'Growth in cities', *Journal of Political Economy*, **100**, 1126–52.

Greif, S. and D. Schmiedl (2002), *Patentatlas Deutschland–Dynamik und Struktur der Erfindungst ätigkeit.* München: Deutsches Patent- und Markenamt.
Griliches, Z. (1995), 'R&D and productivity: econometric results and measurement issues', in P. Stoneman (ed.), *Handbook of the Economics of Innovation and Technical Change*, Oxford: Blackwell Publishing, pp. 52–89.
Henderson, V. (1997), 'Externalities and industrial development', *Journal of Urban Economics*, **42**, 449–70.
Henderson, V., A. Kuncoro and M. Turner (1995), 'Industrial Development in Cities', *Journal of Political Economy*, **103**(5), 1067–90.
Jöreskog, K. and D. Sörbom (2001), *Lisrel 8: User's Reference Guide*, Lincolnwood, IL: SSI Scientific Software International.
Keilbach, M. (2000), *Spatial Knowledge Spillovers and the Dynamics of Agglomeration and Regional Growth*, Heidelberg: Physica Verlag.
Knight, F.H. (1921), *Risk, Uncertainty and Profit*, Boston, MA and New York: Houghton Mifflin.
Lucas, R.E. (1988), 'On the mechanics of economic development', *Journal of Monetary Economics*, **22**, 3–42.
Mankiw, N.G., D. Romer and D.N. Weil (1992), 'A contribution to the empirics of economic growth', *Quarterly Journal of Economics*, **107**, 407–37.
Marshall, A. (1920), *Principles of Economics*, 8th edition, reprinted 1994, London: Macmillan.
Moran, P. (1948), 'The interpretation of statistical maps', *Journal of the Royal Statistical Society, Series B(10)*, **37**, 243–51.
Oxenfeldt, A.R. (1943), 'New firms and free enterprise: pre-war and post-war aspects' (Working Paper), Washington, DC: American Council of Public Affairs.
Putnam, R.D. (1993), *Making Democracy Work: Civic Traditions in Modern Italy*, Princeton, NJ: Princeton University Press.
Reynolds, P., B. Miller and R. Maki (1995), 'Explaining regional variation in business births and deaths: US 1976–1988', *Small Business Economics*, **7**, 389–407.
Reynolds, P., D. Storey and P. Westhead (1994), 'Cross-national comparisons of the variation in new firm formation rate', *Regional Studies*, **28**, 443–56.
Romer, P.M. (1990), 'Endogenous technical change', *Journal of Political Economy*, **98**, S71–S102.
Saxenian, A. (1994), *Regional Advantage*, Cambridge, MA: Harvard University Press.
Scherer, F.M. (1980), *Industrial Market Structure and Economic Performance*, 2nd edition, Chicago, IL: Rand McNally.
Solow, R.M. (1957), 'Technical change and the aggregate production function', *Review of Economics and Statistics*, **39**, 312–20.
Storey, D.J. (1991), 'The birth of new firms: does unemployment matter? A review of evidence', *Small Business Economics*, **3**, 167–78.
US Small Business Administration (1995), *The State of Small Business: A Report of the President*, Washington, DC: US Government Printing Office.
Yamawaki, H. (1990), 'The effects of business conditions on net entry: evidence from Japan', in P. Geroski and J. Schwalbach (eds), *Entry and Market Contestability: An International Comparison*, Oxford: Basil Blackwell.

APPENDIX: A DESCRIPTION OF THE DATA

Output is measured as gross value added in year 2000 of the manufacturing industries corrected for purchases of goods and services, VAT and shipping costs. The stock of physical capital used in the manufacturing industry of the district has been estimated using a perpetual inventory method, which computes the stock of capital as a weighted sum of investments done in the producing industry in the period 1980 to 2000. For a more detailed description of this procedure see for example Audretsch and Keilbach (2004b). Statistics including output and investment are published every two years on the level of the district by the Working Group of the Statistical Offices of the German Länder, under 'Volkswirtschaftliche Gesamtrechnungen der Länder'. Labor is expressed as the number of employees in the manufacturing industries in 2000. This data is published by the Federal Labor Office, Nuremberg that reports number of employees liable to social insurance on the Level of German counties.

Output Productivity: The observed indicators for the latent variable 'output productivity' are the level of average labor productivity (output relative to labor input) and the level of average capital productivity (output relative to capital input) in a region's manufacturing industry. This latent variable is related to well-known measures of total factor productivity (TFP) because the productivity of both labor as well as capital inputs is taken into account (see Solow, 1957). However, while one has to make restrictive assumptions about the payment of inputs and the degree of competition when computing traditional TFP measures, this is not the case for our approach. We have restricted our attention to the productivity of the manufacturing industry because the bulk of private innovation efforts is performed within this industry and we therefore expect the direct as well as indirect effects of technical knowledge on productivity to be stronger in the manufacturing industry than in other industries.

Technological Knowledge: The observed indicators for the latent variable 'knowledge' (technical knowledge) is a region's number of patents relative to our measure of labor. We use German patent data for the years 1995 and 1996. These data are taken from Greif and Schmiedl (2002). These proxy measures for knowledge are taken for periods earlier than 1998 since it is unlikely that R&D takes an immediate effect on entrepreneurship capital and output.

Entrepreneurship: Observed indicators for this latent variable are cumulated numbers of start-ups in high-tech or ICT industries within a county in the years 1998 to 2000, relative to the county's population. Thus, we assume that the higher the entrepreneurship intensity, the higher the level of the latent variable 'entrepreneurship capital'. A high-tech industry is defined as one whose share of R&D employment in total employment is above 2.5 percent. ICT industries comprise products and services that are related to information and communication technologies. For a further discussion of this measure see Audretsch and Keilbach (2004b).

5. The design of industrial models: addressing cooperative behaviours, innovation and public policy

Maria Teresa de Noronha Vaz

5.1 INTRODUCTION

Industrial development has resulted in many changes in the determinants of firm location. The classical approach explains changes that separate leading multinational companies from others and suggests labour savings, investment guarantees or human capital expertise as the main reasons for the more recent location choices of big firms. These changes represent group strategies that give rise to complex firm structures or geographic industrial patterns fixed by informally agreed-upon goals. In the cases of other small and medium-sized firms, locations are mostly dependent on the nature of the activity or sectoral branches they represent. Supply or demand constraints encourage, more or less, the entrepreneurial site of the production plant. Some industries do not conform to either the classical or the activity branch approach and are therefore called 'footloose'. Even if the activity branches of the agro-food industry constitute good examples for observing such locational constraints, Connor and Schiek (1997) suggest that they are infrequently explained by simple supply or demand constraints. Following this line of thinking, this chapter is an exercise in searching for a new causal effect for firm location in the ways in which firm coordination occurs. The emphasis given to innovation shows the need to accept the increasing influence of a new industrial model based on flexible specialization that promotes interrelationships among firms. The lack of clear regulations may result in coordination forms that are neither equilibrated nor long-lasting. This being the case, regional production chains may be determined by the power generated within existent governance structures and, consequently, locational opportunities also. Attending to the characteristics of networking, it can be argued that coexistent different industrial systems will tend to dominate complete subsectors of the industrial chain, particularly when enterprises are small and not able to bargain effectively their role within the system.

The empirical evidence that is the foundation of this study is weak because there are few available time series data sets related to coordination behaviour and location choice. But, from the theoretical framework, one can speculate on a design for future models of industrial geography where firms will have to submit to increasingly specific conditions that restrict their locational choices as a result of the coordination in the systems they integrate. This chapter is organized as follows. Section 5.2 analyses the dynamic character of productive activity and its consequences for the economic space. In this case, innovation and new organizational forms of productive systems are viewed as major factors responsible for change. Section 5.3 identifies two new determinants of firm location, externalities and spatial embeddedness. Section 5.4 introduces the first theoretical contribution of the chapter with the presentation of a typology for firm coordination forms. The theory of contracts starts the discussion which then evolves into an examination of the economics of the networks. Section 5.5 adopts both industrial geography and the notion of governance to explain how firm location, also dependent on agglomeration, scale or scope economies, may combine with different coordination forms. A matrix of empirical observations related to the agro-food system (AFS) is presented in an attempt to illustrate the argument and describe the model framework. Section 5.6 discusses the dynamics of such a model, based on percolation theory, concluding that a tendency to polarization of the diverse governance structures may lead, in the same location and for a given activity branch, to a the loss of a coexistence of different cooperative forms.

5.2 DYNAMICS OF PRODUCTIVE ACTIVITY: INNOVATION AND ORGANIZATIONAL EFFECTS

Productive activity, particularly industrial production, is a dynamic process. The contemporary period deals with increasing competition in a globalized world economy with tensions produced within the system of mass production and positive performance from challenging new systems.

In such a context for which the culture of the firm and its embeddedness in an institutional environment are crucial, it is important to question how the process underlying the selection of certain kinds of strategic responses and the rejection of others occurs.

As Schoenberger (1997) explains when related to the conventional economic-geographic theory, time, space and competition are reduced to a problem of cost minimization with allocated optimal locations. However, given the unrealism of perfect competition conditions, these analytical dimensions are expected to create contradictory strains. There are different forms that can be used to eventually address such conflicts. Among others, innovation and new organizational forms of production systems or regulation may be viewed as options.

Storper and Harrison (1991) defined production systems noting that the basis of such definitions uses several concepts: a production unit physically integrates a set of activities occurring in a single location; a firm is a legal entity where production takes place; an input–output system is a collection of activities that lead up to the production of a specific marketable product; and a branch of production is the statistical aggregate of similar input–output systems.

Production systems are not static representations of economic activity. These systems are characterized by the fact that they are different as a result of the different productive functions of each activity; but they also differ because of their organizational form. The ease with which they change and adapt to the socio-economic environment defines their levels of structural flexibility.

There are many factors responsible for changes in the forms of production systems or the way they interact with each other. In general, making use of the neoclassical approach, one could say that it is the existence of internal economies of scale or scope that justifies choices favourable to increasing size or variety in the productive activity of a system. Increasing competition tends to narrow the margins of internal economies, while technological improvements dilate them. At a certain point, diseconomies start to occur and the disaggregation of the production system takes place. Thus there is a permanent need for innovation and segmentation in the production process.

Smaller firms are generally capable of adjusting to changeable production processes such as labour specialization, strict controls or high quality standards. Providing quick shifts in their productive functions, they are quite able to reply to the technical specificities or segmentation forms of today's markets.

But it is argued that innovative capability of enterprises requires heavy capital flows and not all firms present the same financial potential or maintain the same competencies, knowledge and learning capacity (Keeble and Wilkinson, 1999). Often, vertical coordination through long-term contracting is the way to appropriate benefits for innovation. For example, French millers who have created high-quality flour fitted to the tastes of baguette consumers proposed a technical package and a contractual partnership to bakers (Nicolas, 1999).

Another factor for change is that as Fordist solutions lose strength, local environment specificity becomes more relevant, as it provides essential inputs – like labour force, entrepreneurial capacity, infrastructures, social culture and industrial organization – for the local production organizations (Becattini and Rullani, 1995). This applies mostly to spaces where firms are located, leaving behind scale economies and mass production as determinants of competitive advantages. Industrial districts serve as examples. Here, labour force division among the several specialized small and medium-sized enterprises happens, not due to the coordination of a big enterprise, but to a common entrepreneurial culture and a huge sense of interdependency. Because it is a better adaptation to the environment, this labour force division allows small and medium-sized enterprises (SMEs) located in the industrial districts to have competitive advantages compared to the larger Fordist enterprises.

This study contributes to current thinking about the start of new models for productive systems. Davelaar (1996), in an effort to contribute to the creation of a conceptual framework concerning the spatial patterns that have resulted from systemic changes in production systems, developed an approach on dynamic incubation. In his view, dynamic incubation is how permanent technological change shapes new spatial structures. Davelaar's particular focus is on the emergence of new products and new technological production systems as well as drivers of spatial concentration in the metropolitan areas. His concern focused on both the initial stage and the subsequent dispersion stage.

5.3 DETERMINANTS OF FIRM LOCATION: SPATIAL EMBEDDEDNESS AND ITS EFFECT ON INNOVATION

This study discusses how new production systems shape spatial structures, and is not dissimilar to Davelaar's study (1996). In contrast, however, this study deals with innovation, considering its remote causes (embeddedness) and its nearest effects (forms of systems coordination).

An article from Arena and Romani (1998), in discussing the Marshallian industrial district, calls attention to the fact that small and large firms depend on the historical and institutional environment in which they integrate. This means that considerations related to the way that productive units rely on the possibility of finding external economies have existed for a long time. They have been historically understood as highly linked to organizational capacity and labour specialization.

The present research on innovation dynamics tries to develop more elaborate ideas to help explain the concept underlying spatial embeddedness and its impact on changes in the form of production. There are various aspects to take into account when spatial embeddedness is considered. These are after Avermaete (2004): (1) proximity to and among other related units of production; (2) human capital performance; and (3) perception of regional, national or international facilities and infrastructure. In each case a common factor is the creation of knowledge, currently considered to be the main condition for innovation as a source of sustainable competitive advantage (Nonaka et al., 2000).

An enhanced perception of the different aspects of embeddedness can be obtained by distinguishing codified knowledge from tacit knowledge. While the first one promotes standardized communication, the second is intrinsic to individuals and organizations, helping in the exchange of informal interactions. It concerns experience and insights (Nightingale, 1998).

Recent developments in the area of information and communication technology have made codified knowledge far more easily available than in the past, regardless of location (Malmberg and Maskell, 2002), while tacit knowledge tends to concentrate in certain geographic spaces. For this reason, while codified knowledge is sometimes a source of competitive advantage, tacit knowledge is becoming an increasingly important factor of industrial attraction as firms tend toward spatial proximity so as to benefit from this gain.

Another important factor is related to human capital. It is a fact that the more extensively the labour force or entrepreneurs are rooted in a spatial context, the higher is the probability that they have absorbed historical mechanisms of production, such as previous experience or connections in the regions. Consequently, they are able to produce better opportunities and outcomes (Jack and Anderson, 2002).

In this context, a set of advantages related to the proximity of similar firms surpasses the simple concept of economies of agglomeration and its impact upon innovation. Such proximal or clustered firms tend to observe and compare themselves with each other and learn quickly from the success and failures of others' attempts to improve their own strategy (Antonelli and Calderini, 1999). A resulting reduction of uncertainty in the introduction of new processes or products is therefore expected (Arndt and Sternberg, 2000). Trust becomes a more appreciated attribute as tacit knowledge is transmitted in a personal way, particularly when productive processes are traditional. Proximity of suppliers of materials helps to create a context of certitude and information that helps firms better to accept commitments, often on an informal basis (Grunert and Ottowitz, 1997), while the proximity of firms to research institutes may facilitate easier collaborations and more diffusion of scientific knowledge (Freel, 2000). Searching for a causal relationship between spatial embeddedness

Table 5.1 The firm trajectory to innovation: conceptual framework determinants of innovation

→ Spatial embeddedness	→ Technological learning	→ Inter-firm coordination	→ Entrepreneurial strategies
Involvement of workforce Institutions and infrastructures Local networking	Internal resources	External information	Leaders Followers Traditional firms
Examples: – recruitment – organizations – events – labour availability – employment legislation – access to R&D resources – regional competitors – production for regional markets	Examples: – codified knowledge: staff, training – tacit knowledge: firm experience, labour cultural background	Examples: – use services: consultancy – customers – contracts on R&D	Examples: – historical – firm characteristics – locational choices – marketing targets

↓↓↓↓

Innovation

↑↑↑↑

Efforts →	Activities →	Results →
Based on private R&D	Product	Patents
Based on public R&D	Process	Impact on turnover
Regional policies	Organization	New thinking
Internal requirements	Market	New routines

Source: Vaz elaboration based on Avermaete (2004) and Vaz et al. (2006).

and innovation, the study references two recent conceptual arguments, Avermaete (2004) and Vaz et al. (2006), both developing conceptual frameworks related to the determinants of innovation and its measurement.

The role of spatial embeddedness can be better understood when observing Table 5.1 where determinants of innovation are joined together in a global conceptual framework. Vaz et al. (2006) have tried to quantify the determinants of innovation in a classification of different behavioural patterns of firms. The study suggests that these determinants have irregular impacts on the different forms of innovation in firm location (in this case firms have been grouped by territorial systems) and time, independently of the activity branch to which they belong.

5.4 GOVERNANCE, POWER AND PATTERNS OF INDUSTRIALIZATION: A TYPOLOGY FOR COORDINATION FORMS

There are two principal competing views of the nature of inter-entrepreneurial relationships: the economic point of view and the sociological perspective. The first is supported mainly by the transaction cost approach, a model whose goal is the pursuit of efficiency. Its basic presupposition is that the market and its atomistic organization consolidate all the relations into transactions ruled by rationality and the opportunism of agents (Taylor, 1996). In this model, if transactions involve uncertainty they tend to take place in hierarchically organized firms, saving greater costs in marketing transactions but at the same time using higher levels of bureaucratic organization. Once transactions are moving from markets into hierarchies, there is a specific knowledge that builds up, that is, asset specificity occurs.

Notwithstanding the limitations of the transaction cost model, it may also be used to better understand the functioning of 'production systems' mainly by identifying new industrial spaces. Here flexible specialization and flexible accumulation in the context of agglomeration and Marshallian industrial districts have been identified as processes dismantling hierarchies and replacing them with localized market transactions (Taylor, 1996).

The role of power or unequal power relationships within and between firms may influence patterns of geographical industrialization and therefore speed development in the territories or functional regions. Empiricist tradition in the industrial geography simply separates small firms from large corporations, creating a dichotomy that neglects the appreciation of the full significance of business enterprises, their structures and the type of networks that they integrate. In this context a complete perception of the circuits of power that these relations trace are underestimated, when compared with the capital–labour relationship or job creation. Also, the discussion of the dominance of power is almost exclusively reduced to the neoclassical least-cost location models and/or outcomes.

Literature reviews related to the subject (Benson, 1975; McDermott and Taylor, 1982) show that it has been clear since the 1970s that there is an asymmetric distribution of power occurring in the daily relationships between pairs of corporations, either large or small, displaying elements of supremacy and subordination. The situation may lead to the advantageous management of resources for the most powerful business enterprises, generating a functional and hierarchic network.

To understand networks of power better, theoreticians should depart from the complexity of entrepreneurial 'tissue' and distinguish among all kinds of productive organizations: large firms from small firms, transnational corporations from national-based corporations, foreign-owned from domestic-owned, craft from mass producers, high-technology from low-technology companies, and head offices from branch plants. All these enterprises develop interrelationships, sometimes not necessarily contractual or transactional, at different functional levels, with other organizations or agents in a constellation where place, time and strategic decisions have an influence. Quantitative difficulties in modelling such complex systems hinder the advance of more detailed analytical work.

Production systems integrated in input–output systems are established in a context of relations of power and decision-making structures – the governance of the system. Storper and Harrison (1991) draw attention to the structure of the supply chains where the number of suppliers is different from the number of customers in order to explain the asymmetry of power and develop a typology of governance structures. In this case, governance is defined as a context within which two major types of firms coexist: the core firms and the ring. The core firms have the power to determine the existence of the others, while the second set, the ring, consists of firms that coexist under symmetrical conditions of dominance. These two elementary forces of the governance structures within the different types of input–output systems create different conditions for governance and the interrelationship among enterprises.

The more fragile firms are (for reasons of competition, consumption impositions, thin profit margins, low capital investment, size or age), the more implicated and dependent they become on the local environment and networking they integrate (Kirat and Lung, 1999). Networks serve them not only as channels for market exchanges but also for facilitating collective action, within or outside market contexts. Firm coordination forms represent a vital way to survive. Their managers know it and are able to adapt their decisions to the global interests of the networking system.

However, the main question remains. Who is responsible for decision-making in the networking system? The circuits of power, composed by the firms, other external agents and a huge amount of regulation, to which firms are sensitive, choose the responsible leader, the dominant enterprise.

Indeed, it is possible to assemble a coordination typology based on the structures of governance. Of course, large multinationals or large firms whose product has been clearly defined and is produced for huge consumption segments of the market do not have to submit to external economies and may maintain their production units in dispersed places – this is assumed to be a first model: the vertical integration model.

A second, opposite case focuses on the firms that work in a networking system without a dominant firm. They represent a static relation in the sense that there is no exercise of power and asymmetric relations do not occur. The few examples of this model, the no-leadership model, are mainly located in a few industrial districts. Most other cases represent an intermediary situation that generally moves toward increasing dominance – the leading firm model. Thus the evolution of the third model leans toward the first one in terms of governance.

5.5 FIRM LOCATION AND COORDINATION FORMS: AN EXERCISE WITH THE AGRO-FOOD SYSTEM (AFS)

Choosing the agro-food sector to illustrate how firm locational priorities may combine in different coordination forms is based on its major characteristics. These are:

- It is represented by a very heterogeneous entrepreneurial structure in which many different production systems can be found.
- At both extremes of the spectrum the following entrepreneurial forms can be detected:
  - Local enterprises producing for local demand, some in a traditional way, others making use of strategies of flexible production.
  - Firms integrated in global strategies, oriented to external markets but also very attentive to the needs of local national consumption (Vaz and Urban, 2000). In this case regions should not expect that those firms (often held back by foreign investments) would represent positive improvements in trade balance. Frequently, an increase in consumption or the creation of new expectations among the consumers has been observed, together with increases in regional demand for new imported products.
- The existence of long supply chains composed of multiple circuits and agents that generally undergo tense relations. The circuits

invariably expand from atomistic agricultural structures towards highly concentrated retailer systems. In the presence of a context for difficult relations, business management theory recommends the development of vertical cooperation as the best way to respond to recent market demands and competition tendencies. The adjustments required by the just-in-time or quality control procedures are good examples of the increasing need for vertical coordination.
- As Gallizzi and Venturini (1999) outlined, there is a common tendency toward asymmetric use of power in the AFS. Higher and still increasing concentration in retailing and the shift in the balance of power often result in a greater asymmetry in bargaining power. This contributes to maintain and even reinforce adversarial relationships between food manufacturers and retailers.
- Another important attribute of the AFS is that due to firms' links with the primary industry sector, to labour-intensive techniques and to territorial identity, related industries are important tools of local or regional economic development.

Whatever the form of vertical coordination taken within the systems, at the spatial dimension firms can locate in disperse or in agglomerated forms. The level of dispersion or concentration of the firms is determined mostly by the assets related to productive processes. The common use of equipment or infrastructure, labour force qualification, and research and development facilities may justify agglomeration, as well as technological intensity, or raw material and labour prices could explain diversification. AFS profits derive from strategic choices that are generally related to the first set of factors. In these cases, it is more likely to find agglomerated networks strategically placed to make use of local identities. Of course, multinationals and/or other large firms, whose product has been clearly defined and is produced for huge consumption market segment, do not have to submit to external economies and may maintain their production units in dispersed forms.

Considering the above described characteristics, Table 5.2 combines locational and governance choices in a unique model. The matrix includes different empirical examples. Horizontally, four organizational models (the columns) are identified at the top of the matrix. The first shows the non-existence of scale economies but the existence of scope economies as well as the use of the local identity concept. The next model indicates the presence of benefits from scale economies and suggests the use of the local identity concept. The third model has all the firms using the advantages of scope economies, but being at the national level, generally there is an absence of using the local identity attribute. The last model indicates the

Table 5.2 Examples of locational and governance choices: the case of food enterprises

	No dominant enterprise	One coordinating enterprise and several partners	One leading enterprise and several partners	A set of vertically integrated enterprises
Local level				
Atomistic producers	Wine production Loire Valley (case study)	Nuts production Lamego (case study)	X	X
Network organization of small units	Rice production Mississipi (case study)	Fresh tomato production Brittany (case study)	Carob derivates Algarve	X
Geographic agglomeration of a few but large units	Canned tomato Ribatejo Oeste (case study)	Wine tourism in Tuscany	Roquefort société Roquefort	Pork production North Carolina (case study)
National level				
Network organization of spread-out small units	Grula – small distributors Portugal (case study)	Small distribution of coffee Brazil (case study)	Sunflower oil (HOS) Italy (case study)	X
Network organization of a few but large units	Saucege Production Greece (case study)	Animal feeding France (case study)	Milling industry France (case study)	X
Widely dispersed units	Hog sector Spain (case study)	Wholesale vegetables Montpelier, France	Dairy products Yogurts France	Dairy sector B.G. Food Ltd Kent, UK (case study)

Source: Vaz elaboration based on Storper and Harrison (1991) and supported by referenced case studies.

simultaneous use of scale and scope economies. In this last model, again at national level, it is expected that such firms will not employ local identity attributes. Vertically, simplified governance structures are illustrated: the model of no leadership is exemplified by the cases described in the first column, while the last column illustrates vertical integration. All the other cases represent intermediate situations.

The model described below is extremely simplified and should be viewed as illustrative rather than exhaustive. In theory the matrix should express a much more extended number of rows and columns, all of them describing an evolutionary path for both geographical concentration and coordination forms. However, this would complicate even more the search for empirical cases to fill the resulting boxes, each one illustrative of different spatial systems of production, by sectors.

The exercise, however, enables analysts to investigate whether the production systems remain static in the same cell of this matrix or whether time conditions, namely the power game among organizations, would lead to a change in the relative arrangement of the cells. Ideally, such a matrix could be prepared for certain regions and its dynamic movement followed. This study's argument suggests that a displacement of production systems towards the right side of the matrix would take place, as well as a concentration of firms in the horizontal central area. This movement would happen due to the combined goals of obtaining scale economies, integration or external economies, and cooperation.

5.6 MODEL PROSPECTIVE: IS THE COEXISTENCE OF DIFFERENT COOPERATIVE FORMS IN THE SAME SPACE POSSIBLE?

The models previously described locate in geographical spaces and are part of previously established networking systems. The financial potential, competencies, knowledge and learning capacity of firms are the important instruments for channelling power into such systems, and undergo a dynamic process through which market circuits are defined and settled mostly in the interests of a dominant firm. The other firms are pushed in this fashion, as they have no alternative for surviving outside the networking system.

Given the circumstances, the possibility of trending toward two extreme positions (vertical integration and no leadership) coexisting in the same local conditions is debatable: (1) the model of vertical integration is composed mainly by one structure of governance but expressed in many different functional forms; (2) the model of no leadership enables governance and relational links of the partners that allow an equilibrated distribution of power.

Cohendet's (1998) work on 'percolation modelling' may be helpful in examining this question. He uses the model to analyse the adaptability of economic agents to absorb new technologies when integrated in networking systems. His theoretical conclusion explains that agents included in a networking system accept the irreversibility of the local structure of interaction between potential and actual adopters of the competing technologies. In such cases even the choices of each agent depend on the structure of the system, including those network externalities – the agent's utility increasing with the number of partners adopting the same technology.

This chapter also considers the existence of two classes of models: those where the proximity between agents is symmetrical, and those where the mutual influences between agents are not symmetrical. Percolation can be considered a phenomenon for which a disordered contagion occurs by a continuous aggregation of micro variations on a network. The dynamics of change in this case is a real mutation in a given system. For percolation to occur, a whole set of conditions must occur: the formation of a critical mass, irreversibility, connectivity, receptivity and other concepts that are very difficult to outline in terms of economic agents.

The argument is not valid unless it is demonstrated to have empirical or at least numerical simulation support. However, empirical evidence shows that networking systems do benefit from different socio-economic conditions created by the environment (industrial districts in Italy, and Silicon Valley in the USA) and in each case such conditions are well suited to each of the different models. On the other hand, there is feedback from the enterprises to their environments, generating induced changes that adapt them to firm needs. Labour force specialization and the creation of small new firms based on the research and development (R&D) of new products are good examples. It seems that these may be natural dominance cycles whose dynamic factors help one or the other model to become more competitive at certain geographical spaces.

Only longer-term time series analyses would enable learning with greater certainty about whether or not such models are able to coexist in the same geographical space when representing input–output systems of the same activity branches. Of course there are also questions regarding the scale of such geographic spaces.

5.7 CONCLUSION

The problem raised in this chapter starts with a classical discussion within the forum of regional economics. It concerns the impact that the new industrial model has upon locational choices when firms have to deal with both scale and scope economies.

No doubt, flexible specialization encourages coordination. But how the firms are able to develop cooperative behaviours depends on the environment that they are integrated in (embeddedness), on the market impositions to innovate, and on the regulations supporting competition. The causal effect between spatial embeddedness and innovation has been stressed in this study. The idea has been to demonstrate the symbiotic aspect of these two strategic determinants, emphasizing the role of partnerships.

But partnership and coordination are not trouble-free entrepreneurial attitudes. Brousseau (1993) has presented a model for the dynamics of the organization of production induced by the power of a specific agent in the negotiation of a contract. Even under contractual circumstances (for example, in cases in which regulation may interfere, informal cooperation remains outside of the influence of regulatory controls), the coordination forms are defined by the dominant agents. In other words, production systems should be viewed as unstable elements whose governance structures are neither equilibrated nor, consequently, long-lasting.

To illustrate this idea, this study develops a model that combines different locational and governance choices. Based on empirical examples, the resulting matrix shows two extreme positions: vertical integration and no leadership. The coexistence of these two different systems, in the same local conditions and for the same activity branch, is proposed and debated in the chapter.

Attending to the characteristics of networking, some theoretical arguments speculate that when different industrial systems coexist, they tend to dominate complete subsectors of the industrial chain and design, not the behaviours of the enterprises involved. The dynamics of such a complex model was suggested, but due to limited time series data relating coordination systems to location choices it was not possible to establish empirical evidence to support or disprove it. Further research in this area is recommended.

The theoretical model that has been presented evokes some policy implications at two different levels: development of policy instruments, and their application. The analyses created informed hypotheses suggesting increased vulnerability of firms that are protected from external circumstances such as environment or competition. Their capacity to innovate is therefore linked to uncertainty, which can no longer be considered as an imperfection, but rather as a basic condition (Christensen et al., 2003). Networking decreases this uncertainty but obliges agents to enter into a game of power that, when considered in the geographical space, may define specific behavioural patterns for entrepreneurs. Policy instruments and design should be aware of this reality and become more specific. Under the presented argument, the need for the recognition and creation of regional innovation systems is accentuated. Besides, policy-makers should be able to develop instruments to follow permanently the changes taking place in the productive systems and, if needed, to apply particular incentives.

The second aspect to stress is the modification that this new industrial model suggests for the regulating competition. There is now, more then ever, a tendency for conflict, but cooperation is the rule for survival. In this context legislation should control (in a transversal way) the abuse of power, the use of asymmetrical information and the formation of human capital.

REFERENCES

Antonelli, C. and M. Calderini (1999), 'The dynamics of localised technological exchange', in A. Gambardella and F. Malerba (eds), *The Organisation of Economic Innovation in Europe*, Cambridge: Cambridge University Press, pp. 158–76.

Arena, R. and P-M. Romani (1998), 'Contribution à une Approche Marshalliene de la Petite Enterprise', *Revue d'Economie Industrielle*, **86**, 49–60.

Arndt, O. and R. Sternberg (2000), 'Do manufacturing firms profit from intra-regional innovation linkages? An empirical based answer', *European Planning Studies*, **8**(4), 465–85.

Avermaete, T. (2004), 'Dynamics of innovation in small food firms', PhD thesis in Applied Biological Sciences, University of Gent.

Becattini, G. and E. Rullani (1995), 'Système local et marché global: le district industrial', in A. Raillet and A. Torre (eds), *Économie Industrielle et Économie Spatiale*, Paris: Economica, pp. 173–92.

Benson, J.K. (1975), 'The inter-organisational network as a political economy', *Quarterly Administrative Science*, **20**, 229–49.

Brousseau, E. (1993), *L'Economie des Contrats – Technologies de l'information et coordination interentreprises*, Paris: Press Universitaires de France.

Christensen, P., A.P. Cornett and K. Philipsen (2003), 'Coherence of innovation policy instruments', in B. Asheim, A. Isaksen, C. Nauwelaers and F. Todtling (eds), *Regional Innovation Policy for Small-Medium Enterprises*, Cheltenham, UK and Northampton, MA, USA: Edward Elgar Publishing, pp. 166–90.

Cohendet, P. (1998), 'Network, interactions between economic agents and irreversibilities: the case of the choice among competing technologies', in P. Cohendet, P. Llerena, H. Stahn and G. Umbhauer (eds), *The Economics of Networks*, Berlin: Springer, pp. 93–121.

Connor, J. and W. Schiek (1997), *Food Processing: An Industrial Power House in Transition*, John Wiley & Sons.

Davelaar, E.J. (1996), *Regional Economic Analyses of Innovation and Incubation*, Aldershot, UK and Brookfield, VT, USA: Avebury.

Freel, M. (2000), 'External linkages and product innovation in small manufacturing firms', *Entrepreneurship and Regional Development*, **12**(3), 245–66.
Gallizzi, G. and L. Venturini (1999), 'Towards a theory of successful vertical co-operation', in G. Galizzi and L. Venturini (eds), *Vertical Relationships and Co-operation in the Food System*, Germany: Springer-Verlag, pp. 61–92.
Grunert, K.G. and T. Ottowitz (1997), 'Neumarkter Lammsbräu: brewing beer for Greens', in B. Traill and K.E. Grunert (eds), *Product and Process Innovation in the Food Industry*, London: Blackie Academic & Professional, pp. 99–111.
Jack, S.L. and A.R. Anderson (2002), 'The effects of embeddedness on the entrepreneurial process', *Journal of Business Venturing*, **17**(5), 467–87.
Keeble, D. and F. Wilkinson (1999), 'Collective learning and knowledge development in the evolution of regional clusters for high technology SMEs in Europe', *Regional Studies*, **33**(4), 295–303.
Kirat,T. and Y. Lung (1999), 'Innovation and proximity: territories as loci of collective learning processes', *European Urban and Regional Studies*, **6**(1), 27–38.
Malmberg, A. and P. Maskell (2002), 'The elusive concept of localization economies: towards a knowledge-based theory of spatial clustering', *European Planning A*, **34**(3), 429–49.
McDermott, P. and M. Taylor (1982), *Industrial Organisation and Location*, Cambridge: Cambridge University Press.
Nicolas, F. (1999), 'Globalisation's consequences for vertical coordination and competition in the food system', in G. Galizzi and L. Venturini (eds), *Vertical Relationships and Co-operation in the Food System*, Heidelberg: Physica-Verlag, pp. 157–80.
Nightingale, P. (1998), 'A cognitive model of innovation', *Research Policy*, **27**(7), 689–709.
Nonaka, I., R. Toyama and N. Konno (2000), 'SECI, Ba and leadership: a unified model of dynamic knowledge creation', *Long Range Planning*, **33**(1), 5–34.
Schoenberger, E. (1997), *The Cultural Crisis of the Firm*, Cambridge: Blackwell Publishers.
Storper, M. and B. Harrison (1991), 'Flexibility, hierarchy and regional development: the changing structure of industrial production systems and their forms of governance in the 1990s', *Research Policy*, **20**, 407–422.
Taylor, M. (1996), 'The business enterprise, power and patterns of geographical industrialisation', in S. Conti, E. Malecki and P. Oinas (eds), *The Industrial Enterprise and its Environment: Spatial Perspectives*, Aldershot, UK and Brookfield, VT, USA: Avebury, pp. 99–122.
Vaz, M.T.N., M. Cesário and S. Fernandes (2006), 'Interaction between innovation in small firms and their environments: an explorative study', *European Planning Studies*, **14(1)**, 96–118.
Vaz, M.T.N. and L. Urban (2000), 'Régions périphériques, stratégies agroalimentaires et globalisation', *Economie et Societé*, Série 'Systèmes Agroalimentaires', AG, **24**, 49–60.

6. Differentials in industrial structure and human capital performance across Australia's regions and the settlement system

Robert J. Stimson

6.1 INTRODUCTION

This chapter provides an overview of recent trends and spatial patterns of differentiation in a number of aspects of regional performance in Australia. The focus is specifically on two key aspects of contemporary economic transition, namely:

- changes in industry structure and levels of industry diversification;
- changes in qualifications and occupation levels – or human capital performance – at various levels of spatial scale across the national space economy.

This chapter draws on recently completed research conducted by the Commonwealth Government's Bureau of Transport and Regional Economics (BTRE) (2004a, 2004b) and by a group of researchers at the University of Queensland (UQ) (Stimson et al., 2004). The BTRE research has focused on analysing and modelling trends and patterns over the period 1991–2001 in the characteristics and changing spatial patterns of industry structure and of education, skills and qualifications in Australia, and on the relationship between those phenomena and regional employment size and of changes in regional income. The UQ research was conducted as an Australian National Training Authority (ANTA) National Project (referred to here as the ANTA/UQ study). It focused on analysing and mapping the characteristics and patterns of work, employment, skills, income and other selected socio-economic variables across Australia's cities, towns and urban localities at the 2001 Census, and on developing a typology of statistical local areas (SLAs) to differentiate places according to their position on a 'continuum of opportunity–vulnerability' measuring their performance over the decade 1991–2001 with respect to those dimensions.

The chapter begins with a brief discussion of the rationale for addressing these aspects of regional change and performance, and that is followed by an overview of the recent Australia literature and of the macro context for considering those issues. The bulk of the chapter then follows, in which the implications of the findings of the BTRE and the ANTA/CR-SURF (Center for Research into Sustainable Urban and Regional Futures at the University of Queensland) studies are discussed. The chapter concludes with a brief discussion of the implications of those findings, particularly for regional development and planning policy.

6.2 RATIONALE

It is important to understand the role of regions in a national economy, how different regions perform, and how their structures and performance change over time. There is a huge literature on theory and methods in regional economic development, and over time there has been an evolution of focus in regional economic development theory, from neoclassical theory based on the Solow (1956) model through to 'new growth theory' (see for example Romer, 1986, 1990; Barro, 1990; Arthur, 1994). Increasingly there has been a shift in emphasis from the importance of regional comparative advantage to regional competitive advantage, and a focus on the factors and processes of endogenous growth (see, for example, Johansson et al., 2001).

6.2.1 Economic Growth, Specialization and Diversity

Neoclassical economic theory argues there is a tendency over time for different units of analysis – such as incomes, educational attainment levels and regional performance – to converge over time because of assumed diminishing returns to capital in the long run. However the extent to which convergence (or divergence) is important, and indeed the degree to which it actually occurs, is an important issue as it provides an indication of how different groups of people or regions are changing and growing relative to each other, and of what might be influencing growth rates.

Economic theory also suggests that regional economic growth is derived from regional specialization based on comparative advantage, with stability achieved through diversity by spreading risk across a range of economic activities. The distribution of a region's economic activity across industry sectors, the mix of occupations and the skills mix of jobs all combine to determine the level and distribution of income in a region and the resilience of its economy and its ability to grow (Bureau of Transport and Regional Economics (2004a, p. ix). How the regional industrial mix changes over time is an important consideration for regional performance and competitiveness, and in particular in the context of how that reflects shifts in the structure of the national economy and how the shifts produce an increase or decline in gross value added (GVA) for regions and their industry sectors.

There is considerable debate over the issue of industrial diversification as against specialization, and the nature of locational growth and decline in industry sectors (Gordon and McCann, 2000) and the power of urban scale and agglomeration, particularly for industries such as the advanced producer services (Taylor et al., 2002).

Kaufman (1993) has noted that there is little empirical evidence of a direct relationship between industrial diversity and the economic performance of regions. His study of the relationship between diversity, stability, performance and energy prices in US metropolitan areas found that a diverse employment base creates stability, and that this buffers economic performance against economic shocks. He found that more highly diverse regions outperformed less diverse regions in years when a negative shock occurred, but they underperformed in years where there was a positive shock. However, there was no relationship between diversity and performance for periods when there was no economic shock. Kaufman concluded that increasing diversity does not ensure better regional performance, but rather that it works to insulate the economy from the effects of a shock, either positive or negative. Lande (1994) also notes that diversification does not necessarily reduce instability since employment growth is correlated across industries. Thus, it may be that striving for diversity should reflect a preference for slow and steady growth over a boom-and-bust economy. Policies to encourage stabilizing industries rather than stable industries are thus recommended.

In a study focusing on urban centres, Duranton and Puga (2000) have reviewed national urban systems and they point to five 'stylized facts' concerning industry diversity and specialization, noting that:

- specialized and diversified cities coexist;
- larger cities tend to be more diversified and cities of similar specialization are of similar size;
- individual city-size rankings and individual city specialization are stable over time;
- individual city growth is related to specialization and diversity, and to relative location;

- there is a high rate of firm turnover, most innovations taking place in particularly diversified cities where most new firms are created, with most relocations being from diversified to specialized cities.

The importance of diversity as an attractor of the so-called 'new economy' activities – and in particular the innovative industry sectors – is demonstrated by Henderson et al. (1995), but they do point out that a history of past specialization does seem to matter for the more mature industry sectors.

Of course the industry structure of a region's output can differ greatly from that of its employment because of a whole set of factors, including its resource endowments, and the capital and labour intensiveness and productivity of particular industry sectors. In the Australian context in particular, a region's industry structure, occupation mix and human capital structure are also affected not only by the size of the region's economy, but also by its level of remoteness in the context of the nation's settlement system.

6.2.2 Human Capital

Increasingly the role of human capital, its development and levels, is being given explicit attention in the context of economic transition and regional performance. As stated by the Bureau of Transport and Regional Economics (2004b, p. 4): 'education, skills and qualifications may not be evenly distributed across populations for a number of reasons. Those may relate to the socio-economic background of individuals, opportunities, or location, as well as innate learning capacity'. But in the contemporary era of globalization and the increasingly competitive environment in which both nations and their regions operate, and in particular given the importance of knowledge-based and information-intensive economic activities as the drivers of wealth generation, human capital is assuming increasing significance as an endogenous factor in regional economic growth and development. That is addressed in a number of recent reports by the Organisation for Economic Co-operation and Development (OECD, 1998, 2001a, 2001b, 2001c).

Human capital development has many dimensions. For example, White (1987) sees education as fulfilling two instrumental functions in society:

- an integrative function – primarily through schooling – to transmit cultural norms and values;
- an economic function by equipping people with the skills necessary for participation in the workforce – increasingly achieved through post-school education and training and through lifelong learning.

Higher levels of education and skills are said to have benefits, including higher employability, increased earnings and higher job quality. Among others, Quiggin (1999) has found education to be a significant contributor to economic growth and regional performance, as well as there also being non-monetary benefits, including better health knowledge and health status, transmission of cultural values and reduced criminal behaviour.

Research in the US has long recognized the relationship between educational attainment and economic and regional development (Hanushek and Kinko, 2000). For example, Goetz and Rapasingha (2001) refer to public policy initiatives in several states to attempt to increase the number of college graduates to keep pace with the skills-intensive nature of the 'new economy'.

Two models have been proposed discussing the theoretical impacts of skills and qualifications on economic development. First there is the 'screening model', which assumes that the education system is the process for sorting out individuals into the most difficult and better-renumerated jobs in society, with the outputs of the system ranking the abilities of people and thus providing a signal to potential employers of people's capacity. Then there is the 'human capital model', which argues that education, skills and qualifications form part of a broader economic concept of 'human capital', which refers to the value to the economy of increased economic investment in people.

The Bureau of Transport and Regional Economics (2004b) points out that:

> the links between education, labour quality and productivity are complex. However, education, skills and qualifications are increasingly considered to be central to regional productivity, employment opportunities, personal development and the resilience of communities . . . [Thus the] . . . acquisition, production, distribution and use of knowledge are valued as a contributor to individual and social well-being and economic prosperity. (p. 1)

Over time, the increasing affluence in Western societies – as well as elsewhere – has contributed to higher levels of education for more people. More recently, the transition of production of goods and services to become knowledge-based and information-intensive, along with globalization processes, have raised requirements for labour quality and innovation and entrepreneurship. Increasingly, how knowledge is used is dependent on the skills of the workforce which affects the performance of regions and places.

It is now also argued that the 'new learning economy' (OECD, 2001b) relies on 'lifelong learners' (OECD, 1998), who can adapt positively to changing economic conditions and adopt process and product innovations to improve productivity and performance. That line of argument also suggests that societies (and, by inference, regions and places) with better-educated populations enjoy benefits such as heightened civic participation and volunteering, lower crime rates and social inclusion. Conversely, places with high concentrations of labour force participants with minimal qualifications are more susceptible to social and labour market risks, unemployment and social exclusion (OECD, 2001b).

6.3 RECENT RESEARCH ON REGIONAL ISSUES AND PERFORMANCE IN AUSTRALIA

Over the years many studies have been conducted in Australia investigating regional differentials in, and the interrelationships between population and employment growth, population and employment size, structural shifts in employment distribution across industry sectors, industrial diversification, levels of income, and the characteristics of regional location. However, relatively few studies have incorporated an explicit focus on the nature of occupational structure, occupational status, and education qualifications and skills, all of which are important components in the consideration of human capital differentials in regional development and performance. These have identified a range of factors that influence patterns of regional growth, and the specific conclusions they research or the relationships they identify are not necessarily consistent because of the different focus and methodologies, variations in the level of spatial aggregation/disaggregation in the spatial units of analysis, and the different time periods to which the analyses relate. What follows is a selective summary of some key studies.

In taking a focus on the changing economic roles of cities and towns across the settlement system of Australia, Beer (1999) and Beer and Maude (1995) have conducted a functional classification of regional cities and towns from 1961 to 1996. Their findings show that the highest population growth over the period 1991 to 1996 was recorded by a group of centres characterized by tourism, entertainment and recreation-related industries, with a similar pattern identified for the period 1976 to 1991. An increasing degree of functional specialization was found to have emerged. In 1961 the regional cities and towns could be classified according to just nine categories; that had increased to 12 categories by 1991, and 16 categories by 1996. That fragmentation of functional specialization was seen to reflect the concentration of a number of activities, especially tourism in one set of towns, administration in another, and mining in a third. Beer (1999) suggests that the uneven outcomes for regional cities and towns reflects the way that the broader focus of economic change has impacted upon their specialist functions, which suggests that the days of the country town with a wide range of functions may be passing, and that economic success now calls for specialization in a smaller number of functions.

O'Connor et al. (2001) provide an overview of Australia's changing economic geography up to the mid-1990s, highlighting the multiple divides that are emerging both within the metropolitan cities and across regional Australia. In particular they point to the spatial mismatches that are evident in regional shares of population and population change and shares of investment in economic activity, and they raise a series of challenging implications for people-based policy and for place-based policy in addressing spatial disparities and the infrastructure needs of those segments and places in the space economy that are significant contributors to national wealth and competitiveness.

An early study by the then Department of Home Affairs and Environment (1982) developed a set of urban socio-economic and environmental indicators for urban areas in Australia for the 1970s, and found that urban centres that specialized in manufacturing, electricity and transport showed higher than average income levels. Of course that study was undertaken using data for the time before the post-1970s era of dramatic economic restructuring and deregulation in response to the need for Australia to improve its competitiveness internationally.

More recently a study of structural change over the period 1981 to 1996 by the Productivity Commission (1998) found no systematic relationship between structural change and regional employment growth across Australia's statistical subdivisions, but that high structural change did not mean a low or negative regional employment growth. The study also found that 38 per cent of the variability in actual employment growth in regions could be explained by the national shift component in industry sector employment.

Numerous studies have focused on regional population and employment growth. For example a study by Garnaut et al. (2001) of regional influences on employment and population growth found that metropolitan and coastal regions experienced stronger population and employment growth than did inland and remote regions over the decade 1986 to 1996, with inland and remote growth being strongest in and around the largest towns. The study also found that incomes were high in remote regions, reflecting fast employment growth in the mining and welfare sectors and the need to pay high wages to recruit workers to regions seen to have low amenity.

Bradley and Gans (1998) have used regression analysis of population and labour force growth in Australian cities to demonstrate that labour force growth over the period 1981–91 positively correlates to a city's previous growth and its level of industrial diversity, and that labour force growth was negatively related to the initial size of the city and to government employment share.

Lawson and Dwyer (2002) have conducted a regression analysis of employment growth across 637 regions of Australia, 1986–1996. They found that regions were more likely to experience employment growth if they had high employment in accommodation, cafes and restaurants, or high industrial diversity at the start of the period. They found that regions that experienced high structural change were also more likely to have grown. But less significant factors associated with the likelihood of a region experiencing employment growth included a region having a coastal location, and a high employment share in property and business services. Regions that are relatively remote and regions with high concentrations of employment in electricity, gas and water supply were found to be less likely to experience employment growth.

Trends in regional variations in income distribution have also been studied. For example, research conducted by the National Centre for Social and Economic Modelling (NATSEM) investigating differences in regional performance (Lloyd et al., 2000) reveals a 'hollowing-out' of the income distribution of average household incomes across all regions in Australia between 1991 and 1996. That research shows how four-fifths of households living in the large metropolitan cities and the largest regional towns had about twice as many high-income households and a much smaller population of low-income households. The populations of both high- and low-income households in fact increased across all regions. The regional cities and towns had a similar fall to that in the big cities in the proportion of middle-income households. But the largest change was in the rural towns, where low-income households increased substantially while the proportion of high-income households increased only marginally. The researchers refer to a 'widening income gap' between those living in affluent areas and those living in the middle-ranked areas, with those at the bottom appearing to have fared somewhat better than those at the middle of the income distribution (p. 290).

Baum et al. (1999) have developed a multivariate modelling framework to identify a typology of clusters of community opportunity and vulnerability between 1986 and 1996 across SLAs comprising Australia's mega-metro city regions, and for large regional cities and towns with populations over 10 000, and smaller regional towns with populations between 4000 and 10 000. The key factors differentiating between the places of opportunity and the places of vulnerability in terms of how places were coping with socio-economic transition were found to relate to levels of human capital and income, engagement/disengagement in the workforce, and industry structure, and to population size for the regional towns. That community opportunity–vulnerability framework and typology of SLAs across Australia's cities and towns has been used for further analysis, including a study by Stimson and Baum (2001), to identify the degree to which there are variations between 'opportunity' and 'vulnerable' communities in the incidence of qualifications and skills in the workforce, levels of participation in post-secondary education and training, and the distribution of income including the incidence of household dependence on Commonwealth income support and benefits. Significant spatial and functional disparities were identified across the settlement system.

Draca et al. (2003) have conducted a cross-sectional analysis of the relationship between education, skills and qualifications and the economic performance of five mainland states of Australia, showing that differences in education, skills and qualifications may explain between 10 and 20 per cent of the variation in gross state product (GSP) per capita for Victoria, Queensland and South Australia. Their research concluded that high skill qualifications and jobs are important but do not have to dominate the labour force to achieve economic performance.

The role of education, skills and qualifications in regional economic development and performance is complex but generally favourable (OECD, 2001a, 2001b, 2001c). But there does seem to be some conflicting evidence for the correlation between regional education and skills and employment growth in Australia, with a study by Lawson and Dwyer (2002) using a binomial logit model finding no correlation. However, a complementary regression suggested that a higher proportion of skilled people is associated with higher rates of regional growth in employment. Those researchers also found that regions with low education and skills have stronger rates of out-migration, which may be a reflection of skilled workers being more likely to leave less-educated regions because of diminishing employment opportunities. But the researchers were unable to find a significant correlation between in-migration and education and skills levels.

Garnett and Lewis (2000) suggest that 'an examination of rural education levels, and changes over time, is an important aspect of any analysis of labour markets' (p. 168), particularly in rural and regional areas. They point out that while the proportion of people holding a degree in rural and regional areas is lower than it is in the metropolitan cities, the gap did narrow between 1991 and 1996, even though it still stood at 19.2 per cent for the major urban areas compared to 8.5 per cent in rural localities, and 10.9 per cent in the balance of the rural areas. But the researchers point out that this is not surprising, as many rural occupations are not in professional fields, and thus do not offer the returns to investment in human capital that is the case in the big cities and larger regional centres. The out-migration of people from rural communities to larger towns and to the big cities is due to a number of factors that have been operating for a long time, but it has been exacerbated by low terms of trade for farmers, and a decline in rural services such as banking, health and education in the smaller urban centres and localities.

Garnett and Lewis (2000) refer to research that reveals how 'it has long been recognised that rural [and regional] education facilities are worse than those available in metropolitan areas, and participation rates are also lower' (p. 167). That is demonstrated in work by Harrison (1997), while Norris and Woden (1996) suggest that the difference in quality and levels of formal education might partially explain why people are migrating out of rural and regional Australia, and especially from smaller communities. And it might help to explain why, in general, unemployment rates are higher in rural and regional areas than they are in the metropolitan cities.

6.4 RECENT MACRO TRENDS IN AUSTRALIA

On the basis of the most commonly used indicators of macroeconomic performance, the Main Report from the ANTA/UQ project notes that: 'Australia's economic performance has exceeded that of the G7 economies in all but one of the last ten years' (Stimson et al., 2004: Ch. 2:1). Annual average growth over the decade to 2002/03 was 3.8 per cent, compared with 2.5 per cent for the G7 economies. But despite that strong performance, there are a number of aspects of Australia's economy that make it vulnerable to externally induced fluctuations, chief among these being the fact that it is a small, open economy with a large proportion of it exposed to fluctuating world trading conditions.

The recent strength of the Australian economy is now also being seen in improved employment outcomes. Over the 15 years up to 2000/2001, Australia had a higher unemployment rate than the G7 economies, but that has changed to the reverse situation since that time. The strong growth in employment and the favourable basic macro aggregates of the labour market outcomes appear favourable, but as documented by Stimson et al. (2004, Ch. 2, p. 5), there are some problems, including:

- a high preponderance of non-standard jobs;
- the uneven spatial distribution of employment outcomes;
- below-average outcomes of young males, some migrant groups and indigenous peoples (mainly males);
- issues regarding job quality and satisfaction.

When one takes a long-term historical perspective, then the magnitude of the structural shifts that have occurred in the employment shares of industry sectors in the Australian economy are profound, as highlighted by the following data from the Australian Bureau of Statistics (2002) *Year Book*:

- In 1910/11, agriculture, farming, fishing and hunting accounted for 26 per cent of employment, and this had declined to less than 5 per cent in 2002.
- In 1910/11, 6 per cent of employed persons worked in mining, and this had declined to 2 per cent by 1927/28 and to less than 1 per cent in 2002.
- In 1910/11, manufacturing employed 21 per cent of workers, and this grew rapidly to peak at 33 per cent in the mid-1930s after the 1930s Depression, was 25 per cent in the mid-1960s and fell to 12 per cent in 2002.
- The services industries grew gradually to become the major employers by the end of the twentieth century, with much of the growth occurring since the 1970s. By 2002, retail trade employed 12 per cent of workers, and property and business services also employed 12 per cent.

In common with OECD nations, Australia's economy has thus experienced a decline in the importance of the agricultural and the manufacturing sectors and it has experienced strong growth in the services sectors over recent decades. But, as is also the case in the US, there has been strong growth in Australia in GVA in agriculture, and the decline in employment in manufacturing is linked to strong labour force productivity growth in that sector and a shift in consumer preferences to services as national income has risen (Productivity Commission, 2003). OECD data and research by the Bureau of Transport and Regional Economics (2004a) show that the comparative of the growth in the services sectors in Australia differs from that in other OECD countries in that only Australia has experienced a decline in the GVA share of the OECD's wholesale and retail trade, repairs, hotels and restaurants, and transport sectors. Australia was also the only country in which the GVA shares of the other services activities sector increased. As with other OECD countries, over the three decades from 1970 to 2000, Australia experienced rapid growth in the financial intermediation, real estate, renting and business activities sector.

Using the Malizia and Ke (1993) industry instability index (ISI), the Bureau of Transport and Regional Economics (2004a) has analysed quarterly unemployment data across industry sectors for the period 1985–2002 to measure the extent of deviation of the time series from a long-run linear trend. That analysis shows that the electricity, gas and water and the communication services sectors had the most unstable employment, while employment in health and community services and in retail trade was stable over time (p. 7). At a more detailed level of industry sector disaggregation, it was found that those industries with relatively unstable employment included: 'Machinery and motor vehicle wholesaling and Services to finance and insurance . . . larger industries such as Food retailing, Education and Health services had the most stable employment . . . while Business services employ more people than any other industry, employment is not particularly stable' (p. 8). Agriculture was found to have relatively stable employment.

Turning now to consider human capital levels and performance, expansion in post-secondary education qualification levels in Australia has been substantial but concentrated in the Bachelor or higher degree level, which grew at 47 per cent between 1991 and 1996, and then at a reduced rate of 33 per cent between 1996 and 2001. That contrasts with the certificate or vocational level, which grew at 10 per cent between 1991 and 1996, and then at an increased rate of 31 per cent between 1996 and 2001. But the 2001 Census data show that for the majority (57 per cent) of people in Australia, their highest educational qualification remains at the compulsory schooling or basic vocational level, even though there was a 4.7 per cent decline in their numbers over the decade 1991 to 2001 (Bureau of Transport and Regional Economics, 2004b, pp. 10–11).

The OECD (1998) reports that, while all OECD nations make initial education investments of about 6.3 per cent of gross domestic product (GDP), there are marked differences among member countries in the levels of spending on and in participation in post-compulsory education and training. OECD data show that Australia has slightly more tertiary educated people than the average for OECD nations, but that it has fewer upper-secondary school completions. Its educational expansion has occurred less evenly than is the case for most OECD nations, and in Australia that expansion is concentrated at the university level rather than being spread more evenly across qualifications levels. Draca et al. (2003) have noted that Australia has high levels of educational participation and comparatively low levels of completion. The OECD (1998) data also show that social rates of return to education investment are highest for the upper-secondary level, and they then begin to diminish at tertiary levels. Private rates of return are higher at the tertiary level, and this is the case in Australia in particular (along with Canada and France) where privately borne costs of education are estimated to reap private gains between 15 and 25 per cent higher than initial outlays.

Gregory (1995) points to several labour market conditions in Australia that have contributed to the increased demand for education in Australia since the 1970s. That includes:

- a fall in the effective cost of an additional year of (school) education;
- an increase in part-time employment opportunities that has allowed students to earn an income whilst studying, thus reducing the opportunity cost for further education;
- an increase in the level of government education subsidies providing incentives for education participation.

While education levels have grown strongly in Australia over the decade 1991–2001, with the proportion of people with skilled vocational or higher qualifications having increased from 31 per cent to 43 per cent, such an increase has been in line with comparable OECD nations. But the Bureau of Transport and Regional Economics (2004b) notes that the 'upward trend in education levels was not mirrored in occupation shares' (p. 18), and, 'although there was considerable change in occupation structures within industry sectors, at an aggregate national level relative occupation shares remained similar between 1991 and 2001' (p. ix).

Minimal change in fact occurred in the proportions of workers at the highest and lowest occupation status levels. There was a decrease in the tradespersons, advanced clerical and service workers categories, and there was a more marked decrease in the shares of skilled tradespeople. However, there has been an increase in associate professionals and in all the professional categories (p. 11).

As an economy evolves it is to be expected that different sectors will take on increasing prominence and that the changing nature of work involved will affect the skills levels required. It is important to ascertain where, across industry sectors and across occupational categories, the jobs employing people with different levels of human capital are being created. Research by the Bureau of Transport and Regional Economics (2004a, p. 11) found that, over the decade 1991–2001, all industry sectors did experience growth in the shares of university educated workers, and some sectors have displayed an upward shift towards more highly skilled occupations while offering fewer lower-skilled and unskilled jobs. That has occurred in the mining, finance and insurance, and in the manufacturing sectors. However, the expanding retail trade and the accommodation, cafes and restaurants sectors have increased their shares of relatively unskilled workers. Professional jobs in teaching, health and computing have increased at or above the national level of employment and population growth rates. But the research found that by 2001 all industry sectors with a below-average proportion of highly educated workers were closer to the national average than they were in 1991. In 1991 only six industry sectors were above the average of 10 per cent – education, health and community services, property and business services, government administration and defence, finance and insurance, and cultural and recreation services – whereas by 2001 nine industry sectors were above the national average of 13 per cent, with electricity, gas and water supply, mining, and communication services being added to the list. The fastest growth in jobs for highly educated workers had occurred in mining, communications services, and transport and storage (Bureau of Transport and Regional Economics, 2004b, p. 12).

Analysis by the Bureau of Transport and Regional Economics (2004b, pp. 12–16) also reveals that: 'across all industry sectors, high correlation exists between corresponding education and occupation levels. A negative correlation also exists between high education levels and lower occupation levels, and vice-versa. That is, highly educated workers are unlikely to hold lower level occupations, and workers with minimum qualifications are unlikely to hold higher level occupations' (p. 16).

Reich (1991) has proposed a way to capture better the changes occurring as a result of economic restructuring and the shift from 'old' to 'new' economic activities, the latter involving jobs with advanced human capital skills required by knowledge-intensive industries and occupations. Reich saw those structural changes in employment as being reflected in the changing patterns of jobs across three broad occupational categories, which he proposes represent a way of capturing the changes occurring in modern society. Those three categories are:

- 'Symbolic analyst' occupations, which include jobs held by the professionals and managers who create knowledge and manipulate information. People in those jobs need to be well educated and possess high levels of analytical and technical skills.
- 'Routine production worker' occupations, which are represented by the 'foot soldiers' of the factories and back offices.
- 'In-person service worker occupations', which involve face-to-face contact with customers.

Research by Stimson and Baum (2001) and O'Connor et al. (2001) shows the magnitude of the shifts that have occurred since 1986 in the relative importance of employment in those three broad occupational groupings proposed by Reich. They have reorganized the two-digit occupational categories for which census data are available in Australia. That analysis shows:

- There has been a very significant increase in the share of jobs in the symbolic analyst occupations, from 23.1 per cent of all jobs in 1986 to 26.4 per cent of all jobs in 1996. By 2001 the share of those jobs nationally had increased a little more to comprise 27.5 per cent of jobs.
- The share of routine production workers declined from 36.5 per cent in 1986 to 30.5 per cent of all jobs in 1996. That figure then remained relatively stable at a little under 30.47 per cent by 2001.
- There was a less marked increase in the share of in-person service worker jobs, from 37.8 per cent in 1986 to 40.5 per cent in 1996. By 2000 the share of those jobs had declined marginally to just over 40 per cent.

It is the increase in the proportion of workers in the symbolic analyst occupations that is of particular significance, as these jobs are in activities that increasingly are the drivers of the so-called 'new economy'. The Bureau of Transport and Regional Economics (2004a) notes that: 'in a knowledge based economy, the production, distribution and use of technology and knowledge is an important driver of growth, wealth creation and employment. While all industries generate and/or use new technology to some extent, some are more technology and knowledge-intensive than others' (p. 18). The Bureau estimates that employment in technology and knowledge-based industries in Australia was about 2.9 million, or 37 per cent of persons employed, in 2001 (Bureau of Transport and Regional Economics, 2004a, p. 19).

There is, of course, the issue of changes in the nature of work and in the creation of so-called 'good jobs' and 'bad jobs'. That relates to the issue of job quality related to human capital levels and the incidence of overqualification of people for their job. Tilly (1997) has compiled a set of criteria to provide an overall index of job quality in Australia. As is the case in OECD countries (OECD, 2001b), particularly in the services sectors, Stimson et al. (2004, Ch. 2, p. 6) tell how over the past decade or so Australia has seen the rapid growth of part-time, temporary and casual employment, with full-time jobs having declined from 74 per cent to 61 per cent in recent years. Casual jobs have grown from 10 per cent to 27 per cent of all employees since the early 1990s. During the 1990s, about two-thirds of the growth in employment came from casual jobs, mainly in the retail and hospitality sectors. Now in the first decade of the twenty-first century it is only just under half the nation's employees who work a regular Monday to Friday shift, and those working 35 to 40 hours a week have fallen from about 50 per cent to around 30 per cent of the workforce since the early 1990s. Now almost 40 per cent of male workers work for 50 hours or more a week compared to only 20 per cent in the early 1990s. And in many cases these contemporary forms of employment have been described as low-paid, unstable and dead-end (Gaston and Timcke, 1999). That contrasts sharply with the traditional view of full-time employment as well-paid and secure, with the promise of upward mobility and accompanying rewards (Tilly, 1997).

Inevitably there will be considerable inequalities across groups within a society in their aggregate levels of human capital development, and that will be reflected as well in other social indicators. In Australia, an example of a demographic group whose education, skills and qualifications attainment are still diverging from the rest of the nation's population, are Indigenous Australians. They are characterized – in both aggregate and relative terms – by low rates of progression through secondary school, low rates of participation in post-secondary education, low rates of workforce entry, low levels of literacy and numeracy, poor health status and low socio-economic status.

The foregoing discussion sets the broad macro scene of Australia's contemporary trends and performance with respect to shifts in industry structure, human capital development, changing levels of qualifications, occupational levels and the changing nature of work. It provides the general national context for the focus in the remainder of this chapter on an analysis of regional trends and patterns – at various levels of scale – in industry structure and in human capital and occupation levels. Particular attention is directed towards addressing the effects of population and employment size of regions and of places across the urban hierarchy, and of convergence/divergence in outcomes.

6.5 METHODOLOGY

6.5.1 Data Sources and Scale of Analysis

The BTRE studies of regional industry structure and of regional education, skills and qualifications (Bureau of Transport and Regional Economics, 2004a, 2004b), and the component of the ANTA/UQ study that looked at human capital and industry, occupation and skills specialization/diversification for urban centres and localities (UC/Ls) across Australia's states and territories (Stimson et al., 2004), form the basis of the sections that follow.

The data used in both sets of studies are mostly derived from Australian Bureau of Statistics (ABS) data from the 1991, 1996 and 2001 Censuses. Both sets of studies focused some of their attention on analysis conducted at the level of the states and territories, which provides a coarse aggregated but nonetheless useful basic level of analysis at one step down from the national level of scale. Those states and territories are: New South Wales, Victoria, Queensland, South Australia, Western Australia, Tasmania, Australian Capital Territory and Northern Territory.

The BTRE studies also conduct analysis at another coarse spatial level, the ABS Remoteness Structure, which divides Australia into five broad spatial groupings sharing common characteristics in terms of physical distance from services and opportunities for social interaction. Those five remoteness classes are: major cities of Australia, inner regional Australia, outer regional Australia, remote Australia and very remote Australia.

The BTRE analyses also have been conducted for its labour market regions (LMRs). These are aggregations of the full ABS set of approximately 1350 SLAs into 425 LMRs, based on commuting patterns revealed by data from the 2001 Census. In concept, LMRs reflect the area within which people are willing to commute from their place of work to their place of employment, and for each LMR the majority of employed residents work in the same region in which they live. Thus LMRs represent a reasonably fine level of spatial disaggregation for regional analysis. The beauty of using spatial units based on aggregations of SLAs is that the census data provides change-over-time information for SLAs, 1991 to 2001. Thus, dynamic change-over-time analysis is possible.

The components of the ANTA/CR-SURF study on which this chapter draws refer to the 1519 UC/Ls across Australia's states and territories, as defined by the ABS. UC/Ls range across the urban hierarchy from the capital city metropolitan areas to small regional urban localities with populations as small as 200 people. Sometimes an urban centre may match an SLA, but that is not common across the urban system. The advantage of using UC/Ls is that it is possible to relate analysis to the size of an urban place, while the disadvantage is that the ABS does not provide data on UC/Ls that permits comparison over time for UC/Ls defined on common spatial unit boundaries. Thus, a point-in-time analysis only is possible. The number of UC/Ls for each state and territory at the 2001 census are:

- New South Wales, N = 452.
- Victoria, N = 285.

- Queensland, N = 333.
- South Australia, N = 151.
- Western Australia, N = 152.
- Tasmania, N = 80.
- Northern Territory, N = 58.

For the Australian Capital Territory there is just one urban centre, Canberra.

6.5.2 Industry Structure: Data and Measurement

The BTRE study of regional industry structure (Bureau of Transport and Regional Economics, 2004a) uses a variety of data sources including: ABS National Accounts data to compare the size and growth of industries based on estimates of industry GVA over the period 1984/85 to 2001/02; ABS Labour Force Survey (LFS) data which provide quarterly estimates of employment mix; ABS Census data for 1991, 1996 and 2001; and data derived from the BTRE Industry Structure Database using Australian and New Zealand Standard Industry Classification (ANZSIC) subdivision employment categories for SLAs. Those data are also aggregated to form the LMRs.

Various analytic procedures were used by the Bureau of Transport and Regional Economics (2004a, 2004b) to analyse trends and patterns in regional industry structure, including:

- an industry instability index measuring the extent of deviation of a quarterly time series from a long-run trend;
- the location quotient (LQ) to identify industry sector employment specialization in regions;
- a coefficient of industry localization to determine the extent to which an industry is dispersed across Australia's regions;
- an industrial diversity index is used to provide a general measure of the extent to which a region is characterized by diversified industry structure – a form of shift-share analyses of ANZSIC subdivision employment data for LMRs to investigate the relationship between regional industry structure change and national shifts;
- regression analyses to measure the relationship between regional industry structure change and growth to real taxable income, 1990/91–1999/2000.

The ANTA/UQ study (Stimson et al., 2004) uses ABS 2001 census data measuring employment by industry sector 17 two-digit ANZSIC sectors.

It derives for UC/Ls an industry specialization/diversification index, using the formula set out in Tidswell and Barker (1971). That index theoretically may range from 0 to 100. An index score approaching zero indicates an increasing degree of employment diversification across industry sectors, whereas an index score approaching 100 indicates that employment is concentrated in one or very few industry sectors and that a region has a highly specialized industry structure.

Both the BTRE and the CR-SURF/UQ studies look at the relationship between aspects of regional industry structure and the size of a region's economy measured by employment or by population size of a UC/L.

6.5.3 Human Capital (Education, Qualifications and Occupation Levels): Data and Measurement

The BTRE study of regional education, skills and qualifications (Bureau of Transport and Regional Economics, 2004b) uses a variety of data sources, but focuses in particular on ABS census data for 1991, 1996 and 2001 that are organized into four education qualification level and four occupation level classes.

The BTRE study analyses industry effects on education and skills levels and on occupational composition. There is considerable emphasis placed on trends and patterns for employment in the professions, and there are analyses of the relationship between regional levels of unemployment for Education-1 qualified persons and the log of the working-age population of regions by remoteness classes (Bureau of Transport and Regional Economics, 2004a).

The ANTA/UQ study uses 2002 census data for UC/Ls to derive three indices of human capital performance – university, technical and no qualification – using principal components analysis applied to data on the incidence of people with various levels of educational attainment and the level of participation of the 18 to 24-year cohort in post-secondary full-time education (Stimson et al., 2004, Ch. 5). That study also derives from 2001 Census data an occupation specialization/diversification index and a skills specialization/diversification index for UC/Ls. The ASCO two-digit classes are used to derive an occupation index, while educational qualifications data classes are used to derive a skills index.

The ANTA/UQ study also looks at the urban hierarchy effects on the human capital indices and the occupation and skills specialization/diversification indices across the urban system, using correlation analysis to relate UC/L scores on those indices to the log of population (Stimson et al., 2004, Ch. 5). And the BTRE study also uses regression analysis to look at the relationship between regional growth in taxable income and regional education and occupation levels.

6.6 AGGREGATE TRENDS AND PATTERNS: THE STATES AND TERRITORIES

This section provides an overview of the trends and patterns across the states and territories of Australia and for the Australian remoteness class in terms of industry sector and aspects of human capital.

6.6.1 Industry Structure

As discussed earlier in the chapter, Australia as a nation has experienced structural shifts over time to become less dependent first on agriculture and then on manufacturing for work, and to become more dependent on the services sectors. But the national patterns of structural change are not necessarily reflected uniformly across the states and the territories.

The Bureau of Transport and Regional Economics (2004a, pp. 10–12) analysis of change over time in the employment shares of industry sectors shows that a mixed pattern is evident across the states and territories. Over the decade 1991–2001 the highest rate of employment growth has been in Queensland, closely followed by Western Australia and the Northern Territory, while in Tasmania and South Australia employment growth has been relatively slow but still positive.

That BTRE study found that business services grew strongly across all states and territories, and particularly in the Australian Capital Territory, Victoria and New South Wales. In Queensland and Tasmania, growth in food retailing was most strong, but there was growth in all states and territories. A modest fall in employment shares of personal and household goods retailing occurred in all states and territories. In Victoria and South Australia there was a strong growth in the share of petroleum, coal, chemical and associated product manufacturing. Strong growth occurred in the share of construction in Western Australia and Victoria.

The BTRE study also found that there was growth in all states and territories in property services (and especially in the Northern Territory), community services (especially in Queensland, Tasmania and Western Australia), libraries, museums and arts (especially in the Northern Territory), personal services, and accommodation, cafes and restaurants (except in the Northern Territory).

The BTRE study found that employment shares in agriculture declined in all states and territories, and especially in Queensland and Western

Australia. Employment shares in metal ore mining declined considerably in both the Northern Territory and Western Australia. In all states and territories, there were declines in employment shares for finance and insurance. The share of employment in government administration and defence industries increased in the Northern Territory, but it declined in all the other states and in the Australian Capital Territory, where the decline was particularly marked as it was in Victoria.

Thus, the above summary overview taken from the findings of the Bureau of Transport and Regional Economics (2004a, pp. 10–12) study shows that there is commonality across the states and territories in some of the trends in industry structure shifts, but that some industries in some of the states and territories are experiencing either greater growth or greater decline than in others. There is not an overall pattern of convergence across the industry sectors. That reflects broad historic regional specialization, but also broad regional differentials in the adjustments that the states and territory economies are making vis-à-vis national trends.

LQ analysis of an industry's employment share relative to its national employment share shows that the states and territories have distinctive patterns of specialization. The Bureau of Transport and Regional Economics (2004a, p. 13) notes that 'a number of patterns emerge', and Table 6.1 provides a summary list of those industries in which the states and territories have the highest LQs.

6.6.2 Human Capital and Qualification and Occupation Levels

Earlier reference was made to the rise occurring in qualification levels in Australia and how that is not necessarily being reflected in shifts in occupation shares. Analyses of state and territory performance by the Bureau of Transport and Regional Economics (2004b, pp. 17–18) reveals the patterns of change in education and occupation levels across the states and territories, shown in Table 6.2. The highest qualification and occupation levels are found in the Australian Capital Territory, and the States of Victoria and New South Wales (the most populous states), while Tasmania and Queensland recorded the lowest proportions of highly skilled people at the 2001 Census. Queensland, the Northern Territory and Tasmania have the lowest levels of workers with high-status occupations. South Australia has a similar education structure to Queensland, but an occupation structure a little more balanced towards the higher-status professions. Western Australia and the Northern Territory have the highest proportions of skilled vocational workers.

Queensland, Western Australia and New South Wales have education growth rates that are above the national average. South Australia,

Table 6.1 Top specializations of employment share industry sectors in Australia's states and territories, 2002

State/Territory	Industry sectors with the highest location quotients
New South Wales	Coal mining; Air and space transport; Motion pictures, radio and TV; Services to finance and insurance; Insurance.
Victoria	Textiles, clothing and footwear manufacturing; Petroleum, coal, chemical and associated product manufacturing; Machinery and equipment manufacturing; Storage; Printing, publishing and recorded media.
Queensland	Coal mining; Rail transport; Water transport; Agriculture; Electricity and gas supply.
South Australia	Commercial fishing; Machinery and equipment manufacturing; Oil and gas extraction; Agriculture; FBT manufacturing.
Western Australia	Metal ore mining; Oil and gas extraction; Services to mining; Other mining.
Tasmania	Forestry and logging; Commercial fishing; Wood and paper product manufacturing; Water transport; Electricity and gas supply.
Australian Capital Territory	Defence; Government administration; Libraries, museums and the arts; Business services.
Northern Territory	Defence; Metal ore mining; Government administration; Commercial fishing; Water transport.

Source: Bureau of Transport and Regional Economics (2004a).

Victoria, the Australian Capital Territory and Queensland have growth rates above the average in the highest-status occupations. Over the decade 1991 to 2001, Queensland, Tasmania and the Northern Territory achieved shares of the highest educational category that are closer to the national average, while in South Australia and Western Australia the shares of those people with Education-1 qualifications showed a greater divergence from the national average at the end of that decade.

Analysis of the distribution of skilled workers and professionals across the states and territories shows a decline of skilled trade workers across most states, with growth only in Western Australia, Queensland and the Northern Territory. All states and territories increased their number of professionals in teaching, health and computing, with Western Australia and Queensland leading, and those two states also saw an increase in building engineers (Bureau of Transport and Regional Economics, 2004b, p. 18).

Table 6.2 Shares and growth rates of education and occupation levels in Australia's states and territories, 1991 to 2001

Education and occupation levels 2001 and change 1991–2001		NSW	VIC	QLD	SA	WA	TAS	NT	WA	Australia
Education attainment										
Ed-1	% share 2001	**18.4**	**19.6**	**14.2**	**14.3**	**15.4**	**13.7**	**16.2**	**30.6**	**17.4**
	% growth rate 1991–2001	95.0	89.0	125.5	79.1	97.7	70.9	86.9	63.0	94.7
Ed-2	% share 2001	**8.5**	**8.5**	**7.2**	**7.2**	**8.1**	**7.0**	**7.9**	**8.8**	**8.1**
	% growth rate 1991–2001	34.7	31.9	39.2	10.0	32.1	4.4	25.0	39.1	31.6
Ed-3	% share 2001	**17.9**	**17.0**	**17.0**	**17.8**	**17.6**	**18.0**	**19.0**	**11.8**	**17.5**
	% growth rate 1991–2001	38.8	41.0	59.2	40.6	49.3	40.4	45.9	49.2	44.3
Ed-4	% share 2001	**55.1**	**55.0**	**60.7**	**60.7**	**58.9**	**61.2**	**56.9**	**48.8**	**57.0**
	% growth rate 1991–2001	–12.1	–8.7	12.9	–5.8	6.7	–16.1	–10.6	–7.3	–4.7
Occupation status										
Occ-1	% share 2002	**29.0**	**29.2**	**24.7**	**26.7**	**26.1**	**25.9**	**25.1**	**37.9**	**27.8**
	% growth rate 1991–2001	21.0	26.5	26.1	33.7	7.7	4.5	22.6	26.1	25.1
Occ-2	% share 2002	**11.8**	**11.5**	**12.2**	**11.7**	**12.6**	**11.8**	**14.2**	**14.5**	**12.0**
	% growth rate 1991–2001	90.6	73.0	52.1	96.2	52.5	58.7	66.0	81.9	74.4

Table 6.2 (continued)

Education and occupation levels 2001 and change 1991–2001		NSW	VIC	QLD	SA	WA	TAS	NT	WA	Australia
Occ-3	% share 2002	**16.4**	**16.2**	**16.6**	**15.8**	**17.3**	**15.6**	**16.7**	**11.5**	**16.4**
	% growth rate 1991–2001	–20.8	–15.8	–4.7	–0.6	–19.8	–23.8	–14.0	–0.9	–12.4
Occ-4	% share 2002	**42.7**	**43.1**	**46.6**	**45.7**	**44.0**	**46.7**	**43.9**	**36.0**	**43.9**
	% growth rate 1991–2001	7.0	12.7	25.7	28.7	7.4	5.0	15.6	25.6	16.6

Source: Compiled from Bureau of Transport and Regional Economics (2004b, Tables 9 and 10, derived from ABS 2001 Census data).

6.7 CENTRALITY AND REMOTENESS

The ABS Remoteness Structure provides a further highly aggregated basis on which to obtain a broad regional picture of differentiation across Australia. Those five remoteness classes range from areas that have a high degree of centrality (the major cities of Australia based on locations within or proximate to an urban centre of at least 250 000 population) to those areas that are most remote with no centrality of location (the very remote Australia class).

6.7.1 Industry Structure

The Bureau of Transport and Regional Economics (2004a) has used the Australian remoteness classes to analyse the relative importance of industries by employment across the five classes. That analysis, using 2001 Census data, reveals the following patterns (pp. 13–14):

- Retail trade is the largest employment sector in the major cities and inner regional classes, but it is surpassed by agriculture, forestry and fishing in the outer regional and the remote and very remote classes.

- The relative importance of employment in agriculture, forestry and fishing, mining, and accommodation, cafes and restaurants increases as remoteness increases.
- The importance of employment in manufacturing, wholesale trade, cultural and recreational services, finance and insurance, property and business services, and communication services declines with increasing remoteness, with the last three of those industry sectors being more important sectors of employment in the major cities class.
- The importance of employment in electricity, gas and water supply, retail trade, health and community services, education, and construction peaks in inner regional Australia.
- Government administration and defence employment peaks in the remote and very remote classes, which reflects the participation of Indigenous persons in the Commonwealth government's Community Development Employment Program (CDEP).
- Business services are most important in the major cities class.
- Education is the most important source of employment in the inner regional Australia class.
- Agriculture is the most important source of employment in outer regional and in the remote and very remote Australia classes.

Table 6.2 shows that over the decade 1991–2001, the strongest growth in total employment was found in inner regional Australia (20 per cent), followed by the major cities class (18 per cent), outer regional (10 per cent), and the remote and very remote Australia classes (1 per cent) (Bureau of Transport and Regional Economics, 2004a, p. 14). Business services grew strongly across all the remoteness classes, but not surprisingly it was strongest in the major cities class. The inner regional Australia class experienced very strong growth in food retailing, while community services employment growth was particularly strong in the inner regional and outer regional Australia classes. Construction trade services and accommodation, cafes and restaurants displayed employment growth across all the remoteness classes. Government administration employment had the highest growth in the remote and very remote classes (because of the CDEP). But agriculture showed a decline in its share of employment in the inner regional, outer regional, remote and very remote classes, while remaining unchanged in the major cities class. The share of employment in finance and insurance declined significantly in all the remoteness classes (Bureau of Transport and Regional Economics 2004a, pp. 14–15).

The patterns of specialization of employment in industry sectors would be expected to vary considerably according to centrality and remoteness,

Table 6.3 Top specializations of employment shares for industry sectors in Australia's remoteness classes, 2002

Remoteness class	Industry sectors with the highest location quotients
Major cities	Services to finance and insurance; Insurance; Petroleum; Coal; Chemical and associated manufacturing.
Inner regional	Forestry and logging; Coal mining; Services to agriculture; Hunting and trapping.
Outer regional	Agriculture; Services to agriculture; Hunting and trapping, Commercial fishing.
Remote/Very remote	Metal ore mining; Commercial fishing; Other mining.

Source: Derived from information in Bureau of Transport and Regional Economics (2004a, p. 15).

and this was found to be the case in Australia in the Bureau of Transport and Regional Research (2004a, pp. 15–16) study. Table 6.3 lists the industry sectors with the highest LQs for the remoteness structure classes at the 2001 census.

The Bureau of Transport and Regional Economics (2004a) has paid specific attention to analysing trends in the share of employment in technology- and knowledge-intensive industries. Those shares are seen to decline as remoteness increases. The share is highest for the major cities remoteness structure class (40 per cent), dropping to 32 per cent for the inner regional class, 26 per cent for the outer regional, and 22 per cent for the remote and the very remote Australia classes.

6.7.2 Human Capital: Qualification and Occupation Levels

It was noted earlier how it is common for the big cities to have the highest concentrations of jobs requiring high levels of skills, and for there to be metropolitan–non-metropolitan differences in levels of qualifications. Thus, it is not surprising to see the magnitude of the differences, evident in the data in Table 6.4, in the incidence of the education and occupation levels shares across the remoteness structure of regions in Australia.

The Bureau of Transport and Regional Economics (2004b) analysis of the effects of centrality/remoteness on education and occupation levels in Australia concludes that:

> Overall, the remoteness structure analysis [of Australia] indicates rising levels of educational attainment across all classes, though to a lesser extent for more remote areas. The highest proportion of university educated residents are in

Table 6.4 Shares and growth rates of education and occupation levels in Australia's remoteness classes, 1991 to 2001

Education and occupation levels		Major cities	Inner regional	Outer regional	Remote	Very remote	Australia
Educational attainment							
Ed-1	% share 2001	**19.9**	**12.2**	**10.6**	**10.3**	**9.9**	**17.4**
	% growth rate 1991–2001	95.3	98.1	84.8	78.1	53.5	94.7
Ed-2	% share 2001	**8.6**	**7.4**	**6.6**	**6.1**	**5.8**	**8.1**
	% growth rate 1991–2001	40.3	18.7	4.4	–6.6	5.8	8.1
Ed-3	% share 2001	**16.3**	**20.7**	**20.1**	**19.6**	**17.6**	**17.5**
	% growth rate 1991–2001	39.7	58.4	49.4	33.9	20.6	44.3
Ed-4	% share 2001	**55.3**	**59.7**	**62.7**	**63.9**	**68.8**	**57.0**
	% growth rate 1991–2001	–4.2	–1.6	–9.6	–15.7	–28.5	–4.7
Occupation status							
Occ-1	% share 2002	**28.6**	**24.8**	**28.2**	**31.1**	**24.9**	**27.8**
	% growth rate 1991–2001	31.9	15.8	1.8	–0.5	–4.9	25.1
Occ-2	% share 2002	**12.2**	**11.8**	**11.0**	**10.7**	**10.3**	**12.0**
	% growth rate 1991–2001	76.4	73.9	67.3	53.3	11.0	74.4
Occ-3	% share 2002	**16.0**	**17.8**	**16.1**	**16.0**	**13.3**	**16.4**
	% growth rate 1991–2001	–14.6	–3.3	–6.7	–13.9	–29.0	–12.2
Occ-4	% share 2002	**43.2**	**45.6**	**44.6**	**42.3**	**51.4**	**43.9**
	% growth rate 1991–2001	–16.1	23.6	13.3	1.4	10.4	16.6

Source: Bureau of Transport and Regional Economics (2004b; derived from ABS 2001 Census data).

the major cities groups, while Inner regional areas recorded the highest Ed-1 growth rates. Over the decade [1991 to 2001], Inner regional showed evidence of 'catching up' with the better-educated major cities populations. By contrast, Outer regional, Remote and Very remote areas, while still experiencing growth in their Ed-1 shares, grew at slower rates than Inner regional and Major cities. The majority of the remoteness classes showed some evidence of equalising results within their remoteness category for both education and occupation outcomes. In particular, regions within the major cities, inner regional and very remote classes demonstrated a tendency to equalise outcomes over 1991 to 2001. (p. 23)

6.8 SPATIALLY DISAGGREGATED ANALYSIS

This section provides an overview of the outcomes of the more spatially disaggregated analyses conducted by the BTRE for LMRs and by the CR-SURF/UQ study for State and Territory UC/Ls. Those finer-scale analyses represent more realistic levels of spatial scale at which to investigate regional trends and differentials in patterns of regional performance vis-à-vis industry structure and human capital. They permit both a focus on the degree of variability across regions and a consideration of the extent to which convergence/divergence is occurring across the space economy, and as well a consideration of population size and urban hierarchy effects.

6.8.1 Trends and Patterns in Industry Sector Structure and Diversification

The industry sector structure of employment does seem to be a significant factor in explaining regional differences in economic growth, and considerable variations occur in the industry structure of the LMRs across Australia and as well in the shifts that have been occurring over time in regional industry structure. Indeed, the Productivity Commission (2003) has pointed out that often structural change is essential for regions to take full advantage of new opportunities for growth, even though it can impose costs and disadvantage some groups in a community.

Regional industry structure trends and patterns may be analysed in many ways. For example, the focus can be on looking at the degree of diversity or specialization in the distribution of employment across industry sectors in regions at a point in time, and how, over time, a region's industry structure may have diversified or become more specialized. In that context, where the focus is on the region, it is also possible to identify those industry sectors in which a region tends to specialize and in which there is an above-'average' share of employment in an industry sector relative to the national picture. Or it is possible to focus attention on industry sectors, and to determine the extent to which an industry is dispersed across a nation's regions. Both of those considerations are important to address in developing an understanding of trends and patterns of industry structure in a regional context. In what follows, the second of those considerations will be addressed first.

Industry sector concentration and dispersal across regions

Analysis of industry sector employment structure across the BTRE's 425 LMRs reveals that while agriculture only employed 3.5 per cent of workers nationally in 2001, it is the dominant industry employer in 276 of LMRs, and it was either the second- or third-largest employer in a further 52 LMRs. A number of other industry sectors are also the dominant employment source in 20–30 LMRs, those industries being government administration, metal ore mining, education, health services, and accommodation, cafes and restaurants. Education is among the top three employing industries in over 70 per cent of the LMRs. But, despite its increasing prominence in the national economy, business services was the major employing industry in 2001 in just five LMRs that are centred on five of the capital cities: Sydney, Melbourne, Brisbane, Perth and Darwin (Bureau of Transport and Regional Economics, 2004a, p. 18).

The Bureau of Transport and Regional Economics (2004a) has used the 'coefficient of industry (employment) localization' to measure the extent to which an industry sector is dispersed across LMRs. A coefficient of 100 per cent indicates that employment is fully localized in a single region. Using 2001 Census data the BTRE found that (pp. 20–21):

- Australia's most localized industries are coal mining (with a coefficient of 92 per cent), commercial fishing (78 per cent), agriculture (70 per cent), and forestry and logging (68 per cent) – all primary industries.
- Outside the primary industries, those with the highest degree of localization are defence (56 per cent) and rail transport (43 per cent).
- Service industries have a very low degree of localization, almost all of them having coefficients of 7 per cent or less.
- Manufacturing employment is more localized than the services sector industries, but it is less localized than the primary industries, with manufacturing industry coefficients ranging between 16 per cent and 32 per cent.
- Over the decade 1991 to 2001, employment became much less localized for manufacturing (a decline in coefficient from 36 per cent to 19 per cent); services to agriculture, hunting and trapping (73 per cent to 58 per cent); libraries, museums and the arts (29 per cent to 17 per cent); forestry and logging (77 per cent to 68 per cent); property services (23 per cent to 15 per cent); and metal ore mining (93 per cent to 86 per cent).
- Over the decade 1991 to 2001 there was a marked increase in localization for rail transport (the coefficient increasing from 35 per cent to 43 per cent) and for defence (49 per cent to 56 per cent), that increase being associated with a significant decline in total industry employment.

Of particular interest is what is happening to employment in the technology- and knowledge-based industries: 'Technology and knowledge-based industries are of greatest importance to Australia's largest cities and university towns' (Bureau of Transport and Regional Economics, 2004a, p. 19). The ANTA/UQ study in fact identifies a cluster of larger regional towns with universities, that form one of the 'opportunity' clusters in its analysis of community opportunity and vulnerability in regional cities and towns across Australia to show how they are coping with socio-economic change over the decade 1991–2001 (Stimson et al., 2004, Ch. 8). The BTRE study shows that the LMRs centred on three of the capital cities (Sydney, Melbourne and Adelaide) all have 41 per cent shares of employment in those industries, and the LMR centred on the inland regional city of Armidale in New South Wales (home to the University of New England) has a 40 per cent employment share. Other LMRs with employment shares in technology- and knowledge-based industries above the national average of 37 per cent are those centred on the capital cities of Queensland and Western Australia (Brisbane and Perth) and the regional cities of Orange, Ballarat and Geelong, all with universities (Bureau of Transport and Regional Economics, 2004a, p. 19).

Regional industry structure diversity and specialization

The extent of diversity or specialization that exists in employment across industry sectors in Australia is indicative of the degree to which a local labour market can provide job opportunities for a wide range or a more restricted range of occupation and education skill levels. In general, it is usually hypothesized that the larger a regional economy, the more diverse will be its industry sector employment opportunities; while often in smaller places and places with a specific comparative advantage for particular types of economic production – which may reflect the region's particular resource endowments – the employment opportunities will be more restricted as the regional economy is characterized by a higher degree of industry specialization.

The analysis by Stimson et al. (2004) of UC/Ls across Australia's states and territories uses 2001 Census data to compute an industry specialization/diversification index which shows that across 17 industry sectors the national benchmark index is 35.21, indicating a relatively diverse mix of employment opportunities across industries. But, not surprisingly, as the data in Table 6.5 demonstrate, there is a very wide variation both between the states and territories and within them across their UC/Ls in the degree of industrial employment specialization/diversification.

In their study, Stimson et al. (2004, Ch. 5, pp. 13–14) tell how there are relatively small variations between the capital cities in their degree

Table 6.5 Range in industry employment specialization/diversification in index scores across UC/Ls in Australia's states and the Northern Territory, 2001

Spatial unit	N	Index score	
		Min.	Max.
The urban system	1519	26.32	100.00
Capital cities	8	28.99	34.58
NSW	452	26.32	54.23
Vic	285	27.04	64.91
Qld	331	26.83	95.41
SA	151	28.11	78.56
WA	152	26.62	96.91
Tas	80	27.45	48.60
NT	58	29.16	100.00

Source: Stimson et al. (2004, Ch. 5, p. 13).

of industry specialization/diversification, but that in general the non-metropolitan regional UC/Ls have slightly higher levels of specialization. However, as the data in Table 6.5 show, there are extremely wide variations across the UC/Ls in the degree to which urban centres have diversified or specialized industry structures. The place with most diversified industry employment structure is Forest Hill UC/L in New South Wales with an index score of 26.32, while Duck Creek UC/L in the Northern Territory has an index score of 100, indicating a total concentration of jobs in one industry sector. The range in the index score is thus extreme, and it tends to be greatest in the states and territories with large land areas and sparse populations. For example, the index scores range from the mid-20s to over 90 in Queensland, Western Australia and the Northern Territory, and it is those states that have a considerable preponderance of small, remote towns and urban localities that are mining towns or Indigenous settlements. In contrast, the range in industry specialization/diversification index scores is much more restricted in Tasmania, ranging from only 27 to 48. The largest population states of New South Wales and Victoria have index score ranges from 26 to 64 across their UC/Ls.

The spatial pattern of distribution of the UC/L scores on the industry specialization/diversification index in 2001 is shown in Figure 6.1. On that map the places with the most diversified job opportunities across a wide mix of industry sectors are represented by the highest density of symbols, while those UC/Ls with the highest index scores, representing places with very specialized industry structures and thus a restricted

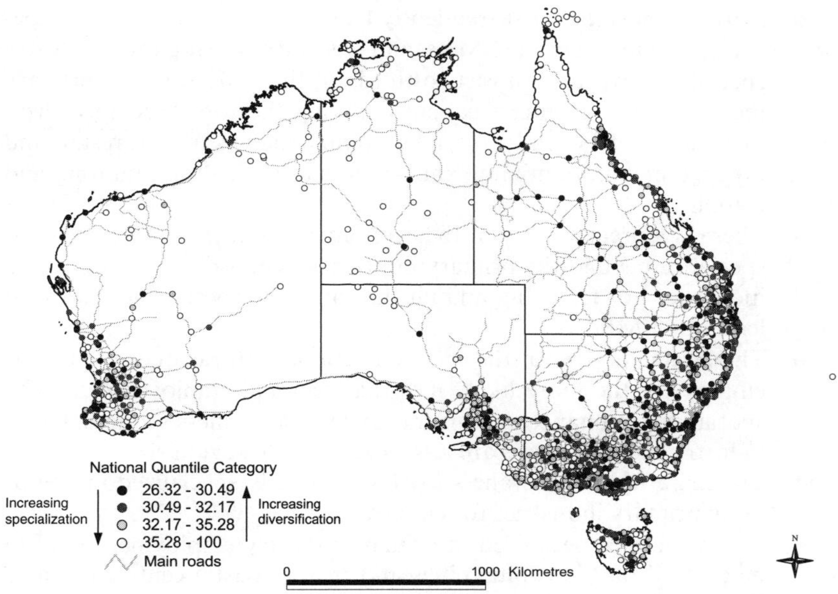

Source: Stimson et al. (2004).

Figure 6.1 Pattern of UC/L scores on the industry specialization/diversification index, Australia, 2001

range of employment opportunities are identified by the lowest density of symbols. The map provides a powerful pictorial representation of the spatial pattern of industry diversity and specialization across the UC/Ls of Australia.

The analysis of regional concentration and dispersion of employment in industry sectors conducted by the Bureau of Transport and Regional Economics (2004a, pp. 21–3) uses 2001 Census data to calculate LQs for LMRs. That disaggregated level of spatial analysis picks up patterns of likely regional level comparative advantage. Such analysis is important, but for many of the LMRs, a particular industry for which a region may have large LQ might, in fact, be based on a very small total employment. However, the LQ analysis does permit the identification of the specific LMRs in Australia that have the top levels of industry specialization by employment concentration relative to the national benchmark as represented by their LQ for an industry sector (see Bureau of Transport and Regional Economics, 2004a, p. 22). The BTRE analysis shows that:

- Agriculture is the most frequently featured industry as the top specialization in 112 of the LMRs, and it is one of the top three industry specializations for almost two-thirds of the LMRs. Other primary industries also feature frequently among the top three specializations for LMRs, and especially commercial fishing, forestry and logging, metal ore mining, and services to agriculture, hunting and trapping.
- There is a great variety in the economic activities in which regions specialize beyond the primary industries, with only seven out of 53 industries not featuring among the top three specializations for at least one LMR.
- The larger the size of the regional economy (measured by persons employed), the more likely it is that regional employment will be specialized in finance and insurance, and in business services. Other industry specializations are less closely tied to region size.
- The majority of Australia's LMRs are highly specialized in one or more primary industries for employment.
- Regions underspecialized in primary industry employment tend to be centred on the capital cities and major coastal centres (such as Geelong, Townsville and Port Augusta).
- There are LMRs in the far northern and central parts of Australia with under-representation of primary industry employment, mainly regions concentrating on mining and tourism.
- Regions with more than half of all their employment in primary industries are especially geographically concentrated in inland south-west and mid-west Western Australia and inland Queensland.
- Regional specializations of employment concentration appear to change relatively slowly over time, although over the decade 1991 to 2001 the number of LMRs where government administration was one of the top three industry specializations (probably due to the CDEP) did increase, and there was a decline in the number of regions specialized in rail transport and in other services.
- Regional dependence on manufacturing specialization has generally declined, being in line with the fall in employment and increased productivity in manufacturing identified by the Productivity Commission (2003).

Industrial diversity and size of a regional economy

Stimson et al. (2004, Ch. 5, pp. 24–5) have specifically looked at the relationship between the urban hierarchy effect and the degree of industrial employment specialization/diversification across UC/Ls in the states and territories, using correlation analysis between the scores of UC/Ls on that index and

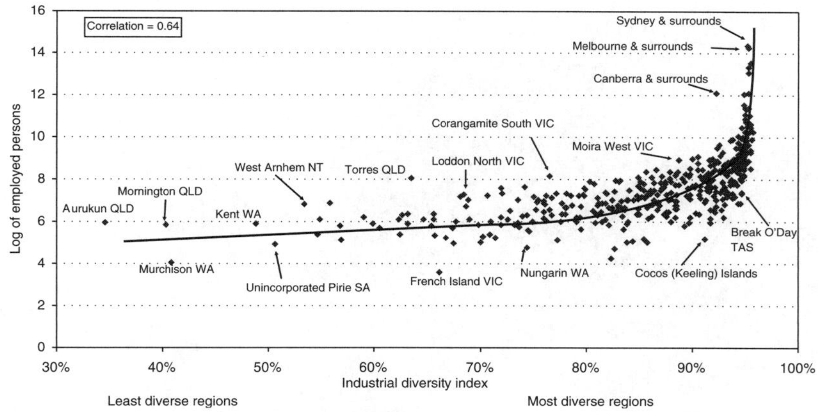

Source: Bureau of Transport and Regional Economics (2004a, p. 25).

Figure 6.2 Industrial diversity and size of regional economy, 2001: distribution for LMRs, 2001

the log of their population in 2001 (Figure 6.1). As expected, there is a negative correlation, confirming the well-established hypothesis that industrial diversification is associated with urban size. However, the correlation coefficients were not particularly high, ranging from only –0.24 in New South Wales (the most populous state with a relatively well-developed urban hierarchy), to a high of –0.37 in both the Northern Territory and Tasmania – which are small-population states (in the case of the Northern Territory, of large geographic size; in the case of Tasmania, of small geographic size).

The Bureau of Transport and Regional Economics (2004a) has looked more explicitly at the relationship between industrial employment diversification and the size of the regional economy for LMRs across Australia. That analysis shows that the larger a region's economy (measured by the log of employed persons) the more likely it is to have a diversified industrial base. The pattern of the relationship is shown in Figure 6.2. The 156 LMRs with more than 3000 employed persons had a diversity index below 85 per cent (that analysis used the Bradley and Gans, 1998 Herfindahl index, where an index of 100 per cent represents complete diversification across all industries). The Bureau of Transport and Regional Economics (2004a) points out that: 'there is considerable variation in industrial diversity across regions of a similar size, particularly amongst the smaller regions' (p. 26), while all the capital cities have 'very dense economies, with an industrial diversity index of 95 per cent or more' (p. 26).

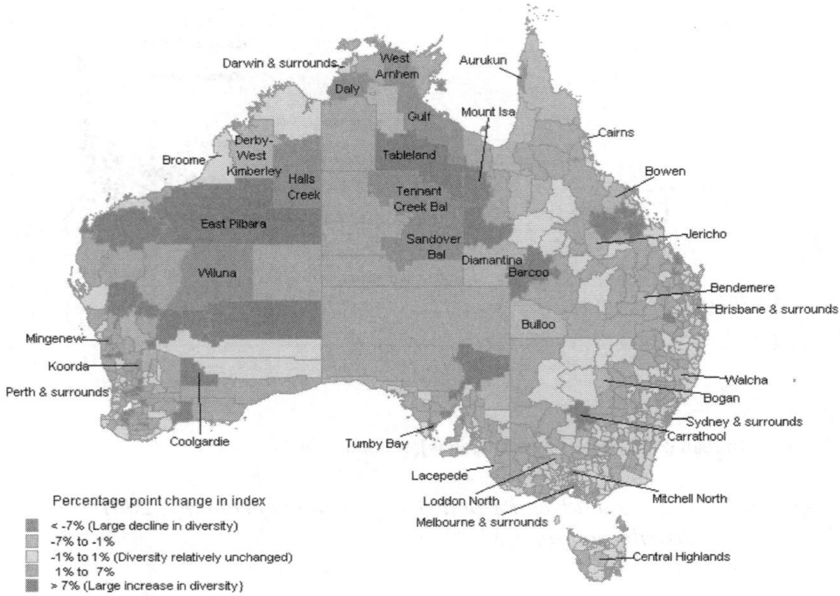

Source: Bureau of Transport and Regional Economics (2004a, p. 27).

Figure 6.3 Change in industrial diversity for Labour Market Regions, 1991–2001

Is Australia's regional industry structure diversifying?

Bradley and Gans (1998), among others, have noted how Australia's regions are becoming more industrially diverse. The Bureau of Transport and Regional Economics (2004a) has calculated a structural change index (SCI) for LMRs to estimate the degree of change in industry structural employment over the two successive inter-censal periods, 1991–96 and 1996–2001, and for the decade 1991 to 2001. An SCI of 100 per cent represents a complete reversal of industry structure. The patterns of change in industrial diversity across LMRs for the decade 1991 to 2001 are mapped in Figure 6.3 which shows the percentage point change in the SCI.

For Australia as a whole, the SCI for the decade 1991 to 2001 was 12 per cent: 'meaning that to restore the employment mix in existence in 1991, 12 per cent of employed persons in 2001 would have to change industries' (Bureau of Transport and Regional Economics, 2004a, p. 28). The structural change was much greater for the inter-censal period 1991–96 than it was for the period 1996–2001, while employment growth was stronger for the 1996–2001 component of that decade.

The Bureau of Transport and Regional Economics (2004a) has also computed an industrial diversity index for its LMRs. It notes that: 'nationally, the diversity index has fallen from 96.2 per cent in 1991 to 95.6 per cent in 2001, indicating a small overall decline in industrial diversity' (p. 26). However, that study shows how:

> 'many more regions experienced an increase in industrial diversity, than experienced a decline . . . [That] . . . seeming contradiction is due to the fact that, of Australia's capital cities, only Darwin experienced an increase in industrial diversity. For example, Sydney's diversity index decreased from 96.2 per cent to 95.2 per cent, meaning employment became rather less evenly distributed across industries over the decade. Between 1991 and 2001, the industry structure of employment has become less diversified for Australia's major cities, while other regions (on the whole) have become more industrially diverse'. (p. 26)

The Bureau of Transport and Regional Economics (2004a) analysis of structural change in industry employment across LMRs highlights a number of significant dimensions of regional variation in industry sector employment growth and decline over the decade 1991–2001. The complexity of change occurring across Australia's regions does seem to be taking on new dimensions, as some areas are experiencing increases in industrial diversity while others are experiencing a decrease in industrial diversity.

The BTRE's SCI analysis shows that all the nation's LMRs experienced some degree of structural change over the decade 1991–2001, with 75 per cent of regions having an SCI of between 10 and 20 per cent. The change was greatest in the remote regions that lack industrial diversity, and in general the larger regions – and especially those centred on the capital cities – experienced relatively little change (Bureau of Transport and Regional Economics, 2004a, p. 28).

The BTRE's detailed SCI analysis of industry structure change in LMRs over the period 1991–2001 suggests that some new dynamics are occurring across Australia's space economy. A much earlier study of structural change in Australia for the period 1961 to 1976 – before the onset of the end of the period of post-Second World War boom and the beginning of the late twentieth-century era of globalization, deregulation and economic restructuring – found that large cities underwent less change than smaller cities (Department of Home Affairs and the Environment, 1982). And more recently a Productivity Commission (1998) study found that smaller regions experienced the greatest rates of structural change. The findings of the Bureau of Transport and Regional Economics (2004a) research would lead one to question that simple dichotomy, and the results would suggest that a more complex picture exists of regional patterns of industry structural change.

6.8.2 Trends and Patterns in Human Capital: Education and Occupation Levels

Earlier in this chapter, reference was made to research that has highlighted the uneven performance across Australia's regions with respect to aspects of human capital and the associated patterns of differentiation in the levels of education and qualifications and the occupation levels of regions. This subsection addresses some of those distributional patterns.

Derived indices of human capital performance across the settlement system
Stimson et al. (2004, Ch. 5) provide a detailed analysis of the degree of variation across the UC/Ls in Australia's states and territories in levels of human capital. Using a principal components analysis of 2001 Census data on the distribution of levels of educational attainment in UC/Ls, three human capital indices were derived relating to:

- university qualified people and post-secondary participation in university education;
- technical qualified people and post-secondary participation in technical education;
- people with no qualifications other than basic schooling.

The range of scores of UC/Ls on those three human capital indices across the states and the Northern Territory are shown in Table 6.6. The scores have been standardized deliberately to range from 0 to 100 nationally.

The national benchmark score on the human capital university index is 28.55, and Table 6.6 shows how the range of scores of UC/Ls on that index varies greatly, and especially across the urban system of Victoria and New South Wales, the two most populous states with the most developed urban hierarchies. Queensland also has a wide range in UC/L scores on this index. Among the metropolitan cities, it is Sydney, Canberra, Melbourne, Brisbane and Perth that have the highest average scores on this human capital index, while Hobart and Adelaide have markedly lower average scores. On average, regional UC/Ls in Victoria have the highest scores on the index, with regional UC/Ls in the Northern Territory and Tasmania having the lowest scores on average. The place with the highest index score in regional Australia is Dinner Plain (index score of 100) in Victoria, with Tarcutta in regional New South Wales having the lowest score in the nation (of 0).

The overall spatial pattern of UC/L performance on the human capital university index is shown in Figure 6.4. There is a marked concentration of

Table 6.6 Range in standardized human capital index scores across UC/Ls in Australia's states and the Northern Territory, 2001

Spatial unit	N	University		Technical		No qualifications	
		Min.	Max.	Min.	Max.	Min.	Max.
Australia							
The urban system	1519	0.00	100.00	0.00	100.00	0.00	100.00
Capital cities	8	48.27	81.91	25.13	33.57	26.48	46.99
Within states and territories							
NSW	452	0.00	97.38	11.69	100.00	0.00	78.58
Vic	285	8.57	100.00	10.56	78.13	3.63	68.81
Qld	331	2.10	87.55	2.36	88.11	3.03	91.65
SA	151	3.70	65.54	13.58	74.52	28.44	95.68
WA	152	5.32	67.30	1.56	67.65	11.02	80.96
Tas	80	3.48	54.88	11.82	68.82	26.55	77.94
NT	58	1.42	61.83	0.00	46.08	15.44	100.00

Source: Stimson et al. (2004, Ch. 5, p. 11).

UC/Ls with low scores on this human capital index across the inland areas and the remote parts of Australia, and many of those places are small towns and Indigenous settlements. But it is also the case that some of the rapidly growing coastal towns in 'sun belt' locations are poor performers on the human capital university index. The map also shows how it is the larger towns in the wheat–sheep belt, some of the large towns along the coast, and the remotely located mining towns that have the highest scores on the human capital university index.

The national benchmark level for the human capital technical index is 34.52. In contrast to the patterns shown for the human capital university index, on the human capital technical index in general the regional UC/Ls tend to do much better. Stimson et al. (2004, Ch. 5) tell how on this index, among the metropolitan cities it is Hobart that has on average the highest score, followed by Perth, Sydney, Canberra and Melbourne, with Darwin having the lowest score. On average, regional UC/Ls in New South Wales have the highest scores on this index, followed by Tasmania, South Australia and Western Australia, with regional UC/Ls in the Northern Territory on average having the lowest scores on the index. Forest Hill in regional New South Wales is identified as the non-metropolitan place with the highest score (100) on this index, while the place with the lowest score (1.56) is Wiluna in Western Australia.

The data in Table 6.6 show that it is New South Wales and Queensland

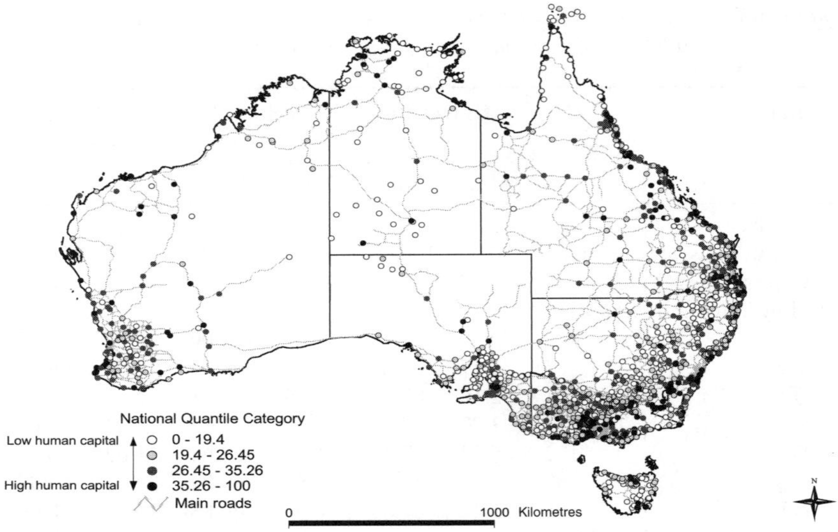

Source: Stimson et al. (2004, Ch. 5, p. 29).

Figure 6.4 Pattern of UC/L scores on the human capital university index, Australia 2001

that have the highest range in the distribution of UC/L scores on the human capital technical index. The data also show that in the Northern Territory the overall level of scores of regional UC/Ls on this human capital index are much lower than for any of the states, reflecting the high preponderance of remote, small Indigenous settlements in the Northern Territory.

Figure 6.5 shows the regional pattern across Australia on the human capital technical index. The striking contrast in the pattern of index scores on this map compared to that for the human capital university index score pattern (in Figure 6.4) is that the incidence of high scores on the human capital technical index is much more common across the towns of the wheat–sheep belt and along the coastal areas. And the remote mining towns and many of the old industrial towns (such as those in South Australia's 'iron triangle' region) have high scores on the human capital technical index. However, the UC/Ls with the lowest scores on the human capital technical index tend to be many of the smaller inland towns and the remote, small Indigenous settlements, along with some of the large regional centres that scored highly on the human capital university index.

The national benchmark score on the human capital no-qualifications

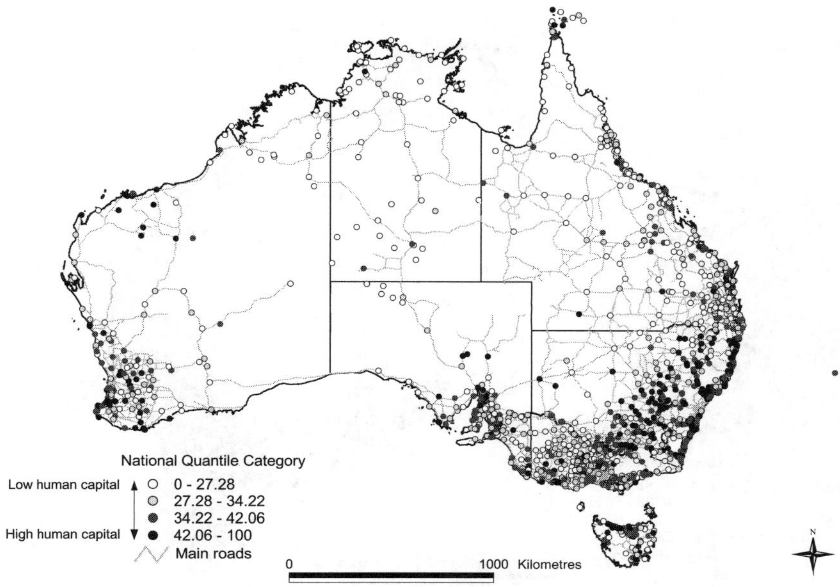

Source: Stimson et al. (2004, Ch. 5, p. 29).

Figure 6.5 Pattern of UC/L scores on the human capital technical index, Australia, 2001

index is 55.80. Stimson et al. (2004, Ch. 5, p. 6) note that in many ways the pattern of UC/Ls scores on this index is the opposite to that for the other two derived human capital indices just discussed. Of the metropolitan cities, Hobart and Adelaide on average have the highest scores on the human capital no-qualifications index, and they are above the national benchmark score. In the regional areas, it is the Northern Territory, Tasmania, Queensland and New South Wales where on average the scores of UC/Ls on this index are highest. The place in Australia with the poorest performance (that is, the highest score of 100) on this human capital index is Umbakwmba, an Indigenous community in the Northern Territory, while the snowfields town of Thredbo in New South Wales has the lowest index score and is thus the strongest performer on this human capital index. The data in Table 6.6 show that both Queensland and the Northern Territory have a very large range in UC/L scores on the human capital no-qualifications index, while New South Wales and Victoria tend to have a base incidence of regional UC/Ls with high scores on this index. Both South Australia and Tasmania tend to have a lesser incidence

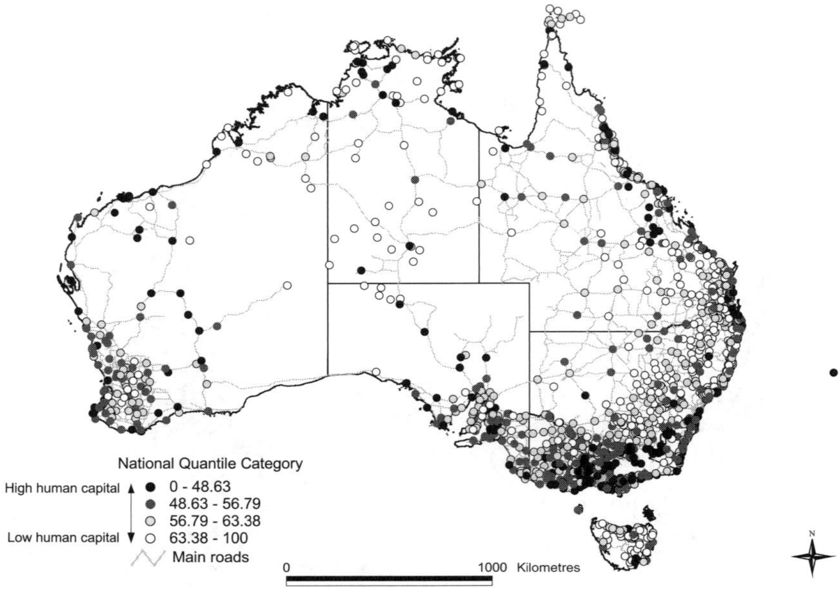

Source: Stimson et al. (2004, Ch. 5, p. 30).

Figure 6.6 Pattern of UC/L scores on the human no qualifications index, Australia, 2001

of regional UC/Ls with low scores on this index, reflecting better human capital performance. The data show that the states of Queensland and South Australia and the Northern Territory – all with a relatively high preponderance of small and remote Indigenous settlements – have a relatively high preponderance of places with high scores on this index.

Figure 6.6 maps the regional pattern across Australia of UC/Ls scores on the human capital no qualifications index. On the map the places with the darkest symbols have the lowest scores on the index representing those UC/Ls with better levels of human capital performance. Those UC/Ls tend to be concentrated in the inland wheat–sheep belt and many of the other agricultural regions, and they also include some of the coastal service and tourism towns. On that map the UC/Ls with the highest scores on this index are represented by the symbols with the darkest shading which indicates very poor levels of human capital performance. They are widely spread across the smaller towns of the inland farming and pastoral areas, parts of the coast, and the small, remote Indigenous settlements.

Labour market areas: analysis of educational attainment

The Bureau of Transport and Regional Economics (2004b, pp. 23–6) notes that a good guide to a region's performance is the quality of its labour market; thus the education, skills and qualifications of its population will be an important consideration. Its study of Australia's LMR with respect to those activities reveals that it is the LMRs in the inland areas – and in particular in the remote locations – that have the lowest proportions of highly educated people, and that is evident especially in Queensland and South Australia. While that is also the case to an extent in the remote areas of Western Australia and the Northern Territory, there nonetheless are some LMRs that have above average proportions of highly qualified people, in particular associated with the mining, health, education, and community services sectors. The pattern of distribution of tertiary-qualified people across the LMRs shows that it is predominantly the east coast region and the capital cities that have the highest concentrations.

The Bureau of Transport and Regional Economics (2004b) has also identified those non-capital city LMRs that have the most highly qualified people in each industry sector. That analysis reveals that: 'many regions lack workers with higher formal qualifications across a range of local industries. However, some non-capital regions are clearly demonstrating high levels of highly educated workers across a variety of local industries' (p. 26).

Some of those regions have been described by Salt (2001) as 'sea-change' towns that are attracting in-migrants from the capital cities, often to retire. They include the LMR surrounding Byron and Wollongong in New South Wales and Augusta–Margaret River in Western Australia, which the Bureau of Transport and Regional Economics (2004b, p. 26) describes as regions that are displaying high levels of knowledge-based economic activity. And the ANTA/UQ study by Stimson et al. (2004, Chs 5, 8) tells how it is the coastal and the inland regions centred on large regional service towns with university campuses that have the highest levels of incidence of people with high levels of human capital outside the metropolitan cities.

6.8.3 Occupational Diversity in Regions

The CR-SURF/UQ study has specifically looked at variations in the degree to which there are spatial variations in the diversity of employment across occupations. Using the standard occupational categories, an occupational specialization/diversification index was calculated for UC/Ls across the urban system. Similarly, using the data on educational attainment levels a skills specialization/diversification index has been calculated

Table 6.7 Range in occupation and skills specialization/diversification index scores across UC/Ls in Australia's states and the Northern Territory, 2001

Spatial Unit	N	Occupation		Skills	
		Min.	Max.	Min.	Max.
Australia					
The urban system	1519	17.57	80.04	17.93	97.90
Capital cities	8	35.63	39.14	50.72	59.68
Within States and Territories					
NSW	452	31.61	52.23	30.66	79.88
Vic	285	33.22	57.08	37.74	76.73
Qld	331	32.31	68.70	17.93	87.36
SA	151	33.69	59.41	52.74	91.79
WA	152	31.89	69.10	38.01	97.84
Tas	80	34.96	43.08	43.25	78.57
NT	58	17.57	80.04	44.28	97.90

Source: Stimson et al. (2004, Ch. 5, p. 13).

for UC/Ls, which is indicative of the degree to which the industry structure of place provides employment opportunities for a wide or a narrow range of skills.

The outcomes of those analyses reveal that the national benchmark score on the occupational specialization/diversification index is 37.2, while on the skills specialization diversification index it is 64.17 (Stimson et al., 2004, Ch. 5). The summary statistics for the distribution across UC/Ls in the states and the Northern Territory on both of those indices are shown in Table 6.7. The data show that there is a much wider variation in the diversity and specialization of both occupation and skills mix across the regional UC/Ls than is the case in the metropolitan cities, and in general the degree of specialization in the mix of skills is greater than it is for the mix of occupations.

On the occupation specialization/diversification index, the most specialized places are usually small and remote mining towns and Indigenous settlements, and in particular across regional areas of Queensland, South Australia, Western Australia and the Northern Territory, as indicated in Figure 6.7, while the larger regional towns across the inland wheat–sheep belt and along the coast tend to have more diversified occupational structures, as indicated in the spatial pattern of the highest density of symbols in Figure 6.7. Also, quite a lot of regional towns that have quite high scores on the occupation specialization/diversification index have

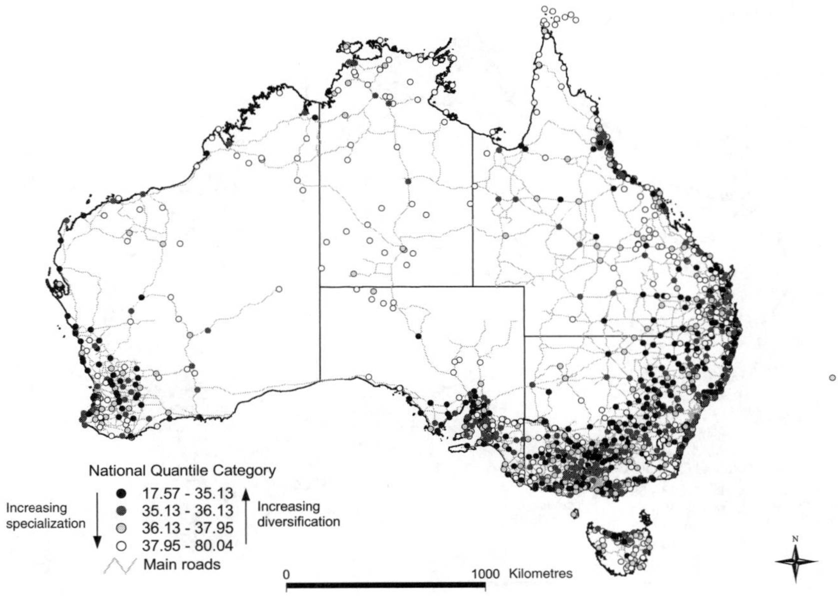

Source: Stimson et al. (2004, Ch. 5, p. 31).

Figure 6.7 Pattern of UC/L scores on the occupation specialization/diversification index, Australia, 2001

specialized industry structures, and those tend to be places dominated by manufacturing and utility industries as well as mining.

For the skills specialization/diversification index analysis, the data in Table 6.7 show that regional UC/Ls tend to have a much greater likelihood of having a more restricted range of employment opportunities for a wide set of skills mixes among workers. Stimson et al. (2004, Ch. 5, p. 15) point to how it is common for a very high degree of skills specialization to be found across the small, remote and Indigenous settlements in Queensland, Western Australia and the Northern Territory, as represented by the predominance of a lower density of symbols on the map in Figure 6.8. The map also shows that higher levels of skills specialization tend to be prevalent across the inland towns of most states; often those are smaller places, and in general that reflects a concentration of low-skill jobs. Some of the remote mining towns and a few of the coastal towns specializing in tourism also have more specialized industry and occupation structures and a restricted skills mix. Figure 6.8 also shows that the more diversified skills mixes are found in some

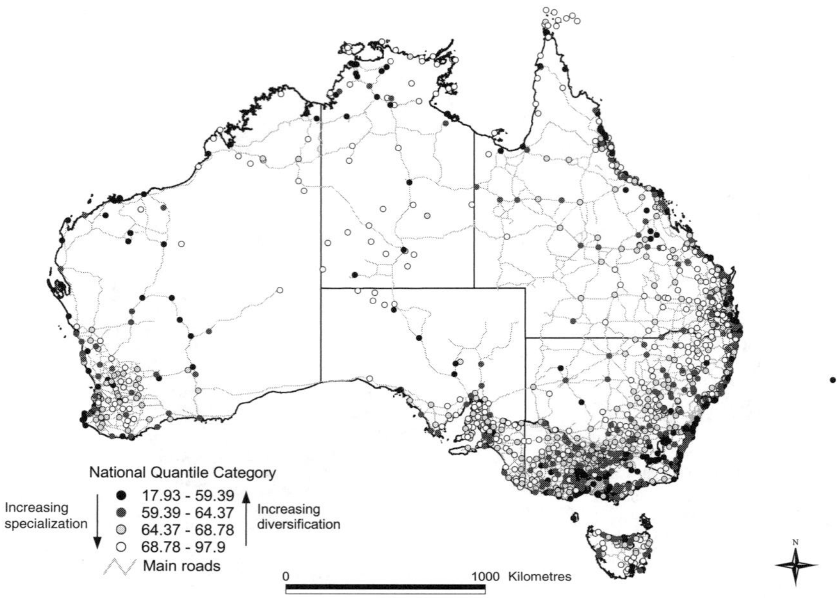

Source: Stimson et al. (2004, Ch. 5, p. 31).

Figure 6.8 Pattern of UC/L scores on the skills specialization/diversification index, Australia, 2001

of the larger coastal towns and also in some of the larger towns in the inland wheat–sheep belt and other agricultural areas. A more diverse skills mix also tends to be found in UC/Ls located in close proximity to the metropolitan cities.

Reference is made in the Bureau of Transport and Regional Economics (2004b) research to the fact that often it is difficult to attract skilled people to regional areas and to retain them; that deficiency is commonly identified as a policy issue for regional development in Australia. An example is the deficiency in health services in many rural and regional areas. But the BTRE research does make the telling point that that deficiency does not hold true across all the professional categories, with modelling for the period 1991–2001 showing that there has been a marginal increase in the proportion of teaching professionals across a wide range of regions, including coastal, inland and remote regions (Bureau of Transport and Regional Economics, 2004b, p. 27). However, that has not actually occurred in many of the regional areas of South Australia and Tasmania.

Of particular noteworthiness is the distribution of skilled tradespeople.

Despite a decline in employment in the trades, shortages in some trades occupations have persisted for a long time. There has been a general decline, with fewer LMRs maintaining their shares of skilled tradespeople over the decade 1991 to 2001, with the sparsely populated and inland regions having the lowest levels of growth in skilled tradespersons (Bureau of Transport and Regional Economics, 2004b, p. 28).

Regional size, the settlement hierarchy and human capital

The analysis of the performance of LMRs with respect to education, skills and qualifications conducted by the Bureau of Transport and Regional Economics (2004b) certainly reveals how LMRs with a greater number of employed people are likely also to have higher shares of tertiary-qualified people, and how in general the LMRs in remote and inland locations tend to have relatively low shares of highly educated and skilled people. The patterns shown in Figures 6.4 to 6.8 certainly show that there are marked regional patterns to the distribution of UC/L scores on the human capital indices and the occupation and skills diversification indices derived in the CR-SURF/UQ study (Stimson et al., 2004, Ch. 5). However, as the Bureau of Transport and Regional Economics (2004b, p. 29) study does point out, some of the LMRs in the sparsely populated areas of Australia – such as mining towns – do have high shares of tertiary-qualified people, and some of the 'sea-change' coastal towns in the 'sun-belt' areas with lifestyle advantages are also attracting relatively high shares of university-qualified people.

Stimson et al. (2004, Ch. 5, pp. 24–5) have conducted a correlation analysis for each of the states and the Northern Territory to measure the nature of the relationship between UC/L scores on the three human capital indices – university, technical and no qualifications – and UC/L scores on the industry, occupation and skills specialization/diversification indices and the log of population of UC/Ls. In that way the urban hierarchy effect may be measured. The results of those correlation analyses are reproduced in Table 6.8.

It is evident that there is a positive correlation between the population size of UC/Ls and their performance on the human capital university and the human capital technical indices, but that that positive relationship is stronger for the university index performance. Conversely, there is a negative correlation between population size of UC/Ls and their performance on the human capital no-qualifications index. Those results show that larger urban places do better in terms of human capital performance. But what the correlation coefficients in Table 6.8 do show is that that relationship is not particularly strong in a statistical sense, except in the Northern Territory, which is alone among the states in having a correlation

Table 6.8 Pearson's correlation coefficients for UC/L scores on the human capital and the specialization/diversification indices and population size (logarithmic) of UC/Ls for the states and the Northern Territory, 2001

Indices	NSW	Vic	Qld	SA	WA	Tas	NT
Human capital: university	+0.27	+0.20	+0.35	+0.24	+0.28	+0.12	**+0.62**
Human capital: technical	+0.11	+0.09	+0.05	+0.18	+0.17	+0.09	**+0.42**
Human capital: no qualification	–0.23	–0.06	–0.29	–0.25	+0.28	–0.14	**–0.50**
Industry specialization index	–0.27	–0.32	+0.24	–0.34	–0.31	–0.29	**–0.42**
Occupation specialization index	–0.29	–0.34	+0.26	–0.36	–0.31	–0.37	–0.37
Skills specialization index	–0.23	–0.13	+0.23	–0.23	–0.32	–0.12	**–0.45**

Note: Significant correlation coefficients in bold.

Source: Stimson et al. (2004, Ch. 5, p. 24).

coefficient in excess of ±0.40 for any of those relationships. Those results, along with some of the findings from the Bureau of Transport and Regional Economics (2004b), do suggest that, while regional size or position up or down the urban hierarchy do matter vis-à-vis human capital performance, there are some smaller size regions in terms of their employment size, and some UC/Ls down the urban hierarchy, that do perform well in terms of human capital dimensions.

Table 6.8 also shows that there is a negative correlation between the population size of a UC/L and its score on the occupation specialization/diversification index, with the correlation coefficients for five of the six states (the exception being Queensland) and the Northern Territory being negative. They range from +0.26 for Queensland to -0.42 for the Northern Territory. But once again those correlation coefficients are not particularly high. The table also indicates how there is similarly a negative correlation between the population size of UC/Ls and their scores on the skills specialization/diversification index for five of the six states (the exception again being Queensland) and the Northern Territory, with the correlation coefficients ranging from +0.23 for Queensland to -0.45 for the Northern Territory. The Stimson et al. (2004) research shows that, while both diversity of occupational opportunity and diversity of employment for local populations with a wide mix of skills is more likely to be found in larger places up the urban hierarchy, that is not necessarily the case in Queensland with its traditionally more diversified regional town structure and many regional centres along the coast, as well as its many small mining towns. The results of the correlation analysis does suggest that there is a degree of both occupation and skills diversification to be found in some smaller places further down the urban hierarchy.

6.9 RELATIONSHIPS BETWEEN REGIONAL GROWTH, INDUSTRY STRUCTURE, HUMAN CAPITAL, AND QUALIFICATION AND OCCUPATION LEVELS

The focus now turns to explore more specifically the relationship between regional growth, industry structure, human capital, and qualification and occupation levels. Relatively little research has been conducted in Australia at a spatially disaggregated level below that of the states and territories or at the statistical division (SD) level, of which there are 56.

6.9.1 Forecasting Regional Growth at the Aggregate Level

One such aggregate level study was conducted by Adams (2002), at the SD level. It predicted that, over the period 1996/97 to 2007/08, all the SD level regions in Australia are predicted to grow, and that growth rates are expected to converge or become more similar over that forecast period compared to the previous decade: 'largely because there are greater differences between the industrial mixes of the sub-state regions than the industrial mixes of the states' (Adams, 2002, p. 12). The level of forecast average growth in real value-added over that period ranged from a top of 4.7 per cent per annum growth in Perth SD, the capital city of Western Australia, to a low of 1.82 per cent per annum growth in the Eyre SD in regional South Australia. That analysis told how 'mining and agricultural concentrations explain the extreme rankings of several regions' (p. 12) – such as the goldfields, wheat belt and mid-west in Western Australia where relatively poor growth was forecast – with a presence of mining not necessarily preventing a region from doing well or poorly. Likewise the absence of agriculture does not prevent a region from having a relatively low forecast, and nor does it ensure strong growth.

Adams's (2002) analysis has been used by Beer (2002) to argue that there are five key determinants of likely growth rates for regions in Australia:

- Local-level demand, with regions in states with strong growth prospects – Western Australia and Queensland – being more likely to grow strongly due to the growth impulses of the state.
- Diversity of the production base, with regions with more diverse and more multi-tiered economies having better prospects because they are not reliant on one or two industries.
- The identification and use of natural advantages for the benefit of the region, which embraces both locational advantages (such as access to major markets) and the use of resources (such as good water supplies and an attractive environment).
- The efficient and sustainable use of natural resources, which is a key determinant of growth prospects, with unsustainable use of resources inhibiting growth.
- The willingness of regions and their leaders to adjust to technological and other external changes, which greatly influences their rate of growth.

6.9.2 Disaggregated Analysis for Labour Market Regions

Disaggregated analysis of regional growth at a level of spatial scale below states or SDs has been undertaken by the Bureau of Transport and Regional Economics (2004a, 2004b), using four approaches. Those approaches look at: the effect of national shifts in employment on regional growth; the effect of initial industry structure on regional growth; the effect of industrial diversity; and the effect of education skills and qualifications.

One explanation given by the Bureau of Transport and Regional Economics (2004a) for the differences in regional employment growth is that the: 'strongly performing regions are specialised in industries that are growing rapidly at the national level, and poorly performing regions are specialised in industries with low or negative growth rate' (p. 33). Shift-share analysis was used to shed light on that proposition through investigation of the national shift component of employment change by industry sectors in LMRs over the decade 1996–2001. It was found that: 'actual regional employment growth rates were much more widely dispersed than the hypothetical growth rates' (p. 33), (that is, those derived from the national component of the shift-share analysis). But: 'despite this, the actual and hypothetical employment growth rates were positively correlated, and the relationship was statistically significant. About 20 per cent of variation in employment growth rates across regions could be explained by the industry structure of regional employment in 1991, and subsequent national growth trends by industry' (p. 33).

That finding of 20 per cent explanation is much below the 38 per cent found in an earlier Productivity Commission (1998) study for the period 1981–96, but the difference may be due to the use of the smaller LMRs in the Bureau's study compared to the large statistical subdivisions used in the Productivity Commission's analysis. But the Bureau's findings also confirm the proposition that the more recent change in growth rates for industry sector employment vary more across regions because of endogenous factors.

The Bureau of Transport and Regional Economics (2004a, 2004b) has also undertaken detailed investigation of regional patterns of growth, measured by growth in real tax income between 1990/91 and 1999/2000 as a proxy for economic growth. Part of that analysis groups LMRs into quintiles based on their rate of growth in total real taxable income. That research highlights how there are differentials in the initial 1991 industry structure of LMRs across the income growth quintiles, with income growth exceeding employment growth in all but the first income quintile, while for the lowest two income quintiles income growth accounts for a relatively small share of employment growth.

The Bureau of Transport and Regional Economics (2004a, 2004b) then undertook multivariate regression analysis of income growth between 1990/91 and 1999/2000 for LMRs which showed that – after controlling for state or territory, size of regional economy, mean income and educational qualifications – the 1991 ANZSIC division industry sector employment shares were a statistically significant grouping of variables in explaining regional variation in income growth. The model used explained about 42 per cent of the variation in income growth rates across labour market regions. Regions with a relatively high share of 1991 employment in communication services, retail trade, health and community services, and electricity, gas and water tended to experience a lower income growth rate. It was also found that industry-intensive variables were significant predictors of income instability across the LMRs.

To test the Australian context applicability of Kaufman's (1993) finding in the US that a diverse employment base creates stability and buffers the economic performance of a region against the effects of an economic shock, the Bureau of Transport and Regional Economics (2004a) has attempted the difficult task of trying to isolate the relationship between industrial diversity and economic growth and stability. The analysis showed that: 'across the labour market regions (LMRs), evidence does exist of a strong and statistically significant association between industrial diversification and income instability ($r = -0.61$)' (p. 39). Thus:

> regions with a low level of industrial diversity in 1991 tended to have relatively unstable incomes between 1990–1991 and 1999–2000. The relationship between industrial diversity and total real taxable income was weaker ($r = +0.26$), but in accordance with the proposition that more diverse [regional] economies tend to experience higher growth. (p. 39)

That bivariate correlation between industrial diversity and income growth is present because the size of a regional economy is closely related to both industrial diversity and to income growth. Thus, the Bureau of Transport and Regional Economics (2004a) also undertook multivariate regression analysis of income growth (and, separately, instability) against the 1991 industrial diversification index, controlling for state or territory, size of the regional economy, average income, bachelor degree qualifications, and ANZSIC division employment shares of LMRs in 1991. The results indicate that the 'initial level of industrial diversity was a statistically significant explanatory of variation on income growth across regions' (p. 40).

Those results are consistent with Kaufman's (1993) findings in the US. The results thus support the conclusion that industrial diversity is closely related to stability of economic performance, rather than to economic growth per se. Regions with a relatively high level of industrial diversity tended to experience more stable income growth between 1990/91 and 1999/2000, holding other factors constant. This conclusion proved to be robust to changes in model specification (such as adding region type or size of largest urban centre variables).

Research by the Bureau of Transport and Regional Economics (2004b) has also examined the relationship between education and occupation levels and economic growth across LMRs and growth in total real taxable income between 1990/91 and 1999/2000. It was found that for all five quintiles of income growth for the LMRs there was a link between high shares of tertiary-qualified people and high-income growth, with income decline and minimal change being associated with relatively low 1991 shares of people with Bachelor or higher degree qualifications for all regions, whether agricultural or regional. And high shares of intermediary and elementary workers were associated with income decline in both agricultural and non-agricultural regions (pp. 33–4). The Bureau says that the result of its analysis 'suggests that the relationship between higher-education levels and income growth does not seem to continue indefinitely. While higher skilled workers and occupations are important, they do not need to dominate the labour force for income growth to occur' (Bureau of Transport and Regional Economics, 2004a, p. 35).

6.10 CONCLUSIONS

This chapter has provided an overview of recent regional trends and patterns in industry structure, human capital, and education and occupation levels in Australia, drawing on recent research conducted by the BTRE and ANTA/UQ. That overview of the findings of the spatially disaggregated analyses conducted by the Bureau of Transport and Regional Economics (2004a, 2004b) and by Stimson et al. (2004) has been put in the context of the broad macro situation in Australia and the implications for regional development and performance evident from other research conducted in recent years.

6.10.1 The Macro Level

At the macro level, it is clearly evident that the industry structure of employment in Australia continues to shift towards a dominance of the services sectors, that educational levels are rising – particularly among younger adults – and that there has been strong growth in the share of jobs in the 'symbolic analyst' occupations, reflecting the increasing importance of the knowledge-intensive activities associated with the 'new economy'. Labour force participants with minimum qualifications are at greater risk of unemployment. However, educational expansion is not seen to be reflected nationally in changing occupations which have remained relatively stable, although there has been considerable internal change in the occupation structures of industry sectors with all industries having experienced growth in their shares of highly qualified workers. It has only been among the skilled tradespeople where there has been a decline relative to the working-age population.

6.10.2 Industrial Structure

The BTRE research reveals that a close tie exists between regional industry structure and the size of a regional economy, and also the degree of remoteness of a region. Not surprisingly, the importance of regional employment in the agriculture, mining, and accommodation, cafes and restaurants industry sectors is seen to rise with increasing remoteness, whereas the relative importance of employment in the technology- and knowledge-intensive industries is seen to decline with remoteness and increase with the size of the regional economy, to be most highly concentrated in the largest of the metropolitan cities.

While these general relationships seem to be strong, nonetheless there remains a considerable degree of variation across Australia's regions in the relative shares of particular industry groups, and there is considerable variety in the industries in which regions specialize. There is also plenty of evidence pointing to considerable variation across regions in the particular industries that are the main sources of employment growth. The Bureau of Transport and Regional Economics (2004a) research in particular shows how the relative shares of employment in particular industries have changed depending on what component of the decade 1991–2001 is considered, with the magnitude of change varying from 1991–96 to 1996–2001.

The data seem to indicate that, over the decade 1991 to 2001, there has been the emergence of a more diverse industrial structure outside the major cities, and the Bureau of Transport and Regional Economics (2004a, p. 46) research shows that only 37 of the nation's 425 LMRs experienced a decline in industrial diversity in excess of one percentage point, while 228 LMR experienced an increase of more than one percentage point in their industrial diversity. However, there is also evidence to show that about 20 per cent of the variation in employment rate that occurred across LMRs over that decade could be explained by the industry structure of regional employment in 1991 and subsequent national growth trends in industry. The Bureau says this finding points 'potentially to other important influences on regional economic growth' (p. 45), and that those may include endogenous factors such as: 'amenity, remoteness, investment, leadership and the region's resource and skills base' (p. 45).

The research evidence also shows that those regions with a more highly diverse industry structure tend to have experienced more stable economic performance than is the case for regions with more specialized industry structures. However, the Bureau of Transport and Regional Economics (2004a) study points out that its modelling 'does not support the claim that a highly diverse industry structure is associated with greater regional growth products' (p. 46).

It would thus seem that the industry structure of employment in regions in Australia does play an important but not necessarily a dominant role in explaining regional differences in performance and economic growth. Some convergence is evident. But regional specialization also remains strong. The ANTA/UQ study and the BTRE research findings both indicate that a larger size per se does not always result in increased industry diversity, just as smaller size does not always create specialization. But increasing diversity of itself does not ensure better performance; rather it might act more to insulate a region's economy from the effects of economic shocks (Bureau of Transport and Regional Economics, 2004a, p. 46).

6.10.3 Human Capital

Turning to human capital issues, it is clear that the rise in education levels nationally is being reflected across all the remoteness classes over the decade 1991–2001, even though the level of educational attainment does continue to decline with increasing remoteness and also with the size of a region or place. It is among the Indigenous population that the decline is most marked. But there does seem to be emerging something of an oversupply of skills in some of the more populated regions, while there has been greater absorption of skills in the regional areas of Australia, and that is reflected through the increasing shares of some employment in some of the professions across some of the regional areas. However, the ANTA/UQ study points to the continuing dichotomy at a general level between the capital cities and regional urban areas in their human capital performance (Stimson et al., 2004, Ch. 10, p. 4).

The results of the BTRE research suggest that a degree of equalization is occurring in educational levels across Australia's regions, there being some evidence of convergence in skills and qualification outcomes for the more populated regions, but that diminishes with increasing remoteness (Bureau of Transport and Regional Economics, 2004b, p. ix). However, professionals in other areas, such as teaching, are becoming more evenly distributed regionally, while some professions, such as computing professionals, are highly concentrated in the major cities and some of the larger regional centres.

The Bureau of Transport and Regional Economics (2004b) research concludes that: 'overall, regions with higher 1991 shares of university educated residents tended to experience higher income growth over the 1991 to 2001 decade' (p. 42). The regions with high shares of managers, administrators and professionals – the highly skilled workers – showed no clear link with income growth. The research findings suggest that: 'the relationship between higher education and income growth does not persist indefinitely' (p. 42).

The ANTA/UQ research (Stimson et al., 2004) shows that, across the urban system, there seems to be a positive relationship between the size of an urban place and its level of performance on the human capital indices derived by that research, and that there is also a tendency for occupation diversity and skills density to increase with increasing size of a place. But the relationships for the latter are of a considerably lesser magnitude than for the former, and it is evident that some larger places do not have high levels of human capital performance, and some of them have specialized occupation and skills structures, while some smaller places have strong human capital performance and reasonably diverse occupational and skill structures. The overall links, then, between education, skills, occupation levels and regional performance and growth are somewhat more complex than might have been expected.

6.10.4 Policy Issues

What implications do the findings of the research reviewed in this chapter have for regional policy and planning? Four key issues are:

- Diversification is important but not a panacea for economic growth, and a 'regional push for greater industrial diversity might better reflect preferences for slow and steady growth over a boom and bust economy' (Bureau of Transport and Regional Economics, 2004a, p. 46).
- Where people live can certainly affect the diversity of job opportunities with respect to the mix of industry, occupation and skill requirements, and it can affect overall levels of labour market participation and engagement. Thus, 'place does matter' (Stimson et al., 2004, Ch. 10, p. 4).
- The level of human capital is a factor differentiating the performance of places. Thus 'people skills do matter' (Stimson et al., Ch. 10, p. 4).
- Population size does matter, as seen in the degree to which large urban places have more diversified job opportunities across both industry sectors and occupational categories, and larger places have higher levels of human capital performance. 'Large urban places also tend to offer employment opportunities for a greater range of educational attainment skill levels. This is not surprising and most likely it represents a self-selection outcome as the best people seek the better performing places so the direction of causation becomes blurred' (Stimson et al., 2004, Ch. 10, p. 5).

Previous studies, as well as the BTRE and ANTA/UQ studies reviewed here, tell us that an important issue for policy is the degree to which the differentiation across regions can be addressed by people-based as against place-based measures, or by a mixture of both approaches (O'Connor et al., 2001; Baum et al., 1999):

- People-based approaches certainly enhance human capital development, and thus post-secondary education and training become critical. 'And enhancing geographical access to those education and training services also became important' (Stimson et al., 2004, Ch. 10, p. 8).

- The overwhelming evidence is that investment in human capital development as a people-based policy is associated with advantageous place-based outcomes, as well as advantages for people (Stimson et al., 2004, Ch. 10, p. 8).
- Place-based interventions are typically oriented towards selective industry assistance, payroll tax exemptions, land deals, and the like. But such measures can have detrimental impacts on the economic welfare of populations in particular regions (Industry Commission, 1993, 1996), and industry assistance packages in reality have limited potential for state and local government regional development policy to impact on regional economic activity in the longer term (Giesecke and Maddern, 1997, p. 17).
- Strategies for regional development 'need to be built upon local comparative advantage, and capitalise on region-specific resources, knowledge and location' (Bureau of Transport and Resource Economics, 2004a, p. 45).

The nature of Australia's space economy is changing rapidly, and the processes of change are impacting upon people and places in differential ways. One of the challenges will be to develop and implement regional policies and strategies that build successful regions and places into even more success. 'Inevitably that will require greater selectivity, but would be more likely to result in enhanced national performance and improved competitiveness, giving a better return on limited government resources' (Stimson, 2002, p. 35).

It is inevitable that tensions result from differential levels of regional performance and that will continue. The challenge is how best might Australia, with its three-tier system of government, respond with appropriate people-based and place-based policies for all the nation's regions.

ACKNOWLEDGEMENT

The author wishes to acknowledge the contribution of his colleagues at the University of Queensland who are the joint authors of the ANTA/CR-SURF study Main Report (Stimson et al., 2004), the results of which are drawn upon for some of the discussion in this chapter. The author also is indebted to the researchers in the Bureau of Transport and Regional Economics who produced the research in the Bureau's studies (Bureau of Transport and Regional Economics, 2004a, 2004b) that are also drawn upon throughout the chapter. The author thanks the Bureau of Transport and Regional Economics for supplying some of the figures reproduced in the chapter. Of course the interpretation of the research findings of others that are both quoted and referred to in this chapter and the context in which those research findings are discussed are entirely the responsibility of the author and may not necessarily be the views and interpretations held by the authors of those studies.

REFERENCES

Adams, P.D. (2002), 'Prospects for Australia's regions', *Sustaining Regions*, **1**(2), 4–16.

Arthur, W.B. (1994), *Increasing Returns and Path Dependency in the Economy*, Ann Arbor, MI: University of Michigan Press.

Australian Bureau of Statistics (ABS) (2002), *Year Book of Australia*, No. 84, ABS: Canberra.

Barro, R.J. (1990), 'Endogenous technological change', *Journal of Political Economy*, **98**, S71–S102.

Baum, S., R. Stimson, K. O'Connor, P. Mullins and R. Davis (1999), *Community Opportunity and Vulnerability in Australia's Cities and Towns: Characteristics, Patterns and Implications*, Brisbane: University of Queensland Press for the Australian Housing and Urban Research Institute.

Beer, A. (1999), 'Regional cities within Australia's evolving urban system, 1991–96', *Australasian Journal of Regional Studies*, **5**(3), 329–48.

Beer, A. (2002), 'Editorial', *Sustaining Regions*, **1**(2), 3.

Beer, A. and A. Maude (1995), 'Regional cities within the Australian urban system, 1961 to 1991', *Urban Policy and Research*, **13**(3), 135–48.

Bradley, R. and J. Gans (1998), 'Growth in Australian cities', *Economic Record*, **74**(226), 266–78.

Bureau of Transport and Regional Economics (BTRE) (2004a), 'Focus on Regions No. 1: Industry structure', Information Paper 49, BTRE, Department of Transport and Regional Services, Canberra.

Bureau of Transport and Regional Economics (BTRE) (2004b), 'Focus on Regions No. 2: Education, skills and qualifications', Information Paper 51, BTRE, Department of Transport and Regional Services, Canberra.

Department of Home Affairs and the Environment (1982), *Australian Urban Environmental Indicators*, Canberra: Australian Government Publishing Service.

Draca, M., J. Foster and C. Green (2003), 'Human capital investment and economic growth in the Australian economy', in C. Williams, M. Draco and C. Smith (eds), *Productivity and Regional Economic Performance in Australia*, Brisbane: Queensland Office of Economic and Statistical Research (OESR), Queensland Treasury, with Queensland Government/Treasury, pp. 155–62.

Duranton, G. and D. Puga (2000), 'Diversity and specialisation in cities: why, where and when does it matter?' *Urban Studies*, **37**(3), 533–55.

Garnaut, J., P. Connell, R. Lindsay and V. Rodriguez (2001), 'County Australia: influences on employment and population growth', ABARE Research Report, 2001.1, Canberra.

Garnett, A.M. and E.T. Lewis (2000), 'Population and labour mobility in rural Australia', *Australasian Journal of Regional Studies*, **6**(2), 157–72.

Gaston, N. and D. Timcke (1999), 'Do casual workers find full-time employment: evidence from the Australian Youth Survey', *Economic Record*, **75**(231), 333–47.

Giesecke, A.D. and J.R. Maddern (1997), 'Regional government economic policy: assessing the policy instruments', *Australasian Journal of Regional Studies*, **3**(1), 3–18.

Goetz, S.J. and A. Rapasingha (2001), 'The returns to higher education: estimates for the contiguous states', paper to Regional Science Association International, North American Annual Meeting, Charleston, SC, November.

Gordon, I.R. and P. McCann (2000), 'Industrial clusters, complexes, agglomeration and/or social networks', *Urban Studies*, **37**(3), 513–32.

Gregory, R. (1995), 'Higher education expansion and economic change', *Australian Bulletin of Labour*, **21**(4), 295–22.

Hanushek, E.A. and D.D. Kinko (2000), 'Schooling, labour-force quality, and the growth of nations', *American Economic Review*, **90**(5), 1187–1208.

Harrison, H. (1997), 'Trends in the delivery of rural health, education and banking services', National Farmers Federation Research Paper, vol. II, Canberra, February.

Henderson, J.V., A. Kuncoro and M. Turner (1995), 'Industrial development in cities', *Journal of Political Economy*, **103**, 1067–90.

Industry Commission (1993), *Impediments to Regional Industry Adjustment*, Canberra: Australian Government Publishing Service.

Industry Commission (1996), 'State, territory and local government assistance to industry', (draft report), Industry Commission, Melbourne.

Johansson, B., Ch. Karlsson and R.R. Stough (2001), *Theories and Endogenous Growth: Lessons for Regional Policy*, Heidelberg: Springer-Verlag.

Kaufman, R. (1993), 'An empirical exploration of the relation among diversity, stability and performance in economic systems', *Structural Change and Economic Dynamics*, **4**(2), 299–313.

Lande, P. (1994), 'Regional industrial structure and economic growth and stability', *Journal of Regional Science*, **34**(3), 343–60.

Lawson, J. and J. Dwyer (2002), *Labour Market Adjustment in Regional Australia*, Sydney: Reserve Bank of Australia.

Lloyd, R., A. Harding and O. Helwig (2000), 'Regional divide? A study of incomes in regional Australia', *Australasian Journal of Regional Studies*, **6**(3), 271–92.

Malizia, E. and S. Ke (1993), 'The influence of economic diversity on unemployment and stability', *Journal of Regional Science*, **33**(2), 221–35.

Norris, K. and M. Woden (1996), *The Changing Australian Labour Market*, Canberra: Australian Government Publishing Service.

O'Connor, K., R. Stimson and M. Daly (2001), *Australia's Changing Economic Geography and Society Dividing*, Melbourne: Oxford University Press.

OECD (1998), *Human Capital Investment: An International Comparison*, Paris: Organisation for Economic Co-operation and Development.

OECD (2001a), *The Well-Being of Nations: The Role of Human and Social Capital*, Paris: Organisation for Economic Co-operation and Development.

OECD (2001b), *Cities and Regions in the Learning Economy*, Paris: Organisation for Economic Co-operation and Development.

OECD (2001c), *Does Human Capital Matter for Growth in OECD Countries? Evidence from Pooled Mean-Group Estimates*, Paris: Organisation for Economic Co-ordination and Development.

Productivity Commission (1998), 'Aspects of structural change in Australia', Research Report, Ausinfo, Canberra.
Productivity Commission (2003), 'Trends in Australian manufacturing', Commission Research Paper, Ausinfo, Canberra.
Quiggin, J. (1999), 'Human capital theory and education policy in Australia', *Australian Economic Review*, **32**(2), 130–44.
Reich, R.B. (1991), *The Work of Nations*, New York: Vintage Books.
Romer, P. (1986), 'Increasing returns and long run growth', *Journal of Political Economy*, **94**, 1002–37.
Romer, P.M. (1990), 'Endogenous technological change', *Journal of Political Economy*, **98**, S71–S102.
Salt, B. (2001), *The Big Shift: Welcome to the Third Australian Culture*, Victoria: Hardie Grant Books.
Solow, R.M. (1956), 'A contribution to the theory of economic growth', *Quarterly Journal of Economics*, **70**, 65–94.
Stimson, R.J. (2002), 'Success and stress: regional performance across Australia', Keynote Address, Inspiring Regional Australia National Conference, Bunbury, October.
Stimson, R. and S. Baum (2001), 'Patterns of advantage and disadvantage across Australia's communities: a focus on education and human capital', *New Horizons in Education, the Journal of World Education Fellowship Australia*, **105**(Nov.), 9–34.
Stimson, R., S. Baum, J. Mangan, Y. Van Gellecum, T-K. Shyy and T. Yigitcanlar (2004), 'Analysing spatial patterns in the characteristics of work, employment and skills in Australia's capital cities and across its regional cities and towns: modelling community opportunity and vulnerability, main report', prepared for the Australian National Training Authority (ANTA), CR-SURF/ANTA 2003 National Project, Centre for Research into Sustainable Urban and Regional Futures, University of Queensland, Brisbane.
Taylor, P.J., G. Catalano and N. Gane (2002), 'A geography of global change: services and cities 2000–01', Globalisation and World Cities Study Group and Network, GaWC Research Bulletin, **77**.
Tidswell, W.V. and S.M. Barker (1971), *Quantitative Methods: The Approaches to Socio-Economic Geography*, London: University Tutorial Press.
Tilly, C. (1997), *Half a Job: Bad and Good Part-Time Jobs in a Changing Labor Market*, Philadelphia, PA: Temple University Press.
White, D. (1987), *Education and the State and Federal Involvement in Educational Policy Development*, Melbourne: La Trobe University.

7. Innovation clusters linking regions

Brigitte Preissl

7.1 INTRODUCTION

The innovation cluster literature of the last few years has shown that innovating firms benefit from regional clustering (see, for example, OECD, 2001; Porter, 1990, 1998; Bergman et al., 2001; Keeble and Wilkinson, 2000; Cooke, 2001b). This chapter will present evidence for innovation activity in a cluster context that links regions by creating knowledge transfer chains. It is based on an analysis of the innovation cluster of the German automotive component sector. This cluster confirms the benefits of regional agglomeration, and it also shows the importance of privileged access to knowledge and expertise that transcends regions, but relies on typical cluster features. This perspective on clusters requires a clear distinction between innovation and production clusters. The essential ingredient for innovation is new knowledge; and to get it at the right time, in exactly the quality needed, is crucial for success. The transfer of knowledge benefits from relations based on trust and informal communication. Hence, access to resources essential for innovation is easier in a cluster than in market transactions. It will be argued that there are specific advantages for innovating firms to act in a cluster context, but not all of them are derived from agglomeration. Other features of cluster configurations that rely on previous interaction play a prominent part here. It is these latter features that provide the main rationale for an integration function of clusters across regions.

In this approach, cluster membership is no longer defined by location in a specific region and a new approach for identifying cluster members had to be found. The method adopted here uses a functional perspective on innovation for the identification procedure.

Empirical evidence has been derived from an analysis of the German automotive components sector and its innovation activities.[1] Taking a 'sector perspective', the concept overlaps to a great extent with 'sectoral innovation systems' (Malerba, 2004). However, it is different from this theoretical approach as it emphasizes both the importance of a sector-specific knowledge base and the benefits of clustering. In addition, automotive components comprise a whole set of industrial sectors or industries ranging from leather goods to glass, from electronic devices to tin and steel products. Hence, it is not a sector in the sense of Malerba's analysis.[2]

Car manufacturing is a competitive and innovation-intensive economic sector. The dynamics of the industry are transmitted to the innovation activity of component suppliers. The configuration of their innovation cluster is mainly determined by patterns of technological development and strategic settings in the automotive industry.

The division of labour between car manufacturers and suppliers has changed substantially since the early 1990s as the result of a reorganization of processes of production and new governance models in supply chains (Hancké, 1997; Lay and Wallmeier, 1999a, 1999b; Peters, 1997; Jürgens and Meißner, 2005). This has determined the dynamics of innovation and growth in the automotive component sector to a large extent. Car manufacturers have shifted resource and development (R&D) tasks to their suppliers; hence, innovation activity has intensified in the component sector without, however, giving the suppliers full control over the process. Innovation strategies in the automotive industry, the rhythm of change, features of competition and new car model policies stimulate and guide innovation at the component supplier level. Clustering in the sense of agglomeration of similar and complementing activities in close proximity plays a major role in achieving innovation targets; however, component supplier firms have developed other links that are also essential for innovation success. These links require a revision of strictly local and regional cluster concepts.

7.2 CLUSTERS AND INNOVATION

An important predecessor of cluster studies was the notion of 'industrial districts' (Marshall, 1952 [1890]). These districts are characterized by the presence of firms belonging to a specific industry in a region which generates economies of scale in procurement and marketing, and in the availability of trained labour (see also Piore and Sabel, 1984; and Krugman, 1991). The rationale of industrial districts depends to a large extent on providing enough critical mass to stimulate infrastructure and the allocation of similar firms along the value chain.

The protagonists of cluster concepts acknowledge the importance of industrial districts but add some features that are of particular relevance under the perspective of gaining competitive advantage in dynamic international markets. Porter describes a scenario in which competition and cooperation combine to promote competitiveness for cluster members as well as for the regions they belong to (Porter, 1998). The linkages resulting from interaction in the cluster are superior to market relations for specific phases of innovative activity. Hence, competition is complemented by cooperation. Porter suggests that it is no longer access to cheap and abundant resources required as factors of production, but the productive use of these resources that creates competitive advantage (Porter, 1998). From this, three basic elements of clusters are derived: (1) access to essential resources; (2) enhancing productivity and ability to innovate; and (3) supporting new business formation. Cooke uses the concept of regional innovation systems, which is quite similar to that of clusters. He points out that members of these regional systems are linking with a wider global context as many firms' activities stretch over a national and international network (Cooke, 2001a). Innovation clusters in particular are dependent on optimal conditions for knowledge transfer and learning.

7.2.1 A Simple Definition

Although based on complex notions of clusters and their effects on the performance of companies and regions, the definition used in this chapter remains rather simple: a cluster is a set of interdependent organizations that contribute to the realization of innovations in an economic sector or industry. This definition has emerged from the analysis of the innovation cluster of German automotive component suppliers. It is specific to this sector, but other cluster studies suggest that it might also be used for analysis of innovation in other sectors (Whalley and den Hertog, 2000). The definition lays down important characteristics. It does not give any geographical orientation, that is, cluster actors are not confined to a territorial space. The cluster perspective is that of an industry or industrial sector. This implies concentration on a set of relevant technologies and innovation service providers, given by the nature of the products or services in this industry. This feature is also used as the central anchor for cluster identification, which rests on innovation activity of firms in a specific industry. On the other hand, the definition allows for the inclusion of manufacturing as well as service innovation, and it comprises all actors contributing to innovation. Thus, it also abandons a strictly technological- or R&D-oriented notion in favour of a more comprehensive approach.

The concept is sector-specific, not firm-specific. From the point of view of a single firm, the cluster is a potential, a set of resources that develops with the firm's participation or without it. Some actors might cooperate only with a small number of other actors and for certain types of

Table 7.1 Cluster benefits

Benefits related to . . .	
Agglomeration	Knowledge spillovers
	Transaction cost
	Shared infrastructure
Level of activity	Economies of scale
	Network externalities
	Specialization
Interaction	Tacit knowledge
	Trust
	Competition and cooperation

Source: Preissl and Solimene (2003).

innovation, others appear more often as protagonists in innovations. As technology develops and market dynamics change, innovation functions and, consequently, the actors will also change. For example, the introduction of electronic navigation systems in cars or the development of alternative energy sources, such as fuel cells, requires the introduction of new fields of knowledge in the cluster.

Many cluster characteristics and benefits relate to the production activity of the firms involved (economies of scale, access to transport infrastructure, specialization). Innovation clusters require a somewhat modified perspective, since here a different set of resources is essential – more specifically, (tacit and explicit) knowledge and expertise, access to high-tech research results, and various implementation services for new technologies. As innovation clusters are characterized by the generation of new products and services or new processes, they typically rely on resources that may not already be available in the cluster. Hence, innovation clusters must be open for the inclusion of new actors and for expansion beyond strictly defined geographic limits.

7.2.2 Cluster Characteristics

The advantages of clustering can be related to three groups of phenomena: those attributed to agglomeration, those deriving from a certain activity level and those emerging from interaction, as listed in Table 7.1.

While agglomeration favours relations between identical actors as well as those between complementary actors, advantages from a high level of activity are due to the presence of many actors of the same type (or a critical mass of actors) in the cluster. Interaction in innovation clusters again refers to complementary competencies of actors. Benefits of agglomeration and of interaction are not always easily separated, because proximity stimulates interaction, and interaction often results in knowledge spillovers.

The location of automotive component manufacturers in Germany reflects advantages of geographical proximity, and the actors in the sector are well aware of this. For example, the automotive technology research institutes linked with the technical university of Aachen benefit from the vicinity of large car manufacturers. The generation of spin-offs, growth and diversification of activities has led to a complex set of competencies on automotive production in and around this university which is intensively used by firms in the region. The establishment of a faculty for machine construction and automotive technologies in the University of Applied Sciences in Zwickau is an example of knowledge infrastructure that serves local companies; it is meant to keep manufacturers in the region and to attract new investment from firms specializing in the automotive sector. Thirteen firms in the city are engaged in the manufacturing of car parts and components, and can thus benefit from the specialization in the university. In addition, the local cluster comprises many firms in the service sector, such as computer services, engineering and technology support services, which deliver services to the component supplier companies.

Cluster benefits are also derived from the level of activity present in a certain region. Economies of scale can be developed, if demand is substantial. A critical mass of demand allows firms to specialize and thus to develop expertise and qualifications which cannot easily be imitated. Network externalities are likely to occur the more firms participate in a cluster.

However, the most important features of the automotive component sector's innovation cluster are advantages derived from previous interaction. Throughout the innovation process component supplier firms cooperate with partners that they can trust because of a positive common experience in the past or because of personal connections. In particular, cooperation partners for innovation projects are found through the following links (see Preissl and Solimene, 2003):

- clients with whom a long-term supplier–customer relationship exists;
- university institutes that have delegated practitioners and PhD candidates to the firm;
- partners that have been met in industry associations and related committees;

- acquaintances from university years;
- engineers that had previously worked for the company and then set up their own research institutes;
- suppliers known from long-term cooperation;
- personal recommendations within automotive engineers' peer groups.

Interaction is favoured by proximity. For example, students from a nearby university look for jobs in component supplier firms or link their theses with a company project. Cluster participants meet frequently on the occasion of local events. However, the links created by these encounters tend to be quite stable, and they persist even if an actor moves away. Similarly, relationships built up in other contexts are the basis of cooperation in an innovation cluster regardless of the location of actors. Here the two attributes of 'competence' and 'trust' are more important than geographical closeness.

Complementarities and cooperation between the various participants in the innovation process generate routines and rituals that are specific to the cluster and provide the instruments and catalysts for the exchange of knowledge. Despite the enormous increase in the availability of information due to the automation of search processes and the international linking of information systems, tacit knowledge seems to play an increasing role in company strategies (see, for example, Bergman and Feser, 1999). Selecting relevant information from a vast supply and judging the reliability of data from anonymous sources are problems often resolved by referring to knowledge exchanged in peer groups. Tacit knowledge helps to contextualize more or less random information. It constitutes part of the assets of specific companies and individuals. Thus, it is bound to organizational and geographic locations and to persons. This specificity increases circulation of information and the spread of knowledge within the cluster, but prevents external actors from accessing it (Keeble and Wilkinson, 1999). Cluster interaction is likely to create an atmosphere that favours the exchange of tacit knowledge because it enhances trust between business partners.

The distinction between benefits that derive from proximity, those that are due to critical mass and bundling and those emerging from interaction shows that not all cluster advantages are linked to spatial clustering. Technical progress in transportation and communication systems might lead to an enlargement of the area that a cluster encompasses. Bergman and Feser see a potential 'spatial dispersal of cluster firms' and 'reduction in geographic clustering' as a result of more efficient means of transport (Bergman and Feser, 1999).

Processes of innovation in the automotive component industries rely on highly specialized knowledge; they are characterized by leaps in technology, materials used and model strategies (see Jürgens and Meißner, 2005). A shift of R&D tasks from the automotive manufacturing industry to the component suppliers has created a need for the latter to build up R&D capacity. While the larger firms such as Siemens, Bosch or ZF Friedrichshafen can rely on their own R&D departments, smaller firms have to use external sources of technology.

Component suppliers emphasized that the essential feature for the selection of partners in innovation was the quality of input and the trust established in the relationship that made cooperation successful. The identification of pieces of knowledge needed at an early stage of the innovation process is followed by the establishment of relations with the supplier of such knowledge. This is the step in which cluster relations are mobilized. The use of research facilities and the patterns of cooperation in innovation in the sector show a preference for local partners, but if successful cooperation with more distant actors already exists or if the necessary resources cannot be provided locally, the partner with the best quality of service and a history of good collaboration is approached. Innovating companies thus aim for the most appropriate and highest quality of inputs, which might be available only from distant sources; in this case, cluster relationships with the provider of inputs guarantee privileged access to these resources. In this sense, clusters are enhancing cross-regional links.

An important element of cluster membership, that has been mentioned by several interviewed cluster actors, is access to knowledge about 'what is going on in the sector'. This comprises technological advances, but also knowing 'who does what', which projects have been taken up or have failed, who cooperates with whom, and so on. Such knowledge is shared between cluster members; the units of reference are the component supplier's industry and industry associations, the car manufacturing community, and – last but not least – the personal knowledge network of senior engineers and researchers.

7.3 INNOVATION SERVICES PROVIDERS

7.3.1 Innovation as a Set of Services

Cluster analysis faces the problem of defining cluster membership in geographical, sectoral and/or institutional terms. The challenge here is not only to produce lists of cluster participants, but also to explain their roles and the dynamics of interaction between them.

A functional perspective on innovation and clusters provides an instrument for cluster analysis that allows for a dynamic perspective on cluster membership and, at the same time, determines the roles of actors in the cluster. In the approach chosen here, each innovation is characterized by a unique set of services leading to its successful realization. The different steps of the innovation process can be interpreted as a set of services that fulfil specific functions and take the process closer to completion.[3] Each function is provided by one (or several) actors. All actors contributing to the provision of an innovation function are cluster members. Any innovation requires a different set of functions to be covered: in some cases basic research might be negligible, in others training of personnel might be a marginal function; sometimes innovation might call for the introduction of other functions altogether, for example environmental checks in the case of a new car engine.

Innovation functions are exercised in the form of innovation services. These services can be provided by internal and external agents. If innovation functions change with the development of new technologies, new materials or knowledge-generating strategies, new actors will have to come in, while others (temporarily) lose importance within the cluster. The distinctive advantage of using an innovation service approach in cluster analysis (apart from its straightforward criterion for cluster membership) is its flexibility with respect to cluster actors, their entrance and exit into the cluster and their location.

Table 7.2 gives a list of functions and a list of actors to pursue these functions in processes of innovation in the automotive component sector. Component suppliers were asked to describe the attribution of tasks to actors in innovation. Although the division of labour varies from innovation to innovation, the table gives an illustration of the composition of the cluster and the interaction of cluster members with the innovating firm.

Contrary to our expectations and to common beliefs, the larger automotive component suppliers did not attribute an extraordinary importance to cooperation in R&D in innovation. Many innovation service functions were provided in-house, and only R&D related to small details in a new tool or process were delegated to research and technology organizations (RTOs) or other partners. Smaller component suppliers often interacted with universities, but some of them also complained about a lack of opportunities for cooperation.

7.3.2 Cluster Actors

The cluster of innovation service providers in the sector shows groups of actors with very different institutional settings. They belong to different

Table 7.2 Innovation functions and service suppliers in the component supplier cluster

Functions	Innovating firm	Client	Supplier	RTO	KIBS	Agent	Partner	Others
Basic research	++	o	o	+++	+	o	+	Universities
Applied research	+++	o	o	+++	o	o	o	
Innovation idea	+++	+++	+	++	o	++	o	Production units, literature
Information gathering	+++	o	o	++	+	+	o	
Feasibility studies	+	+	o	++	o	+	+	Production/ purchasing units
Product development	+++	o	+++	+++	o	+	+	
Process development	++	o	+	+++	+	o	+	Software firms
Technological advice	o	+	+	o	o	+	+	
Planning	+	o	o	o	o	o	o	
Implementation	+	o	o	o	+	o	+	
Training/HRM	+	o	o	++	+	+	o	
Quality control	+	o	o	o	+	o	o	Students
Testing	+	o	o	++	++	o	+	Students
Prototypes	+++	o	+	+	+	o	o	Universities
Documentation	+	o	o	+	+		o	
Certification	+ +	o	o	o	o	+	o	Service firms, public authorities
Marketing	+	+	o	o	o	+	o	
Project management	+	o	+	+	+	o	o	Service firms
Financing	++	+	o	+	+	+	o	Government

Note: +++ strong role ++ active role + moderate role o not active in this function

Source: Preissl and Solimene (2003).

industries, there are private as well as public organizations, small and large units, actors that only serve the automotive component industries and others that also work for clients in other sectors. The complexity of cars and the resulting heterogeneity of component suppliers requires that a wide range of RTOs specializing in different fields become part of the cluster. Apart from actors within the innovating companies, the cluster comprises six groups of participants:

1. The clients in the automotive manufacturing industry.
2. The suppliers of inputs to component manufacturing.
3. RTOs (specializing in certain technologies, in specific components, in general engineering or in various fields of car-related technology).
4. Knowledge-intensive business service (KIBS) firms.
5. University research institutes.
6. Federal and regional government agencies.

Links vary with respect to frequency and intensity of interaction. Subclusters may form with more intense cooperation, while the links between many cluster members may remain loose. At the core of the cluster, the component suppliers activate cluster members for the purposes of their innovations. However, cluster members also communicate between each other, cooperate in various innovation projects for different clients or meet at sector events, such as fairs, industry association meetings and so on. The constituting element of the cluster is interaction, which can be effected in physical encounters, through electronic communication or indirectly (by reading another cluster member's publications).

The technological knowledge needed is provided by several partners, and the major fields of technical progress shape the configuration of the innovation cluster. Technical trends and advances push some research institutions to the cluster margins or out of the cluster altogether, and place others in the centre. It is therefore useful to look at the major technological trends in car manufacturing in order to identify the relevant competencies required in innovation and the actors representing these competencies. Four major paths of technological development are prevalent in the evolution of car manufacturing at the beginning of the twenty-first century, and they are also likely to occupy a prominent role over the next few years (see also Jürgens and Meißner, 2005 and Preissl and Solimene, 2003):

- introduction of information and communication technology;
- lightweight construction;

- environmental concerns and fuel cell technology;
- safety concerns.

This indicates that knowledge from different highly specialized sources is needed. The providers of such knowledge may form their own technology-specific geographical clusters. For example, research facilities in the field of alternative energy sources, in particular fuel cells, is clustering in the Baden-Württemberg area close to the component supplier Bosch. A high level of specialization in each of the four relevant fields means that each regional component supplier cluster cannot comprise research facilities of the required quality for all four technological fields. Knowledge suppliers in the cluster are either specializing in specific technologies (informaton technology, construction materials, car safety), in distinct components (brakes, car electronics, gear systems) or possess competencies for 'cars' as complex systems.

Crucial for applied and theoretical knowledge creation in the cluster are the knowledge-intensive and highly specialized RTOs that have specific competencies in all car-related technologies. The expertise that they accumulate is a particularly scarce resource in the cluster, as they offer unique sets of knowledge. In order to fit the pieces of knowledge delivered by the RTO into the innovating company's R&D and production facilities, close cooperation is required. Forms of cooperation can range from medium- to long-term stays of RTO personnel in the innovating company, to frequent meetings and intensive electronic communication, depending on the nature of the project and the phase in the innovation process. Besides, RTOs have an important function in disseminating knowledge as the expertise gained in a research contract is then used to serve the next client in another project. No confidentiality clause can prevent the results of learning from spreading to other clients.

Of particular relevance are combinations of RTOs and KIBS firms that are located in one organizational setting, usually a university. Typically, the KIBS firms are private spin-offs of the RTO. RTOs and KIBS organizations combine basic research competence with directly applicable knowledge of high relevance for car manufacturers and suppliers. They typically interact with component suppliers in early research and development functions of an innovation. Other than most RTOs, however, KIBS firms are not subject to restrictive rules about the range of activities that they are allowed to engage in. Hence, they have more flexibility than partly government-supported RTOs to shift between innovation functions.

The clients in the automotive industry play an active role in the identification of innovation opportunities. Usually major innovation projects (for example a new gear system) are developed in accordance with a main client. On the other hand, component suppliers cooperate with their clients when conceiving their own innovation ideas in order to minimize the risk involved. The client's interest is confirmed and specified in a series of meetings. Agreement about the course of development of an innovative product is reached between customer and supplier in these meetings, whereas more routine communication is effected via electronic links. In the initial and final phases of an innovation, cooperation is intense, and often engineers from the client firm stay with the component supplier for weeks or months.

As regards suppliers of parts and raw materials (in short, suppliers): if the realization of innovations requires new inputs, suppliers may enhance the innovation process by investing in the development of these inputs; or innovations may be impeded by a lack of adequate inputs and reluctance of suppliers to generate them. The typical form of interaction between innovating firms and their suppliers is physical in the negotiation phase; later, simultaneous engineering between the component manufacturer and its supplier's computer systems is a routine procedure. Suppliers clearly play a subordinate role (reflected, for example, in the conditions for appropriation of research output). The selection of cooperation partners is based on experience: the supplier has proven that he is capable of delivering reliable inputs.

In this cluster, KIBS firms (engineering firms, software and IT consultants, management consultants) only play a role as contractors for smaller development tasks in construction and design, mainly for larger component suppliers. Business service firms are service providers which contribute to the innovation process but do not transmit any significant innovation-related knowledge into the innovating firms (tax consultants, banks, patent lawyers, marketing firms, and so on).

The links of 'university' professors with automotive component manufacturers are generally based on personal contacts between the holder of the chair and engineers in the companies. Two patterns of interaction with component suppliers are typical. First, students who cooperate with the innovating firm as practitioners and, thus, transfer academic knowledge into the company and receive practical knowledge while observing and participating in firm activities. The second pattern consists of contributions of academics, usually delivered as research papers or specific problem solutions. These two patterns have usually been observed between innovating firms and universities in the same region. A location-independent, indirect form of innovation service provision by universities is the development of the base of theoretical knowledge by their publication activities.

Two types of agents are present in the cluster: those that promote technology diffusion, and those that communicate policy targets from the political to the economic system. Some agents are private, usually managed by industry associations and serving the interests of all companies in an industry. These services can be delivered over larger distances, which increases the efficiency of operations of agents. Federal and regional governments act as sponsors of R&D and technology transfer as well as drivers of regulatory changes that induce innovative activity. They stimulate research and support technical and structural change. Governments can be active supporters of cluster generation by investing in (knowledge) infrastructures.

7.3.3 Geographical Aspects of Cluster Configuration

The geographical reach of the cluster stretches from regional links to the national economy and to foreign partners. One determining factor for the location of cluster actors is the sector-specific agglomeration of component suppliers and car manufacturers. This agglomeration sometimes emerges in the course of time; it may also result from outsourcing practices or strategic decisions of firms. Examples for regional clustering in automotive production and innovation are the Zwickau area and the Köln–Aachen area, as well as Frankfurt–Rüsselsheim and Stuttgart. However, there are important RTO/KIBS combinations allocated in Berlin, in Stuttgart and in Aachen that serve the automotive and the component industries all over Germany and beyond.

Another feature that influences the location of innovation cluster activity for the sector is the existence of research capacities. This explains the importance of Berlin for R&D services, and some other locations where reorganized institutes of academies of science of the former German Democratic Republic are trying to establish a reputation as sources of knowledge for the automotive industry. Such institutes can be found, for example, in Dresden and Leipzig.

Wengel and Shapira found for the machinery and equipment sector in Germany, which delivers a large part of its output to the automotive industry, that cooperation in R&D was not more pronounced locally than nationally or internationally (Wengel and Shapira, 2004). While 26 per cent of firms in a sample of 1400 firms said that they engaged in R&D cooperation with regional clients, 45 per cent cooperated with clients internationally. The figures for R&D cooperation with suppliers were 30 per cent for regional partners and 35 per cent for international partners (Wengel and Shapira, 2004, p. 261). This shows that proximity is not the dominant criterion for selecting R&D partners.

7.4 CROSS-REGIONAL LINKAGES AND CLUSTERS

7.4.1 Location and the Innovation Cluster Rationale

Michael Porter has based his research on cluster phenomena and their relation to competitiveness on the observation that despite a growing international integration of markets, firms still rely on close cooperation in a regional context. These local links even seem to become stronger as 'globalization' gains momentum (Porter, 1998). The phenomenon of clusters that link regions is based on a similar set of arguments. The local cluster context allows firms to make productive use of resources; however, the sourcing of knowledge and other inputs and the marketing of products and services are embedded in global links (see also Cooke, 2001a).

In the case of the automotive components sector the relevant innovation cluster is formed by a group of actors which benefit from advantages deriving from physical proximity on the one hand, and trusted relationships based on interaction on the other. The heterogeneity of the sector implies that knowledge needed for innovation in the automotive component sector comes from very different backgrounds. It is quite unlikely that this knowledge will be agglomerated in one region (and it would be economically inefficient to replicate the organizations that generate these resources in each cluster). Cars combine a whole set of highly sophisticated technologies; this means that component suppliers cannot purchase innovation input 'off the shelves'. Path-dependent relationships with well-tested work styles, trusted partners in terms of confidentiality and in terms of service/product quality, are essential. These relationships form and flourish in a cluster context.

Cluster actors with specific competences that belong to local or regional clusters themselves are linked with the innovation cluster of the automotive component supplier sector. There is no obvious reason why these clusters should be dissolved to form other (regional) clusters around automotive component suppliers.

The new division of labour between component suppliers and car manufacturers implies that with the exception of a few large producers, such as Bosch, Siemens or Sachsenring, there are only a few historically grown regional clusters of innovation service providers around component suppliers and, thus, the relevant knowledge is accessed elsewhere.

As innovation cycles become shorter and technological requirements tend to be more sophisticated, specialization is becoming more important to guarantee high quality. This means that only one or two research facilities with specific competencies are to be found in the whole country, and they are, thus, shared by local and non-local users.

Innovation clusters are by their very nature likely to change the configuration of existing production clusters by introducing new knowledge and additional resources that were previously not present, but are essential for the realization of a new product or process. This might lead to a relocation of firms, if the innovation causes a long-term change in the character of essential inputs (as, for example, the allocation of software firms in close proximity with automotive manufacturers, or of genetics laboratories close to food-producing companies). It can also imply more cross-regional links between innovating firms and innovations service providers (at least in a transition period). Whether distance creates a problem with respect to generating the advantages typically attributed to clustering depends on the nature of the innovation, the history of relationships within the cluster, and technical progress in means of communication.

7.4.2 Virtual Cluster Links

The relationships that firms establish through communication via electronic networks have been interpreted as the end of local or regional clustering (Passiante and Secundo, 2002; Kaufmann et al., 2002; Maignan et al., 2003). Though none of these authors would go so far as to claim completely 'virtual' clusters, an increasingly strong role of virtual links in company strategies seems to be generally assumed. In the context of cluster analysis, the crucial question following from this is whether virtual links can show the same characteristics that define geographically circumscribed clusters. Whether communication in virtual environments will allow firms to generate relationships based on trust, or stimulate the exchange of informal information, is still an open question. It can be assumed that knowledge spillovers as well as the transfer of tacit knowledge will always require personal encounters. As Maignan et al. put it: 'it is possible to transform into bit strings only the codifiable knowledge, while tacit knowledge, embodied in practices, people or networks of relationships cannot [*be*]' (Maignan et al., 2003, p. 5). Empirical studies have revealed that virtual exchange of information plays an important part in processes of innovation, but in most cases the communicating partners know each other from previous work (or study) experience or have at least met once (see Preissl and Solimene, 2003).

7.5 SUMMARY AND A NOTE ON CLUSTER POLICY

Cluster relations tend to be more stable and more intense than market relations, and therefore integrate regions more effectively. With the growing internationalization and specialization of knowledge creation, these cross-regional cluster links expand more often across national boundaries. Information and communication technologies are enablers that facilitate the establishment of cluster relations between distant partners.

Clustering affects the visibility of a region as well as its attractiveness. The existence of one or more industry-, technology- or science-related clusters in a region therefore enhances the intensity of communication and stimulates business links with this region. The more active and dynamic the cluster is, the more it promotes the reputation of the region to which its core belongs.

Observations on local connotations of innovation clusters depend on the particular perspective on a cluster. In the present case, the German automotive component suppliers' cluster has been conceived and identified using innovating firms (that are not locally clustered) as the core of the cluster. The identification procedure led to the inclusion of innovation service providers outside local and regional boundaries. These service providers, in turn, may form local clusters; for example, clusters of car-related software producers.

Apart from the practical difficulty to establish clusters using regional policy instruments, it would be inappropriate to induce a software company to move closer to a component supplier, if it can get more advantages from its current local software cluster. From the perspective of regional innovation policy, any measure that helps to form clusters by providing infrastructure (including research and education facilities) will enhance the generation of a knowledge base of the highest quality. This may support the allocation of similar institutions. Aiming at the formation of purely local clusters by supporting the relocation of existing cluster members, on the contrary, would not make much sense. Innovating firms will always go for the most appropriate innovation service provider in terms of quality and reliability. Hence, supporting excellence in public services is the best way to ensure that the best innovation service provider is a local firm or other organization.

NOTES

1. For a detailed documentation of the innovation cluster of the German automotive component suppliers see Preissl and Solimene (2003). The analysis is based on interviews with 40 cluster participants and experts.
2. In this chapter the term 'industry' is used for companies producing the same product or service; 'sector' is the more comprehensive term which describes the set of industries delivering products and services to the automotive manufacturing industry.
3. This does not imply that a linear innovation model is assumed. The procedure can be characterized by loops and backward movements and still the innovation functions are performed that are necessary for progression towards success.

REFERENCES

Bergman, E., D. Charles and P. den Hertog (2001), 'In pursuit of innovative clusters', in OECD (ed.), *Innovative Clusters: Drivers of National Innovation Systems*, Paris: OECD Publications, pp. 7–18.

Bergman, E.M. and E.J. Feser (1999), 'Industry clusters: a methodology and framework for regional development policy in the United States', in OECD (ed.), *Boosting Innovation: the Cluster Approach*, Paris: OECD Publications, pp. 243–68.

Cooke, P. (2001a), 'Regional innovation systems, clusters, and the knowledge economy', *Industrial and Corporate Change*, **10**(4), 945–74.

Cooke, P. (2001b), *Knowledge Economies: Clusters, Learning and Co-operative Advantage, Studies in International Business and the World Economy*, London: Routledge.

Hancké, B. (1997), 'Vorsprung, aber nicht länger (nur) durch Technik', in F. Naschold, D. Soskice, B. Hancké and U. Jürgens (eds), *Ökonomische Leistungsfähigkeit und Institutionelle Innovation*, Berlin: WZB-Jahrbuch, pp. 213–34.

Jürgens, U. and H.R. Meißner (2005), *Arbeiten am Auto der Zukunft – Produktinnovationen und Perspektiven für die Beschäftigten*, Berlin: Edition sigma.

Kaufmann, A., P. Lehner and F. Tödtling (2002), 'Effects of the Internet on the spatial structure of innovation networks', Paper presented at the ERSA Conference, 27–31 August, Dortmund.

Keeble, D. and F. Wilkinson (1999), 'Collective learning and knowledge development in the evolution of regional clusters of high technology SMEs in Europe', *Regional Studies*, **33**(4), 295–303.

Keeble, D. and F. Wilkinson (2000), *High-Technology Clusters, Networking and Collective Learning*, Aldershot: Ashgate.

Krugman, P. (1991), 'Increasing returns and economic geography', *Journal of Political Economy*, **99**, 483–99.

Lay, G. and W. Wallmeier (1999a), 'Stand und Entwicklungstendenzen der Produktionsmodernisierung in der Automobilzulieferindustrie', FhG-ISI, November, Karlsruhe.

Lay, G. and W. Wallmeier (1999b), 'Automobilzulieferer – Quo vadis. Mitteilungen aus der Produktionsinnovationserhebung 14', Oktober.

Maignan, C., D. Pinelli and G. Ottaviano (2003), 'ICT, clusters and regional cohesion: a summary of theoretical and empirical research', Nota di Lavoro 58, Fondazione Eni Enrico Mattei.

Malerba, F. (2004), 'Sectoral systems of innovation: basic concepts', in F. Malerba (ed.), *Sectoral Systems of Innovation: Concepts, Issues and Analyses of Six Major Sectors in Europe*, Cambridge: Cambridge University Press, pp. 9–41.

Marshall, A. (1952). *Principles of Economics*, London: Macmillan, 1st edition 1890.

OECD (2001), *Innovative Clusters: Drivers of National Innovation Systems*, Paris: OECD Publications.

Passiante, G. and G. Secundo (2002), 'From geographical innovation clusters towards virtual innovation clusters: the innovation virtual system', paper presented at the ERSA Conference, 27–31 August, Dortmund.

Peters, J. (1997), 'Zur technologischen Leistungsfähigkeit deutscher Automobilzulieferer', Bericht zum Forschungsprojekt Automobil & Innovation an der Universität Augsburg.
Piore, M. and C.F. Sabel (1984), *The Second Industrial Divide: Possibilities for Prosperity*, New York: Basic Books.
Porter, M. (1990), *The Competitive Advantage of Nations*, New York: Free Press.
Porter, M. (1998), 'Clusters and the new economics of competition', *Harvard Business Review*, **6**, 77–90.
Preissl, B. and L. Solimene (2003), *The Dynamics of Clusters and Innovation*, Heidelberg: Springer/Physica.
Wengel, J. and P. Shapira (2004), 'Machine tools: the remaking of a traditional sectoral innovation system', in F. Malerba (ed.), *Sectoral Systems of Innovation: Concepts, Issues and Analyses of Six Major Sectors in Europe*, Cambridge: Cambridge University Press, pp. 243–86.
Whalley, J. and P. den Hertog (2000), 'Clusters, innovation and RTOs. Research report of the RISE project' (Research and Technology Organisations in the Service Economy), http://centrim.bus.brighton.ac.uk/open/we/do/proj/rise/risewp/wp1synth.pdf.

PART II

Case studies including practice and policy

8. Explaining China's economic growth: does entrepreneurship matter?

Junbo Yu, Shaoming Cheng and Roger R. Stough

8.1 INTRODUCTION

Entrepreneurship has been gradually incorporated into neoclassical economic analyses and widely accepted as one of the most important factors for economic growth. Strong empirical evidence of the significant impact of entrepreneurship on economic performance has been found at the firm establishment level (Audretsch, 1995; Caves, 1998; Sutton, 1997) and at the country level, particularly in Organisation for Economic Co-operation and Development (OECD) countries (Audretsch and Fritsch, 2002; Audretsch and Keilbach, 2004, 2005; Fritsch, 1997). However, the existing literature has not paid close attention to two urgent questions. The first one is: 'How does entrepreneurship endowment and entrepreneurship policy shape regional economies': and the other is: 'To what extent does entrepreneurship development contribute to economic growth in transitional countries.'

The purpose of this chapter is, therefore, to provide analysis on how entrepreneurship has contributed to regional economic growth in China, the largest transitional country, from a planned to a more market-oriented economy. This chapter focuses on China's provincial economic growth from 1996 to 2001, and entrepreneurship is explicitly included into an aggregate production function to test empirically for its contribution to growth. This chapter is important because it complements earlier literature and provides a theoretical and methodological foundation for future comparative studies. This chapter is also important because it offers a timely evaluation of China's previous entrepreneurship development policies and performance, and thus provides valuable insights for China's ongoing and future policy adjustment and improvement.

8.2 ENTREPRENEURSHIP AND ECONOMIC GROWTH

Entrepreneurship was not an integral component in earlier leading economic theories, particularly neoclassical theories. From the French economist Richard Cantillon who first used the word 'entrepreneur' in the early eighteenth century, and on through to both Schumpeter and Opie (1934) and Kirzner (1973, 1979) who established their own influential entrepreneurship theories, entrepreneurship and entrepreneurial activities have been left out of mainstream neoclassical economic analyses, primarily because the neoclassical perfectly competitive equilibrium models precluded the necessary role or even the existence of entrepreneurs and entrepreneurship. This exclusion determined that entrepreneurship theories were at a 'complementary' if not 'secondary' position to leading neoclassical theories of the twentieth century.

The growing interest in entrepreneurship in economic analysis, particularly in the economic growth literature, results from the unsatisfactory explanatory power of neoclassical growth accounting exercises. Following Solow (1956) and Swan (1956), traditional neoclassical growth accounting studies leave the major part of economic growth – that is, the Solow residual – unexplained. These latter studies attributed the residual portion to exogenous factors, for example technological progress, and suggested that public policies have little or no effect on long-term economic growth. This is particularly unsatisfactory from a policy-making perspective.

The emergence and development of endogenous growth theory provides a good framework to explain the unexplained residual in traditional growth models and literature. Endogenous growth studies state that economic growth is determined and influenced by economic agents' decisions made within an economic system, and is not merely the outcome of some exogenous processes as presented in the more traditional analyses. These endogenous growth studies stress issues that were overlooked in traditional research, for example knowledge production and spillovers (Romer, 1990), human capital accumulation (Lucas, 1988; Uzawa, 1965), learning-by-doing (Arrow, 1962), and research and development (R&D) (Aghion and Howitt, 1992). Established endogenous growth theories 'endogenize' knowledge production and growth and therefore regard knowledge spillovers as one of the most prominent engines of economic growth. Even though these theories successfully identify knowledge spillovers as one of the sources of growth, they fail to elaborate how knowledge diffuses within an economic system by implicitly assuming that spillovers happen automatically. In particular, these endogenous theories overlook the active and critical role of entrepreneurs in knowledge spillovers and economic growth.

In order explicitly to fill this 'missing link' between entrepreneurship and economic growth, Acs et al. (2004) proposed that entrepreneurship and entrepreneurial activities are the major knowledge diffusion mechanism within an economic system and explicitly established a linkage between entrepreneurship and growth. In other words, the creation of knowledge is a merely necessary condition for economic growth. Acs et al. (2004) further added, based on the Schumpeterian 'new combinations' element, that new knowledge in terms of new products, processes or organizations leads to opportunities that economic agents (entrepreneurs) can exploit. In so doing, entrepreneurial activities serve as the knowledge transmission function within a society.

Guided by theory and a hypothesis that there is a direct linkage between entrepreneurship and economic growth, empirical research to test for this link was conducted. Audretsch and Keilbach (2005) introduced a new variable, entrepreneurship capital, into the traditional production function growth accounting approach and confirmed that entrepreneurship endowments significantly affect economic growth across regions in Germany. Acs and Plummer (2005) focused on incumbent firms and entrepreneurial new ventures and their roles in localized knowledge spillovers and thus regional economic growth. They concluded that the contribution of knowledge to growth depends on new ventures that emerge from the entrepreneurial process in a given region. Despite the initial support and evidence for the positive effect of entrepreneurship on economic growth, empirical research is still limited, particularly in the context of China's economic growth, and more generally in transitional economies. One of the purposes of this chapter is, therefore, to help fill the void in the literature by explicitly examining the relation between China's entrepreneurship development and regional economic growth.

8.3 RESEARCH QUESTIONS AND HYPOTHESES

The purpose of this chapter is to test whether the development of entrepreneurship contributes to economic growth in China. The launch of Gai Ge Kai Fang (Reform and Opening) policy in China since the late 1970s turned China, a centrally planned economy, into a widely recognized transitional country. Privatization was gradually implemented in both rural and urban areas, and from tertiary industries to almost all the business sectors. Although the decentralization and deregulation process moved slowly in China's political system, the development of entrepreneurship has been legitimized and increasingly encouraged since the mid-1990s.

The distinctive attribute of the Chinese reform is its abandonment of bureaucratic coordination of the economy through a process of gradually 'growing out of the plan' and reaching the goal of a full-fledged market economy (Naughtong, 1992). Both Li (1997) and Krug and Hendrischke (2003) suggested that this attribute effectively supported the development of entrepreneurship with China's 'gradualist' and optimizing institutional system, while the 'big bang' privatization strategies in Eastern European socialist economies unexpectedly impeded entrepreneurial activities in those chaotic societies. As a consequence, the motivating effect of entrepreneurship development to economic growth is perceived to be more significant in China than in other transitional economies, especially in the late 1990s, which was only a short period after 'shock therapy' had been implemented in Eastern Europe.

Recent entrepreneurship studies surfaced a new concept of entrepreneurship that sheds more light on the role of government. As a system necessary for economic growth, entrepreneurship consists of three components: entrepreneurs who desire to achieve their goal of economic survival and advancement; the social constitution that grants that the right for 'free enterprises' is assumed; and the government that has the ability to induce entrepreneurs' motivation toward social development and growth outcomes, and to adjust the constitution system so that it works at its best to protect each individual entrepreneur (Audretsch et al., 2002; Lowrey, 2003). Compared with the OECD countries where small government and a mature market economy have existed, the Chinese government's support in fostering an entrepreneurial environment is far more crucial and decisive than any other determinant. Here, we can conduct entrepreneurship determinants and policy analysis so long as we can distinguish the unique role of government policy in affecting entrepreneurship development and economic growth in China.

8.3.1 Hypotheses

Most of the recent empirical studies that have investigated the source of economic growth in China suggest that the accumulation of physical capital and labor account for the majority of the output growth from the early 1950s to the late 1980s (Chow, 1993; Krugman, 1994). However, both Borensztein and Ostry (1996) and Hu and Khan (1997) showed that productivity has become the primary driving force of China's rapid economic growth, while capital and labor accumulation still plays an irreplaceable role, particularly since China's economic reform in 1978. Hence, physical capital and labor are expected to explain significantly the variation of the annual gross domestic product (GDP) data.

In addition, Wang and Yao (2001), applying endogenous growth analysis, found that the accumulation of human capital was quite rapid in China and contributed significantly to growth and welfare during the reform period 1978–99. Hereby, we also expect a significant contribution from the knowledge capital variable in our model.

The Fourteenth National Congress of the Chinese Communist Party (CCP) in 1992 clearly showed the nature of the economic reform is to change the mechanism of resource allocation, so that China could move from a planned economy to a market economy in which the market plays a critical role in the allocation of resources. The declaration of this congress was regarded as a complete legitimization of China's market economy. Since 1979, the revival of the entrepreneurship spirit has been tracked into an institutionally protected freeway. Several studies based on the material of the late 1990s, for example the Global Entrepreneurship Monitor (GEM, 2003) and Li (1997), suggested that the increasingly intensified entrepreneurial activities have clearly been influencing economic growth in China. It is thus reasonable to expect a significant value of the entrepreneurship capital variable from the estimation of our model.

Furthermore, as we have discussed, the evolution of Chinese national, regional and local policies are expected to disturb the homogeneity of the panel data. Therefore, our additional hypothesis is that a random effects model for analyzing the panel data will not be appropriate in our case, while a fixed effects model might be more effective to extract the systematic variance of the data (Davidson and Mackinnon, 1993; Greene, 2003).

8.4 METHODOLOGY AND DATA

This chapter adopts the Cobb–Douglas-type production function in which the constant return to scale is assumed. By further assuming labor-augmenting technological progress, we obtain equation (8.1):

$$Y_{it} = K_{it}^{\alpha} H_{it}^{\beta} E_{it}^{\gamma} (AL_{it})^{1-\alpha-\beta-\gamma} e^{\varepsilon_{it}}, 0 < \alpha < 1, 0 < \beta < 1, 0 < \gamma < 1 \quad (8.1)$$

where Y, K and L represent GDP, physical capital stock and labor, respectively. H represents human capital, E represents entrepreneurship capital, and A represents labor-augmenting technological progress (Audretsch and Keilbach, 2005). α, β, and γ are parameters to be estimated. As we have assumed constant return to scale in the model above, the output elasticity of L will be actually calculated from $1 - \alpha - \beta - \gamma$ instead of being estimated like other parameters. $e^{\varepsilon_{it}}$ is the error term. The subscript i refers to different provinces in China, and t refers to different years from 1996 to 2001.

Dividing both sides of equation (8.1) by labor, we obtain the intensive Cobb–Douglas production function as follows:

$$y_{it} = A_{it}^{1-\alpha-\beta-\gamma} k_{it}^{\alpha} h_{it}^{\beta} e_{it}^{\gamma} \quad (8.2)$$

where $y = Y/L$, $k = K/L$, $h = H/L$ and $e = E/L$ are quantities per labor. Accordingly, the logarithm regression equation is:

$$\ln y_{it} = a_{i0} + \alpha \ln k_{it} + \beta \ln h_{it} + \gamma \ln e_{it} + a_{1i}T + \varepsilon_{it} \quad (8.3)$$

where a_{i0} represents the intercept term, a_{1i} is the parameter and ε_{it} is the error term. T is the time trend variable, capturing exogenously determined technological changes over the data period (Fraser, 2002).

Income and Labor: regional GDP data are from China's National Bureau of Statistics. Labor statistics are drawn from the statistical yearbooks of China from 1997–2002. The total numbers of people employed are used instead of man-hours due to the lack of data on the latter.

Capital stock: the estimation of capital stock distribution across China's provincial administrative regions has generated considerable literature since the early 1990s (Chow, 1993). The debate among different final results mostly lies in the estimation of the initial capital stock and the choice of the rate of depreciation (Maddison, 1998; World Bank, 1997; Wu, 2003). In this chapter, we first adopt China's total capital stock which Chow (1993) estimated as 175 billion yuan in 1952. This figure is decomposed to the provincial level according to the Perpetual Inventory Method proposed by Goldsmith (1951). Since the value of yearly net capital stock can be estimated from annual incremental capital stock which is available for the period 1952–2002 for all regions, the value of capital stock for the *ith* region in the *tth* year can be expressed as

$$K_{it} = K_{i,1952}(1 - \delta)^{t-1952} + \sum_{0}^{t-1952-1} (1 - \delta)^{t-1952-1} \Delta K_{i,t-1952-1} \quad (8.4)$$

where δ is a given rate of depreciation and ΔK_{it} is the value of incremental capital. All variables are expressed in constant price. Also assumed is a depreciation rate $\delta = 0.05$ for provincial capital stock from 1996–2001, consistent with Wu's (2003) sensitivity analysis.

Human capital: this chapter uses a proxy for the stock of human capital that measures the education duration approximately for each province's population. Thus the equation is of the form:

$$H_{it} = \sum_{l} P_{itl} \times D_{itl} \quad (8.5)$$

where the value of human capital stock for the *ith* region in the *tth* year (H_{it}) is calculated by two multipliers: duration of education at a certain level and the population that has been enrolled accordingly. The reason we propose this approach instead of following the 'knowledge capital' path laid by Audretsch and Keilbach (2005) is twofold. First, in existing empirical studies of China, the knowledge capital measured by R&D personnel seldom appeared to be a significant variable which is conformable to Jones's (2001) comment that technological progress driven by R&D only describes the growth model of advanced countries as a whole. Second, the work of Mankiw et al. (1992) and Barro and Lee (1993) implied that indicators of education attainment may be more compatible for measuring human capital in developing countries.

Entrepreneurship capital: in any case, entrepreneurship capital, like all of the other types of capital, is multidimensioned and heterogeneous. However, the measurement of entrepreneurship capital is not an easy task primarily because it is extremely difficult to develop a comprehensive index to capture the various dimensions of entrepreneurship let alone the fact that data that could be used for the construction of the comprehensive index are not available. In the existing literature, the prevailing approach for measuring entrepreneurship is through new firm start-up rates (Acs and Plummer, 2005; Audretsch and Keilbach, 2005). Compared to such dynamic measurement of entrepreneurship, Stough (2006) recently intended to develop a stock counterpart by measuring the amount of small enterprises across US major metropolitan areas under specific size thresholds. Due to the issue of data availability, we simply test our hypothesis from the dynamic measurement approach. Accordingly, we construct a data set with comparatively short time series (1996–2001) since number of start-ups is subject to a greater level of stochastic disturbance over short time periods; the longer the time period in which we compute the measure of entrepreneurship capital based on start-up rates, the more this indicator will deviate from reality (Audretsch and Keilbach, 2005).[1] The sources and descriptions of the variables are shown in Table 8.1.

With respect to the causality issue, which means that the number of newly created firms depends on the regional economic performance and the entrepreneurship capital may thus become an endogenous variable, we compared the regression results using lagged output value and current output value to make sure that economic performance is 'caused' by entrepreneurship capital and not vice versa. Therefore, the corrected measurement could be regarded as consistent with our empirical approach.

Table 8.1 Definition and sources of the data

Independent variables	Descriptions	Data sources
Output (Y_{it})	Provincial GDP measured in 1979 constant price.	National Bureau of Statistics of China
Physical Capital (K_{it})	Provincial capital stock measured in 1979 constant price.	The author's calculation based on the data from National Bureau of Statistics of China, using the Perpetual Inventory Method (Goldsmith, 1951)
Human Capital (H_{it})	Provincial population's education attainment duration in terms of year.	National Bureau of Statistics of China
Labor (L_{it})	Provincial number of employees as the equivalent of labor.	National Bureau of Statistics of China
Entrepreneurship Capital (E_{it})	The number of start-ups in the respective province relative to its population.	China Second National Census of Basic Units

8.5 EMPIRICAL RESULTS

Before estimating the models, it is important to determine how to incorporate panel data effectively and efficiently, yet avoid specification errors. Although the principal models of panel data analysis have been summarized as the fixed-effects and the random-effects models (Greene, 2003; STATA, 2003), it is important to clarify several relevant econometric issues in an effort to justify the estimations and results to follow.

8.5.1 Spatial Autocorrelation as a Specification Bias

Consider fitting our model after a logarithm transformation of the form:

$$Y_{it} = X_{it} \times \beta + \varepsilon_{it} = X_{it} \times \beta + \mu_i + v_{it} \tag{8.6}$$

In equation (8.6), β is the coefficient vector to be estimated while $\varepsilon_{it} = \mu_i + v_{it}$ is the residual item. A random effects model assuming that ε_{it} is uncorrelated with X_{it} while the unit-specific residual $u_i \neq 0$. A Breusch and Pagan (1980) Lagrange multiplier (BP-LM) test for $u_i \neq 0$ has been performed after the regression, indicating that a simple ordinary least squares (OLS) estimation will be unsuitable. Furthermore, the result of the

Table 8.2 Estimation results of random-effect and fixed-effect production function models

	Random-effects specification	Fixed-effects specifications		
		(1)	(2)	(3)
Intercept	−1.69***	−0.82***	−1.87***	−1.84***
	(−14.31)	(−59.70)	(−13.93)	(−13.94)
Physical capital	0.64***	0.91***	0.58***	0.56***
	(16.10)	(22.96)	(10.86)	(10.63)
Human capital	0.30***		0.38***	0.35***
	(7.12)		(7.84)	(7.32)
Entrepreneurship capital	0.03***			0.03***
	(2.84)			(2.62)
Time trend	0.01	−0.01*	0.01***	0.01***
	(1.47)	(−1.68)	(2.89)	(2.66)
Summary statistics				
Number of observations	168	168	168	168
Number of groups	28	28	28	28
R^2	0.986	0.980	0.986	0.987
BP-LM test	$p = 0.00$; H_0 rejected			
Hausman test	p = 0.00; H_0 rejected			

Hausman (1978) specification test, which compares the consistent fixed-effects model with the efficient random-effects model, rejects the random-effects specification and suggests the existence of systematic heterogeneous variances among the explanatory variables (see Table 8.2).

This specification problem, that is, heterogeneity, actually attributed to the developmental gap has existed in China since the mid-1980s. The uneven development strategy since China's Opening and Reform on the one hand resulted in enlarged economic inequality between coastal and interior regions, and on the other hand induced significant differences regarding the magnitude and quality of production elements in corresponding regions (Yang et al., 2006). Consequently, we expect systematic variation primarily based on a spatial dimension and thus apply Moran's *I* test to diagnose spatial attributes of the independent variables.

Indicated by Table 8.3, all the independent variables in our model show spatial autocorrelation, which clearly manifests their systematic variation

Table 8.3 Global spatial autocorrelation test for independent variables in production function

Variables	I	E(I)	Sd(I)	z-statistic	p-value
K	0.435	−0.006	0.019	23.654	0.000
L	0.437	−0.006	0.019	23.740	0.000
H	0.399	−0.006	0.019	21.802	0.000
E	0.541	−0.006	0.019	29.382	0.000
ε	0.000	−0.006	0.019	0.322	0.747

Notes:
Null hypothesis is that there are no spatial autocorrelation in tested variable. P-values denote the probability of spatial autocorrelation not to differ significantly from zero.
ε is the error term predicted by fixed-effects model.

by location. The solution of this outcome was proposed by Hoch (1962) who proposed the estimation of a production function parameter with a panel data set using fixed-effects model specification. We follow his approach with a fixed-effects model attempting to capture μ_i and suppressing the specification bias to correct our model. The bottom row in Table 8.3 shows that tests on spatial autocorrelation for the error term after the re-estimation using a fixed-effects model do not reject the null at the 99 percent level, indicating the cure of the specification bias.

8.5.2 Collinearity Diagnostics

Another obstacle to correctly interpreting the estimation results is the clarification of some collinearity problems (Fraser, 2002). Here we employ the 'condition indexes' approach developed by Belsley (1991) to examine collinearity.

If there are near linear dependencies among columns of **X** this will result in a small eigenvalue (λ) of the cross-product matrix $\mathbf{X}^T\mathbf{X}$. By sorting the eigenvalues in descending order we can assess the smallness of the minimum eigenvalue relative to the maximum eigenvalue. It is this information that is used to define condition indexes.

The *k*th condition index of **X** is defined as

$$\eta_k = \frac{\lambda_{max}}{\lambda_k} \qquad (8.7)$$

for $k = 1 \ldots p$. Therefore, it follows that an eigenvalue (λ_k) that is small relative to the maximal eigenvalue (λ_{max}) will yield a high condition index. By way of experimental observation, Belsley (1991) states that weak dependencies are associated with condition indexes between 5 and 10 and very strong linear dependencies for values greater than 30. After standardizing our **X** which is necessary for condition indexes to provide stable information, we calculate the condition indexes for equation (8.3) and get $\eta_1 = 1.00, \eta_2 = 2.45, \eta_3 = 14.5$. It is therefore suggested that the collinearity problem among independent variables is rather limited.

8.5.3 Explanation of the Empirical Results

The estimation results of three fixed-effects model specifications are summarized in Table 8.2. Column 1 within the fixed-effects group first estimates the traditional Solow model; from column 2 to column 3, human capital as well as the entrepreneurship capital are gradually incorporated into the production function.

The value of goodness of fit (R^2) in columns 1 to 3 reaches 98–99 percent, showing a good explanation for China's economic growth in associated years and the competitiveness of specification 3 as well (99 percent). With the exception of the time trend coefficient in column 1, all the t-values for coefficients of other independent variables in columns 1 to 3 are significant at 1 percent level. The coefficients of the labor variable $(1 - \alpha - \beta - \gamma)$ vary from 0.04 to 0.09 across all specifications, which is odd in terms of conventional judgments yet consistent with recent studies' observations of China's productivity change since the late 1990s. While China still utilizes comparatively abundant labor resources, the marginal contribution to GDP from a pure increase in labor amount has been rather limited.

On the other hand, it is estimated that physical capital is one of the most important production factors determining output across Chinese provinces. According to Table 8.3, the contribution of capital accumulation to economic growth in this study (0.91–0.56) is mostly consistent with Chow's (1993) 0.628 and other relevant studies' average value, 0.6. However, those results we cited normally base their regression on time series data through the whole reform period or even longer, while our research is concentrating on the late 1990s (Zhang, 2002; Zheng and Hu, 2005). Capital deepening has become a most prominent phenomenon in China's economic growth since the mid-1990s. Thus we consider our estimation (0.58 in column 2 and 0.56 in column 3) to be more consistent with the real situation where the marginal output of capital drops due to the effect of decreasing returns to scale.

In addition, the positive and statistically significant coefficient of human capital is consistent with Lucas's (1988) view that education matters as a factor of production. We also note that the time trend regressor's significant coefficient implies a slight contribution to economic growth from technology change. While such a phenomenon of slowdown in terms of technical progress in China since the mid-1990s has been addressed as well as explained by Zheng and Hu (2005) and Zhang (2002) from different perspectives, we also suspect that a rather limited time series which had been included in the data set may account for difficulties in observing an explicit technology progress.[2]

Estimation result of the constant term which is used to be interpreted as the technological item turns out to be negatively significant, implying technical regress. Our explanation of this outcome exists in the nature of panel data estimation and the feature of our independent variables. Hoch (1962) noted that the constant in production function estimation with panel data was actually the combination of a region constant which will reflect different technical efficiency between regions, and a time constant which will reflect the change in technical efficiency over time and differences in external environment between years. Accordingly, a single constant without proper decomposition will not be economically meaningful, but merely a statistical item.[3] Moreover, an important drawback for employing proxies to measure human capital and entrepreneurship capital, as we did in this chapter, is that if the proxies are ideally proportional to our target variables, the factor of proportionality will affect only the constant term (Mankiw et al., 1992). This also reinforces our conclusion that the constant term in our estimation is pointless.

Column 3 shows the results when entrepreneurship capital is also included in the production function. The positive and statistically significant coefficient indicates that entrepreneurship is becoming a valid factor in explaining variations of output across China. Those provinces with a greater degree of entrepreneurship capital exhibit higher levels of output. There might be concerns on the exaggeration of entrepreneurship capital's contribution to economic growth, especially taking its small coefficient into account. However, one should also be aware of the facts that entrepreneurship capital's impact has been suppressed due to the overlap effects from other independent variables (that is, physical capital and human capital), and largely constrained due to its measurement's limitation.

8.6 POLICY IMPLICATIONS

While there is an abundant literature which attributes China's outstanding macroeconomic performance to the timely and suitable government regulations, few examples shed light on a national-level improvement of microeconomic adaptability to fluctuations. Fortunately, the result of our empirical study may serve as a reminder that without an adequate development of entrepreneurship at the individual level and the firm level, even an incisive and scientific policy still would not fully exert its energy when the society responds dully (Carree and Thurik, 2003; Lowrey, 2003). Hence, it is obviously reasonable for Chinese local governments to re-evaluate their entrepreneurship environment and relevant policies so as to build or complete a dynamic regional growth system through continuous creative destruction (Acs et al., 1998).

A review of modern regional development theories also instructs us to visualize regional growth to be determined by specialization, diversity and competition (Glaeser et al., 1992). In our empirical finding, the replacement of labor by human capital reflects a smaller or even negative gain from the marginal labor input, urgently indicating a reconsideration of the nation's comparative advantage which is conventionally taken as the lower labor cost. Meanwhile, the significance of entrepreneurship capital, its positive coefficient and its well recognized push effect to specialization, diversity and competition (Audretsch and Keilbach, 2004; Carree and Thurik, 2003) predict an irreplaceable role of entrepreneurship in China's future economic growth. But the realization of sustainable economic growth in China requires more than a spontaneously formed entrepreneurship environment constructed by market and ownership reform. In other words, the unconscious intervention of the Chinese government in fostering entrepreneurship will not be sufficient for continued economic growth in the future. Lowrey (2003) argues that although Romer's explanation of long-term economic development due to human capital accumulation of such factors as knowledge and skill, scientific knowledge and technical skills is central to economic growth in the twenty-first century, these factors merely determine potentialities. The realization of ideas, such as business formation or economic advancement, crucially depends on the cost and the risk factors related to the quality of the labor force. Entrepreneurship is the crucial mediator that transforms 'knowledge' from the labor force via profit motivation and therefore it turns out to be the key determinant of sustainable economic growth. The very slight increase of R^2 after the involvement of entrepreneurship capital clearly demonstrates more space for government policy to promote entrepreneurship in China.

While it has already been shown above that non-economic conditions such as value systems and institutions that are not hostile to entrepreneurial activity, and a government that is able to maintain law, power and policy consistency, are necessary for the development of entrepreneurship (Baumol, 1990; Papanek, 1962), the Chinese government still appears to be struggling with the paradox created by its communist ideology and the demand for encouraging or pressuring entrepreneurship development. Such hesitation in the construction of an entrepreneurial society

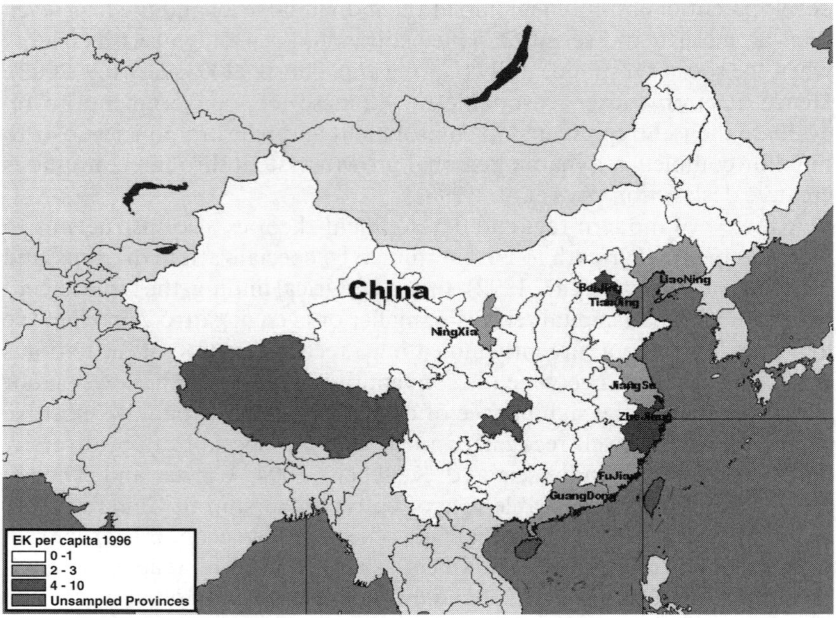

Note: Entrepreneurship capital is measured by the number of start-ups in the respective province relative to its population.

Source: National Bureau of Statistics (NBS, 2003).

Figure 8.1 The distribution of China's entrepreneurship capital in 1996

has greatly delayed the study of entrepreneurship in China and in turn weakened its voice. Moreover, the ambiguous attitude of the Chinese government to entrepreneurship development has increased uncertainty about entrepreneurial activity and may thus ultimately have suppressed the growth of its entrepreneurial niche (Li, 1997). Knowing this, the future effect of the Chinese government's intervention in entrepreneurship development becomes more unpredictable and is tightly linked to the direction that its political reform takes.

Finally, inspired by our Hausman specification test result and the high correlation between **X** [i,t] and u[i], we attempt to trace the imbalanced distribution of entrepreneurship capital as an explanation for the heterogeneity among individual provinces regarding the influence of entrepreneurship development on economic growth. As is shown in Figure 8.1 and Figure 8.2, the distribution of entrepreneurship capital in China through 1997 to 2001 exhibits a sharp gap between the coastal provinces and the

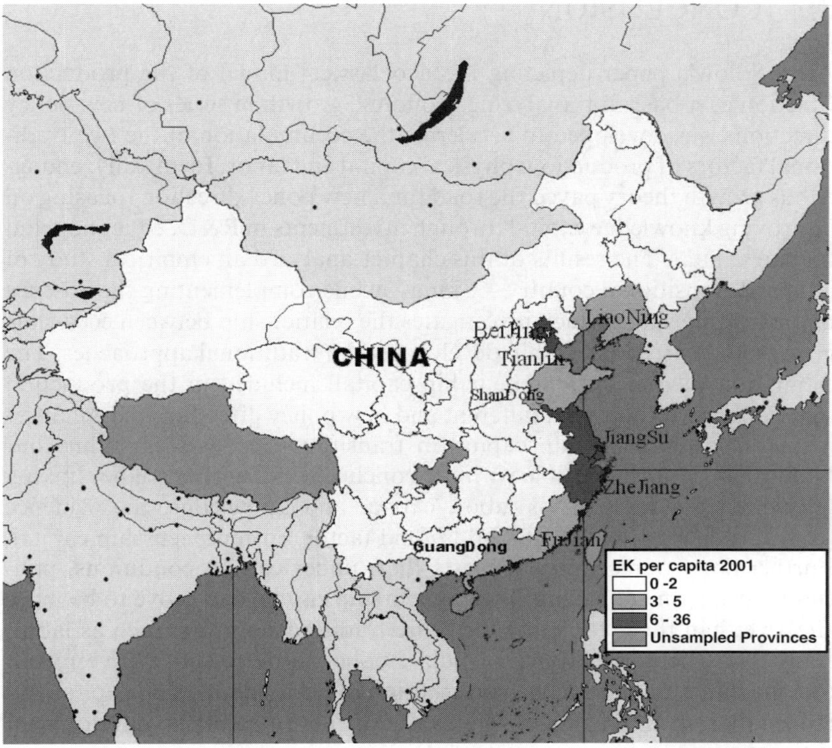

Note: Entrepreneurship capital is measured by the number of start-ups in the respective province relative to its population.

Source: National Bureau of Statistics (NBS, 2003).

Figure 8.2 The distribution of China's entrepreneurship capital in 2001

interior provinces. The existence of this gap can on the one hand explain the fixed effect of regions in our model, together with the systematic variations of other variables; on the other hand, it brings up a serious question that the expansion of this gap will greatly impede the convergence of economic growth speed among different regions, and threaten the realization of the so-called Harmonious Society which has been set as a goal for future development by the Chinese government. Consequently, a comprehensive comparison and analysis on the determinants of entrepreneurship development in China, especially the determinant of government policy, should be carried out in the near future in order to encourage entrepreneurial activity in lagging regions.

8.7 CONCLUSION

After Solow's paper depicting the neoclassical model of the production function as a basis for analyzing economic growth, a series of new policy directions was developed to accelerate the accumulation of the two traditional factors of production: physical capital and labor. Identically, endogenous growth theory paved the road for a new policy direction focusing on improving knowledge capital through investments in R&D, education and human capital. The results of this chapter analyzed an empirical study of a typical transitional country – China – while complementing the absence of current literature which investigates the relationship between economic growth and entrepreneurship development in traditional approaches. The estimation of our 'entrepreneurship capital' included in the production function model suggests a different and new policy direction: the enhancement of entrepreneurship capital in transitional economies. While our findings are still compatible with the conclusions of earlier studies linking growth to factors such as labor, capital and knowledge, the evidence from this chapter leads to an additional factor, entrepreneurship capital. Furthermore, our chapter suggests that, under certain conditions, policies focusing on enhancing entrepreneurship capital can prove to be more effective than those targeting the more traditional factors, such as labor. As regards the implications for public policy, a more active government role in China to increase the contribution of entrepreneurship capital and reduce the gap among regions in respect of entrepreneurship development is encouraged, taking account of the institutional uniqueness of transitional societies.

NOTES

1. Note that ChongQing, the fourth directly governed city of China, and HaiNan, Tibet are dropped from the data sample due to their data inconformity.
2. We thank Schintler Laurie for her helpful comments regarding the explanations to associated empirical results as a discussant at the Uddevalla Symposium 2006.
3. This explanation accords with the discussant's suggestion that we may separately estimate the model by coastal and inland regions.

REFERENCES

Acs, A., D. Audretsch, P. Braunerhjelm and B. Carlsson (2004), 'The missing link: the knowledge filter and entrepreneurship growth', Discussion paper no. 4783, London: Centre for Economic Policy Research.

Acs, Z.J., B. Carlsson and C. Karlsson (1998), *Entrepreneurship, Small and Medium-Sized Enterprises, and the Macroeconomy*, New York: Cambridge University Press.

Aghion, P. and P. Howitt (1992), 'A model of growth through creative destruction', *Econometrica*, **60**, 323–51.

Acs, Z.J. and L.A. Plummer (2005), 'Penetrating the "knowledge filter" in regional economics', *Annals of Regional Science*, **43**(4), 989–1012.

Arrow, K. (1962), 'Economic welfare and the allocation of resources for invention', in *The Rate and Direction of Incentive Activity: Economic and Social Factors*, Washington, DC: National Bureau of Economic Research, pp. 607–26.

Audretsch, D.B. (1995), *Innovation and Industry Evolution*, Cambridge, MA: MIT Press.

Audretsch, D.B. and M. Fritsch (2002), 'Growth regimes over time and space', *Regional Studies*, **36**, 113–24.

Audretsch, D.B. and M. Keilbach (2004), 'Entrepreneurship capital and economic performance', retrieved 24 August 2004, from ftp://ftp.zew.de/pub/zew-docs/dp/dp0276.pdf.

Audretsch, D.B. and M. Keilbach (2005), 'Entrepreneurship capital and regional growth', *Annals of Regional Science*, **39**(3), 457–69.

Audretsch, B.D., Roy Thurik, Ingrid Verheul and Sander Wennekers (eds) (2002), *Entrepreneurship: Determinants and Policy in a European–US Comparison*, London: Kluwer Academic Publishers.

Barro, R.J., and J.W. Lee (1993), 'International comparisons of educational attainment', *Journal of Monetary Economics*, **32**, 363–94.

Baumol, W.J. (1990), 'Entrepreneurship, productive, unproductive and destructive', *Journal of Business Venturing*, **8**, 197–210.

Belsley, D.A. (1991), *Conditioning Diagnostics: Collinearity and Weak Data in Regression*, New York: John Wiley & Sons.

Borensztein, E. and J.D. Ostry (1996), 'Accounting for China's growth performance', *American Economic Review*, **86**(2), 224–8.

Breusch, T. and A. Pagan (1980), 'The Lagrange multiplier test and its applications to model specification in econometrics', *Review of Economic Studies*, **47**, 239–53.

Carree, M.A. and R. Thurik (2003), 'The impact of entrepreneurship on economic growth', in Z.J. Acs and D.B. Audretsch (eds), *Handbook of Entrepreneurship Research: An Interdisciplinary Survey and Introduction*, Boston, MA, USA and Dordrecht, the Netherlands: Kluwer, pp. 437–71.

Caves, R.E. (1998), 'Industrial organization and new findings on the turnover and mobility of firms', *Journal of Economic Literature*, **36**, 1947–1982.

Chow, G. (1993), 'Capital formation and economic growth in China', *Quarterly Journal of Economics*, **108**(3), 809–42.

Davidson, R. and J.G. Mackinnon (1993), *Estimation and Inference in Econometrics*, New York: Oxford University Press.

Fraser, I. (2002), 'The Cobb–Douglas production function: an Antipodean defence?' *Economic Issues*, **7**(1), 39–58.

Fritsch, M. (1997), 'New firms and regional employment change', *Small Business Economics*, **9**, 437–48.

Glaeser, E.L., H.D. Kallal, J.A. Scheinkman and A. Shleifer (1992), 'Growth in cities', *Journal of Political Economy*, **100**, 1126–52.

Global Entrepreneurship Monitor (GEM) (2003), 'Executive report', retrieved 3 November 2004, from http://www.gemconsortium.org.

Goldsmith, R.W. (1951), 'A perpetual inventory of national wealth', *Studies in Income and Wealth*, **14**, 5–61.

Greene, W.H. (2003), *Econometric Analysis*, 5th edition, Upper Saddle River, NJ: Prentice Hall.

Hausman, J.A. (1978), 'Specification tests in econometrics', *Econometrica*, **46**, 1251–71.

Hoch, I. (1962), 'Estimation of production function parameters combing time-series and cross-section data', *Econometrica*, **30**(1), 34–53.

Hu, Z. and M.S. Khan (1997), 'Why is China growing so fast?', *IMF Staff Papers*, **44**(1), 103–31.

Jones, C.I. (2001), *Introduction to Economic Growth*, 2nd edition, New York: W.W. Norton & Company.

Kirzner, I.M. (1973), *Competition and Entrepreneurship*, Chicago: University of Chicago Press.

Kirzner, I.M. (1979), *Perception, Opportunity and Profit: Studies in the Theory of Entrepreneurship*, Chicago: University of Chicago Press.

Krug, B. and. H. Hendrischke (2002), 'Entrepreneurship in China: institutions, organizational identity and survival. Empirical results from two provinces', in H. de Bettignies (ed.), *New Models on Management and New Managers in Asia*, Fontainebleau: INSEAD, pp. 231–68.

Krugman, P. (1994), 'The myth of Asia's miracle', *Foreign Affairs*, **73**, 62–78.

Li, F. (1997), 'A social organization of entrepreneurship: the rise of private firms in China', retrieved 3 November 2004, from http://wwwlib.umi.com/dissertations/gateway.

Lowrey, Y. (2003), 'The entrepreneur and entrepreneurship: a neoclassical approach', *Small Business Administration*, retrieved 22 February 2005, from http://www.kluweronline.com/issn/0921-898X/.

Lucas, R.E., Jr. (1988), 'On the mechanics of economic development', *Journal of Monetary Economics*, **22**(1), 3–42.

Maddison, A. (1998), *Chinese Economic Performance in the Long Run*, OECD Development Centre Studies, Paris: OECD.

Mankiw, G., D. Romer and D. Weil (1992), 'A contribution to the empirics of economic growth', *Quarterly Journal of Economics*, **107**, 407–37.

Naughtong, B. (1992), 'Implications of the state monopoly over industry and its relaxation', *Modern China*, **18**, 14–41.

National Bureau of Statistics (NBS) (ed.) (2003), *China Second National Census of Basic Units*, Beijing: China Statistics Press.

Papanek, G.F. (1962), 'The development of entrepreneurship', *American Economic Review*, Supplement.

Romer, P.M. (1990), 'Endogenous technological change', *Journal of Political Economy*, **98**, S71–103.

Schumpeter, J.A. and R. Opie (1934), *The Theory of Economic Development: An Inquiry into Profits, Capital, Credit, Interest, and the Business Cycle*, Cambridge, MA: Harvard University Press.

Solow, R.M. (1956), 'A contribution to the theory of economic growth', *Quarterly Journal of Economics*, **70**(1), 65–4.

STATA (2003), *Cross-Sectional Time-Series Reference Manual*, College Station, TX: STATA Corporation.

Stough, R. (2006), 'Entrepreneurship and public policy: measurement, analysis, and public policy implications', presented at the 45th Western Regional Science Association Annual Meeting, Santa Fe, NW.
Sutton, J. (1997), 'Gibrat's legacy', *Journal of Economic Literature*, **35**, 40–59.
Swan, T.W. (1956), 'Economic growth and capital accumulation', *Economic Record*, **32**, 334–61.
Uzawa, H. (1965), 'Optimum technical change in an aggregate model of economic growth', *International Economic Review*, **6**, 18–31.
Wang, Y. and Y. Yao (2001), '*Sources of China's economic growth, 1952–99: incorporating human capital accumulation*', retrieved 3 May 2005, from http://www-wds.worldbank.org/servlet/WDS_IBank_Servlet?pcont=details&eid=000094946_01080904131761.
World Bank (1997), *China 2020: Development Challenges in the New Century*, Washington, DC: World Bank.
Wu, Y. (2003), 'Has productivity contributed to China's growth?', *Pacific Economic Review*, **8**(1), 15–30.
Yang, Y.H., A.G. Hu and N. Zhang (2006), 'Regional disparities of China's human development', *China Economic Quarterly*, **5**(21), 456–78.
Zhang, J. (2002), 'China's capital formation and economic growth since the reform: empirical results and explanations', *World Economic Forum*, **1**, 18–37.
Zheng, J.H. and A.G. Hu (2005), 'An empirical analysis of provincial productivity in China (1979–2001)', *China Economic Quarterly*, **4**(15), 263–96.

9. Knowledge accessibility and new firm formation

Charlie Karlsson and Kristina Nyström

9.1 INTRODUCTION

It is obvious that knowledge plays a fundamental role for successful entrepreneurial activities. To have the chance to succeed, new firms must be based on a new combination of knowledge that is at least marginally superior to existing combinations in terms of product characteristics and/or price. Thus, knowledge flows[1] play an important role in fostering innovative and entrepreneurial activities (Sorensen and Audia, 2000).

However, the generation of new knowledge by means of both university and company research and development (R&D) is strongly concentrated in a limited set of regions (Gråsjö, 2005). Hence, there are substantial spatial variations in the accessibility to existing as well as new knowledge, since flows of knowledge are often spatially bounded. The fact that knowledge can diffuse between locations does not imply that it transmits costlessly across geographic space. Accessing and absorbing knowledge is costly, and geographic proximity reduces these costs. Thus, we have reason to expect a substantial variation in entrepreneurial activities between regions, since the prospects for starting new firms are greater in locations offering higher accessibility to knowledge. The reason is, of course, that potential entrepreneurs can access external knowledge at a lower cost in locations with high knowledge accessibility than in locations with low knowledge accessibility. We expect, *ceteris paribus*, higher frequency of new firm start-ups in regions with high knowledge accessibility.

There are (to our knowledge) relatively few empirical studies which analyse the effects of knowledge accessibility on entrepreneurship and new firm start-ups. Among existing studies, most concentrate on the influence of accessibility to university R&D, and few studies consider the combined effects of accessibility to both university and company R&D. Since these earlier studies use the term spillover, we will also use the term when we give an overview of their results. We will discuss later in the chapter why we are critical of the manner in which the term is used. Strong evidence that regional spillover effects stimulate new firm start-ups, in particular in regions with high specialization, was found by Harhoff (1999). However, he did not explicitly include university spillovers. Analysing the frequency of high-technology start-ups, Bania et al. (1993) find only a small effect of university research funding on the start-up rate in the electrical equipment and electronics sector, and no considerable effect in the instruments and related products sector.

Using data from the biotechnology sector, Audretsch and Stephan (1996, 1999) show that knowledge spillovers to a new firm start-up facilitate the appropriation of knowledge for the individual scientist – but not necessarily for the organization creating the new knowledge in the first place. Also using data from the biotechnology sector, Zucker et al. (1998) explain how spillover effects in research can improve entrepreneurship. They demonstrate that it is not spillovers per se, but rather the intellectual capital of the star scientist that plays a fundamental role in determining both location and timing of new firms. Assuming that universities create technological spillovers, Shane (2001a, 2001b) uses a patent database from Massachusetts Institute of Technology (MIT) to explore determinants of new firm formation and new firm creation. Analysing cross-industry patent citations, Dumais et al. (2002) provide general evidence of spillover effects on firm foundation but without providing specific evidence of university spillovers. Lazear (2002), analysing another kind of university spillover, provides evidence that new firm start-up activity (among other things) can be explained by the amount of general human capital possessed by individuals.

Taken together, these earlier studies indicate that universities generate spillover effects which positively stimulate entrepreneurial activity. However, we consider these earlier studies suffer from a number of limitations besides their often dubious spillover concepts. They do not consider the combined effects of flows of knowledge from both university and company research. This is a serious limitation since most directly applicable knowledge, measured for example as the number of patents generated, is produced by company research. Secondly, there are strong spatial variations in knowledge spillover potential, that is, in knowledge accessibility. However, these earlier studies fail to model spatial variations in knowledge accessibility in a consistent and meaningful way.

Against this background, the purpose of this chapter is to analyse to what extent variations in accessibility to scientific and technological knowledge (measured in an analytically consistent and meaningful way) can explain variations between Swedish municipalities in entrepreneurial activities (measured in terms of entry of firms).

The outline of the chapter is as follows. In section 9.2 we discuss the conditions for entrepreneurship and the conditions for knowledge-based entrepreneurship in particular. The concept of knowledge accessibility is introduced and defined in section 9.3. Section 9.4 presents the data and econometric model. In section 9.5 we present our empirical results. Our conclusions and suggestions for future research are presented in section 9.6.

9.2 KNOWLEDGE-BASED ENTREPRENEURSHIP

A fundamental question in entrepreneurship research concerns how entrepreneurs discover new knowledge-based business opportunities. In contrast to the knowledge concept used in standard endogenous growth theory, we follow the approach in regional economics and economic geography where authors often work with a knowledge concept that adheres to Marshall's ideas, which comprise a broader concept. In the case of Marshall (1920) as well as Schumpeter (1934), knowledge includes phenomena such as market and organizational knowledge. Within this general broad concept, we find it useful to distinguish three main types of knowledge:

1. Scientific knowledge in the form of basic scientific principles that can form a basis for the development of technological knowledge.
2. Technological knowledge – implicit and explicit blueprints – in the form of inventions (or technical solutions) that either materialize in new products or can be readily used in the production of goods and services.
3. Entrepreneurial knowledge that comprises business relevant knowledge about products, business concepts, markets, customers, and so on.

Concerning the production of new knowledge, we expect that most new scientific knowledge is produced by means of university R&D, while most new technological knowledge is produced by means of company R&D. With regard to the generation of new knowledge-based business opportunities, we expect that they can be based on new technological knowledge, new entrepreneurial knowledge or new combinations of existing technological and/or entrepreneurial knowledge. However, knowledge stocks as well as the generation of new knowledge are concentrated in space, mainly in large functional urban regions. Since the diffusion of knowledge in geographical space is neither instantaneous nor complete, it is obvious that knowledge to a varying degree is localized (Karlsson and Manduchi, 2001). To a large extent, it is localized to large functional urban regions. The diffusion of knowledge takes place in spatial networks, that is, 'knowledge networks' (Batten et al., 1989; Kobayashi, 1995) consisting of a set of nodes and a set of links connecting them. At a coarse spatial resolution, these nodes are represented by human settlements such as towns, cities and metropolitan regions, providing different instances of functional regions.[2] At a finer geographical scale, we can observe network links between and within firms, and between individuals. The nodes can be characterized by their endowment of knowledge production capacities and related activities, including knowledge infrastructure such as universities, meeting infrastructure, stocks of knowledge and human capital, local knowledge networks, and so on. The links include transportation as well as communication channels. The spatial perspective highlights the importance of spatial frictions as a factor limiting knowledge diffusion, and makes it clear that excludability of knowledge is not only a result of patents, business secrets, and so on but also a consequence of limited physical accessibility.

Much of the discussion and analysis of knowledge diffusion and its pertinent knowledge flows have become contaminated because of unclear and fuzzy definitions. In particular, many scholars have employed the concept of 'spillovers' in an unfortunate way (Echeverri-Carroll 2001; Gordon and McCann, 2000). As a step towards more clarity and precision in the analysis, we suggest separation into the three groups of knowledge flows: (1) transaction-based knowledge flows; (2) transaction-related knowledge flows; and (3) knowledge spillovers. Table 9.1 presents the three categories and identifies eight types of knowledge flows.

The distinctions made in Table 9.1 are important for several reasons. First, when the flows are transaction-based the participating economic agents have, in their own hands, market-like instruments to influence the resource allocation. Second, the mechanisms that generate the flows are different for the three main categories, which have implications for policy formation. Third, externalities that can arise in all eight cases vary in nature (for example pecuniary and non-pecuniary) and should not be confused with each other.

We can observe that existing and often larger firms engage in the search for and/or the production of economically useful technological (and entrepreneurial) knowledge as inputs into their ongoing innovation processes. The possibility of turning localized knowledge into innovations depends on the capacity of existing firms in a region to appropriate existing learning opportunities by means of both R&D and internal learning, and also by systematic absorption of specific knowledge externalities available in the regional environment (Antonelli, 1998). This is stimulated in areas

Table 9.1 Classification of knowledge flows to a firm

Main categories of knowledge flow	Different types of knowledge flows
Transaction-based flows	1. Flows from knowledge providers that sell knowledge that is used as an input to the firm's R&D activities.
	2. Flows in the form of inventions (innovations) that are sold to the firm (e.g. by licensing a patent).
	3. Knowledge flows between firms that cooperate in an R&D project, where costs and benefits are regulated by explicit or implicit contracts.
Transaction-related flows	4. Flow of knowledge that is embodied in the delivery of inputs from an input supplier to the firm.
	5. In the course of supplying inputs to the firm, knowledge from the input supplier spills over unintentionally to the input-buying firm.
	6. In the course of supplying inputs to another firm, knowledge from the input-buying firm spills over unintentionally to the input-selling firm.
Spillover flows	7. Unintentionally, knowledge spills over from one firm to a competing firm in the same industry.
	8. Unintentionally, knowledge spills over between firms belonging to different industries.

Source: Karlsson and Johansson (2006).

where monopolistic competition prevails, which makes it possible for innovative firms to earn a (temporary) monopoly profit.

Turning now to explanations of the dynamics of entrepreneurial initiatives and the pertinent entry of new firms, such explanations traditionally rely on the combination of profit opportunities determined by the level of market concentration and structural entry barriers originating in the existence of scale economies and other cost advantages of established firms with respect to potential entrants (Bain, 1956). According to this tradition, innovative activities in R&D laboratories of established firms are regarded as barriers to entry (Orr, 1974). Following Schumpeter, other authors more recently have stressed that innovation may represent a vehicle for new firms to enter the market successfully. Innovative entry is now widely regarded as a central force driving competition among firms (Dosi et al., 1997; Geroski, 1999). One might observe that small, new companies have certain market advantages in terms of new technologies, since they tend to develop in low-volume, high-price niches at early stages, which are less attractive for large firms (Stankiewicz, 1986).

However, since new firms by definition have done no R&D of their own (Acs and Audretsch, 1988), the question arises: how can potential entrepreneurs get access to the innovation-creating inputs, that is, the technological and entrepreneurial knowledge necessary for generating innovations? The obvious mechanism is that old as well as new technological and entrepreneurial knowledge is diffusing in various knowledge networks for possible exploitation by economic agents other than those who created it. However, it is not obvious that economic agents, which possess a mix of technological and entrepreneurial knowledge (which with a certain probability can be transformed into an innovation) should appropriate the returns from that knowledge by becoming entrepreneurs. Of course, the potential innovation could be sold to an existing firm or to another potential entrepreneur. But the problem with asymmetric information (Akerlof, 1970) often implies that the best way to appropriate returns from such mixtures of technological and entrepreneurial knowledge is entrepreneurial action. Entrepreneurial initiatives or entrepreneurship generate an entrepreneurial act of organizing resources to initiate commercial activity (Bhide, 1999).

It seems natural to assume that different economic agents have different endowments of technological and entrepreneurial knowledge. It is also natural to assume that it is exactly this uneven distribution of knowledge, together with variations in regional market potential and demand, which creates opportunities for discovering potential new goods and services, that is, potential innovations. Of course, individual economic agents also differ in their capacity to discover, create and exploit innovations, that is, to create new combinations out of existing technological and entrepreneurial knowledge, and thus to be organizers of change. One important reason for capacity differences among economic agents is differences in terms of integration in personal, social and professional networks (Birley, 1985; Aldrich and Zimmer, 1986; Szarka, 1990). Capacity differences are important, since modern entrepreneurship is based on associated skills of a varied nature. An entrepreneur is an opportunity seeker, and in this endeavour he or she needs to have an eye for and a readiness to respond to an often rapidly changing external environment (Nijkamp, 2003).

Generally speaking, two factors must converge for a nascent entrepreneur to found a new firm in a functional region to exploit a potential innovation, that is, for an entrepreneurial event (Shapero, 1984) to occur (Sorensen, 2003).

The first is a personal knowledge network. The potential entrepreneur must perceive an opportunity for profit in a particular segment or market niche of the regional economy, that is, have enough incentive to start a new firm. Since much of the relevant technological and entrepreneurial knowledge only exists privately, awareness of potentially profitable opportunities requires connections to those with pertinent knowledge, typically currently engaged in R&D or a business in a particular industry. Entrepreneurs that can access existing technological and entrepreneurial knowledge in the actual industry enjoy a large advantage (Klepper and Sleeper, 2002; Klepper, 2001). The importance of the personal knowledge network increases with the knowledge intensity in the actual industry where the potential entrepreneur intends to found a new firm.

The second factor is a personal resource network. The individual who perceives an opportunity must build a firm – assemble the necessary capital, skilled labour and knowledge – to exploit it. Social relations and networks play a crucial role in acquiring tacit knowledge and in convincing resource holders to join the new venture, whether as employees or as investors. However, the wealth position of the individual (Lindh and Ohlsson, 1996, 1998; Holtz-Eakin et al., 1994) as well as the supply of venture capital in the region (Malecki, 1997) also have important effects for the probability of becoming an entrepreneur (and propensity to grow).

If we summarize the discussion in this section, we claim that the most critical factor, in particular for entrepreneurial activities in knowledge-intensive sectors, is accessibility to technological and entrepreneurial knowledge. Unfortunately, we have no good measures of entrepreneurial knowledge, so in the next sections we will only be able to test the influence of accessibility to technological and scientific knowledge by using accessibility to university and company R&D, respectively, as proxies.

9.3 KNOWLEDGE ACCESSIBILITY

We turn to the problem of how it is possible to operationalize accessibility to technological and scientific knowledge. If we start with the accessibility concept as such, based on earlier experiences we claim that it is meaningful to distinguish different types of accessibility with different spatial reach, which correspond to the spatial interaction patterns of firms and households. For our purposes, we observe that a national economy can be divided into functional regions that consist of one or several localities. In this chapter, such localities are labelled municipalities. Functional regions are connected to other functional regions by economic and infrastructure networks. The same is true for different localities (or municipalities) within a functional region. Moreover, each municipality can also be seen as a number of nodes connected by the same type of networks. The borders between functional regions are characterized by a decline in intensity of economic interaction, including commuting compared to intra-regional interaction. Thus, functional regions can be approximated with labour market regions.

With reference to such a structure, it is possible to define three different spatial levels, with different characteristics in terms of mobility and interaction opportunities. Because of this, it is also possible to construct three different categories of accessibility. Johansson et al. (2002) distinguish between: (1) intra-municipal accessibility, (2) intra-regional accessibility; and (3) extra-regional accessibility. Based on commuting data, they show that the time sensitivity parameter λ is different for intra-municipal, intra-regional and extra-regional interaction. Inside a municipality, parameter λ^1 applies, inside the pertinent region parameter λ^2 applies, and for contacts outside the region, parameter λ^3 applies.

In order to explain the three accessibility measures in more detail, one has to start at the municipality level. The focus is on municipality s in a functional region R, so that $s \in R$. The average time distance between zones in municipality s is denoted by t_{ss} and the size of the opportunity D in the same municipality is given byD_s. From this, the intra-municipal accessibility to the opportunity D_s is calculated as follows:

$$A^D_{sM} = \exp\{-\lambda^1 t_{ss}\} D_s \tag{9.1}$$

However, economic actors in municipality s also have accessibility to the opportunity D in all other municipalities r that belong to region R. By letting t_{sr} denote the time distance between municipality s and r, the intra-regional accessibility of municipality s can be expressed as:

$$A^D_{sR} = \sum_{r \in R,\, r \neq s} \exp\{-\lambda^2 t_{sr}\} D_r \tag{9.2}$$

Finally, economic actors such as firms and households in municipality s also have accessibility to the opportunity D_k in the k municipalities outside region R. This extra- or inter-regional accessibility is specified in equation (9.3):

$$A^D_{sE} = \sum_{k \notin R} \exp\{-\lambda^3 t_{sk}\} D_k \tag{9.3}$$

D_i is here a measure of opportunities in each municipality and can relate to opportunities such as suppliers, customers, supply of producer services, supply of educated labour, universities and R&D institutes, R&D activities, higher education patents, and so on (see, *inter alia*, Klaesson, 2001). The accessibility measure of the type discussed here satisfies certain criteria of consistency and meaningfulness (see for example Weibull, 1976).

Table 9.2 Categories of accessibility, travel time distances and contact types

Accessibility	Approximate time distance	Type of contacts
Local	5–15 minutes	Several unplanned contacts per day
Intra-regional	15–50 minutes	Contacts and travels made on regular basis (commuting), once per day
Inter-regional	>50 minutes	Planned contacts, low frequency

Source: Johansson et al. (2002).

Table 9.3 Knowledge accessibility measures

Variable	Interpretation
A^C_{sM}	Intra-municipal accessibility to company R&D in municipality *s*
A^C_{sR}	Intra-regional accessibility to company R&D in municipality *s*
A^C_{sE}	Inter-regional accessibility to company R&D in municipality *s*
A^U_{sM}	Intra-municipal accessibility to university R&D in municipality *s*
A^U_{sR}	Intra-regional accessibility to university R&D in municipality *s*
A^U_{sE}	Inter-regional accessibility to university R&D in municipality *s*

The time distances used are travel time distances by car according to the National Road Authority in Sweden. The relevant time distance ranges are illustrated in Table 9.2. The time sensitivity parameters are taken from Johansson et al. (2002). These differ in size in the following way: $\lambda^2 > \lambda^3 > \lambda^1$, which means that time friction is greatest for time intervals of the magnitude 15–50 minutes, smaller for intervals longer than 50 minutes and smallest for very short time periods.

Having established our three types of accessibility, we are now able to define six different measures of knowledge accessibility (see Table 9.3). These six measures are assumed to give a good picture of general accessibility to scientific and technological knowledge.

The general hypothesis tested in this chapter is that new firm formation at the municipal level is a positive function of our six knowledge accessibility measures. Given our basic theoretical assumption that knowledge is spatially bounded and diffuses in geographical space, we expect intra-municipal knowledge accessibility to have the strongest influence on new firm formation, and inter-regional knowledge accessibility to have the weakest influence. We also expect accessibility to company R&D generally to have a stronger influence than university R&D, since the former contains a much higher share of its R&D directed towards generating technological knowledge.

This is our first tentative study in this field using an accessibility approach. For this purpose we have chosen the following nine sectors for study:

1. All private sector industries.
2. Manufacturing industries.[3]
3. Knowledge-intensive manufacturing industries.[4]
4. The private service sector.[5]
5. Knowledge-intensive private services.
6. Producer services.
7. Knowledge-intensive producer services.
8. Producer and mixed services.
9. Knowledge-intensive producer and mixed services.

Knowledge intensity is measured here as the share of employees with a long[6] university education. The knowledge-intensive part of a sector is defined as including one-third of the industries with the highest knowledge intensity. This approach makes it possible to see differences between different parts of the private sector related to knowledge-driven new firm formation.

9.4 DATA, DESCRIPTION OF VARIABLES AND ECONOMETRIC MODEL

9.4.1 Knowledge-accessibility

In the previous section our general accessibility concept was presented and we now turn to our measures of company and university R&D. As our measure of company R&D we use the volume of company R&D measured in man-years per year, and as our measure of university R&D also measured in man-years per year. Instead of a flow measure one could consider a stock measure, but in a steady-state situation, flow measures probably are a good indicator of current stocks of knowledge. Furthermore, one might assume that it is the newest knowledge that is most critical for new entrepreneurial initiatives. As mentioned above, we use accessibility to firms as our measure of accessibility to entrepreneurial knowledge. The measure for accessibility is available for the years 1993, 1995, 1997 and 1999. In the regressions the average accessibility over these years is used.

9.4.2 New Firm Formation

Regarding the measure for new firm formation, data collected by Statistics Sweden are used. The data set consists of firm-level data including information from the profit and loss account and the balance sheet. Each firm in the data set is classified according to the Standard Industrial Classification (SIC) system at the five-digit level.[7] Since 1996, all non-financial enterprises in the corporate sector[8] are included. This means that all non-financial joint-stock companies, cooperatives, partnerships, limited partnerships, associations and some foundations are included. However, it is unfortunately not possible to distinguish between these types of ownership structures in the data set. The firms reported as entering or exiting may be spin-offs from larger companies or independent firms. Data from 1996 to 2001 are available and used in the empirical part of this chapter.

In order to ensure that the analysis covers only firms with real economic activity, firms that did not report any sales or any employees were removed from the data set. After these firms were removed, about 200 000 of the original 300 000 firms remained, for each year. Each firm is assigned a unique identification code. If a new identification code appears, this is identified as a firm entry. Using the data available from 1996 to 2001 implies that new entering firms can be identified for the years. Further information about this data set can be found in Nyström (2006).

The number of new firms established in a region can of course also be expected to depend on the size of the region. Hence the size of the region, measured by the population, is included as a control variable. Table 9.4 presents definitions of variables. Table A9.1 in the Appendix presents some descriptive statistics regarding variables for 1999.

9.4.3 Econometric Model

In order to estimate the impact of accessibility, we estimate a simple additive model. Ordinary least squares (OLS) was used to estimate the models. White's robust variance estimator was used in all estimations in order to control for heteroscedasticity. The model initially estimated is presented in equation (9.4):

$$E_{i,s} = \beta_0 + \beta_1 A^U_{sM} + \beta_2 A^U_{sR} + \beta_3 A^U_{sE} + \beta_4 A^C_{sM} + \beta_5 A^C_{sR} + \beta_6 A^C_{sE} + \beta_7 S_s + \varepsilon_{i,s} \tag{9.4}$$

Since there might be problems with multicollinearity in the regression specified above due to highly correlated variables, the correlation between

Table 9.4 Definition of variables

Variable	Definition
$E_{i,s}$	Number of entering firms in industry *i*, in municipality *s*
A^U_{sM}	Intra-municipal accessibility to university R&D in municipality *s* (Average)
A^U_{sR}	Intra-regional accessibility to university R&D in municipality *s* (Average)
A^U_{sE}	Inter-regional accessibility to university R&D in municipality *s* (Average)
A^C_{sM}	Intra-municipal accessibility to company R&D in municipality *s* (Average)
A^C_{sR}	Intra-regional accessibility to company R&D in municipality *s* (Average)
A^C_{sE}	Inter-regional accessibility to company R&D in municipality *s* ((Average)
S_s	Logarithm of population in municipality *s*

variables is presented in the Appendix, Table A9.2. The only variables with a particularly high correlation are intra-regional university R&D and intra-regional company R&D (0.845). In order to check robustness of the results, the model was therefore estimated without accessibility to intra-regional university R&D variable. This model is specified in equation (9.5):

$$E_{i,s} = \alpha_0 + \alpha_1 A^U_{sM} + \alpha_2 A^U_{sE} + \alpha_3 A^C_{sM} + \alpha_4 A^C_{sR} + \alpha_5 A^C_{sE} + \alpha_6 S_s + \mu_{i,s} \quad (9.5)$$

9.5 KNOWLEDGE ACCESSIBILITY AND NEW FIRM FORMATION: EMPIRICAL EVIDENCES

Table 9.5 presents the results of estimating equation (9.4) using data for 1999. The table shows a very clear pattern across all types of industries. It is accessibility to intra-municipal university and company R&D that has a positive impact on the number of new firms established in the municipality. This finding supports our hypothesis that close and local interaction has the strongest effect on new firm formation. In fact, the empirical result shows that increased accessibility to inter-regional accessibility to company R&D actually has a negative impact on new firm formation. An interpretation is that a potential new firm considering locating in a municipality which has rather good accessibility to inter-regional company R&D actually might prefer to locate in that particular region.

Table 9.5 Accessibility to university and company R&D and new firm formation 1999 (reduced model)

Industry	Constant	Size	Intra-municipal accessibility to university R&D	Intra-regional accessibility to university R&D	Inter-regional accessibility to university R&D	Intra-municipal accessibility to company R&D	Intra-regional accessibility to company R&D	Inter-regional accessibility to company R&D	R^2
1 All industries	−377.930*	43.073*	0.225*	0.033	0.035	0.361*	−0.015	−0.131*	0.867
	(−3.100)	(3.248)	(1.975)	(0.520)	(0.584)	(4.555)	(−0.466)	(−2.078)	
2 Manufacturing industry	−35.343*	4.149*	0.013	0.002	0.002	0.024*	−0.002	−0.009*	0.853
	(−4.166)	(4.494)	(1.615)	(0.454)	(0.446)	(4.720)	(−1.121)	(−2.109)	
3 Knowledge-intensive manufacturing industry	−8.046	0.910	0.007	0.002	0.002	0.015*	−0.001	−0.005*	0.861
	(−1.774)	(1.846)	(1.850)	(0.805)	(0.939)	(4.657)	(−0.754)	(−2.016)	
4 The private service sector	−263.346*	29.909*	0.175*	0.028	0.027	0.273*	−0.102	−0.010*	0.863
	(2.788)	(2.910)	(1.975)	(0.569)	(0.589)	(4.511)	(−0.414)	(−2.117)	
5 Knowledge-intensive private services	−148.159*	16.792*	0.139*	0.027	0.027	0.237*	−0.055	−0.085*	0.867
	(−1.997)	(2.076)	(2.022)	(0.673)	(0.690)	(4.561)	(−0.263)	(−2.080)	
6 Enterprise services	−114.742	13.031*	0.107	0.027	0.022	0.179	−0.005	−0.067	0.863
	(−1.948)	(2.031)	(1.964)	(0.840)	(0.756)	(4.512)	(−0.341)	(2.103)	
7 Knowledge-intensive enterprise services	−50.958	5.763	0.069*	0.015	0.015	0.109*	−0.001	−0.039*	0.872
	(−1.549)	(1.609)	(2.217)	(0.784)	(0.823)	(4.574)	(−0.122)	(−2.060)	
8 Enterprise and mixed services	−193.747*	21.988*	0.141	0.031	0.026	0.244*	−0.008	−0.089*	0.864
	(−2.366)	(2.469)	(1.906)	(0.716)	(0.657)	(4.538)	(−0.350)	(−2.077)	
9 Knowledge-intensive enterprise and mixed services	−56.374	6.358	0.068*	0.015	0.015	0.118*	−0.002	−0.042*	0.869
	(−1.545)	(1.602)	(2.167)	(0.757)	(0.794)	(4.563)	(−0.177)	(−2.054)	

Note: * indicates significance at the 5 per cent level; t-values in parenthesis.

The estimations in Table 9.5 also show that the effect of intra-municipality company R&D is generally larger than the effect of intra-municipality university R&D (since the coefficients are generally larger). This confirms our hypothesis that this kind of R&D is a more important determinant of new firm formation. The variable controlling for size of the municipality has, as expected, a positive and significant effect on new firm formation. If we look at differences across industries, we can observe that the impact of intra-municipality company and university R&D is generally larger for firms in the service industry compared to the manufacturing industry. On the other hand, if we compare the parts defined as knowledge-intensive parts of different types of service industries, the influence of intra-municipality R&D seems lower in knowledge-intensive parts of the sectors. A possible explanation is that these firms need to make sure that they have access to knowledge within the firm and, therefore, less need to access knowledge produced in other firms. Hence, accessibility to knowledge is even more critical to firms that do not have the knowledge themselves.

Table 9.6 presents the results of estimating equation (9.5), which is the somewhat reduced model excluding intra-regional accessibility to university R&D. The results show that the findings presented earlier are robust in the sense that intra-municipality university R&D and company R&D still have a positive and significant influence on new firm formation. Again, inter-regional accessibility to company R&D has a negative influence on new firm formation.

In order to check the robustness of the results presented regarding the data from 1999, the same two models were estimated using data from 1997. Results from these estimations are presented in the Appendix, Tables A9.3 and Table A9.4. These estimations also show in this case that intra-municipality university and company R&D have a positive effect on new firm formation. The negative influence of inter-regional accessibility to company R&D on new firm formation is also significant in these estimations.

9.6 CONCLUSIONS AND SUGGESTIONS FOR FUTURE RESEARCH

In this chapter, it is suggested that since knowledge is spatially bounded and diffuses in space, close local knowledge interactions will have the strongest influence on new firm formation. This hypothesis is supported by empirical analysis, which finds that both intra-municipality accessibility to university and intra-municipality company R&D have a positive effect on new firm formation, whereas intra-regional and inter-regional accessibility has no or even a negative effect on new firm formation.

Table 9.6 Accessibility to university and company R&D and new firm formation 1999

Industry	Constant	Size	Intra-municipal accessibility to university R&D	Inter-regional accessibility to university R&D	Intra-municipal accessibility to company R&D	Intra-regional accessibility to company R&D	Inter-regional accessibility to company R&D	R^2
1 All industries	−384.863*	43.839*	0.222*	0.024	0.362*	−0.001	−0.126*	0.867
	(−3.018)	(3.161)	(1.974)	(0.456)	(4.592)	(−0.077)	(2.105)	
2 Manufacturing industry	−35.699*	4.188*	0.013	0.001	0.024*	−0.002	−0.008*	0.852
	(−4.051)	(4.369)	(1.611)	(0.356)	(4.761)	(−1.664)	(−2.142)	
3 Knowledge-intensive manufacturing industry	−8.423	0.952	0.007	0.002	0.015*	−0.000	−0.005*	0.860
	(−1.775)	(1.8459	(1.843)	(0.796)	(4.695)	(−0.285)	(−2.025)	
4 Private service industries	−269.165*	30.551*	0.173*	0.018	0.274*	0.001	−0.098*	0.863
	(−2.724)	(2.842)	(1.971)	(0.439)	(4.548)	(0.148)	(−2.134)	
5 Knowledge-intensive service industries	−153.885*	17.423*	0.137*	0.018	0.238*	0.006	−0.081*	0.867
	(−1.977)	(2.053)	(2.018)	(0.525)	(4.598)	(0.678)	(−2.094)	
6 Enterprise services	−120.298	13.644*	0.106	0.014	0.180*	0.006	0.062*	0.862
	(−1.940)	(2.021)	(1.950)	(0.527)	(4.549)	(0.850)	(−2.083)	
7 Enterprise and mixed services	−200.282*	22.709*	0.139	0.016	0.246*	0.006	−0.084*	0.863
	(−2.324)	(2.424)	(1.897)	(0.456)	(4.576)	(0.632)	(−2.074)	
8 Knowledge-intensive enterprise services	−53.992	6.098	0.063*	0.009	0.110*	0.005	−0.036*	0.871
	(−1.559)	(1.617)	(2.213)	(0.636)	(4.611)	(1.204)	(−2.064)	
9 Knowledge-intensive enterprise and mixed services	−59.597*	6.713	0.066*	0.010	0.119*	0.005	−0.039*	0.869
	(−4.550)	(1.606)	(2.164)	(0.607)	(4.600)	(1.060)	(−2.060)	

Note: * indicates significance at the 5 per cent level; t-values in parenthesis.

In the theoretical section, it was also argued that accessibility to company R&D can be expected to have a stronger influence on new firm formation compared to university R&D, because this type of R&D can be expected to contain a higher share of knowledge directly aimed at generating technological knowledge. This hypothesis was also confirmed in the empirical analysis, which showed that intra-municipality accessibility to company R&D has a stronger influence than university R&D on new firm formation.

The empirical analysis in this chapter used a cross-section setting. However, the cross-sections for two years, 1997 and 1999, were used to validate results. For future studies, it would be valuable to be able to use panel data, which makes it possible to control for individual heterogeneity and differences across time.

ACKNOWLEDGEMENT

The authors gratefully acknowledge the assistance with the data analysis by Lina Bjerke.

NOTES

1. For reasons explained in section 2 we prefer to use the term 'knowledge flows' rather than the term 'knowledge spillovers' used in a routine fashion in the literature.
2. Functional regions are delimited based upon the spatial interaction patterns of the economic agents in a country. A functional region is fundamentally characterized by its size, by its density of economic activities, social opportunities and interaction options, and by the frequency of spatial interaction between the actors within the region (Johansson, 1997).
3. SIC code 15–37.
4. SIC codes 22, 23, 24, 30, 32, 33 and 35.
5. SIC codes 50–64 and 70–74.
6. More than three years of university education.
7. The SIC code at the four-digit level corresponds to NACE Rev. 1.
8. Financial intermediation (SIC codes 65–67), real estate activities (SIC code 70) and activities of membership organizations (SIC code 91) are not included in the data set.

REFERENCES

Acs, Z.J. and D.B Audretsch (1988), 'Innovation in large and small firms: an empirical analysis', *American Economic Review*, **78**, 678–90.

Akerlof, G.A. (1970), 'The market for "lemons": qualitative uncertainty and the market mechanism', *Quarterly Journal of Economics*, **84**, 488–500.

Aldrich, H. and C. Zimmer (1986), 'Entrepreneurship through social networks', in D. Sexton and R. Smilor (eds), *The Art and Science of Entrepreneurship*, Cambridge, MA: Ballinger, pp. 101–23.

Antonelli, C. (1998), 'Localised technological change, new information technology and the knowledge-based economy: the European evidence', *Journal of Evolutionary Economics*, **8**, 177–98.

Audretsch, D.B. and P.E. Stephan (1996), 'Company–scientist locational links: the case of biotechnology', *American Economic Review*, **86**, 641–52.

Audretsch, D.B. and P.E. Stephan (1999), 'Knowledge spillovers in biotechnology: sources and incentives', *Journal of Evolutionary Economics*, **19**, 97–107.

Bain, J. (1956), *Barriers to New Competition*, Cambridge, MA: Harvard University Press.

Bania, N., R. Eberts and M.S. Fogarty (1993), 'Universities and start-up of new companies: can we generalize from Route 128 and Silicon Valley?', *Review of Economics and Statistics*, **75**, 761–6.

Batten, D.F., K. Kobayashi and Å.E. Andersson (1989), 'Knowledge, nodes and networks: an analytical perspective', in A.E. Andersson, D.F. Batten and C. Karlsson (eds), *Knowledge and Industrial Organization*, Berlin, Heidelberg and New York: Springer, pp. 31–46.

Bhide, A.V. (1999), *The Origin and Evolution of New Businesses*, Oxford: Oxford University Press.

Birley, S. (1985), 'The role of networks in the entrepreneurial process', *Journal of Business Venturing*, **1**, 107–18.

Dosi, G., F. Merba, O. Marsili and L. Orsenigo (1997), 'Industrial structures and dynamics: evidence, interpretations and puzzles', *Industrial and Corporate Change*, **6**, 3–24.

Dumais, G., G. Ellison and E.L. Glaeser (2002), 'Geographic concentration as a dynamic process', *Review of Economics and Statistics*, **84**, 193–204.

Echeverri-Carroll, E. (2001), 'Knowledge spillovers in high technology agglomerations: measurement and modelling', in M. Fischer and J. Fröhlich (eds), *Knowledge Complexity and Innovation Systems*, Berlin: Springer Verlag, pp. 146–61.

Geroski, P. (1999), 'Innovations as an engine of competition', in D. Mueller, A. Haid and J. Weigand (eds), *Competition Efficiency and Welfare*, Dordrecht: Kluwer, pp. 13–26.

Gordon, I.R. and P. McCann (2000), 'Industrial clusters: complexes, agglomeration and/or social networks', *Urban Studies*, **37**, 513–32.

Gråsjö, U. (2005), 'Accessibility to R&D and patent production', Jönköping International Business School, Sweden, mimeo.

Harhoff, D. (1999), 'Firm formation and regional spillovers – evidence from Germany', *Economics of Innovation and New Technology*, **8**, 27–56.

Holtz-Eakin, D., D. Joulfaian and H.S. Rosen (1994), 'Sticking it out: entrepreneurial survival and liquidity constraints', *Journal of Political Economy*, **102**, 53–75.

Johansson, B. (1997), 'Regional differentials in the development of economy and population', in O. Sörensen (ed.), *Empirical Evidence of Regional Growth: The Centre–Periphery Discussion*, Copenhagen: Expert Committee of the Danish Ministry of the Interior, pp. 107–62.

Johansson, B., J. Klaesson and M. Olsson (2002), 'Time distances and labor market integration', *Papers in Regional Science*, **81**, 305–27.

Karlsson, C. and B. Johansson (2006), 'Regional development and knowledge', CEISIS Electronic Working Paper series, Paper No. 76, Jonkoping International Business School.

Karlsson, C. and A. Manduchi (2001), 'Knowledge spillovers in a spatial context: a critical review and assessment', in M.M. Fischer and J. Fröhlich (eds), *Knowledge Complexity and Innovation Systems*, Berlin and Heidelberg: Springer, pp. 101–23.

Klaesson, J. (2001), 'Spatial interaction models and concepts: a review of the gravity theory', Jönköping International Business School, Sweden, mimeo.

Klepper, S. (2001), 'Employee startups in high-tech industries', *Industrial and Corporate Change*, **10**, 639–74.

Klepper, S. and S. Sleeper (2002), 'Entry by spinoffs', Papers on Economics and Evolution 2002–07, Jena: Max Planck Institute for Research into Economic Systems, Evolutionary Economics Group.

Kobayashi, K. (1995), 'Knowledge network and market structure: an analytical perspective', in D.F. Batten, J.L. Casti and R. Thord (eds), *Networks in Action: Communication, Economics and Human Knowledge*, Berlin: Springer, pp. 127–58.

Lazear, E.P. (2002), 'Entrepreneurship', NBER Working Paper No. 9109.

Lindh, T. and H. Ohlsson (1996), 'Self-employment and windfall gains: evidence from the Swedish lottery', *Economic Journal*, **106**, 1515–26.

Lindh, T. and H. Ohlsson (1998), 'Self-employment and wealth inequality', *Review of Income and Wealth*, **44**, 25–42.

Malecki, E. (1997), 'Entrepreneurs, networks and economic development: a review of recent research', in J.A. Katz (ed.), *Advances in Entrepreneurship: Firm Emergence and Growth*, vol. 3, Greenwich, CT: JAI Press, pp. 57–118.

Marshall, A. (1920), *Principles of Economics*, 8th edition, London: Macmillan.

Nijkamp, P. (2003), 'Entrepreneurship in a modern network economy', *Regional Studies*, **37**, 395–405.

Nyström, K. (2006), 'Entry and exit in Swedish industrial sectors', Dissertation, Jönköping International Business School, Sweden.

Orr, D. (1974), 'The determinants of entry: a study of the Canadian manufacturing industry', *Review of Economics and Statistics*, **56**, 58–66.

Schumpeter, J. (1934), *The Theory of Economic Development*, Cambridge, MA: MIT Press.

Shane, S. (2001a), 'Technological opportunities and new firm creation', *Management Science*, **47**, 205–20.

Shane, S. (2001b), 'Technology regimes and new firm formation', *Management Science*, **47**, 1173–90.

Shapero, A. (1984), 'The entrepreneurial event', in C.A. Kent (ed.), *Environment for Entrepreneurship*, Lexington, MA: D.C. Heath, pp. 21–40.

Sorensen, O. (2003), 'Social networks and industrial geography', *Journal of Evolutionary Economics*, **13**, 513–27.

Sorenson, O. and G. Audia (2000), 'The social structure of entrepreneurial activity: geographic concentration of footwear production in the US, 1940–1989', *American Journal of Sociology*, **106**, 324–62.

Stankiewicz, R. (1986), *Academics and Entrepreneurs. Developing University–Industry Relations*, London: Frances Pinter.

Szarka, J. (1990), 'Networking and small firms', *International Small Business Journal*, **8**, 10–22.

Weibull, J. (1976), 'An axiomatic approach to the measurement of accessibility', *Regional Science and Urban Economics*, **6**, 357–79.

Zucker, L.G., M.R. Darby and J. Armstrong (1998), 'Geographically localised knowledge: spillovers or markets?' *Economic Inquiry*, **36**, 65–86.

APPENDIX

Table A9.1 Descriptive statistics

	Mean	Std. dev.	Skewness	Kurtosis	Minimum	Maximum	N
Size	9.837	0.879	0.749	3.897	7.942	13.497	288
Intra-municipal accessibility to university R&D	52.524	320.824	7.552	61.976	0	3012.260	288
Intra-regional accessibility to university R&D	114.450	299.235	3.299	14.5953	0	1990.380	288
Inter-regional accessibility to university R&D	96.478	164.142	2.933	13.1279	0.0004	1022.650	288
Intra-municipal accessibility to company R&D	115.565	605.806	12.795	188.954	0	9335.980	288
Intra-regional accessibility to company R&D	227.026	644.125	4.584	27.920	0	5503.450	288
Inter-regional accessibility to company R&D	199.180	217.047	2.245	10.338	0.002	1448.730	288
E (All industries)	88.917	318.959	12.882	187.842	4	4922	288
Manufacturing industry	7.31359	18.6469	11.113	146.362	0	270	287
Knowledge-intensive manufacturing industry	2.28819	10.5993	13.205	196.265	0	165	288
The private service sector	66.559	251.843	12.835	186.230	2	3872	288
Knowledge-intensive private services	44.941	204.259	13.692	207.556	0	3226	288
Enterprise services	27.7049	125.458	13.5821	204.456	0	1973	288

Knowledge-intensive enterprise services	14.6736	73.4444	13.9882	214.830	0	1169	288
Enterprise and mixed services	55.9063	219.718	13.029	191.027	2	3400	288
Knowledge-intensive enterprise and mixed services	55.9063	219.718	13.029	191.027	2	3400	288

Appendix A9.2 Correlation Matrix 1999

	Size	Intra-municipal accessibility to university R&D	Intra-regional accessibility to university R&D	Inter-regional accessibility to university R&D	Intra-municipal accessibility to company R&D	Intra-regional accessibility to company R&D	Inter-regional accessibility to company R&D
Size	1.000						
Intra-municipal accessibility to university R&D	0.444	1.000					
Intra-regional accessibility to university R&D	0.289	0.067	1.000				
Inter-regional accessibility to university R&D	0.266	0.108	0.250	1.000			
Intra-municipal accessibility to company R&D	0.367	0.634	0.084	0.125	1.000		
Intra-regional accessibility to company R&D	0.282	0.080	0.845	0.400	0.050	1.000	
Inter-regional accessibility to company R&D	0.200	0.183	0.040	0.405	0.083	−0.011	1.000

Appendix A9.3 Accessibility to university and company R&D and new firm formation 1997

Industry	Constant	Size	Intra-municipal accessibility to university R&D	Intra-regional accessibility to university R&D	Inter-regional accessibility to university R&D	Intra-municipal accessibility to company R&D	Intra-regional accessibility to company R&D	Inter-regional accessibility to company R&D	R^2
1 All industries	−502.005*	56.968*	0.252*	0.019	0.026	0.357*	−0.009	−0.133*	0.867
	(−3.930)	(4.102)	(2.018)	(0.308)	(0.428)	(4.535)	(−0.293)	(−2.086)	
2 Manufacturing	−56.820*	5.743*	0.014	0.002	0.000	0.019*	−0.065	0.006	0.081
industry	(−3.652)	(4.766)	(1.346)	(0.545)	(0.044)	(4.039)	(−0.291)	(0.420)	
3 Knowledge-	−10.234*	1.155*	0.008*	0.002	−0.000	0.012*	−0.001	−0.004	0.845
intensive manufacturing industry	(−1.925)	(2.016)	(2.130)	(0.890)	(−0.141)	(4.573)	(−0.410)	(−1.073)	
4 The private	−381.530*	43.087*	0.202*	0.014	0.021	0.281*	−0.004	−0.107*	0.869
service sector	(−3.746)	(3.886)	(1.974)	(0.268)	(0.424)	(4.528)	(−0.170)	(−2.017)	
5 Knowledge-	−205.773*	23.164*	0.153*	0.022	0.018	0.242*	−0.002	−0.084*	0.869
intensive private services	(−2.603)	(2.693)	(2.080)	(0.547)	(0.451)	(4.576)	(−0.100)	(−2.017)	

Appendix A9.3 (continued)

Industry	Constant	Size	Intra-municipal accessibility to university R&D	Intra-regional accessibility to university R&D	Inter-regional accessibility to university R&D	Intra-municipal accessibility to company R&D	Intra-regional accessibility to company R&D	Inter-regional accessibility to company R&D	R^2
6 Enterprise services	−122.607* (−2.522)	13.849* (2.611)	0.096* (2.005)	0.014 (0.591)	0.017 (0.698)	0.147* (4.506)	−0.0004 (−0.032)	−0.056* (−2.137)	0.864
7 Knowledge-intensive enterprise services	−48.359 (−1.787)	5.482 (1.852)	0.052 (1.962)	0.010 (0.778)	0.008 (0.566)	0.089* (4.569)	(0.001 (0.175)	−0.031* (−1.970)	0.865
8 Enterprise and mixed services	−301.485* (−3.385)	34.010* (3.509)	0.173* (1.972)	0.018 (0.418)	0.018 (0.428)	0.249* (4.523)	−0.003 (−0.119)	−0.091* (−2.045)	0.863
9 Knowledge-intensive enterprise and mixed services	−303.745* (−3.413)	34.249* (3.537)	0.172 (1.970)*	0.018 (0.415)	0.018 (0.428)	0.248* (4.526)	−0.003 (−0.121)	−0.092* (−2.052	0.863

Note: * indicates significance at the 5 per cent level; t-values in parenthesis.

Appendix A9.4 Accessibility to university and company R&D and new firm formation 1997

Industry	Constant	Size	Intra-municipal accessibility to university R&D	Inter-regional accessibility to university R&D	Intra-municipal accessibility to company R&D	Intra-regional accessibility to company R&D	Inter-regional accessibility to company R&D	R^2
1 All industries	−506.037*	57.413*	0.251*	0.020	0.357*	−0.001	−0.130	0.867
	(−3.815)	(3.981)	(2.022)	(0.365)	(4.572)	(−0.102)	(−2.140)	
2 Manufacturing industry	−57.278*	5.792*	0.014	−0.001	0.019*	0.000	0.006	0.081
	(−3.579)	(4.641)	(1.331)	(−0.161)	(4.068)	(0.137)	(0.438)	
3 Knowledge-intensive	−10.646*	1.200*	0.008*	−0.001	0.012	0.306	−0.004	0.844
manufacturing industry	(−1.895)	(1.982)	(2.116)	(−0.467)	(4.614)	(0.525)	(−1.649)	
4 Private service industries	−384.375*	43.401*	0.201*	0.016	0.281*	0.001	−0.105*	0.863
	(−3.637)	(3.775)	(1.977)	(0.373)	(4.564)	(0.120)	(−2.172)	
5 Knowledge-intensive service	−210.383*	23.672*	0.151*	0.010	0.242*	0.007	0.081*	0.869
industries	(−2.549)	(2.636)	(2.082)	(0.308)	(4.614)	(0.808)	(−2.046)	
6 Enterprise services	−125.625*	14.182*	0.095*	0.013	0.147*	0.006	−0.054*	0.864
	(−2.485)	(2.572)	(2.003)	(0.576)	(4.543)	(1.140)	(−2.159)	
7 Enterprise and mixed	−305.298*	34.431*	0.171*	0.012	0.250*	0.005	−0.089*	0.864
services	(−3.292)	(3.413)	(1.972)	(0.323)	(4.560)	(0.551)	(−2.078)	
8 Knowledge-intensive	−50.493	5.717	0.051	0.005	0.090*	0.005	−0.029*	0.865
enterprise services	(−1.798)	(1.862)	(1.958)	(0.389)	(4.607)	(1.833)	(−1.978)	
9 Knowledge-intensive	−307.536*	34.667*	0.171**	0.012	0.250*	0.005	−0.089*	0.863
enterprise and mixed services	(−3.319)	(3.440)	(1.970)	(0.324)	(4.563)	(0.542)	(−2.086)	

Note: * indicates significance at the 5 per cent level; t-values in parentheses.

10. Migrant female entrepreneurship: driving forces, motivation and performance

Tüzin Baycan-Levent and Peter Nijkamp

10.1 SCOPING THE SCENE

The main feature of economic restructuring in recent decades has been a marked shift from employment in large firms to self-employment in small firms. This trend has been most pronounced among members of two different groups: immigrants and women. The increasing rate of business ownership among both immigrant groups and women has become one of the driving forces of the growth of national economies, in particular the US and in many countries in Europe (Barrett et al., 1996; Borjas, 1986, 1990; Center for Women's Business Research, 2004, 2005; Cross, 1992; GEM, 2004; Gorter et al., 1998; Kloosterman et al., 1998; OECD, 2001a, 2001b, 2006; Pearce, 2005; Weeks, 2001). Actually, both ethnic and female participation in terms of self-employment and entrepreneurship are seen as powerful economic forces and contributors to a solution to structural labor market problems in many industrialized countries.

When we look at the position of women, some available data clearly show the increasing trend in female self-employment over the years. In the 1990s between one-quarter and one-third of the formal sector businesses were owned and operated by women – in the US 38 percent (1999), in Finland 34 percent (1990), in Australia (1994) and Canada (1996) 33 percent, in Korea 32 percent (1998) and in Mexico 30 percent (1997) (Weeks, 2001) – while in the 2000s the female share in total entrepreneurial activity has approached almost 50 percent in many countries. According to Verheul et al. (2004), who explain female and male entrepreneurship across 29 Global Entrepreneurship Monitor (GEM), countries, the share of women in total entrepreneurial activity is over 40 percent in many countries. On the basis of 2002 data, the female share in entrepreneurship is 44.3 percent in South Africa, 41.5 percent in Mexico, 41.2 percent in Brazil, 40.8 percent in Poland and Argentina, 39.4 percent in India,

38.8 percent in the US, 38.7 percent in Finland and 38.3 percent in the Netherlands.

The report titled 'Top facts about women-owned businesses' by the Center for Women's Business Research (2005) claims that nearly half (48 percent) of all privately held US firms are women-owned, meaning that one out of 11 adult women in the US is an entrepreneur. The report states that the estimated growth rate in the number of women-owned firms is nearly twice that of all firms (17 percent vs. 9 percent). These firms employ 19.1 million people, meaning that one out of seven employees in the US works in a woman-owned business. Besides the employment of 19.1 million people, these firms generate nearly $2.5 trillion value in sales and thus make an important contribution to the US economy.

However, research also shows that women have substantially lower levels of self-employment than men. Although female self-employment rates have risen drastically in recent decades, the prevalence of business ownership among women is only 50–60 percent of that for men. Self-employment is male-dominated in most countries and several countries have female self-employment rates that are roughly one-third of male rates (Fairlie, 2005; Lohmann, 2001; OECD, 2001b). The analysis of the dynamics of self-employment by gender, race and education by Fairlie (2005) shows that women are substantially less likely to be self-employed than men, and have lower rates of entry into self-employment and higher exit rates from self-employment than men. The probability of self-employment increases with an individual being older, married, widowed, divorced, separated, having more children or having a disability (Fairlie and Meyer, 1996; Lohmann, 2001). Therefore, the motives to choose self-employment are also different for men and women. While self-employment is a successful employment option for men, self-employment for women is a way to combine business and domestic responsibilities. Overall, compared to other types of employment, self-employment offers women the desirable and valuable element of time and space flexibility to combine family with work, while different institutional settings create differing opportunities, leading to different outcomes for self-employment (Baycan-Levent et al., 2006; Brush, 1992; CEEDR, 2000; Constant, 2004; Fischer et al., 1993; Koreen, 2001; Letowski, 2001; Lohmann, 2001; Nielsen, 2001; OECD, 1998, 2001a; Weeks, 2001). While being married increases the probability of working in flexible types of employment, married women are likely to have higher occupational prestige and wage rates, since an alternative source of income (the husband's) is generally available and the value of the married woman's time in the home may be higher. Therefore, a married woman is less likely to take a job, if she cannot earn high wages or attain a reasonably high level of occupational prestige (Kossoudji and Ranney,

1984). Another explanation for the choice towards self-employment is given by Constant (2004) on the basis of some critical factors such as age, education, parenthood and self-employed parents. According to the findings of Constant's research, women choose self-employment over a business career in the salaried sector when they are older, less educated, have young children and parents who are self-employed themselves. When women are younger and more educated but have children, they choose self-employment as a way to circumvent unemployment. Women who are more educated and do not have young children are more likely to be businesswomen in the paid sector, suggesting a clear choice for a secure job. The results of the study show also that while businesswomen in paid employment earn the highest wages, women in self-employment earn more than women in lower dependent employment categories.

When we look at the immigrant groups, according to the *International Migration Outlook* published by the Organisation for Economic Co-operation and Development (OECD, 2006), immigrants account for a large proportion of the total labor force in the OECD countries. The numbers have increased by over 10 percent over the five years 1999–2004 in almost all OECD countries. While the increase is especially large in Southern European countries – for instance, six times in Italy and 3.5 times in Spain – the increase reached levels of 46 percent in Ireland, 42 percent in Sweden and 30 percent in the US. In 2004, the foreign-born labor force accounted for 45 percent of the total labor force in Luxembourg, 25 percent in Switzerland, 13 percent in Sweden, 12 percent in Germany and 11 percent in Belgium, France, the Netherlands and Spain. The report states that immigrants have contributed to job creation in many countries. Immigrants contributed to and benefited from over 30 percent of net job creation in the UK, whereas the percentage was 20 percent in Spain, the Netherlands, Portugal, Italy and Sweden. Self-employment among immigrants also increased in almost all countries in 1999–2004 in both numbers and as a percentage of overall self-employment. The share of foreign-born in total self-employment accounted for 38.7 percent in Luxembourg, 17.5 percent in Switzerland, nearly 14 percent in Sweden and 12 percent in Belgium in 2004.

According to another report, *Global Entrepreneurship Monitor United Kingdom* (GEM, 2004), UK ethnic minorities lead on entrepreneurship. The report states that the UK forms Europe's most entrepreneurial economy and that people from ethnic minorities make a large and important contribution to the success of the UK economy.

The increasing number of self-employed migrants and the results of many studies show that the tendency or ability to become self-employed differs between native people and immigrants (Borjas, 1986; Fairlie and Meyer, 1996; Verheul et al., 2001). In general, immigrants are more likely to be self-employed than similarly skilled native-born workers, while in many countries self-employment rates of immigrants exceed those of native-born. While assimilation has a positive impact on self-employment probabilities (Borjas, 1986), the level of education and time since immigration are important determinants of self-employment (Fairlie and Meyer, 1996).

The literature on migrant entrepreneurship explains the driving forces and motivations (see for example Bull and Winter, 1991; Danson, 1995; Davidsson, 1995) to become self-employed by structural factors (such as social exclusion and discrimination, poor access to markets and high unemployment), and cultural factors (such as specific values, skills and cultural features including internal solidarity and loyalty, flexibility, personal motivation, strong work ethics, informal network contacts with people from the same ethnic group, and flexible financing arrangements and so on), or a blend of these factors (included in the so-called 'interaction' model formulated by Waldinger et al., 1990). In general, the motives for migrant entrepreneurship are to be found largely in the challenges imposed by their less-favored position (social exclusion, discrimination, lack of education and skills, high levels of unemployment and so on). The existence of ethnic and social networks also plays a major role in motivating immigrants towards entrepreneurship (van Delft et al., 2000; Johnson, 2000; Kloosterman et al., 1998; Masurel et al., 2002; Ram, 1994a, 1994b; Wilson and Portes, 1980). Such networks provide, on the one hand, rotating credits, a protected market and a proper labor force (Basu, 1998; Deakins et al., 1997; Deakins, 1999; Kloosterman et al., 1998; Lee et al., 1997; Rettab, 2001), while on the other hand they create above-average loyalty between the ethnic firm and its clients (Donthu and Cherian, 1994; Dyer and Ross, 2000). Although there are some similar motives and driving forces among different migrant groups, self-employment rates differ enormously between migrant groups, a situation that can be explained between cultural factors.

In parallel to the increasing trend in self-employment among immigrants and women, a new trend, increasing business ownership by migrant females, has emerged. Although the available data are limited, this new information highlights some interesting facts in migrant female entrepreneurship.

According to the report published by the Center for Women's Business Research (2004), as of 2004 there were an estimated 1.4 million privately held firms majority-owned (51 percent or more) by women of color (include African Americans, Asian American/Pacific Islanders, Hispanics, and Native American/Alaska Natives) in the US, employing nearly 1.3 million people and generating nearly $147 billion in sales. Firms owned by women of color now represent 21.4 percent of all privately held, women-owned firms in the US – meaning that one out of five women-owned firms is owned by a woman of color. The number of firms owned by women of color is estimated to have increased six times faster than the number of all US firms (55 percent vs. 9 percent); employment has increased by 62 percent; and sales by 74 percent between 1997 and 2004. The report also states that women of color own 35.6 percent of all firms owned by persons of color. Women of color also employ 20.1 percent of the workers and generate 16.3 percent of the sales of all firms owned by persons of color.

According to another study which examines the rise of immigrant women entrepreneurs in the United States (Pearce, 2005), today immigrant women comprise one of the fastest-growing groups of business owners. The study states that the number of immigrant women business owners has increased 468 percent since 1980, and nearly 190 percent since 1990. During the same 20 year period, the number of entrepreneurial ventures among immigrant men has increased by 300 percent. It seems that although immigrant men continue to have the highest rates of business ownership, the ownership among immigrant women is moving closer to that of their male counterparts. On the other hand, the results of the study also show that, although they represent a small portion of women's business ownership overall, immigrant women are more likely than non-immigrant women to own their own business. In 2000, 9.3 percent of employed immigrant women were business owners, compared to 6.2 percent of employed native-born women in the US. The *Global Entrepreneurship Monitor United Kingdom* report (GEM, 2004) observes the same trend for the UK. According to the report, women from ethnic minorities are substantially more entrepreneurial than their white female counterparts. While female total entrepreneurial activity (TEA) is 3.6 percent amongst white people, it is two and a half times higher amongst women from mixed backgrounds (10.2 percent), Bangladeshis (10.9 percent), other Asians (10.3 percent) and black Caribbeans (10.5 percent). According to the report, the most entrepreneurial group is that of 'other black', at some 29.2 percent of all women (GEM, 2004). These figures clearly show that migrant females have become more entrepreneurial than their migrant male and native female counterparts.

This new emerging trend at the intersection of migrant and female entrepreneurship, so-called 'migrant female entrepreneurship', has drawn the attention of several researchers to focus more on migrant females than on migrant males (Baycan-Levent et al., 2003, 2006; Center for Women's Business Research, 2004; Constant, 2004; Dallalfar, 1994; Gilbertson, 1995; Hillman, 1999; Pearce, 2005; Schoeni, 1998; Wright and Ellis, 2000). These studies highlight very interesting trends in migrant female entrepreneurship and explain some prominent characteristics of migrant females in the labor market. However, much research is needed to understand better the driving forces, motivations and success conditions or performance of migrant female entrepreneurs.

Against this background, the present study investigates and analyses migrant female entrepreneurship on the basis of driving forces, motivation and performance of migrant female entrepreneurs. Which factors push migrant females towards entrepreneurship and determine their entrepreneurial performance? In order to understand the determinant factors behind the motivation towards entrepreneurship as well as the economic and survival performance of migrant female entrepreneurs, this chapter addresses Turkish female entrepreneurs in Amsterdam.

The study is organized as follows. In section 10.2 an overview of migrant female entrepreneurship is given, and migrant female entrepreneurship is described on the basis of a comparison of migrant and female entrepreneurship. Section 10.3 contains a description of our case study and our data material from in-depth interviews. Various empirical results are given to describe the general profile of Turkish female entrepreneurs and enterprises. Section 10.4 then offers an explanatory framework of the characteristics of migrant female entrepreneurs and enterprises, by using a recently developed artificial intelligence method – rough set analysis. Section 10.5 concludes with a summary discussion on migrant female entrepreneurship.

10.2 MIGRANT FEMALE ENTREPRENEURSHIP: AN OVERVIEW

Although much research effort has been put into the study of migrant entrepreneurship and female entrepreneurship, there is little comprehensive or solid research on migrant female entrepreneurship, while studies of the gender dimensions of ethnic employment niches remain generally case-based. In general, less attention has been paid to the vital role of gender resources in ethnic economies; the focus has been on the status of women as either unpaid or underpaid family members. Women's involvement in ethnic economies is often regarded as an extension of their domestic, maternal or socially reproductive activities in the household. Having access to cheap or unpaid family labor and, in many cases, married women's labor has been a critical factor in determining the economic success of the small business to accumulate capital.

The reasons for this lack of attention to gender dimensions of ethnic employment depend, on the one hand, on the belief that the number of female labor migrants is relatively small and that any potential impact they might have is insignificant; and on the other hand, on the assumption that women primarily follow men in migration and when they work they find jobs working alongside their husbands, filling the same labor market functions (Kossoudji and Ranney, 1984). However, many studies suggest clearly that women are not simply following men in migration and that their labor market functions are quite distinct from men's (Dallalfar, 1994; Kossoudji and Ranney, 1984; Wright and Ellis, 2000). Women's migration patterns may be distinct from those of men in both the timing and the directionality of the flow. Gendered obligations often make it more difficult for women to migrate than men, or require that they move for reasons other than employment. Dallalfar (1994) and Wright and Ellis (2000) emphasized that women and men have differential access to both ethnic and gender resources within the immigrant community, and that they tend to access different networks for finding work or obtain differential information from networks because of gender characteristics of jobs. They explained this fact by the gendered social capital in immigrant communities as well as different migration information systems of women compared to men.

The lack of attention to gender dimensions of the ethnic economy has prompted in recent years an increasing interest among researchers in addressing women as entrepreneurs in the ethnic economy, in parallel to the increasing number as well as the higher shares of migrant females in business ownership compared to migrant male and native counterparts (Baycan-Levent et al., 2003, 2006; Center for Women's Business Research, 2004; Constant, 2004; Dallalfar, 1994; Gilbertson, 1995; Hillman, 1999; Pearce, 2005; Schoeni, 1998; Wright and Ellis, 2000). In general, these investigations describe migrant or ethnic female entrepreneurship on the basis of two dichotomies: male–female (gender) and ethnic–native (ethnic).

'Are ethnic female entrepreneurs special ethnic entrepreneurs or special female entrepreneurs?' On the basis of this research question Baycan-Levent et al. (2003) described the dual character of ethnic female entrepreneurs and the characteristic indicators of ethnic female entrepreneurship that are critical in the two-sided effects of ethnic and female entrepreneurship. For this identification they compared the characteristics, advantages/opportunities and problems/barriers of these two groups. This comparison shows that there are many similarities between these two groups in terms of characteristics and opportunities, specific barriers and problems, but also clear differences in terms of ethnic or gender-based obstacles, needs and networks (Figure 10.1). However, the results of their study show that ethnic female entrepreneurs are not special ethnic entrepreneurs, but that they are special female entrepreneurs particularly in terms of their personal and business characteristics, and their driving forces and motivations.

The findings of many studies show that gender has become more

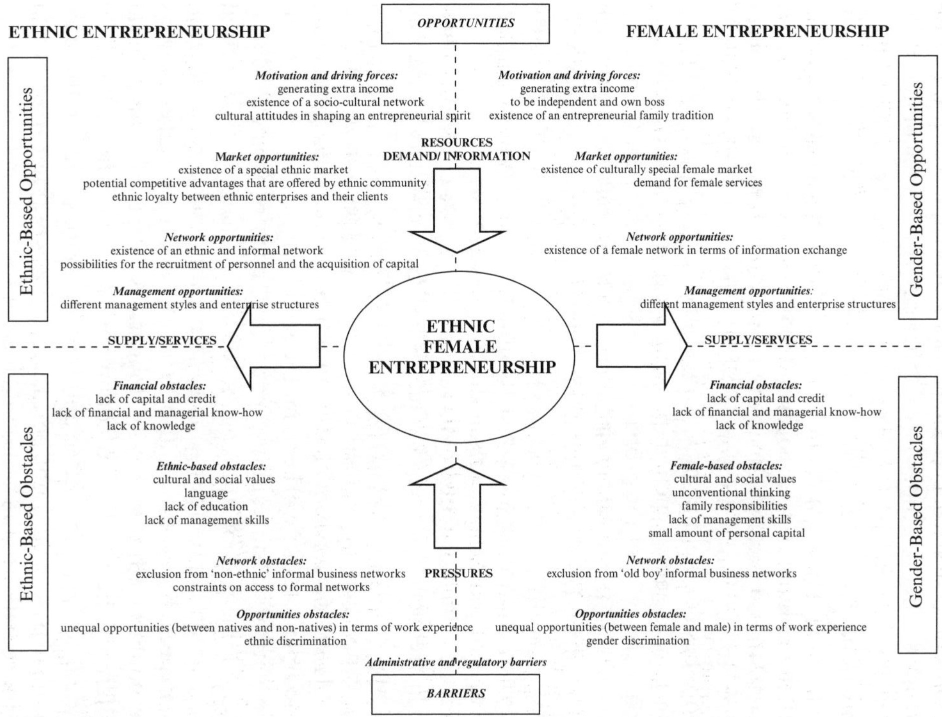

Source: Baycan-Levent et al. (2003).

Figure 10.1 Opportunities and barriers in ethnic female entrepreneurship

important than race in determining occupation (Albelda, 1986; Baycan-Levent et al., 2003, 2006; Dallalfar, 1994; Wright and Ellis, 2000). Ethnicity matters less than gender in the labor market. According to the study of Baycan-Levent et al. (2006), 'gender' as a factor has a higher importance than 'ethnicity' in the characteristics and behavioral attitudes of migrant entrepreneurs, while gender-based differences in migrant entrepreneurship are similar to gender-based differences observed commonly in entrepreneurship. It seems that the changes in the economy over time have led to occupational convergence by gender. Gender is a definitive factor in determining immigrant entrepreneurial activity, as well as types of ethnic resources that immigrants use to form and maintain their small businesses (Dallalfar, 1994). Immigrant women are more likely to funnel into occupations where other immigrant women work, regardless of place of birth, than into jobs beside co-ethnic men (Wright and Ellis, 2000). As generally observed in female entrepreneurship, being married, widowed, divorced or separated increases also the probability of self-employment for migrant females. For example, the study of Dallalfar (1994) on Iranian women entrepreneurs in the US shows that many Iranian immigrant women who are divorced, separated, widowed or never married, or immigrant women who are married and whose husbands are underemployed or unemployed, are sole owners of small businesses in the ethnic economy.

The literature on the structure of female work in ethnic economies highlights certain frequently found characteristics. Gender-focused research shows that the enclave economy does not necessarily support the professional advancement of women as much as it does for men (Zhou and Logan, 1989). Occupational segregation by gender; discrimination; women's multiple roles as workers, mothers and wives; lack of access to information networks and capital account for much of women's disadvantage vis-à-vis men (Zhou and Logan, 1989; Gilbertson, 1995). Cultural factors also play an important role in fostering this tendency. In general, women are expected (and expect also themselves) to earn wages in ways that do not conflict with their family obligations. Depending on cultural values, welfare of the family and community may have higher priority than individual achievement (Zhou and Logan, 1989), so that in this case the women's purpose would not be to develop a working career but to contribute immediately to the household income for the benefit of younger members. Enclave employment provides women with low wages, minimal benefits and few opportunities for advancement (Gilbertson, 1995). Discrimination, occupational segregation and work–family conflicts result in lower wages and fewer opportunities for women, regardless of labor market sector. Although a key advantage of enclave employment is access to resources that facilitate entrepreneurship, research shows that women in the mainstream economy encounter more barriers to self-employment than men. Therefore, enclave employment may be more exploitative of women (Gilbertson, 1995). On the other hand, as most studies indicate, the professional activities of women in an ethnic economy did not change their family-related workload, but actually increased their workload overall (Gilbertson, 1995; Hillman, 1999; Zhou and Logan, 1989).

The findings of several studies show that many immigrants start their business after a discouraging experience in the traditional labor market, where they face language barriers, low wages, racial or ethnic discrimination, and sometimes exploitation. In general, for immigrant women self-employment is a potential way to escape from unemployment after having worked in industry or after the failure of the more qualified second generation to integrate in the general labor market (Hillman, 1999). Therefore, self-employment is more of an advancement than a starting point of emancipation or an adaptation process. Or, self-employment for immigrant women is a way of achieving a respectable social status, even though it does not necessarily mean that they achieve high earnings (Constant, 2004).

According to a study by Pearce (2005), motivations for business ownership display varying patterns among immigrant women entrepreneurs according to national origin. For example, in the US several Chinese and Vietnamese women open their businesses in response to 'pull factors', whereas Korean women open their businesses because business ownership was their only option to survive economically, and Latinas do so in response to 'push factors'. Therefore, ethnic differences among entrepreneurs' motivations can vary from one location to another, and depend on social class differences, opportunity structures and ethnic group relations in a particular location.

Morokvasic's (1988) study on self-employed immigrant women in five European countries distinguished two groups of women entrepreneurs. A first group of self-employed women followed an individual strategy having had previous experience of institutionalized training. A second group adopted a more traditional strategy, by continuing the same activity they were engaged in before becoming self-employed. Very few women were housewives before starting their own business.

According to Dallalfar (1994), entrepreneurial immigrant women are using the ethnic economy to engage in work activities that are more profitable than working as low-paid and devalued workers in businesses often owned by men. However, the results of research by Morokvasic (1988) and Hillman (1999) show that the majority of self-employed immigrant women offered 'non-ethnic' products and services, and they overwhelmingly addressed 'non-ethnic' consumers. For example, Turkish female entrepreneurs in Berlin (Hillman, 1999) did not consider themselves as part of the 'ethnic economy', nor as 'typical of other Turkish women'. The trend towards a mainly non-ethnic orientation of Turkish female entrepreneurs was confirmed by the nationality and the specialization of the suppliers of the sold goods, the composition of the clientele and the frequently mentioned disadvantages of the involvement of family members (hierarchical problems) in the business.

As observed in both migrant and female entrepreneurship, the orientation to the service sector is also the main feature of migrant female entrepreneurship. According to a report published by the Center for Women's Business Research (2004), in the US 61 percent of firms owned by women of color are in the service sector, whereas 12.4 percent are in retail trade, and 4 percent are in goods-producing industries including construction, mining, manufacturing and agriculture. The greatest growth by industry in the number of firms owned by women of color from 1997 to 2004 has taken place in the services industry (55.8 percent growth), followed by transportation, communications and public utilities (47.3 percent) and agriculture (34.8 percent). Pearce's (2005) study states that the top industry for immigrant women business owners is working in private households, followed by child day-care centers, and restaurants and other food services in the US. Nineteen of the top 20 industries in which these entrepreneurs work are service industries. Two of the top service industries for immigrant women business owners are real estate and management, scientific and consulting services where the potential for earnings is much higher than in many other service industries.

Pearce (2005) explained the higher concentration of entrepreneurial women in service industries by a number of factors: (1) women enter fields related to services they already know (health care, cooking, cleaning, beauty care); (2) women often do not have access to the amounts of start-up capital needed for many industries; and (3) women may not be trained in the particular expertise needed for other fields. She emphasized that another possible explanation may be that entrepreneurial women stimulate or help to incubate the businesses of other women.

The findings of several studies show that immigrant women entrepreneurs represent a potential source of continued new business growth that brings a broad range of international skills to the work force. They are not only creating jobs for themselves, but they also stimulate job creation by hiring employees. It is estimated that businesses owned by women across nationalities today provide 12 million jobs in the US (Pearce, 2005). Their economic contributions also include: interest paid on loans; purchases of raw materials and wholesale goods; contracts for ancillary services; education and training for young entrepreneurs through internships and mentoring; purchase or leasing of business space, homeownership and rent for residences; and charitable contributions (Pearce, 2005).

This overview shows that the earlier phase of self-employment experience of immigrant women was a part of family strategy, whereas this trend has changed over the years after experiencing lower wages, minimal benefits and the multiple impacts of an enclave economy towards a new phase to escape from the subordination of women in patriarchal control mechanisms. Several examples of success stories illustrate that immigrant women are swiftly moving beyond their roles as small store owners and unpaid workers in their husbands' businesses (Hillman, 1999; Pearce, 2005). Hillman (1999) states in a speculative way that, while men dominate the ethnic economy through their activities and their orientation towards primarily ethnic clientele, women have to leave it if they do not want to remain in a subordinate position. Consequently, they are making inroads into fields outside of the traditional 'ethnic' and 'feminine' occupations.

10.3 TURKISH FEMALE ENTREPRENEURS IN AMSTERDAM: EMPIRICAL RESULTS OF A CASE STUDY

10.3.1 Preparatory Remarks

In the present section, we will evaluate the empirical results of our case study research in two parts. In subsection 10.3.2 we will examine the profile of Turkish female entrepreneurs in terms of personal characteristics, motivation, driving force and entrepreneurial family tradition. And next, in subsection 10.3.3 we will examine the profile of Turkish female enterprises in terms of enterprise features, performance, and profiles of employees and clients. After this evaluation of the empirical results of our case study research, we will in Section 10.4 present an explanatory framework of the profiles for Turkish female entrepreneurs and enterprises based on a recently developed artificial intelligence method, viz. rough set analysis.

10.3.2 Profile of Turkish Female Entrepreneurs

The empirical data of our research are based on in-depth personal interviews held among 34 Turkish female entrepreneurs who own and operate firms in Amsterdam. In other words, all entrepreneurs in our sample are self-employed. As there are no disaggregated data in terms of ethnicity and gender at the Amsterdam Chamber of Commerce, much information about the entrepreneurs was provided during the survey in an informal way by using the ethnic networks and relations among entrepreneurs. Although there is no official or business organization for ethnic business, these ethnic networks and relationships were very useful to reach other entrepreneurs, especially those in the same sector. As a result, our sample represents all Turkish female entrepreneurs in Amsterdam that can be reached by using the ethnic networks among entrepreneurs.

Personal characteristics of Turkish female entrepreneurs

Female entrepreneurs are a heterogeneous and diverse group, but also share some common personal characteristics. Usually, female entrepreneurs are aged between 35 and 45, married with children and well educated (Brush, 1992; CEEDR, 2000; Fischer et al., 1993; Koreen 2001, Letowski, 2001; Nielsen, 2001; OECD, 1998; OECD, 2001a; Weeks, 2001). The results of our survey show that the personal characteristics of the Turkish female entrepreneurs in Amsterdam are largely the same as the personal characteristics of female entrepreneurs in other countries. An examination of the personal characteristics of the entrepreneurs (Table 10.1) shows that more than half of the entrepreneurs (61.76 percent) fall between the ages of 31 and 40, and that most of them are married (73.53 percent) with children (82.35 percent, including divorced entrepreneurs). Almost 75 percent of the entrepreneurs graduated from secondary vocational schools and have no language problems in the Netherlands: more than 80 percent can speak Dutch fluently or well. This language ability also depends on their arrival year in the Netherlands. When we look at the arrival year in the Netherlands, we see that almost half of the entrepreneurs came between 1970 and 1980, and this rate increases to 70 percent for those who were born and came between 1961 and 1970. It means that the majority of the entrepreneurs have been in the Netherlands for more than 20 years, and they have also had educational opportunities in the Netherlands.

Motivation, driving force and entrepreneurial tradition of Turkish female entrepreneurs

In the literature on entrepreneurship it is often mentioned that both migrant and female entrepreneurs start an enterprise with less labor market experience and less entrepreneurial experience than that of either non-migrant entrepreneurs or of all male entrepreneurs (Brush, 1992; Fischer et al., 1993; CEEDR, 2000; Kalleberg and Leicht, 1991; OECD, 1998, 2001a). Both migrant and female entrepreneurs start their business with a strong economic motivation such as generating extra income, and are attracted by an entrepreneurial opportunity (Brush, 1992; Fischer et al., 1993; Kloosterman et al., 1998; Masurel et al., 2002; OECD, 1998,

Table 10.1 Personal characteristics of Turkish female entrepreneurs

	Number of entrepreneurs	Share in total (%)
Age		
21–25	5	14.71
26–30	5	14.71
31–35	8	23.53
36–40	13	38.23
41–45	3	8.82
Marital status		
Single	2	5.88
Married	25	73.53
Divorced	7	20.59
Family status		
Without children	6	17.65
With children	28	82.35
Education level		
Primary school level	2	5.88
Secondary school level	2	5.88
Middle vocational training	25	73.53
Higher vocational training	4	11.77
University	1	2.94
Language ability (Dutch)		
Fluently	21	61.76
Good	7	20.59
Moderate	6	17.65
Arrival year in the Netherlands		
Born	3	8.82
1961–70	5	14.71
1971–80	16	47.05
1981–90	6	17.65
1991–2000	4	11.77
Total	34	100.0

2001a; Weeks, 2001). However, some studies show the contradictory result that non-economic motives, like being independent, are more important in some countries (Letowski, 2001; Nielsen, 2001). It is often argued that migrant entrepreneurs tend to use their own capital or to obtain capital from their ethnic networks such as family members and friends (Deakins et al., 1997; Van Delft et al., 2000; Kloosterman et al., 1998; Lee et al., 1997; Masurel et al., 2002), while female entrepreneurs also tend to use their own capital or to obtain capital from family members (Bruce, 1999; CEEDR, 2000; OECD, 1998, 2001a; Verheul and Thurik, 2001). On the other hand, some studies (Bruce, 1999; Brush, 1992; Letowski, 2001) indicate that if female entrepreneurs have a self-employed husband or family members, the probability to become an entrepreneur increases.

When we look at the position and the previous experience of Turkish female entrepreneurs in Amsterdam before start-up (Table 10.2), we see that the majority (70.59 percent) of the entrepreneurs were employed and 20.59 percent were already active as entrepreneurs in their previous positions. While 38.23 percent of the entrepreneurs had experience through employment, 32.35 percent had experience through school or study and 17.65 percent as entrepreneurs in their previous professional experience. The entrepreneurs who had no experience constitute only 11.77 percent of the total. These figures show that Turkish female entrepreneurs often start an enterprise with prior experience.

On the other hand, we see a very high rate of family members who are also entrepreneurs. This is one of the most important results of this study. Almost 80 percent of Turkish female entrepreneurs have at least one entrepreneur family member (Table 10.2). The high rate of parents (41.18 percent), brothers or sisters (44.12 percent) and other relatives (47.05 percent) who are entrepreneurs shows that entrepreneurial family tradition is a very important driving force for Turkish female entrepreneurs. It seems plausible that besides their personal experience in the labor market, they also benefit from this entrepreneurial experience of the family, and this entrepreneurial spirit pushes or encourages them to become entrepreneurs. These figures also show that the entrepreneurial spirit of Turkish female entrepreneurs is not a husband matter, but a strongly parental matter.

The other indicator supporting this entrepreneurial tradition is the motivation of the entrepreneurs. The results of our study show that economic motivation, such as generating extra income, was not the first reason for Turkish females to become entrepreneurs (Table 10.2). On the contrary, the most important reasons are to be independent (67.65 percent) and to be their own boss (70.59 percent), which can be interpreted as an entrepreneurial spirit. Only 26.47 percent of the entrepreneurs indicate that extra income is also a reason in their preference list to become entrepreneurs. The low rate of continuation of family business tradition (11.77 percent) is a very interesting result, when it is compared with the rate of the entrepreneur's family members. Although 80 percent of the Turkish female entrepreneurs have entrepreneur family members, only 11.77 percent indicate that their motivation originated from this tradition. This situation can be

Table 10.2 Motivation, driving force and entrepreneurial tradition of Turkish female entrepreneurs

	Number of entrepreneurs	Share in total (%)
Position before starting		
Employed	24	70.59
Unemployed	2	5.88
Entrepreneur	7	20.59
Student	1	2.94
Previous experience		
Through employment	13	38.23
Through entrepreneurship	6	17.65
Through school or study	11	32.35
None	4	11.77
Entrepreneur's family members	27	79.41
Husband	8	23.53
Parents	14	41.18
Brothers/sisters	15	44.12
Relatives	16	47.05
The reasons to be an entrepreneur		
To be independent	23	67.65
To be own boss	24	70.59
Work experience	11	32.35
Extra income	9	26.47
Family tradition	4	11.77
Dissatisfaction with previous employment	3	8.82
Capital sources		
Own capital	15	44.12
Family or friends	14	41.18
Financial institutions	11	32.35
Other	3	8.82
Total	34	100.0

explained in that they separate the motivation to be independent or to be their own boss from this tradition.

When we look at the tendencies observed in the use or acquisition of capital, we see that 44.12 percent of the entrepreneurs have used their own capital, while 41.18 percent have obtained it from family or friends (Table 10.2). Sometimes, they have combined these two sources. Generally, they prefer to obtain capital from family rather than from financial institutions, because of the high interest rates. When they obtain capital from family members, they do not pay interest. On the other hand, 32.35 percent of the entrepreneurs have taken credit from financial institutions. However, most of them indicated that they have taken this credit in the names of their husbands or family members, for two reasons. The first is that, when they applied to the financial institutions, they had stopped their previous job and were actually unemployed at that stage. And the second reason concerns the difficulties in obtaining credit as a result of a lack of experience as an entrepreneur. Most of them tried to obtain credit from financial institutions in their own names, but after their first failed attempts, they used this second way and they obtained credits in the names of their husbands or family members.

If we evaluate all our findings, we can say that the profile of Turkish female entrepreneurs shows the following characteristics. Turkish female entrepreneurs are entrepreneurs who are between the ages of 30 and 40, married with children, were born or came to the Netherlands at least 20 years ago, and therefore received vocational and language education in the Netherlands; they have an experience as employee or entrepreneur in their previous position, have entrepreneur family members who support them morally and also financially, and originate from an entrepreneurial family tradition encouraging an entrepreneurial spirit to be independent or their own boss.

10.3.3 Profile of Turkish Female Enterprises

The features of Turkish female enterprises

In the literature on migrant and female entrepreneurship it is often mentioned that there are various similar characteristics between migrant and female enterprises (Brush, 1992; CEEDR, 2000; Deakins, 1999; Fischer et al., 1993; Kloosterman et al., 1998; Koreen, 2001; Lee et al., 1997; Letowski, 2001; Nielsen, 2001; OECD, 1998, 2001a; Weeks, 2001). The research shows that most migrant and female enterprises belong to the service sector, are small-sized and relatively young, while family ownership for migrant enterprises and sole proprietorship for female enterprises are the legal form of most of the enterprises.

When we examine the features of Turkish female enterprises (Table 10.3), we see that all enterprises are in the service sector, except for one in manufacturing (textiles), and that 80 percent of the enterprises are in four sectors: driving school, hairdresser, fashion shop, and human resource management and temporary job agency. The specific activities of several enterprises show some distinct ethnic and female entrepreneurial

Table 10.3 Features of Turkish female enterprises

	Number of enterprises	Share in total (%)
Activities of the enterprise		
Driving school	12	35.29
Hairdresser	5	14.71
Fashion shop	6	17.65
Human resource management/temporary job agency	4	11.77
Flowershop	1	2.94
Finance/insurance/tourism/real estate	2	5.88
Laundry	1	2.94
Press agency	1	2.94
Transport	1	2.94
Textile manufacturing	1	2.94
Foundation year of enterprise		
1986–1990	3	8.82
1991–1995	10	29.41
1996–2000	14	41.18
2001–	7	20.59
Starting situation of the enterprise		
Newly started	25	73.53
Taken over from family or friends	3	8.82
Taken over from alien in the same sector	6	17.65
Proprietorship		
Sole proprietorship	30	88.24
Shareholder/husband/children	1	2.94
Shareholder/parents-sisters/brothers	1	2.94
Shareholder/other family members	1	2.94
Shareholder/alien	1	2.94
Number of employees		
No employee	17	50.00
1–5 employees	14	41.18
13 employees	1	2.94
23 employees	1	2.94
48 employees	1	2.94
Total	34	100.0

opportunities. For example, in our sample more than one-third of the enterprises (35.29 percent) are made up of driving schools, and this sector has appeared to serve clearly ethnic and female needs. The clients of these enterprises are Turkish women, and they prefer to learn from other Turkish women for two reasons. The first one is of course the language problem, related to learning more easily from women, and the second one depends on cultural and religious reasons such as jealousy by their husbands. This market opportunity has attracted many women to this sector, while female entrepreneurs who work in this sector also constitute role models for their clients. Besides this market opportunity, related opportunities such as the low capital intensity of this sector and the flexibility of working hours also cause growth in this sector. This kind of ethnic and female opportunity is less evident for the other sectors: some of them clearly serve ethnic and female needs – for example, special hairdressing for religious women by female hairdressers – but this is not a general trend for the entire sector. It can be said that they manage their businesses for economic reasons, and if there are some special market opportunities, they benefit from them; otherwise they do not take into consideration ethnic and female needs, and they address other groups. For example, most fashion shop owners and hairdressers have indicated that they do not prefer Turkish clients because of their consumer behaviour – they do not spend as much money on clothing, hair care and cosmetics – and therefore they address other groups. Most entrepreneurs in other sectors were attracted by their work experience in relation to their knowledge of the market structure of the sector, while some have even taken over the firm they were employed by in the past. In summary, all entrepreneurs are attracted by an entrepreneurial opportunity.

On the other hand, we observe that there is an increase in start-up enterprises after 1990. Between 1996 and 2000, 14 enterprises (41.18 percent of the total) started, and this number is higher than the number of the enterprises that started in the previous two periods. This increasing trend has also continued after 2000 and constitutes more than 20 percent of the enterprises. Therefore, we can say that a clear trend for female entrepreneurship in Turkish immigrant groups has occurred in the last decade and that more than 90 percent of the Turkish female enterprises have started after 1990.

When we look at the starting position of the enterprises, 73.53 percent of the enterprises were newly started and 17.65 percent were taken over from immigrants in the same sector. Sole proprietorship forms the legal form of most of the enterprises (88.24 percent). On the other hand, most of the enterprises are small (91.18 percent), while 50 percent of the enterprises have no employees, and 41.18 percent have less than five workers.

Performance of Turkish female enterprises

It is often argued that migrant entrepreneurs and female entrepreneurs show a low performance and success rate (Brush, 1992; Brush and Hisrich,

Table 10.4 Performance of Turkish female enterprises

	Number of enterprises	Share in total (%)
Development of sales		
Increase	15	44.12
Decrease	4	11.77
Same	8	23.53
Don't know	7	20.59
Profit last year		
Positive	21	61.76
Negative	1	2.94
Same	5	14.71
Don't know	7	20.59
Total	34	100.0

1999; Buttner and Moore, 1997; Fischer et al., 1993; Kalleberg and Leicht, 1991; Rietz and Henrekson, 2000; Rosa et al., 1994); in particular, the success of migrant entrepreneurs depends on their ethnic networks and support obtained from this network (Deakins, 1999; Kloosterman et al., 1998; Lee et al., 1997; Masurel et al., 2002).

When the development of sales and the profit of the previous year is examined for Turkish female enterprises in terms of their performance, almost half of the enterprises (44.12 percent) have an increase in sales, while 23.53 percent have about the same level (Table 10.4). In particular, mature enterprises do not exhibit a rise in sales, which can be explained by a balanced and stable development level. The entrepreneurs of these mature enterprises emphasized the duration of their economic activities in explaining their sales or development. Only 11.77 percent of the enterprises have a declining profit position. For the enterprises that have recently started (20.59 percent), there is no unambiguous information; however, several entrepreneurs indicated a positive and increasing trend. Nevertheless, when we examine the profits of the previous year, their success can be seen more clearly: 61.76 percent of the entrepreneurs had an increased profit, while 14.71 percent had the same profit. The rate of negative profit is only 2.94 percent. Here there is no available profit and loss information for recently started enterprises (20.59 percent). These figures show a rather high economic performance.

Profile of employees and clients of Turkish female enterprises

In the literature on migrant entrepreneurship, it is often argued that migrant entrepreneurs tend to hire employees of their own ethnic group

Table 10.5 Profile of employees and clients of Turkish female enterprises

	Number of employees	Share in total (%)
Composition of employees		
Total employees	121	100.00
Nationality of employees		
Turkish employees	74	61.16
Non-Turkish employees	47	38.84
Sex of employees		
Male employees	50	41.32
Female employees	71	58.68
	Number of enterprises	**Share in total (%)**
Composition of clients (%)		
Types of clients		
Individual clients	28	82.35
Male clients	28	25.00
Female clients	28	75.00
Firms	6	17.65
Nationality of clients (individual clients + firms)		
Turkish clients	34	44.00
Non-Turkish clients	34	56.00
Total	34	100.0

and they tend to use their personal and ethnic networks in order to recruit new employees (Deakins et al., 1997; van Delft et al., 2000; Kloosterman et al., 1998; Lee et al., 1997; Masurel et al., 2002). In general, they tend to run their enterprises with partners who are family members or relatives.

In discussing the features of Turkish female enterprises, it is noteworthy that most of the enterprises are small: 50 percent of the enterprises have no employees, and 41.18 percent have less than five workers. When we examine the composition of the employees, it is seen that almost two-thirds of the employees are Turkish (61.16 percent) (Table 10.5). The high rate of Turkish employees clearly shows that Turkish female entrepreneurs tend to hire employees of their own ethnic group. On the other hand, while female workers constitute 58.68 percent of the total employees, the share of male workers is 41.32 percent. Although the rate of female workers is higher than the rate of male workers, there is no big difference between these two groups and no clear evidence for the preferences for the female employees. Their preferences depend also on the sectors' structures and needs.

As emphasized in the previous section on the features of Turkish female enterprises, the specific activities of several enterprises show some distinct ethnic and female entrepreneurial opportunities. Some activities have appeared to serve clear ethnic and female needs; others address other groups. When we examine generally the composition of the clients regardless of the sector, we see that most enterprises serve individual clients (82.35 percent), while few others serve firms (17.65 percent). And female clients constitute the majority, with a rate of 75 percent of the individual clients. On the other hand, when we look at the nationality of the clients, we see that although there is no big difference, the rate of non-Turkish clients (56 percent) is higher than that of Turkish clients (44 percent). Thus, it can be said that the orientation on clients of the Turkish female enterprises has changed in most activities. However, the services that the enterprises offer to their clients are largely provided by their ethnic employees.

If we evaluate all our findings, we can say that the profile of Turkish female enterprises shows the following features. Turkish female enterprises are small enterprises which have emerged in the last decade, belong to the service sector, show a rather high economic performance, serve clear ethnic and female needs on the one hand, and non-ethnic but clearly female needs on the other hand. These features, however, which are in a stage of change in terms of orientation on clients from ethnic towards non-ethnic, are still supported by the ethnic network in hiring employees.

10.4 EXPLANATORY FRAMEWORK FOR THE PROFILES OF TURKISH FEMALE ENTREPRENEURS AND ENTERPRISES

10.4.1 Rough Set Analysis: Introduction

Our explanatory framework for the identification of the most prominent characteristics of ethnic female entrepreneurs is based on a specific recently developed artificial intelligence method, viz. rough set analysis. Rough set data analysis (RSDA) is a classification method developed by Pawlak (1991) for the analysis of non-stochastic (including qualitative and nominal) information. RSDA is an application of Knowledge Discovery in Databases which is concerned with extracting useful information from a complex multivariate database (Fayyad et al., 1996). Rough set data analysis is based on minimal model assumptions in terms of formal causal specifications and admits ignorance when no proper conclusion can be drawn from the data at hand (Ziarco, 1998). Hence, it is more exploratory and heuristic in nature. RSDA draws all its information from the a priori given data set. In other words, RSDA remains at the level of an empirical system: more precisely, the implicit formal and the empirical system coincide and the multidimensional scaling acts then as the identity function. In RSDA, there is no numerical system that is different from the operationalization of the observed data, and there are no outside parameters to be chosen, nor is there any deductive statistical model to be fitted. RSDA can be viewed as a pre-processing device to recognize the potentially important explanatory variables. Data reduction is the main feature of RSDA, as it allows the representation of hidden structures in the database. It should be stressed here that rule induction in itself is not a part of rough set theory. It can rather be seen as a tool for preparing data for induction, especially for defining classes for which rules are generated. The final outcome of the database is a decision table from which decision rules can be inferred by using rough set analysis. The rules are logical statements (if . . . then) which represent the relationship between the description of objects and their assignment to particular classes (see Pawlak, 1991, 1992). Details on rough set analysis both from a methodological and from an applied perspective can be found *inter alia* in Deogun et al. (1997), Famili et al. (1997), Fayyad et al. (1996), Pawlak (1991, 1992), Slowinski (1995), van Delft et al. (2000), van den Bergh et al. (1998) and Ziarco (1998).

The rough set analysis in our study is carried out with the help of the computer program Rough Set Data Explorer (ROSE).[1] This software system is able to deal with the basic elements of rough set theory and the related rule discovery techniques. We use the ROSE software in our study to identify the determinant factors behind the driving forces, motivation and performance in ethnic female entrepreneurship. In our study, the data system on ethnic female entrepreneurs can be regarded as a mixed (qualitative and quantitative) database that is suitable for classification and explanation. Rough set analysis then acts as a specific multidimensional classification approach that appears to be able to identify various important factors that are responsible for motivation and performance of ethnic female entrepreneurs. In the next subsection, we will offer the results of the rough set analysis applied to Turkish female entrepreneurs in Amsterdam.

10.4.2 Empirical Results: Driving Forces, Motivation and Performance of Turkish Female Entrepreneurs

As mentioned above, rough set analysis is essentially a classification method devised for non-stochastic information. The application of rough set analysis proceeds in two successive steps: the construction of an information survey, and the classification of information contained in the survey. In our case, the information survey consists of experiences of Turkish female entrepreneurs in terms of driving forces, motivation and performance. This information survey which contains characteristics (attributes) of Turkish female entrepreneurs is given in the previous section in Tables 10.1 to 10.5. The next step, the classification of information contained in the survey, is one of the most problematic issues in the application of rough set analysis, as the chosen thresholds are not always unambiguous and hence may also lead to information loss. In general, some sensitivity analysis on the classification used is meaningful, as a balance needs to be found between homogeneity and class size. In our case, after some sensitivity analyses the categories for each relevant attribute are defined and listed in Table 10.6. Next, on the basis of these categories, the resulting coded information table is constructed (Table 10.7).

Our rough set framework consists of 18 variables; 16 of them are attribute variables, three of them decision variables. The variable 'reasons to be entrepreneur' is used as both an attribute and a decision variable. As a decision variable, 'reasons to be entrepreneur' refers to motivation and driving forces, while the other two decision variables, 'development of sales' and 'profit last year', constitute performance variables. The ROSE software is applied for each of these three decision variables independently and the results of the analysis are evaluated on the basis of these decision variables in order to highlight the determinant factors (attribute variables) behind the motivation and performance of Turkish female entrepreneurs.

In the application of the rough set analysis, three main sets of indicators and outputs can be calculated: the reducts and the core; the lower and upper approximation; and rules.

The reduct – in other words, a minimal set of attributes – is the least minimal subset which ensures the same quality of classification as the set of all attributes. Intersection of all reducts/minimal (in other words, an attribute that appears in all minimal sets) is defined as the 'core'. The core is a collection of the most significant attributes for the classification in the system. The reducts and core for each set of data on the basis of three decision variables are given in Tables 10.8, 10.9 and 10.10.

Ten sets of reducts for each data set and two different core attributes are found. The core attribute of the first data set, reasons to be entrepreneur, is A3 (language (Dutch ability)) whereas the core attribute of the following two data sets, development of sales and profit last year, is A8 (foundation year of the enterprise). As can be seen in Tables 10.8, 10.9 and 10.10, without these two core attributes it is impossible to classify the results of the reasons to be entrepreneur, development of sales and profit last year. This means that these attributes strongly influence the motivation and performance of the entrepreneurs.

Next, the relative frequencies of appearance of the condition attributes

Table 10.6 Classification of variables investigated

Variable	Categories
Arrival year in the Netherlands	1 born 2 1961–80 3 1981–2000
Education level	1 primary 2 medium vocational and secondary 3 higher vocational and university
Language (Dutch ability)	1 fluently 2 good 3 moderate
Position before starting	1 employed 2 unemployed 3 entrepreneur 4 student
Entrepreneur family members	1 yes 2 no
Reasons to be entrepreneur	1 to be independent and own boss 2 other reasons
Foundation year of the enterprise	1 1986–90 2 1991–95 3 1996–2000 4 2001–
Starting situation of the enterprise	1 newly started 2 taken from alien 3 taken from family and friends
Capital sources	1 own+family and friends 2 financial institutions 3 other
Number of employees	1 no employee 2 1–5 employees 3 5+ employees
Nationality of employees	1 no employee 2 only Turk 3 only non-Turk 4 mixed
Gender of employees	1 no employee 2 male 3 female 4 mixed
Nationality of clients	1 Turk majority 2 non-Turk majority 3 mixed
Gender of clients	1 male majority 2 female majority 3 firm 4 mixed
Sector	1 human resource management 2 driving school 3 fashion shop 4 hairdresser 5 other services
Development of sales	1 increase 2 non-increase
Profit last year	1 positive 2 non-positive

Table 10.7 Codified information table on Turkish female entrepreneurs

	Turkish female entrepreneurs																	
	Entrepreneur characteristics							Enterprise features										
	A1	A2	A3	A4	A5	A6	A7 / D	A8	A9	A10	A11	A12	A13	A14	A15	A16	D1	D2
No	Arrival year in the Netherlands	Education level	Dutch ability	Position before starting	Previous experience	Entrepreneur family members	Reasons to be entrepreneur	Foundation year of the enterprise	Starting situation of the enterprise	Capital sources	Number of employees	Nationality of employees	Gender of employees	Nationality of clients	Gender of clients	Sector	Development of sales	Profit last year
1	2	3	1	1	1	1	1	3	1	2	2	3	3	2	3	1	1	1
2	3	2	2	1	1	2	2	1	2	2	2	4	3	2	2	2	1	1
3	3	1	3	2	4	2	2	3	1	1	1	1	1	2	2	3	2	1
4	2	3	1	1	4	1	1	3	1	3	3	4	4	3	3	1	1	1
5	2	2	1	1	1	1	1	3	3	1	1	1	1	2	4	4	1	1
6	2	2	1	1	4	1	1	3	1	3	2	4	2	1	1	5	1	1
7	2	3	1	3	2	2	1	3	2	3	2	3	4	2	4	5	1	1
8	2	2	1	3	2	1	2	1	3	1	2	3	3	2	2	3	1	1
9	2	2	1	1	1	2	2	4	1	1	1	1	1	1	1	5	2	2
10	3	1	3	3	2	1	1	4	2	1	1	1	1	2	4	5	2	2
11	3	2	2	1	1	1	1	3	2	2	2	2	3	2	2	4	1	1
12	1	2	1	1	1	1	1	4	1	1	1	1	1	2	2	3	2	2
13	2	2	2	3	2	1	2	3	1	1	1	1	1	2	2	3	2	1
14	3	2	3	1	3	1	1	2	1	1	1	1	1	1	2	2	1	1
15	3	2	2	1	1	1	1	4	1	1	3	2	4	2	3	1	2	2
16	3	2	2	3	2	1	1	2	2	1	2	3	4	2	2	4	1	1
17	3	2	3	3	3	1	1	2	1	2	1	1	1	1	2	2	1	1
18	2	2	1	1	3	1	1	3	1	1	1	1	1	1	2	2	1	1

Table 10.7 (continued)

	Turkish female entrepreneurs																	
	Entrepreneur characteristics							Enterprise features										
	A1	A2	A3	A4	A5	A6	A7 / D	A8	A9	A10	A11	A12	A13	A14	A15	A16	D1	D2
No	Arrival year in the Netherlands	Education level	Dutch ability	Position before starting	Previous experience	Entrepreneur family members	Reasons to be entrepreneur	Foundation year of the enterprise	Starting situation of the enterprise	Capital sources	Number of employees	Nationality of employees	Gender of employees	Nationality of clients	Gender of clients	Sector	Development of sales	Profit last year
19	3	2	3	2	4	1	1	2	1	2	1	1	1	1	2	2	1	1
20	2	2	2	1	3	1	2	2	1	1	1	1	1	1	2	2	1	1
21	3	3	1	4	3	1	2	3	1	1	2	3	2	2	3	5	2	2
22	2	2	1	1	1	1	2	2	2	1	2	2	4	2	4	4	1	1
23	2	2	1	1	1	2	2	2	1	1	2	3	2	2	4	4	1	1
24	1	2	3	1	3	1	2	4	1	2	1	1	1	1	2	2	2	2
25	2	2	2	1	3	1	1	1	1	2	2	2	4	1	2	2	1	1
26	2	3	1	1	1	1	1	3	1	1	1	1	1	2	3	1	2	1
27	2	2	1	1	1	1	1	3	1	1	2	2	3	1	1	5	1	1
28	2	2	1	3	2	2	1	3	1	1	2	2	4	2	3	5	1	1
29	2	2	1	1	3	1	1	4	1	1	1	1	1	1	2	2	2	2
30	1	2	1	1	3	1	1	3	1	1	1	1	1	1	2	2	1	1
31	2	2	1	1	1	1	1	4	3	1	2	3	2	2	1	3	2	2
32	2	2	1	1	3	1	1	2	1	1	1	1	1	1	2	2	1	1
33	2	2	1	1	1	1	2	2	1	1	3	4	4	2	2	3	1	1
34	2	2	1	1	3	2	1	2	1	1	1	1	1	3	2	2	1	1

Table 10.8 Reducts and core: reasons

	Core reason sets
Reduct	Set no. 1 {A3, A5, A8, A16}
	Set no. 2 {A3, A6, A8, A15, A16}
	Set no. 3 {A3, A8, A10, A12, A16}
	Set no. 4 {A3, A4, A10, A12, A16}
	Set no. 5 {A3, A8, A12, A15, A16}
	Set no. 6 {A3, A8, A10, A13, A16}
	Set no. 7 {A3, A8, A12, A13, A16}
	Set no. 8 {A3, A8, A13, A14, A16}
	Set no. 9 {A3, A4, A10, A13, A16}
	Set no. 10 {A3, A8, A13, A15}
Core	{A3}

Table 10.9 Reducts and core: development

	Core reason sets
Reduct	Set no. 1 {A5, A8, A13, A16}
	Set no. 2 {A5, A8, A10, A16}
	Set no. 3 {A6, A8, A10, A15, A16}
	Set no. 4 {A8, A12, A13, A16}
	Set no. 5 {A8, A10, A12, A16}
	Set no. 6 {A8, A13, A14, A16}
	Set no. 7 {A5, A8, A11, A16}
	Set no. 8 {A6, A8, A11, A15, A16}
	Set no. 9 {A8, A12, A15, A16}
	Set no. 10 {A8, A13, A15, A16}
Core	{A8}

in the reducts for each data set are given in Tables 10.11, 10.12 and 10.13. After core attribute A3, two other attributes, A8 (foundation year of the enterprise) and A16 (sector) in the reasons to be entrepreneur; and after core attribute A8, another set of attributes, A13 (gender of employees), A15 (gender of clients) and A16 (sector) in the development of sales and profit last year, appear as relatively important attributes with higher frequency rates.

The lower and upper approximation – and derived accuracy of relationships for each value class of the decisional variable – is another indicator from a rough set analysis. The latter is the lower divided by the upper approximation of each class. Accuracy and quality of classification can also be derived from the choice of thresholds. The results are shown in

Table 10.10 Reducts and core: profit

	Core reason sets
Reduct	Set no. 1 {A2, A8, A13}
	Set no. 2 {A4, A8}
	Set no. 3 {A5, A8, A13}
	Set no. 4 {A8, A10, A13}
	Set no. 5 {A8, A12, A13}
	Set no. 6 {A8, A13, A14}
	Set no. 7 {A5, A8, A16}
	Set no. 8 {A6, A8, A15, A16}
	Set no. 9 {A8, A12, A15, A16}
	Set no. 10 {A8, A13, A15}
Core	{A8}

Table 10.11 Frequency of attributes in reducts: reasons

Attribute	Frequency	Frequency %
A3. Language (Dutch ability)	10	100
A4. Position before starting	2	20
A5. Previous experience	1	10
A6. Entrepreneur family members	1	10
A8. Foundation year of the enterprise	8	80
A10. Capital sources	4	40
A12. Nationality of employees	4	40
A13. Gender of employees	5	50
A14. Nationality of clients	1	10
A15. Gender of clients	3	30
A16. Sector	9	90

Tables 10.14, 10.15 and 10.16. For all classes of reasons, development of sales and profit last year the accuracy appears to be 1. Also, the accuracy and quality of classification are equal to 1. This value is the maximum value in all these cases. This means that on the basis of the chosen characteristics, female entrepreneurs and enterprises in our sample are fully discernible regarding the classes of decision variables.

The 'rules' – exact or approximate relationships between explanatory variables and dependent variables – offer the possibilities to extract conditional causal structures from our data set. Decision rules are conditional statements that are expressed in the form of 'if–then' statements. A rule may be exact or approximate. An exact (or deterministic) rule guarantees

Table 10.12 Frequency of attributes in reducts: development

Attribute	Frequency	Frequency (%)
A5. Previous experience	3	30
A6. Entrepreneur family members	2	20
A8. Foundation year of the enterprise	10	100
A10. Capital sources	3	30
A11. Number of employees	2	20
A12. Nationality of employees	3	30
A13. Gender of employees	4	40
A14. Nationality of clients	1	10
A15. Gender of clients	4	40
A16. Sector	10	100

Table 10.13 Frequency of attributes in reducts: profit

Attribute	Frequency	Frequency (%)
A2. Education level	1	10
A4. Position before starting	1	10
A5. Previous experience	2	20
A6. Entrepreneur family members	1	10
A8. Foundation year of the enterprise	10	100
A10. Capital sources	1	10
A12. Nationality of employees	2	20
A13. Gender of employees	6	60
A14. Nationality of clients	1	10
A15. Gender of clients	3	30
A16. Sector	3	30

that a particular combination of categories of the condition attributes results in only one particular category of the decision attribute (same conditions, same decisions). An approximate (or non-deterministic) rule, on the other hand, states that a particular combination of categories of the condition attributes corresponds to more than one category of the decision attribute (same conditions, different decisions). Therefore, only in the case of exact rules, using the information contained in the decision table, is it always possible to state with certainty whether an object belongs to a certain class of the decision variable. The quality of the decision rule is indicated by its strength. The strength of a rule represents the number of observations or cases that are in accordance with that rule. Tables 10.17,

Table 10.14 Accuracy and quality of the classification of the reasons to be entrepreneur

Reasons class	Accuracy	Lower approximation	Upper approximation
Independent	1	23	23
Other factors	1	11	11
Accuracy of classification:	1		
Quality of classification:	1		

Note: The accuracy for each class is the lower divided by the upper approximation.

Table 10.15 Accuracy and quality of the classification of the development of sales

Profit class	Accuracy	Lower approximation	Upper approximation
Increase	1	26	26
Non-increase	1	8	8
Accuracy of classification:	1		
Quality of classification:	1		

Note: The accuracy for each class is the lower divided by the upper approximation.

Table 10.16 Accuracy and quality of the classification of the profit

Development class	Accuracy	Lower approximation	Upper approximation
Increase	1	23	23
Non-increase	1	11	11
Accuracy of classification:	1		
Quality of classification:	1		

Note: The accuracy for each class is the lower divided by the upper approximation.

Table 10.17 Rules generated by the rough set analysis: reasons

Rules	Description of rules	Strength (#)	Strength (%)
Rule 1	(A4 = 1) & (A8 = 3) => (D = 1)	9	39.13
Rule 2	(A3 = 1) & (A4 = 1) & (A5 = 3) => (D = 1)	5	21.74
Rule 3	(A6 = 1) & (A8 = 4) & (A10 = 1) => (D = 1)	5	21.74
Rule 4	(A3 = 1) & (A8 = 2) & (A14 = 2) => (D = 2)	3	27.27
Rule 5	(A3 = 2) & (A13 = 1) => (D = 2)	2	18.18
Rule 6	(A1 = 3) & (A6 = 2) => (D = 2)	2	18.18

Table 10.18 Rules generated by the rough set analysis: development

Rules	Description of rules	Strength (#)	Strength (%)
Rule 1	(A8 = 2) => (D1 = 1)	10	43.48
Rule 2	(A8 = 3) & (A14 = 1) => (D1 = 1)	4	17.39
Rule 3	(A13 = 3) => (D1 = 1)	5	21.74
Rule 4	(A1 = 2) & (A13 = 4) => (D1 = 1)	6	26.09

10.18 and 10.19 show the rules and their strengths that can be generated from our data set. This information enables us to classify female entrepreneurs according to under which conditions they are successful and which kind of similarities can be found among them.

As can be seen in Tables 10.17, 10.18 and 10.19, all rules generated in the reasons to be entrepreneur and development of sales and profit of our information survey (using the classes of Table 10.17) are deterministic; in other words, all rules generated from our data set are exact rules. Therefore, we can say that these exact rules offer a sufficient condition of belonging to a decision class.

An overall evaluation of the decision rules shows that especially six condition attributes – A3 (language (Dutch ability)), A4 (position before starting), A6 (entrepreneur family members), A8 (foundation year of the enterprise), A11 (number of employees) and A13 (gender of employees) – determine the motivation and performance of female entrepreneurs. While a relatively higher language ability, a working experience and entrepreneur family members motivate women positively to become entrepreneurs (Table 10.20); a longer stay in the Netherlands and longer entrepreneurial activity contribute positively to the performance of relatively older entrepreneurs; whereas an entrepreneurial family tradition,

Table 10.19 Rules generated by the rough set analysis: profit

Rules	Description of rules	Strength (#)	Strength (%)
Rule 1	(A8 = 2) => (D2 = 1)	10	38.46
Rule 2	(A1 = 2) & (A8 = 3) => (D2 = 1)	10	38.46
Rule 3	(A11 = 2) & (A15 = 2)=> (D2 = 1)	5	19.23
Rule 4	(A8 = 3) & (A11 = 1) => (D2 = 1)	6	23.08

Table 10.20 Empirical results: rules / reasons

	If				Then
Rule 1	employed	+ 1996–2000 foundation		⟶	independent
Rule 2	fluent Dutch	+ employed	+ school experience	⟶	independent
Rule 3	entrepreneur family	+ 2001– foundation	+ family capital	⟶	independent
Rule 4	fluent Dutch	+ 1991–95	+ non-Turk clients	⟶	other factors
Rule 5	good Dutch	+ no employee		⟶	other factors
Rule 6	1981–2000 arrival	+ no entrepreneur family		⟶	other factors

family capital and ethnic clients contribute positively to the performance of relatively younger entrepreneurs and enterprises (Tables 10.21 and 10.22).

10.5 RETROSPECT AND PROSPECT

In recent years, we have observed the first signs of a new stage in the urban economy, where migrant females look for new opportunities in business. In parallel with the increasing trend in self-employment among immigrants and women, a new trend, namely an increasing business ownership by migrant females or, in other words, migrant female entrepreneurship, has emerged as a novel phenomenon. The question is whether the new niche of migrant female entrepreneurship opens new perspectives for socio-economic cohesion or even integration. Although the number of studies

Table 10.21 Empirical results: rules / development

	If			Then
Rule 1	1991–95 foundation			⟶ increase
Rule 2	1996–2000 foundation	+	Turk clients	⟶ increase
Rule 3	female clients			⟶ increase
Rule 4	1961–80 arrival	+	mixed (♀ + ♂) clients	⟶ increase

Table 10.22 Empirical results: rules / profit

	If			Then
Rule 1	1991–95 foundation			⟶ positive
Rule 2	1961–80 arrival	+	1996–2000 foundation	⟶ positive
Rule 3	1–5 employees	+	female clients	⟶ positive
Rule 4	1996–2000 foundation	+	no employee	⟶ positive

on migrant female entrepreneurship is limited, the available literature highlights new perspectives for socio-economic cohesion and integration.

Firstly, the available data show that migrant females comprise one of the fastest-growing groups of business owners and that they are more entrepreneurial than their migrant-male and native-female counterparts. Although migrant males continue to have the highest rates of business ownership, the ownership among migrant females is moving closer to that of their male counterparts.

Secondly, although the orientation in migrant entrepreneurship is generally internal and depends on ethnic sources in terms of products, clients and employees, the orientation of migrant female entrepreneurs is generally towards non-ethnic products and services. An escape from an enclave economy as well as subordination in patriarchal control mechanisms is commonly observed among migrant females in the labor market. The trend towards a mainly non-ethnic orientation by migrant female entrepreneurs is a novel and interesting perspective for the future labor market.

Thirdly, migrant female entrepreneurs may break not only their 'ethnic' chain, but also their 'feminine' chain, and they are making inroads into fields outside of the traditional 'ethnic' and 'feminine' occupations.

And fourthly, the findings of several studies show that migrant women entrepreneurs represent a potential source of continued new business growth that brings a broad range of international skills to the workforce. They are not only creating jobs for themselves, but they also stimulate job creation by hiring other employees.

The present chapter has investigated migrant female entrepreneurship and the driving forces and motivations that push or pull migrant females towards entrepreneurship, on the basis of case study research among Turkish female entrepreneurs in Amsterdam. The findings from this study are the following.

The results of our analysis, based on rough set analysis, show that the critical conditions in the driving forces, motivation and performance of migrant female entrepreneurs have emerged in six factors and attributes: (1) arrival year in the Netherlands; (2) education (language) and working experience; (3) foundation year of the enterprise; (4) size of the enterprise; (5) gender and nationality of clients; (6) family support (capital and entrepreneurial tradition).

While 'a longer stay in the Netherlands' and 'a longer lasting entrepreneurial activity' contribute positively to the performance of relatively older entrepreneurs, 'an entrepreneurial family tradition' and 'family capital' as well as 'ethnic clients' contribute positively to the performance of relatively younger entrepreneurs and enterprises. The reasons to become entrepreneur also stem from both 'language ability' and 'working experience', which are directly related to the years lived in the Netherlands.

The above findings are certainly provisional and call for more solid research. First, there is a need for a proper behavioral cultural–economic foundation of the emerging phenomenon of migrant female entrepreneurship. The opportunity costs of a regular market versus those in a risky entrepreneurial environment have to be weighed against each other. From an empirical perspective, it ought to be examined whether several motives and achievements of migrant female entrepreneurs are country-, gender- or culture-specific. In this framework, there is a need for solid comparative research from different cities, using for example meta-analytic research techniques. This would also require a further analysis of regulations (formal and informal) and their impacts on the entrepreneurial market. So it is clear that the field of migrant female entrepreneurship may offer fertile ground for original and policy-relevant research.

NOTE

1. The ROSE software is available at: http://www-idss.cs.put.poznan.pl/rose/.

REFERENCES

Albelda, R.P. (1986), 'Occupational segregation by race and gender, 1958–1981', *Industrial and Labor Relations Review*, **39**(3), 404–11.

Barrett, G.A., T.P. Jones and D. McEvoy (1996), 'Ethnic minority business: theoretical discourse in Britain and North America', *Urban Studies*, **33**(4–5), 783–809.

Basu, A. (1998), 'An exploration of entrepreneurial activity among Asian small business in Britain', *Small Business Economics*, **10**(4), 313–26.

Baycan-Levent, T., E. Masurel and P. Nijkamp (2003), 'Diversity in entrepreneurship: ethnic and female roles in urban economic life', *International Journal of Social Economics*, **30**(11), 1131–61.

Baycan-Levent, T., E. Masurel and P. Nijkamp (2006), 'Gender differences in ethnic entrepreneurship', *International Journal of Entrepreneurship and Innovation Management*, **6**(3), 173–90.

van den Bergh, J.C.J.M., K. Button, P. Nijkamp and G. Pepping (1998), *Meta-analysis in Environmental Economics*, Dordrecht: Kluwer.

Borjas, G.J. (1986), 'The self-employment experience of immigrants', *Journal of Human Resources*, **21**(4), 485–506.

Borjas, G.J. (1990), *Friends or Strangers: The Impact of Immigrants on the US Economy*, New York: Basic Books.

Bruce, D. (1999), 'Do husbands matter? Married women entering self-employment', *Small Business Economics*, **13**, 317–29.

Brush, C.G. (1992), 'Research on women business owners: past trends, a new perspective and future directions', *Entrepreneurship Theory and Practice*, **17**(4), 5–30.

Brush, C. and R.D. Hisrich (1999), 'Women-owned businesses: why do they matter?' in Z.J. Acs (ed.), *Are Small Firms Important? Their Role and Impact*, Washington, DC: US Small Business Administration, Kluwer Academic Publishers, pp. 111–27.

Bull, E. and F. Winter (1991), 'Community differences in business births and business growths', *Journal of Business Venturing*, **6**, 29–43.

Buttner, E.H. and D.P. Moore (1997), 'Women's organizational exodus to entrepreneurship: self-reported motivations and correlates with success', *Journal of Small Business Management*, **35**(1), 34–46.

CEEDR (2000), 'Young entrepreneurs, women entrepreneurs, ethnic minority entrepreneurs and co-entrepreneurs in the European Union and Central and Eastern Europe', Final Report to the European Commission, DG Enterprise, Centre for Enterprise and Economic Development Research (CEEDR), Middlesex University Business School, UK.

Center for Women's Business Research (2004), 'Business owned by women of color in the United States, 2004: a fact sheet', http://www.womensbusiness research.org.

Center for Women's Business Research (2005), 'Top facts about women-owned businesses', http://www.womensbusinessresearch.org/topfacts.html.
Constant, A. (2004), 'Immigrant versus native businesswomen: proclivity and performance', IZA Discussion Paper No. 1234.
Cross, M. (ed.) (1992), *Ethnic Minorities and Industrial Change in Europe and North America*, Cambridge: Cambridge University Press.
Dallalfar, A. (1994), 'Iranian women as immigrant entrepreneurs', *Gender and Society*, **8**(4), 541–61.
Danson, M.W. (1995), 'New firm formation and regional economic development', *Small Business Economics*, **7**, 81–7.
Davidsson, P. (1995), 'Culture structure and regional levels of entrepreneurship', *Entrepreneurship and Regional Development*, **7**, 41–62.
Deakins, D. (1999), *Entrepreneurship and Small Firms*, 2nd edition, London: McGraw Hill.
Deakins, D., M. Majunder and A. Paddison (1997), 'Developing success strategies for ethnic minorities in business: evidence from Scotland', *New Community*, **23**, 325–342.
van Delft, H., C. Gorter and P. Nijkamp (2000), 'In search of ethnic entrepreneurship in the city', *Environmental Planning C*, **18**, 429–51.
Deogun J., V. Raghavan, A. Sarkar and H. Sever (1997), 'Data mining: trends in research and development', in T.Y. Lin and N. Cercone (1997) *Rough Sets and Data Mining: Analysis for Imprecise Data*, Dordrecht: Kluwer, pp. 4–46.
Donthu, N. and J. Cherian (1994), 'Impact of strength of ethnic identification on Hispanic shopping behaviour', *Journal of Retailing*, **70**(4), 383–93.
Dyer, L.M. and C.A. Ross (2000), 'Ethnic enterprises and their clientele', *Journal of Small Business Management*, **38**(2), 48–66.
Fairlie, R.W. (2005), 'Entrepreneurship among disadvantaged groups: an analysis of the dynamics of self-employment by gender, race, and education', in S.C. Parker, Z.J. Acs and D.R. Audretsch (eds), *Handbook of Entrepreneurship*, Kluwer Academic Publishers, pp. 437–75.
Fairlie, R.W. and B.D. Meyer (1996), 'Ethnic and racial self-employment differences and possible explanations', *Journal of Human Resources*, **31**(4), 757–93.
Famili, A., W.M. Shen, R. Weber and E. Simoudis (1997), 'Data preprocessing and intelligent data analysis', *Intelligent Data Analysis*, **1**(1), 33–47.
Fayyad, U., G. Piatetsky-Shapiro and P. Smyth (1996), 'From data mining to knowledge discovery: an overview', *Artificial Intelligence Magazine*, **17**, 37–54.
Fischer, E.M., A.R. Reuber and L.S. Dyke (1993), 'A theoretical overview and extension of research on sex, gender, and entrepreneurship', *Journal of Business Venturing*, **8**(2), 2151–68.
Gilbertson, G.A. (1995), 'Women's labor and enclave employment: the case of Dominican and Colombian women in New York City', *International Migration Review*, **29**(3), 657–70.
Global Entrepreneurship Monitor (GEM) (2004), *Global Entrepreneurship Monitor United Kingdom*, London: London Business School.
Gorter, C., P. Nijkamp and J. Poot (eds) (1998), *Crossing Borders*, Aldershot: Ashgate.
Hillman, F. (1999), 'A look at the "hidden side": Turkish women in Berlin's ethnic labor market', *International Journal of Urban and Regional Research*, **23**(27), 267–82.

Johnson, P.J. (2000), 'Ethnic differences in self-employment among Southeast Asian refugees in Canada', *Journal of Small Business Management*, **38**(4), 78–86.
Kalleberg, A.L. and K.T. Leicht (1991), 'Gender and organizational performance: determinants of small business survival and success', *Academy of Management Journal*, **34**(1), 136–61.
Kloosterman, R.C., J. van der Leun and J. Rath (1998), 'Across the border: economic opportunities, social capital and informal businesses activities of immigrants', *Journal of Ethnic Migration Studies*, **24**, 367–76.
Koreen, M. (2001), 'Women entrepreneurs in SMEs: realising the benefits of globalisation and the knowledge-based economy: synthesis', *OECD Conference on Women Entrepreneurs in SMEs: Realising the Benefits of Globalisation and the Knowledge-Based Economy*, OECD Proceedings.
Kossoudji, S.A. and S.I. Ranney (1984), 'The labor market experience of female migrants: the case of temporary Mexican migration to the US', *International Migration Review*, **18**(4), 1120–43.
Lee, Y., T. Cameroen, P. Schaeffer and C.G. Schmidt (1997), 'Ethnic minority small business: a comparative analysis of restaurants in Denver', *Urban Geography*, **18**(7), 591–621.
Letowski, M.A. (2001), 'Improving statistics on women entrepreneurs', *Second OECD Conference on Women Entrepreneurs in SMEs: Realising the Benefits of Globalisation and the Knowledge-Based Economy*, OECD Proceedings.
Lohmann, H. (2001), 'Self-employed or employee, full-time of part-time? Gender differences in the determinants and conditions for self-employment in Europe and the US', MZES Working Papers No. 38.
Masurel, E., P. Nijkamp, M. Tastan and G. Vindigni (2002), 'Motivations and performance conditions for ethnic entrepreneurship', *Growth and Change*, **33**(2), 238–60.
Morokvasic, M. (1988), *Minority and immigrant women in self-employment and business in France, Great Britain, Italy, Portugal and Federal Republic of Germany*. Commission of the European Communities, V/1871/88-EN, Paris.
Nielsen, P.B. (2001), 'Statistics on start-ups and survival of women entrepreneurs: the Danish experience', *Second OECD Conference on Women Entrepreneurs in SMEs: Realising the Benefits of Globalisation and the Knowledge-Based Economy*, OECD Proceedings.
OECD (1998), *First OECD Conference on Women Entrepreneurs in SMEs*, OECD Proceedings.
OECD (2001a), *Second OECD Conference on Women Entrepreneurs in SMEs: Realising the Benefits of Globalisation and the Knowledge-Based Economy*, OECD Proceedings.
OECD (2001b), '*Issues related to statistics on women's entrepreneurship*', Workshop on Firm-Level Statistics, 26–27 November, DSTI/EAS/IND/SWP/AH(2001)11.
OECD (2006), *International Migration Outlook*, SOPEMI 2006 Edition, Paris: OECD.
Pawlak, Z. (1991), *Rough Sets: Theoretical Aspects of Reasoning About Data*, Dordrecht: Kluwer.
Pawlak, Z. (1992), 'Rough sets: introduction', in R. Slowinski (ed.), *Intelligent Decision Support: Handbook of Applications and Advances of the Rough Set Theory*, Dordrecht: Kluwer, pp. 1–2.
Pearce, S.C. (2005), 'Today's immigrant woman entrepreneur', *Immigration Policy in Focus*, **4**(1), 1–17.

Ram, M. (1994a), *Managing to Survive: Working Lives in Small Firms*, Oxford: Blackwell.

Ram, M. (1994b), 'Unravelling social networks in ethnic minority firms', *International Small Business Journal*, **12**(3), 42–53.

Rettab, B. (2001), *The Emergence of Ethnic Entrepreneurship: A Conceptual Framework*, Zoetermeer: EIM/Business & Policy Research.

Rietz, A.D. and M. Henrekson (2000), 'Testing female underperformance hypothesis', *Small Business Economics*, **14**, 1–10.

Rosa, P., D. Hamilton, S. Carter and H. Burns (1994), 'The impact of gender on small business management: preliminary findings of a British study', *International Small Business Journal*, **12**(3), 25–32.

Schoeni, R.F. (1998), 'Labor market outcomes of immigrant women in the United States: 1970 to 1990', *International Migration Review*, **32**(1), 57–77.

Slowinski, R. (1995), *Intelligent Decision Support: Handbook of Applications and Advances of Rough Set Theory*, Dordrecht: Kluwer.

Verheul, I., P. Risseeuw and G. Bartelse (2001), 'Gender differences in strategy and human resource management', Rotterdam Institute for Business Economic Studies 2001/3.

Verheul, I., A. van Stel and R. Thurik (2004), 'Explaining female and male entrepreneurship across 29 countries', EIM Business & Policy Research, SCALES-paper N200403.

Verheul, I. and R. Thurik (2001), 'Start-up capital: "Does gender matter"', *Small Business Economics*, **16**, 329–45.

Waldinger, R., H. Aldrich and R. Ward (eds) (1990), *Ethnic Entrepreneurs*, Newbury Park, CA: Sage Publishers.

Weeks, J.R. (2001), 'The face of women entrepreneurs: what we know today', *Second OECD Conference on Women Entrepreneurs in SMEs: Realising the Benefits of Globalisation and the Knowledge-Based Economy*, OECD Proceedings.

Wilson, K.L. and A. Portes (1980), 'Immigrant enclaves: an analysis of the labour market experiences of Cubans in Miami', *American Journal of Sociology*, **86**, 295–319.

Wright, R. and M. Ellis (2000), 'The ethnic and gender division of labor compared among immigrants to Los Angeles', *International Journal of Urban and Regional Research*, **24**(3), 583–600.

Zhou, M. and J.R. Logan (1989), 'Returns on human capital in ethnic enclaves: New York City's Chinatown', *American Sociological Review*, **54**(5), 809–20.

Ziarco, W. (1998), 'Rough set as a methodology for data mining', in A. Skowron and L. Polkowski (eds), *Rough Set in Knowledge Discovering*, Heidelberg: Physica Verlag, pp. 554–76.

11. Industrial effects on resource acquisition: immigrant enterprises in Kista, Stockholm

Tobias Dalhammar and Terrence E. Brown

11.1 INTRODUCTION

The number of companies run by immigrants and ethnic minority entrepreneurs in Sweden is almost three times the level of 10–15 years ago (SOU, 1999). In 1998, there were about 65 000 immigrant enterprises in Sweden. Proportionally, the number of immigrant and ethnic businesses is still below the general population. However, the number of ethnic enterprises is rising, since around 20 per cent of all new firms in Sweden in 2001 were founded by people 'descending from other countries', which is the official definition for an immigrant entrepreneur.[1] These companies are slightly over-represented in the service sector compared to the manufacturing sector, 21 and 17 per cent, respectively. Furthermore, there are important regional differences. The highest numbers are found in the four counties (*'län'*) of Stockholm, Södermanland, Västmanland and Skåne, where the number of immigrant start-ups was about 25 per cent in 2001. Reasons for starting businesses are similar to those of mainstream (that is, majority) entrepreneurs, for example independency and fulfilling one's ambitions, with the exception that a higher amount of immigrant and ethnic entrepreneurs start a business as a means of avoiding or escaping unemployment (ITPS, 2002).

However, research shows that there are great differences in business activity, behaviour and performance between ethnic groups, in Sweden as well as internationally (Waldinger et al., 1990, 2000; Najib, 1999; NUTEK, 2001a, 2001b; Abbasian, 2003; Mitchell, 2003). Obviously, differences also occur at the individual level (Ram and Smallbone, 2001; Abbasian, 2003). Consequently, a person is not predetermined to a certain kind of business activity just because they belong to a definable ethnic group. And voices have been raised asserting that immigrant entrepreneurship is no homogeneous phenomenon (Najib, 1999; Ram and Smallbone, 2001; Chaganti and Greene, 2002), despite previous policy documents that have been presented (SOU, 1999; NUTEK, 2001a, 2001b). For example, Najib (1999) states that immigrants run businesses in all kinds of industries and settings, including high-technology environments. This also implies that there are contextual aspects to immigrant and ethnic entrepreneurship (Waldinger et al., 1990, 2000; Abbasian, 2003). This presents a view different from the established one, where restaurants and other service-related businesses, such as corner shops, are common references (Najib, 1999).

Immigrant and ethnic entrepreneurship have been researched from a variety of angles. In principle, two basic variables are commonly employed in order to explain differences in entrepreneurial activity between ethnic minority groups (Waldinger et al., 1990, 2000; Najib, 1999). The first one concerns cultural (pull) factors, which derive from ethnicity, above all collective ethnic properties. This view emphasizes the meaning of entrepreneurship in different cultures, such as the propensity to enterprise in the homelands. Cultural factors in this sense equate the concept of ethnic group characteristics. The structural (push) perspective, on the other hand, studies the differences in business activities in structural factors on the labour market. One example is that immigrants in general are discriminated against on the labour market. This implies that structural factors equate to contextual opportunity structures.

Still, both cultural and structural theories have difficulty in explaining why ethnic minority groups show such great differences in business activities despite the fact that discrimination generally means that ethnic minorities are treated in a similar manner (Waldinger et al., 1990, 2000; Light and Gold, 2000). Therefore, a third view deals with a combination of cultural and structural factors. Some researchers (for example Waldinger et al., 1990, 2000) argue that cultural and structural factors overlap each other and therefore are difficult to divide.[2] By this view, either culture or structure is dominant, and the other is complementary (Najib, 1999). This situational approach – also known as the interactive theory – deals with the relationship between cultural or social characteristics and the circumstances of immigrants' arrival and settlement (Mitchell, 2003). The decisive factors could be different for each ethnic minority group, which diminishes the possibility of using a general theoretical approach as a means of understanding immigrant and ethnic entrepreneurship.

11.2 AN INDUSTRIAL PERSPECTIVE ON IMMIGRANT AND ETHNIC ENTREPRENEURSHIP

In the literature and debate about immigrant and ethnic entrepreneurship there is often a lack of clarity concerning what these conceptions mean and include. Waldinger et al. (1990, p. 3) define ethnic entrepreneurship as: 'a set of connections and regular patterns of interaction among people sharing common national background or migration experiences'. In general, 'ethnic entrepreneurship' means entrepreneurship referring to certain ethnic groups, whereas 'immigrant entrepreneurship' refers to entrepreneurship performed by all groups of immigrants in a country (Waldinger et al., 1990, 2000). This means that in the past and at present, entrepreneurs' self-reported ethnic origin is the most commonly used definition of ethnicity (Light, 1973; Waldinger et al., 1990, 2000; Najib, 1999).

However, Chaganti and Greene (2002) convincingly argue that instead of ethnic origin, the owner-manager's degree of personal involvement in the ethnic community is a more accurate measure of the 'ethnicity' of a business. As a result, what decides how to categorize an entrepreneur is the level of involvement among co-ethnics, that is, utilization of ethnic resources and thus ethnicity as a resource. The level of ethnic community involvement is a useful indicator, since it points at the dependence of a business on the ethnic community. And dependence is likely to determine whether resources available in the ethnic community determine boundaries to growth of ethnic businesses, or if owners will seek and can access and exploit opportunities available in the larger mainstream economy. In the longer run, this determines how the ethnic minority background of the individual(s) involved influences the operation of their business.

As mentioned above, what ethnic entrepreneurs access by ethnic involvement is commonly referred to as 'ethnic resources' (Waldinger, 1990, 2000; Light and Gold, 2000; Ram and Smallbone, 2001). Ethnic resources are socio-cultural features that co-ethnic business owners utilize in business or from which their businesses passively benefit. If used strategically, ethnic resources could become a competitive advantage (Ram and Smallbone, 2001). In this sense ethnicity in itself becomes a resource (Pripp, 2001). Despite many benefits of ethnic resources and connections (financial capital, advice, labour and so on), ethnic resources may operate within a context that may limit freedom and impose restrictions that constrain gainful activities (Light and Gold, 2000). In fact, if no other 'mainstream' resources are available, entrepreneurs may be left with no choice but to utilize ethnic resources. And these ethnic resources (for example labour) may not be the most qualified or suitable for the business.

Chaganti and Greene (2002, p. 141) argue: 'A high tech business run by a highly educated ethnic entrepreneur is likely to seek rapid growth and need the same types of resources as those needed by a "mainstream" owner's high tech business.' And although there may be greater hindrances for immigrant and ethnic entrepreneurs, the authors claim that the chances are great that they would obtain the resources necessary. This implies that high-tech immigrant and ethnic entrepreneurs have similar rationales and face similar conditions as their mainstream counterparts. At the same time, Chaganti and Greene (2002) propose that small service firms anchored in ethnic communities may not have the same needs as their high-tech counterparts. These service-based firms face other conditions, not to mention different rationales for engaging in business activities. Therefore, they have a tendency to draw more on ethnic resources. This suggests that type of industry or firm has an impact on the degree of ethnic community involvement, which in turn influences the utilization of ethnic resources.

In opposition to Chaganti and Greene's (2002) suggestions above, Saxenian (2001, p. 82) concludes: 'It appears that the most successful high tech immigrant entrepreneurs in Silicon Valley today are those who have drawn on ethnic resources while simultaneously integrating into mainstream technology and business networks.' The problem is that Saxenian's (2001) findings are based on research in a certain context, namely Silicon Valley in the USA. In Silicon Valley today, there exist large ethnic communities of Chinese and Asian Indian high-tech enterprises, and these are the two groups Saxenian has researched. There is a great possibility that results would be different when researching high-tech immigrant entrepreneurs with other ethnic backgrounds in other business contexts in the world. Thus, the value of Saxenian's (2001) study is to a great extent context-specific and cannot merely be transferred to conditions in Sweden. However, her findings imply that focus should be put on the resources needed (including ethnic resources) in relation to the industry and context within which immigrant and ethnic entrepreneurs are embedded.

11.2.1 Science- and Technology-based versus Service-based Firms

As discussed earlier, conditions for immigrant and ethnic businesses in high-technology settings are likely to be different from those of immigrant and ethnic businesses in more 'traditional' sectors. However, the term 'high-technology' has been used with little care over the years. According to Bozkaya et al. (2003), technology-based small firms (TBSFs) are innovative enterprises also widely known as 'high-technology' start-ups. In a definition proposed by Allen (1992, in Bozkaya et al., 2003, p. 6)[3] TBSFs are: 'businesses whose products or services depend largely on the application of scientific and technological knowledge, or as businesses whose activities embrace a significant technology component as a major source of competitive advantage'. These start-ups are normally based on unique characteristics (as in terms of professional knowledge) of the individual venture, and these businesses are generally located in industries such as aviation, communications, information technology, biotechnology, electronics and medical life sciences (Bozkaya et al., 2003).

In a similar manner, Keeble and Wilkinson (2000, pp. 3–4) apply 'high-technology' (as opposed to other firms and industries) to:

> firms and industries whose products or services embody new, innovative and advanced technologies developed by the application of scientific and technological expertise. Such firms almost invariably regard such expertise and resultant technological leadership as the firm's leading competitive advantage, and are usually identified in practice by high R&D-intensity (high levels of research and development expenditure and/or employment relative to turnover or total workforce).

Note that by this definition, service firms could also be high-tech businesses, albeit that they need to involve innovative and advanced technologies to meet the requirements. Still, when including the aspect of advanced technology, we find this definition useful as a means of making a distinction between technology-based and service-based firms. From now on we equate the terms of high-tech and science- and technology-based firms, and put them in opposition to service-based firms.

Gartner (1985) concludes that many research samples in entrepreneurship are selected without accounting for type of firm or industry. And of those studies that have taken an industrial perspective, few attempts have been made to compare firms in different industries to find out what difference the type of firm might make in the process of venture creation and development. Entrepreneurs form very different kinds of organizations and it is about time that entrepreneurship researchers stopped talking about entrepreneurial organizations as a certain type. Differences in industrial settings and other issues mean that the kind of organization emerging has an important impact on the development of firms.

Samuelsson's (2001) research shows there are significant systematic differences between firms exploiting innovative and those exploiting equilibrium (imitative) venture opportunities. His empirical findings reveal that innovative venture opportunities are characterized by a 'specialist' strategy and tacit knowledge, and are more likely to acquire specific resources needed to exploit the opportunity (utilitarian reinforcement). This activity involves the creation of new transactions. Accordingly, exploiting innovative venture opportunities is more oriented towards risk and new markets, where first-mover advantage is a potential opportunity and 'liability of newness' (Stinchcombe, 1965) a potential threat. In opposition to this, exploiting equilibrium venture opportunities involves existing market transactions and such activities tend to imitate existing ventures. A market is in place and a ready concept can often be used when setting the course for the business, which means that the potential pitfalls are less. This implies that exploiting equilibrium venture opportunities should be a shorter and more straightforward process. The big threat is the existence of heavy competition.

In relation to type of industry or firm, it seems that the division between exploiting innovative and equilibrium (imitative) venture opportunities is applicable also to the division between science-and technology-based and service-based firms, although it does not correspond in all ways. As an example, a firm that exploits an ethnic niche could be innovative in the sense that it creates a new market and explores previously unexplored terrain. However, in principle the division between innovative and equilibrium venture opportunities is applicable to the type of industry or firm. Innovative ventures are generally high-tech, science- and technology-based firms, and equilibrium ventures are generally service-based firms.

11.3 RESOURCE ACQUISITION AND THE RESOURCE-BASED VIEW

Firms interact with the surroundings because they need resources (Gartner, 1985; Light and Gold, 2000; Alvarez and Busenitz, 2001). In fact, Light and Gold (2000) regard the concept referred to as 'entrepreneurial capacity' as just a cipher for the resources that create it. A new firm emerges when the individual(s) involved identify, assemble and configure resources; thus resources are one of the defining properties of new ventures, contributing to the character of the emerging organization (Katz and Gartner, 1988; Barney, 1991; Alvarez and Busenitz, 2001). Over time, some resources are reorganized, new ones are acquired, some become specialized and others may become idle (Brush et al., 1997).

A resource acquisition perspective has its roots in the resource-based view (Penrose, 1959 [1985]; Barney, 1991; Brush et al., 1997). According to this view, organizations are comprised of heterogeneous bundles of resources, defined as: 'all tangible and intangible assets that are tied to the firm in a relatively permanent fashion' (Brush et al., 1997),[4] or as 'all assets, capabilities, organizational processes, firm attributes, information, knowledge, etc. controlled by a firm that enable [it to] improve its efficiency and effectiveness' (Barney, 1991, p. 101). The acquisition of resources and their combinations provide a firm's strengths, and optimally are a source of competitive advantage (Penrose, 1959 [1985]; Barney, 1991; Alvarez and Busenitz, 2001). The acquisition of resources then becomes a key activity for new ventures, since these normally start out with a scarce resource base (Aldrich, 1999; Johannisson, 2000).

11.3.1 Resources in Relation to Immigrant and Ethnic Entrepreneurship

Different researchers have defined a number of resources (Greene and Brown, 1997; Greene et al., 1997). All resources are forms of capital (Light and Gold, 2000). In immigrant and ethnic entrepreneurship literature, resources commonly have been discussed in a way that deals with how immigrant and ethnic entrepreneurs possess and acquire so-called 'mainstream' resources in relation to ethnic resources (Waldinger et al., 1990, 2000; Pripp, 2001; Saxenian, 2001; Chaganti and Greene, 2002; Abbasian, 2003). Light and Gold (2000, pp. 83–4) develop this further and make the distinction between 'class resources' and 'ethnic resources'. While class resources refer to social status and not to ethnic origin, ethnic resources are acquired differently and cannot be applied to resources dependent on class, which numerous examples show (Light and Gold, 2000; Pripp, 2001; Saxenian, 2001; Chaganti and Greene, 2002). Light and Gold (2000) refer to four types of capital in relation to class resources: financial, cultural, social and human capital. Immigrant and ethnic enterprises are expected to utilize both class and ethnic resources in different proportions.

Ethnic resources are socio-cultural and demographic features of a whole ethnic group from which co-ethnic entrepreneurs benefit actively or passively. Ethnic resources characterize a whole group, not just isolated members and not just high-status members:

> Typical ethnic resources include kinship and marriage systems, relationships of trust, ethnic-derived social capital, cultural assumptions, religion, native language fluency, a middleman heritage, entrepreneurial values and attitudes, rotating credit associations, relative satisfaction arising from nonacculturation to prevailing labor and living standards, reactive solidarities, multiplex social networks, employer paternalism, an ideology of ethnic solidarity, and a generous pool of underemployed and disadvantaged coethnic workers. (Light and Gold, 2000, p. 102)

In practice, money from co-ethnics (financial capital), co-ethnic labour, ethnic traditions of business ownership and business expertise, and ethnic consumer demand are the most useful measures of ethnic involvement and dependency. These resources are normally built on mutual trust (Light and Gold, 2000).

Financial capital is basically the economic resources tied to the business activity. For ethnic entrepreneurs, the ethnic community and the ethnic network often provide opportunities for financial assistance (Waldinger et al., 1990, 2000; Light and Gold, 2000). Typically, such arrangements have the character of informal borrowing and lending, sometimes with interest, based on mutual tacit understanding of the rules of the game. Although this kind of credit-giving activity has been regarded and stated as a valuable resource exclusive to certain ethnic groups, these loans have to be paid back sooner or later, just as any other loans. And examples show that the very existence of such arrangements could indicate that these people have problems in borrowing money from 'mainstream' sources (Light and Gold, 2000).

Human capital means an individual's investment in personal productivity. Formal education such as university education, and informal education such as work experience, are the basic forms of human capital. Besides, non-formal education, like adult education, may increase an individual's human capital (Light and Gold, 2000; Davidsson and Honig, 2003). Human capital also includes a number of other variables, where for example language skills are suggested to be important for immigrant and ethnic entrepreneurs. These are referred to as knowledge, and knowledge may be defined as either tacit (know-how) or explicit (know-what). Davidsson and Honig (2003, p. 306) state that: 'tacit knowledge refers to know-how, the often noncodified components of activity. Know-what consists of the explicit type of information normally conveyed in procedures, processes, formal written documents and educational institutions'. Previous studies show that formal education increases the individual's likelihood of engaging in nascent activities, but that it does not determine success in the exploitation process (Davidsson and Honig, 2003).

Bourdieu (1979, in Light and Gold, 2000, p. 91) defines cultural capital: 'as competence in a society's high-status culture'. For the study of immigrant and ethnic entrepreneurship, cultural capital is best translated as the knowledge of how to acquire 'mainstream' forms of capital in a society. Human capital, for example, increases its owner's productivity, a competence rewarded with higher productivity and income, whereas cultural capital reflects prestige recognition for which people get for example desirable education and business contacts. This means that education or work experience could have value as both human and cultural capital. The difference depends upon the priorities of the entrepreneur as to whether the emphasis is on the real vocational experience or the importance of prestige recognition (Light and Gold, 2000).

One definition of social capital is: 'the arrangement of human resources to improve flows of future income' (Light and Gold, 2000, p. 94). And Davidsson and Honig (2003, p. 307) state: 'Social capital theory refers to the ability of actors to extract benefits from their social structures, networks and memberships. Social networks provided by extended family, community-based or organizational relationships are theorized to supplement the effects of education, experience and financial capital.' A fruitful way is to utilize social capital broadly in terms of social exchange to examine the effects of exchange ties on performance. Ties that result in social capital can occur at both individual and organizational levels, although they are commonly attributed to the individuals involved (Aldrich, 1999; Davidsson and Honig, 2003). Thus, access to social relations that facilitate entrepreneurship increases a person's entrepreneurial social capital, and the simplest form of social capital is a network of strong (bonding) and weak (bridging) social ties (Ardichivili et al., 2003; Davidsson and Honig, 2003). 'The contribution of social networks to entrepreneurship is the most important discovery in the last generation. Entrepreneurs make extensive and important use of social networks when starting and running a business' (Light and Gold, 2000, p. 264). Cultural capital includes the knowledge of what social capital is, how to obtain it and how to use it. Nevertheless, cultural capital and social capital are distinguished by the fact that cultural capital means the knowledge of how to obtain and use 'mainstream' resources, and social capital means the actual acquisition and possession of those resources. Unlike financial capital, which decreases with use, social capital increases with use. And unlike human and cultural capital, which a learner absorbs, social capital remains an external resource (Light and Gold, 2000).

Although all types of resources are important, when looking at resource acquisition aspects, social capital stands out as being extraordinarily crucial (Davidsson and Honig, 2003). A lack of social capital generally leads to a lack of other resources as well. Many researchers have emphasized the importance of social and professional networks, and for businesses with scarce resources, networking more or less equates to actions of resource acquisition (Aldrich, 1999; Johannisson, 2000, 2001; Saxenian, 2001).

11.4 CONCEPTUAL FRAMEWORK

Gartner (1985) presents a framework including four perspectives or dimensions in order to understand early firm development: the characteristics of the individual(s) involved; the organization under creation; the environment surrounding the new venture and its influence; and the very process by which the new venture is started. Although he does not claim this framework to be complete, Gartner (1985) convincingly argues that no description of a venture is complete without taking these four perspectives into account. He suggests that an integration of these perspectives is needed to describe the multidimensional phenomenon of new venture creation. Thus, the framework provides a systematic means of comparing and contrasting complex ventures, that is, conceptualizing variation and complexity. The value of such an approach is also applicable in a narrowly selected research sample in order to avoid making too hasty conclusions about the virtual sameness of businesses in a sample (Gartner, 1985).

In our conceptual framework for this study, we use Gartner's (1985) framework and specifically focus on some aspects related to each dimension in the framework. Those aspects will be emphasized in the remainder of this chapter. They are all connected to the discussions conducted above. Although many matters are of interest, we specifically focus on aspects that can be related to: type of industry or firm (the organizational dimension); proactive behaviour of the individual(s) involved (the individual dimension); interaction with actors in the business support system (the environmental dimension); and firm-specific aspects of resource acquisition (the process dimension). Figure 11.1, which is an elaboration of Gartner's (1985) framework, illustrates the conceptual framework for this study.

The conceptual framework incorporates important aspects of the theoretical discussion conducted above and is the 'lens' through which we study the empirical context. The four cornerstones summarize a number of interactions among the dimensions: various types of resources in the resource acquisition efforts of the organization; the individual(s) involved; the interaction with the environment; and the very process by which the resource acquisition process takes place. And according to Alvarez and Busenitz (2001), who discuss the connection between entrepreneurship and the resource-based view, resources can be used as the unit of analysis in entrepreneurship studies. Resources can be studied at each dimension, since a resource acquisition perspective makes it practically possible to organize these at an overall firm level. Therefore, combining the four perspectives with a resource acquisition perspective represents a theoretical as well as a methodological tool.

Type of industry or firm (industry and business logics) represents the organizational or firm level. As previously discussed, service-based immigrant and ethnic businesses are expected to draw on ethnic resources to a higher degree than high-tech immigrant and ethnic businesses, which instead are expected to draw more on 'mainstream' resources (Chaganti and Greene, 2002). 'Proactivity' deals with the attitudes and behaviour of the individual(s) involved. The terms proactive and reactive behaviour

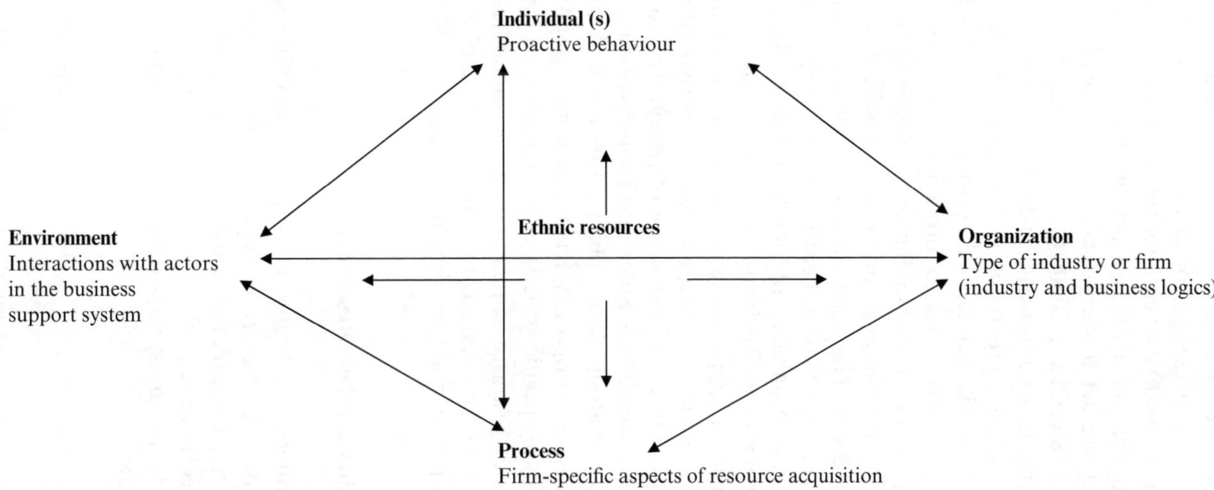

Figure 11.1 The conceptual framework for this study. An elaboration on Gartner's (1985, p. 698) framework for describing new venture creation

reflect different behaviours towards venture opportunities (Bateman and Crant, 1993; Becherer and Maurer, 1999). A person that exerts proactive behaviour acts toward and exploits or creates opportunities, regardless of whether these are innovative or equilibrium in character. On the other hand, reactive behaviour means that a person does not have the same alertness to perceive and act toward opportunities (Kirzner, 1973) or to create opportunities (Swedberg, 2000; Gartner et al., 2003). Although there is practical value in separating individuals and firms, these still are intertwined and can be said to represent two sides of the same coin. Every venture opportunity, regardless of type of industry or firm, involves people, and these can exhibit various degrees of proactive and reactive behaviour. In this sense, action is one of the fundamental aspects in the process of starting up, developing and running a firm (Johannisson, 2000; Holmquist, 2003; Gartner et al., 2003). The importance of actions and behaviours of individuals gives recognition to what Penrose (1959 [1985]) states: management is the most critical resource of all for a firm (Pitelis, 2002).

Further, the influence of the environment is incorporated in interaction with actors in the business support system. This includes how individual(s) involved in a business engage in relationships and networking activities, above all with actors in the business support system, to acquire crucial resources (see Johannisson, 2000). Since new businesses usually start out with scarce resources (Aldrich, 1999), the interactions with and support from actors in the business support system are of utmost importance. The fourth dimension is the specific process each venture goes through, and firm-specific aspects of resource acquisition. A deeper understanding of this dimension can only be obtained by using a methodology that pays attention to the complexity and variation in each case, as well as listens to the individual(s) involved in the cases.

11.4.1 Operationalizing Ethnic Resources

In the conceptual framework (Figure 11.1) we include ethnic resources as a means of investigating the importance of ethnic minority background in the process of acquiring resources for the development of a firm. Utilizing ethnic resources affects the acquisition of all other types of resources. As mentioned before, the five most important kinds of resources in relation to ethnic resources are:

- Ethnic sources for financial capital, for example rotating credit associations.
- Ethnic sources for organizational capital, mainly labour and crucial internal business skills.

- Ethnic origin of human capital of the individual(s) involved, for example a historical proclivity towards business activities in certain industries, and thereby through 'ethnic training' acquisition of adequate business skills.
- Ethnic consumer demand, for example a certain kind of food or products targeted at or wanted by a definable ethnic group.

Further, one additional dimension can be added that emphasizes the importance of social capital:

- Ethnic sources for social capital, for example business expertise and crucial intermediary relations.

These five aspects are in focus when studying the importance of ethnic resources among the firms in the empirical case studies.

11.5 STUDY

This chapter is based on empirical case studies of seven businesses located in Kista in Stockholm, the capital of Sweden. Kista is the most northern district of Stockholm. It includes the units Kista, Akalla and Husby. Almost 30 000 people live in the Kista district and about as many people work there. Kista is an interesting area for more than one reason. First, it hosts a large concentration of ICT (information and communications technology) industry. Over a longer life cycle, the industry in Kista has expanded steadily, and by 2004 there were more than 2000 companies in the Kista district.[5] During the first quarter of 2004, 26 433 people worked in Kista: 17 360 in ICT companies and 9073 in other kinds of firms.[6] A common reference for this ICT focus is Kista Science City.[7] This technology focus is further emphasized by the fact that many ICT and knowledge-intensive companies – both big (such as Ericsson, Nokia) and small (such as those presented below in our study) – have offices located in Kista. This effort is also underlined by the joint foundation of the IT University by KTH (the Royal Institute of Technology) and Stockholm University.

Second, Kista is also a district with great variation. The Kista galleria ('Kista-gallerian') shopping mall divides Kista into two different parts: 'working Kista' (the area where people work) and 'residential Kista' (the housing area where people live). Kista has an international aspect in that many people have roots from countries all over the world. In fact, the number of people with foreign citizenship is 44 per cent.[8] And immigrants start many business initiatives.

In our search for firms, we tried to find businesses that cover a certain scope of business activities in different industries. Apart from high-tech firms, we wanted to study service-based firms as a comparison. We contacted a number of actors, mainly in the business support system in Kista, who function as intermediaries to the firms. Of the seven firms in this study, four are categorized as high-tech firms and three represent service-based firms. All businesses are run by individuals with an immigrant background. All firms are anonymous and named after their respective line of business. The science- and technology-based firms are called 'Glass', 'Digital', 'Smart Cards' and 'TV Advertising'. The service-based firms are called 'Health', 'Food' and 'Translations'.

Methods used include different qualitatively inspired techniques, such as ethnographic approaches and observations. Meetings, conversations, interviews and discussions with the individuals involved are the main sources of information. Further, experts in different areas and people with insights into each of these firms were also interviewed. This is a means of increasing the credibility of the cases and the certainty that we do not just take the stories of the individuals involved for granted without checking them with people without a stake in the firms. Thus, all cases include inputs from at least two people – one of them external – in order to get a more representative and adequate view of each firm. Altogether, we spoke to nine experts, and we also had discussions with them about the general climate for businesses in Kista and Sweden. Their experiences and insights provided valuable input in the process of trying to understand the role of support systems for small firms in Sweden today. For further details on data gathering, see Dalhammar (2004).

We use the dimensions in the conceptual framework – as presented in section 11.4 – as a guideline to construct the empirical cases in the next subsection and to interpret and analyse these texts in section 11.6. Using the conceptual framework is a means of introducing a more general approach to entrepreneurship studies for studying the subfield of immigrant and ethnic entrepreneurship. The only thing the firms in our study have in common is that they involve people with immigrant backgrounds. While it is not our intention to predestine and predetermine these firms, how ethnic resources contribute to the resource acquisition of the firms is a question that will be dealt with empirically.

11.5.1 Firms

The firms are studied from the perspective of what sources they use and utilize for their resource acquisition. The presentations are written about the specific process that each firm goes through and in each case we provide examples of how ethnic resources have or have not been crucial in the firms' resource acquisition.

High-tech firms

Glass (developing new glass material) Glass is a research and development firm based on a newly discovered and patented advanced glass material with commercially interesting properties. The entrepreneurial team consists of three men, all originating from Iran: two childhood friends, S and A, both around 30 years old, and S's father N. S is the inventor of the material and A works with the market. S and A own 50 per cent of the shares each and N functions as a consultant since he has extensive business experience in industries relevant for product applications based on the material.

A has actively sought access to settings where they are able to find the specific resources they need. In 2003, Glass was accepted onto an incubator programme in Kista Science City. A's contact with this organization was based on recommendations from other people at other business support organizations and the team considered several alternatives before they decided to proceed and join this particular setting. They stayed there for six months, but then they moved to a new location in central Stockholm. A talks positively about their new business advisor and the person they work closest to in their new location. 'We need him right now', A says. 'He can help us since he understands the industry and applications we're involved in. He's good at patents!' And their new advisor is positive: 'Glass follows a development that's very good!'

The team also has contacted top people within the Swedish industry, and according to A this makes it easier to find financial capital. These people act like 'door openers' and add to the legitimacy of their business idea. 'We've got many influential people to support our firm, both as references but also as board members', A says. 'We think it's important to have these people supporting us if we want to get credibility for our business!' And Glass has managed to get the money they need for the complicated and complex patent process of the glass material. Further, they have gained legitimacy for their business idea in that they won first prize in Vinnova's Vinn Nu contest.

A says that he and S have always been entrepreneurially driven and that this can partly be attributed to their cultural background. He says that the Iranian culture is 'elitist and competitive'. 'The families helped us when the corporation was founded. These were no big amounts – just to cover the corporate capital requirement.' However, A states that the success of the business does not depend on ethnic resources of any kind since their ethnic network cannot provide them with the resources they need. 'That's not central in this business. I actually haven't thought much about it!' And their former business coach at the incubator programme in Kista Science City concludes: 'On the whole, Glass was like working with any firm. I can't say that it was particularly different because they have Iranian origin.'

Digital (digitally monitoring remote systems) Digital develops new digital technology for monitoring, regulating and controlling remote systems. At the moment, the firm is focused on the process industry, where the technology can be used to control remote machines and robots. However, the technology is very much adapted for the telecom industry and efforts will be put there in the future as well. The founding team consists of two people who each own 50 per cent of the shares. S, a 36-year-old man originating from Iran and the inventor of the technology on which the firm is based, works on technology and product development. H is a 43-year-old native Swedish woman who works on the market side.

In S's family, many people have had their own businesses. He has also run two firms before. 'It's completely different to work in this type of business and industry compared to the firms I've run before', S says. He says it involves more long-term partnerships. 'This is the kind of business I've always dreamed of! I want to have stable relations to a couple of partners and work closely with them to develop products in various projects.' Despite the fact that his family has a strong entrepreneurial focus, he has not had any help from his family with Digital. 'I haven't needed it!' There are also traditions of business activities in H's family, and she previously ran a firm together with her husband. However, she carefully explains that she draws a straight line between business and friendship, and has not involved her family in this business.

There are people helping S with the technical development of the digital platform. These are friends of his with Iranian backgrounds. They have agreed to sign a contract which says that they will get paid if the firm becomes profitable. 'They do this on their free time since they think it's fun to work with this product. They enjoy technical solutions', S says. Still, S utilizes this cheap ethnic labour since the financial situation is tough. But generally, both S and H state that S's immigrant background has not affected the activities of the firm. 'I haven't thought of it before', S states when asked about it. But both H and S state that they want diversity in terms of people. 'We need both the right competences and the right people', S asserts.

Digital has taken measures to find resources connected to its specific business idea. The firm was also accepted onto the same incubator programme as Glass in Kista Science City. S first contacted Stockholm Innovation as a matter of getting assistance concerning where to go with his idea. 'The person I contacted there was a person I knew from before. She told me about the programme in Kista.' 'I know how to write applications', H fills in. 'We had about 4–5 meetings with people there. It was a long process and it was far from certain that we would get accepted.' However, they eventually got in. 'We believed in the idea and the people', their business coach in the programme says. 'It's all about legitimacy and legitimacy opens the door to new valuable contacts and relations', H says. 'When we've talked to other actors and potential partners, I've noticed that it is positive to mention that we sit in this environment!'

'Digital has had a very fast progress', H says. One month after they entered the incubator programme, the joint-stock company was founded. One month later, they received contribution from ALMI to develop their innovation. One month after that they received the first prize in Vinnovs's Vinn Nu contest, a competition limited to new R&D companies. And about six months after the firm was founded, they had a prototype ready for demonstration. Still, the industry is demanding. Their business coach at the programme says: 'What Digital needs is knowledge about and within the process industry. Further, they need more developers for faster technological progress. There are people with the right competences, but since they don't have money they can't pay them for their work. This means they are forced to use solutions like they do right now – that S's Iranian friends work here for free with the development of the platform.'

Smart Cards (developing smart card chips) Smart Cards is a firm engaged in the smart card industry and develops the next generation of new smart card chips. It is organized as a corporation. The aim is to build and maintain relationships with smart card vendors globally. The idea is to improve and increase the performance of the cards with more efficient tailor-made hardware solutions on the chip. O, a 41-year-old man originating from Iran, is the founder and owner of the firm. He mainly works with technology and product development. O owns all the shares and runs the firm together with an assistant, L, a 60-year-old native Swedish man, who mainly handles business contacts.

In Iran, O ran a firm together with his father, and when his father died, O took over the firm. L has previously worked with sales, translation and education. Further, he has helped one friend and his former wife to build up two separate firms. Right now L does not get any compensation for his work: he does unpaid work. L assures us that O *is* Smart Cards. 'I just help him out. I do this because I think it's fun', he says.

In order to finance the expensive product development, O has invested a large sum of his own money, including money he borrowed from family and friends. But he has also succeeded in finding other sources of financing.

'When I presented all my work for SIC (Stiftelsen Innovationscentrum), they gave me money after just a few days, a loan of 400 000 SEK. They were impressed that I had already done market analyses and that the idea was ready to go.' Altogether, the firm has raised about 2 million SEK from different institutions (SIC, ALMI, Vinnova and NUTEK). 'It's different to start a firm like this compared to other kinds of businesses', O says. 'The money I've raised doesn't cover much and the applications for patents consume much of it. This means I generally can't pay potential partners for their work. No one works for free – one has to create incentives! One way is to reward them later if my firm succeeds.' They have a business contact and advisor at ALMI who says: 'Today, many immigrants are dependent on that family and relatives help them financially. In mature industries, families and friends often have the ability to help, but in high tech the same possibilities don't exist.'

The team experiences difficulties in having an income while developing a firm like this. According to L, this is the major problem. 'Financing, personnel resources – although this is not up for discussion yet – and to find the right people to work with is crucial for success.' Their contacts and network relations symbolize a way of solving problems. 'Networking is problem-solving – that's what it is. This is true not just for us but for all developing firms. But it has to do with personal engagement, not just formal contacts. In these contexts people are incredibly important! Formal competence, yes, but it also has to do with competence in relations. The people Smart Cards works with represent such competence', L asserts. O explains there are 6–10 people in a network that help him concerning specific matters. 'I buy the competence I don't have', he says. Further, O says that one has to be careful: 'There are many charlatans in this industry. Many firms try to look much better than they really are.'

Smart Cards applied for a place in an incubator programme in Kista but did not get in. The project leader at that support organization says: 'They came to us and applied for a coaching relation but we rejected their application. We didn't believe in their business idea! We had doubts along a few of the dimensions we use for evaluating the innovations. This has to do with competences, resources and focus of the venture.' However, Smart Cards has managed to find an office in facilities run by this organization. According to O, this setting has still been helpful for Smart Cards since it gives credibility and provides access to a network of potential partners and customers. 'Financing and customer and partner contacts have to do with credibility and this setting provides trustworthiness. This is even more important for me as an immigrant entrepreneur, since I may not have the same contact network as native Swedes.'

L says that a European Union (EU) project with a number of partners is about to be launched. 'O is the originator of this project. Some parties involved in this partnership network are quite big.' Further, although O is a bit secretive about the future since no deals are official yet, he tells us he has 'discussions with business angels and venture capitalists right now', so he thinks the future looks prosperous.

TV Advertising (developing systems for targeted advertising solutions) TV Advertising is a firm directed towards the television and broadcasting market. The product is a combination of a chip and a management system. The firm focuses on digital TV and its domain is in the general area of 'targeted advertising solutions'. K, the founder of the firm, originates from Iran and is in his mid-thirties. He owns all the shares in the firm. Until now, he has run the firm completely on his own from his home in Kista.

K has previously run businesses and still has a firm working with photography and editing for the television industry. In order to support himself, he does various work. 'I do extra work with completely different things. I have many jobs on the side! This is the way I support myself.' His business activities do not reflect a heritage of any kind. 'We have no tradition of business ownership or entrepreneurship in my family. This is more a personal thing. I have a personal motivation towards entrepreneurship.'

K has acquired much money from family and friends to apply for international patents. 'In Iran people don't make the same distinction between my money and your money as in Sweden. When it comes to your parents you'll inherit their money anyway sooner or later.' When borrowing money, he is sometimes obliged to listen to opinions from family and friends, but he solves that by 'choosing what opinions I should listen to'. And despite the fact that friends would provide cheap or even free help, he refuses such help. 'I don't want to work with friends!' he says. He has had bad experiences from this, where it has even led to losing friendship because they have not been able to separate work from pleasure.

Apart from the money he borrowed from family and friends, K has a small loan from SIC (Stiftelsen Innovationscentrum). K has talked to several actors in the business support system, both public and private, who have introduced him to further contacts. 'I contacted a few patent bureaus and a couple of engineers at another firm helped me develop the idea technically.' Still, he needs much seed capital in order to develop and realize his idea. 'I have estimations indicating that I need about 10–20 million SEK to develop all the solutions for the complete solution.' K is currently looking for a setting where he can find the assistance and the contacts he needs to develop his innovation. He has taken the start-up programme offered by a business support system in Kista – the first step in the support programme – and he has applied for a place in the next step in this programme where he would get access to an office space in the business incubator. 'They can give me contacts and assistance. They provide credibility and legitimacy! The economic relation is less important. I can sit somewhere else and I don't save that much money to sit there.'

K talks about the specific condition in the high-tech industries. 'If you start a company too early you won't have the persistence to be in business until the market is ready and you can commercialize the idea', he says. 'If a native Swede would go to partners and investors and present the idea I have it would be much easier for him or her! Immigrants have small and limited networks. Native Swedes have easier access to important contacts than immigrants, because they commonly know someone who knows someone etc.' And he says he gets treated differently compared to native Swedish people. 'When I talk to someone, first of all I'm foreign, then entrepreneur. A Svensson is first of all an entrepreneur! Personally, I have experienced some difficulties with the language, but I know that others have had much worse problems. You have to know either Swedish or English if you want to talk to people. Otherwise you have problems.' Here, a native Swedish partner would help, K says. 'Sometimes, it's good to have a person that takes care of external contacts – one that masters the language. Today, I don't have such a contact, and I don't need it right now, but it will be needed in the near future.' And his contact at the incubator programme confirms that K needs partners in TV Advertising: 'K runs this on his own and that's one thing we generally don't recommend.'

Service-based firms

Health (health care store) Health's business idea is to sell health care products and provide massage and spa services to private and corporate customers. The turnover from selling products in the store and giving massage and treatments go hand in hand. However, a majority of the revenue comes from providing massage and spa treatments. The founding team consists of spouses R, a 48-year old woman who originates from Iran, and S, a 38-year-old man originally from Bangladesh. R is officially the firm owner (sole proprietor) and the one who leads the firm, but they work a lot together and in many ways drive the firm as a team.

R and S do not have traditions of business activities in their families and they have not run businesses before. However, they both have previous experiences from the health care sector. 'The initial plan was to have people employed, but we couldn't afford that. Instead, we have independent contractors. They provide different treatments and services to customers. It's not profitable for these people to rent a space here so the deal is that we share their revenues 50–50. We're all part of a team!', R concludes. Around five people work at Health on a somewhat regular basis.

'The big problems are money and contacts', both R and S state. R says that they have problems for two reasons: the disadvantage of being an immigrant, and starting a business. 'We don't have good contacts. I mean contacts with authorities. When you're an immigrant you don't know where to turn.' R and S applied for business loans, but both ALMI (Sweden's lead partner in financing new business and business ideas in cooperation with local municipalities) and the bank turned their idea down. 'They said they didn't believe in the business idea', R says. Since they did not get any support, they have mainly financed the firm with their own money. They have also borrowed from family and friends in their home countries. They have a contact at the Kista administration who says: 'R is interesting, because she managed to start her firm without any support from the surrounding community. She hasn't got any money from here [for example banks or public institutions] but had to bring these from her home country.'

A masseur who works in the store says that this is a tough industry for a new business. 'It takes one year – then people know where you are. After two years, people know who you are.' He adds: 'The tragic thing in this business – and then I talk about small private firms – is: if ten satisfied customers leave this store, we get one additional customer. If one dissatisfied customer leaves this store, ten customers disappear!'

The firm has plans for expansion. They have got permission to have an outdoor cafe during the summer. 'We'll serve sandwiches and hot and cold drinks. We think this is a way for us to attract customers. It seems like people are afraid to enter the store. They might think that it costs 2000–3000 SEK to go in and buy something, I don't know. With the outdoor cafe we believe it will feel more natural for customers to come here.'

Food (catering firm with exotic food) Food is a catering firm located close to Kista centre. It serves food with an exotic touch, such as African buffets. Catering arrangements is the main activity, but it also serves lunches, salads, main courses and desserts. Z, a 48-year-old woman originating from Iran, is the leader and runs the firm, although it is still organized as an economic association. At present, the firm employs four people: Z and another woman, A, are full-time, and Za and E are part-time workers. Further, Z's daughter and son occasionally help out in the firm. Besides, Z brings in people she knows when they have higher workloads or big orders, for example. These people are generally Iranians. 'It's easier to come in contact with people I know, personally or through contacts.' This means the chance is greater that Iranians and other immigrants are included.

From the beginning, this was a cooperative project initiated by the Kista administration. Their contact there says: 'It was targeted at unemployed immigrant women. Twelve women, all registered at the unemployment office in Kista, were recruited.' People quickly started to leave and Z took the role as the leader of the business. Although naturally there is an ethnic market for this food, most customers are native Swedish, since these are the ones most interested in the food. 'This food is more exotic to them. For us, this food is normal. We cook it at home, so why couldn't we do that here as well!? The people that come from other countries already know how to cook this food!' Z says: 'Business clients are the most profitable ones, but all customers are important!'

The firm still gets help from the Kista administration and its contact there actually is a board member. This contact provides much help when it comes to external relations. The contact agrees that Food has received much support and informal help as a consequence of personal relations. 'Formal assignments were developed into informal over time', the contact says. Further, she states that in order to be successful, immigrant enterprises need mentors who they can call upon when they have questions about various issues. Further, network relations are important: 'They need a network with different parties. I'm a link into the Swedish society, and they need people in their networks with different backgrounds.'

Z has utilized media contacts to promote the business. Food has been mentioned in papers and magazines at several occasions. 'This has definitely been good for us!' she states. She keeps a large number of articles from various newspapers in her office. It is a big pile of documents. 'Apart from this I've also been interviewed on the radio about our business a couple of times.' Z says that the reason for this attention is that they have stayed in business for so long, and at the same time people in the Kista administration have supported and promoted Food at different occasions. 'The writing in the newspapers and the positive marketing we've got are very helpful! After the article in Svenska Dagbladet[9] we've got many orders. We're also represented in various guides on the Internet. We're visible – that's good marketing!'

Z has plans for expansion. She hopes the firm can close deals with one big public actor. 'When they have seminars and conferences, we will deliver food to them.' Further, the firm will probably go from an economic association to a corporation quite soon. 'Many of the former people who worked here from the beginning want to buy shares, so it shouldn't be a problem to find enough capital', Z says.

Translations (translation and interpretation broker service) Translations is a broker service firm that mainly offers interpretation and translation services to clients. The business concentrates on big public customers, and focuses on long-term contracts. R, a 46-year-old woman originating from Turkey (Kurdistan), leads the firm and mainly deals with business contacts. She also owns all the shares in this firm. Apart from R, four people – G, K, H and T – are employed in the firm. They all work on practical day-to-day issues concerning the interpretation broker service.

R speaks both Kurdish and Turkish as well as Swedish. 'Before I started my own firm I worked extra for different translator firms when possible. This was the only industry where I could start a business, so it was an easy choice to start within interpretation and translation. Naturally, I gained from my previous experiences in this area.' R says the success of the firm is due to her own work, and she had no help from family or friends. Still, she received much assistance when the firm was started. She was accepted onto a start-up programme in her neighbourhood and that was crucial for founding the firm: 'But the decisive thing was the project to which I was accepted! If not for that, I probably would have studied instead.' The person in charge of the project at the local administration explains that the project was a transnational EU project. 'I'm definitely proud of R!' he says. 'She and another guy are the ones that have done well.' R says: 'I had big support in the project: office, copier, furniture and telephone. I had no support from my family and no business experience. I didn't ask anyone, but made the decision myself to start the business!' Further, R makes it clear that she started with zero financing. 'I got business start-up subsidies (*starta eget bidrag*) for one year that I was allowed to keep even though I had income from the firm. During the first years, there was much marketing and hardly any assignments. I worked much with contacts to media. TV, papers, weekly and monthly magazines etc. Sometimes, the facts weren't correct, but it's important to be seen! Today, there are some people that contact me and want to talk to me about my business. These are researchers, students and different kinds of organizations. I don't have time to meet them all!' R has a contact in the Kista administration and he likes R's initiative: 'R has proved that she's not dependent on anyone to succeed. I like her because she's a strong woman, and being a woman is a handicap in the Swedish society today.'

A majority of the people who work in R's firm at present are immigrants. 'That's a coincidence!' she tells us. 'It's just happened that I have taken in people with immigrant background. I've had many people on vocational training, at least ten. These vocational training places are distributed by the unemployment agency. Many of them have been for a limited time, normally 3–6 months. After that, some of them have been offered jobs here.'

R says she has big plans for the future:

Table 11.1 Utilization of ethnically derived resources of the firms in this study

	Financial capital	Organizational capital	Human capital	Social capital	Ethnic market
Glass	X		X		
Digital		X	X		
Smart Cards	X		X		
TV advertising	X				
Health	X				
Food	X	X		X	X
Translations			X		

> I want this to become big. I want to be able to breathe and not having this hanging over me every day. As it is now, I have no time for myself. I don't have time to go out and meet my friends – the social life is neglected. I work 55–60 hours/week. I bring work home with me, mainly during weekends; invoices, wages. I'm the only one who can do certain jobs. I have an accountant and bookkeeping consultant that does some of this work, but I do a lot myself!

And the way to become bigger is more volume. 'We need bigger volumes – that's where our competitors have an advantage! We get bigger volumes by getting big long-term contracts with public clients. Then I could hire more people and work less myself.'

11.5.2 Resource Acquisition and Ethnic Resources

In Table 11.1 we present an overview of the utilization of ethnic resources among the firms. The limited number of cases could explain the relatively low utilization of social capital and focus on ethnic markets among the firms. If there had been restaurants and grocery stores, these firms would possibly have shown different results. Still, with this limited number of cases, all types of important ethnic resources are represented. This indicates that these variables are useful as a means of understanding the nature of ethnic resources.

Utilizing ethnic resources generally means utilizing ethnicity as a resource. However, utilizing ethnicity as a resource does not always mean that the individual(s) involved use ethnic sources for their resource acquisitions efforts. They may also utilize the fact that they are part of an ethnic minority: for example, that they can get certain subsidies (like *starta eget-bidrag*[10]) or gain admission to business or incubator programmes targeted at immigrants and/or ethnic minorities. This is the case for R in Translations. The Translations case provides a concrete example where ethnic minority background may have an important impact on the resource acquisition process of immigrant and ethnic businesses. R did not utilize ethnic resources, but her ethnicity facilitated her acceptance onto the business support programme. This is actually the opposite of community involvement. The point we want to emphasize is that utilizing ethnic resources and ethnicity as a resource does not necessarily mean the same thing, and that there are pros and cons with both.

11.6 INTERPRETATION AND ANALYSIS

In this section we go through the dimensions in the conceptual framework, and giving concrete examples from the cases we present how ethnic resources and ethnicity as a resource are used to acquire crucial resources for the firms. Since this is an exploratory study whose goal is to generate new theoretical assumptions for further research, we do not interpret and analyse each firm separately. Instead, we look for patterns in resource acquisition of the firms in relation to their business logics.

11.6.1 Organization: Type of Industry or Firm

Using Samuelsson's (2001) definitions, all four high-tech firms (Glass, Digital, Smart Cards and TV Advertising) in one sense or another are engaged in creating new market transactions, thus exploiting innovative venture opportunities. In Glass, it is the glass material which is expressed as an important breakthrough. Digital's new digital platform is described as a 'shift in technology'. Smart Cards's smart card chips 'enables handling of more applications' and 'improves overall performance'. And TV Advertising's broadcast solution is a means of using digital technology in a new way. In contrast, the service-based firms (Health, Food and Translations) are more oriented toward the exploitation of imitative venture opportunities.

In the cases there are several examples where sources for acquiring resources are affected by industry and business logics. Even though ethnicity – in terms of country of origin and sense of 'immigrant belonging' – is not unimportant in the high-tech firms, it is not an issue concerning the acquisition of crucial resources. Instead, technology and characteristics specific for the individual ventures are brought up in high-tech cases. Individual(s) involved in the ventures as well as external advisors and business coaches give examples of conditions quite specific for firms in the high-tech sector. The cases show that the specific resources needed (large sums of financial capital or specific vocational skills) cannot be acquired by utilizing ethnic resources.

For the service-based firms, our analysis seems to reveal that ethnic resources contribute to a higher degree to the acquisition of crucial resources. Translations's business is based on R's ethnic resources of language and her knowledge about other cultures is also helpful. Food's very business idea reveals that the firm draws on specific ethnic knowledge about cooking and serving exotic food. Health's health care store draws strongly on ethnic resources to acquire financial capital since, in addition to the founders' own money, additional financial resources for the start-up were borrowed from family and friends. For a science- and technology-based firm, it is generally not possible to acquire either sufficient financial capital or, for example, organizational capital (mainly labour) by merely utilizing ethnic relations. Essentially, in our study the division between innovative and imitative ventures equates to the division between high-tech and science- and technology-based firms, and service-based firms. This suggests that ethnic sources for resource acquisition are more important for the service-based firms.

11.6.2 Individuals: Proactive Behaviour

Looking at the second dimension – the individual(s) driving the ventures – there are examples of different attitudes toward action and risk, issues that do not depend on business logics, that is, type of industry or firm. In Glass's case, the people involved show that they have constantly looked for opportunities to develop the business, which has resulted in choices to move to different settings. Digital utilized contacts to enter a business support system and the founders quickly focused on finishing the prototype and bringing it to the market. And both Glass and Digital handed in applications and received prizes in organized business contests.

Z at Food also exhibits proactive behaviour, in the sense that she has utilized contacts in the media to promote the firm. Further, she has managed to get continued support long after the termination of the initial cooperative project. R at Translations managed to access a supportive project aimed at immigrant businesspeople that was crucial for the start-up. R also utilized contacts to media to promote the business. Further, she is involved in business societies in the borough where she lives. K at TV Advertising has contacted several actors, both in Sweden and internationally, in order to find a setting where he can acquire resources and develop his business solution. O at Smart Cards has gone through several parties in order to find an adequate setting, and his networking activities have led to involvement in an EU project with big potential. In Health's case, the founders exhibit behaviours somewhere in between. They have tried to access some settings for support, but do not seem to have utilized all possibilities at hand. Although there are no absolute borders regarding definitions in this matter, in our study there is no example of a firm where the individual(s) involved clearly show reactive behaviour.

11.6.3 Environment: Interactions with Actors in the Business Support System

Not surprisingly, business support aspects have been shown to have crucial impact on the progress and development for all firms in our study. Translations is a good example of this, even though it in fact represents a case where the presentation is rather ambiguous. Her case is the following: although R puts herself and her own work in focus and regards this to be the important factor for the creation and development of the firm, the project she was accepted onto and the support she got have been crucial for the start-up and development of her business. If it were not for this support, the firm would not have come into existence at all and R would have done something else. In fact, her strivings show how proactive behaviour makes it possible to utilize ethnicity as a resource. And Translations is not alone in this study. Food has a similar story, where the initial cooperative project received and the firm still receives much support, not the least by the Kista administration. In contrast to these two firms – as well as to Glass and Digital – Smart Cards, TV Advertising and Health represent three voices that have experienced greater difficulties in gaining adequate support in their interactions with the surroundings. They clearly express the need for better assistance. However, there seem to be fewer alternatives for Health than for the other two.

11.6.4 Summary of Findings

The interpretations and analyses of the cases point at differences regarding the resource acquisition between the high-tech and the service-based firms. These differences can be attributed to the organizational perspective on type of industry or firm, that is, the industry and business logic. However, the aspects of proactive behaviour and the interactions with actors in the business support system are not related to type of industry or firm per se. And these aspects also affect the utilization of ethnic resources.

Type of industry or firm affects what resources are available in the environment and what resources can be acquired using ethnic sources and ethnicity as a resource. Proactivity reflects the behaviour to act toward and mobilize resources, whether ethnic resources or 'mainstream'

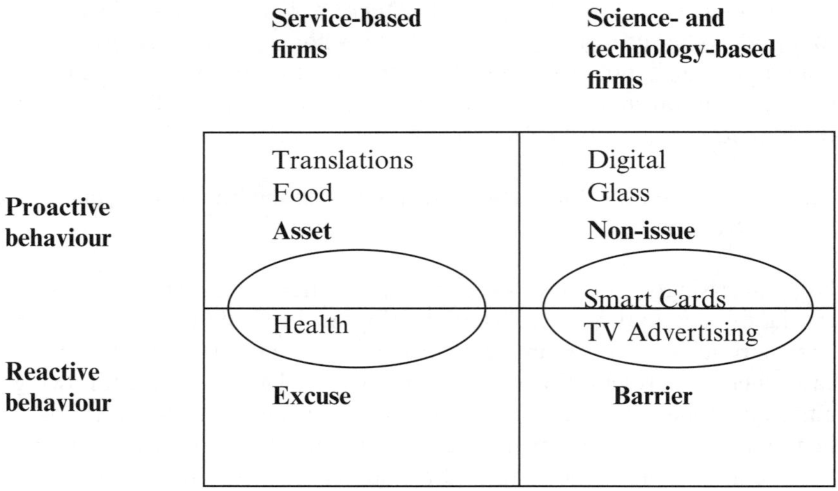

Figure 11.2 Model 1: The influence of ethnic background for the firms in our study in relation to type of industry or firm and proactive behaviour of the individual(s) involved

resources in the general business support system. And the interactive dimension reflects the activity to acquire resources through business actors in the surroundings, which is closely related to proactive behaviour. Thus, these three dimensions affect and interact with each other. Our elaboration on Gartner's (1985) framework assists in understanding and generating knowledge about the resource acquisition of immigrant and ethnic firms. As a consequence, this conceptual and methodological tool justifies its use in this study – and in future studies as well, we believe.

11.7 CONCLUSIONS

In this chapter, we start from the assumption that type of industry or firm affects the utilization of ethnic resources and thereby the importance of ethnic background for immigrant and ethnic businesses. As discussed in section 11.6, type of industry or firm is important, but other aspects – the degree of proactive behaviour of the individual(s) involved and interaction with actors in the business support system – also affect resource acquisition. Based on our interpretations and analyses, in Figure 11.2, Model 1, we present different ways to view the influence of ethnic background for the firms in our study. First, we introduce a model that combines the individual and organizational dimensions: type of industry or firm; and proactive behaviour of the individual(s) involved. Thereafter, we continue by adding the environmental dimension on interactions with actors in the business support system.

Figure 11.2, Model 1 addresses the question of how ethnic background affects new venture creation in science- and technology-based firms and service-based immigrant firms. This model mainly represents the experiences of key people – as in founders or founding teams – complemented with insights from experts such as mentors and business advisors.

The model proposes that in high-tech ventures where individual(s) involved exhibit proactive behaviour, ethnic background is of minor importance and becomes a non-issue (Glass and Digital). In the service-based ventures where the individual(s) involved exhibit proactive behaviour, ethnic background becomes an asset, mainly in the sense that ethnic resources can provide resources that may lead to a competitive advantage. Utilizing ethnic resources and ethnicity as a resource often go hand in hand. But as discussed before, this is not the case with Translations, where the utilization of ethnicity as a resource is not connected to utilization of ethnic resources. On the other hand, Food represents a business that recognizes the value of ethnic resources and utilizes them. Because of the uncertainty connected to the other three businesses (Health, Smart Cards and TV Advertising), these are placed in between possible fields in the model.

In order to understand the situation for these three firms, one more dimension needs to be added. This refers to interactions with actors in the business support system. Unlike the other four firms (Glass, Digital, Food and Translations), Smart Cards, TV Advertising and Health have not gained necessary support in their interactions with the environment. Concerning these three uncertain firms, the individual(s) involved exhibit (at least partly) examples of proactive behaviour. Above all, O at Smart Cards and K at TV Advertising continually seek new opportunities and look for help in the support system in order to develop their business ideas. However, they still feel that they lack sufficient support. The fact that they fall under the category of 'ethnic minority background as a potential barrier or excuse' in the model, reflects problems in relation to the support system rather than reactive behaviour. Thus, this reflects a shortage of resources. These concern social and cultural capital aspects, which in turn lead to a shortage of other types of resources, mainly financial capital. Although both O (Smart Cards) and K (TV Advertising) state that they have not been directly discriminated against, in their own words they say that they lack 'knowledge of the codes' (O) and 'language' (K). But these problems cannot merely be attributed to them as individuals, but rather to relations to the support system around them, including a number of actors. In the same manner as these firms are expected to adjust to the nature of the support system, one can argue that the support system ought to adjust to the competences of the firms. In other words, the environment does not address their needs in acquiring new competences and resources for their firms.

The actors in the support system seem to agree. Today, there exists no support organization comprehensive enough to address specific needs for different venture opportunities. NyföretagarCentrum offers more general help, and according to Smart Cards's contact at ALMI, this support organization does not have enough resources on its own to help firms the way it wants to.[11] This implies that there may be shortages in the support system contributing to the difficulties that firms in this study face. And several people we have interviewed – both businesspeople and experts – express that an immigrant business needs more specific support due to lack of knowledge about how to start and run businesses in Sweden. Gaining confirmation and legitimacy therefore seems to be even more important for immigrant entrepreneurs in comparison to 'mainstream' entrepreneurs. This discussion about complexity in relations with actors in the surroundings supports Gartner's (1985) idea that there is a range of individual needs to address in supportive actions. It also confirms Van de Ven's (1993) view that the entrepreneurial process is a collective effort that demands actions during a long period from many parties, both within the industry and the public sector.

11.8 IMPLICATIONS AND DISCUSSION

The results of the research presented in this chapter have implications for different kinds of stakeholders.

11.8.1 Academics

This study shows that structural and cultural theories both play important roles when researching immigrant and ethnic entrepreneurship from a resource perspective. The field of immigrant and ethnic entrepreneurship should not be treated or regarded as homogeneous. Immigrant entrepreneurship could be used as the overall concept in order to grasp business activities by individuals who have immigrant backgrounds, whereas the concept of ethnic entrepreneurship could be used when the acquisition of ethnic resources and ethnicity as a resource are studied. However, every study should be clear about what aspects of immigrant or ethnic entrepreneurship are studied.

11.8.2 Practitioners

Business advisors should note the importance of encouraging proactive behaviour of immigrant and ethnic entrepreneurs. Further, they should encourage their business clients to find creative ways for resource acquisition. This includes ethnic resources, that is, resources that the advisors themselves usually cannot provide or mediate. They should also make their clients aware of the importance of assessing ethnic sources for resource acquisition, since there are costs involved in such operations, not the least social costs.

From a practical perspective, this means that supportive actions must address different needs depending on the type of industry or firm and to what degree the individual(s) involved exert proactive or reactive behaviour. The degree of confirmation and legitimacy, and thus recognition, from actors in the environment is crucial for all businesses, but maybe even more crucial for immigrant and ethnic businesses, as they often lack sufficient social capital on their own.

11.8.3 Public Policy

Policy-makers should ask themselves a number of important questions. Are there certain business activities that they want to encourage, for example high-tech immigrant and ethnic entrepreneurship? And are there certain measures that should be taken to achieve higher levels of business activity in these sectors? These questions deal with views on ethnicity and ethnic resources. As previously discussed, ethnic resources could be both a blessing and a curse, depending on the relative competitive advantage or disadvantage they provide.

At the moment, those few ethnic minority businesses in Kista are just fragmented voices. But in a not too distant future, they may be part of a whole ethnic high-tech cluster and society. Whether this ethnic high-tech entrepreneurship will be similar or different to what it looks like in Saxenian's (2001) description of Silicon Valley is an open matter. However, there is a great likelihood that there will be spillover effects to the rest of Stockholm and the Greater Stockholm region. Then we will experience developments that affect economic activity as well as matters of integration. This is why the high-tech industry is so interesting and important in relation to other industries where there is often an overestablishment of ethnic firms: it creates possibilities to turn ethnicity (and the view on ethnicity) into a potential resource instead of a burden.

11.8.4 Final Reflections

Our study shows that there is representation among immigrant and ethnic businesses in Sweden today for a more complex picture than the views on immigrant and ethnic entrepreneurship commonly presented. Both the conceptual framework and Model 1 are contributions of this chapter. However, since this is an exploratory study, it is up to future research to investigate further the appropriateness of these findings. While it is reasonable to assume that the topic of immigrant and ethnic entrepreneurship will be highly relevant in the future as well, it is our belief that our work can be further elaborated upon and researched. We hope that future studies will further contribute to this field of research in similar or different contexts to Kista. One example would be to compare immigrant and non-immigrant businesses in the same type of industry, like science- and technology-based firms, engaged in similar or different contexts. Further, identity of entrepreneurs is another interesting dimension that some researchers previously have studied (Fletcher, 2003; Hytti, 2003). This dimension is interesting in relation to immigrant and ethnic entrepreneurship, since it is likely that the business identities of the individual(s) involved affect resource acquisition of their firms.

NOTES

1. In immigrant and ethnic entrepreneurship literature (SOU, 1999; Najib, 1999; NUTEK, 2001a) it is concluded that if a person has at least one parent born abroad, they should be defined as an immigrant too. If that person founds a business, they by definition become an immigrant entrepreneur and the business an immigrant business. However, the Swedish Central Bureau (SCB) for statistics has now changed that definition: in order for a person to be labelled 'immigrant', both her/his parents have to be born abroad (see http://www.uppsala.se/uppsala/templates/StandardPage____3260.aspx).
2. Waldinger et al. (1990, 2000) present an interactive model of ethnic entrepreneurship that incorporates both opportunity structures (market conditions, access to ownership) and group characteristics (predisposing factors, resource mobilization). Ethnic strategies are assumed to arise in response to these exogenous (structural) and endogenous (cultural) factors.
3. http://www.iir.hit-u.ac.jp/file/WP03-23bruno.pdf.
4. Source: http://www.babson.edu/entrep/fer/papers97/brush/bru3.htm#BACKGROUND
5. Source: intranet of the municipality of Stockholm, http://info.kista.stockholm.se/1.htm. According to recent statistics, of these 2000 around 400 are ICT companies, http://www.idg.se/ArticlePages/200401/16/20040116125725_CS/20040116125725_CS.dbp.asp?s=0222222222222222333333333333300133333333333333001111111111111&nolimit=true.
6. Source: http://www.kista.com/artikel/95/001004/se.
7. Kista Science City is an image concept but also connected to a definable geographical area which includes other parts of Stockholm municipality as well as parts of other municipalities in the greater Stockholm area. Apart from Kista, Southern Järva

(Södra Järva) and parts of the municipalities Sollentuna, Järfälla and Sundbyberg are included in the Kista Science City concept. Around 120 000 people live in the area defined as Kista Science City, more than 6000 companies are established there (http://www.kista.com/foretagsregister.html?soktyp=f&mid=007004), and about 65 000 people work in this region (http://www.kista.com/artikel/105/014009/se). Although Kista Science City is a bigger concept than Kista, the Kista district is the focus in this chapter.

8. Source: website of the Swedish public television news programme, http://www.svt.se/nyheter.
9. A widely read national Swedish newspaper.
10. This is a subsidy that people who have been unemployed for a longer period of time can get in order to start up their own firms. In Sweden, it is generally easier to get this source of financing if you are an immigrant and/or belong to an ethnic minority.
11. Expressed during a phone conversation, 30 January 2004.

REFERENCES

Abbasian, Saeid (2003), 'Integration på egen hand – En studie av invandrade kvinnoföretagare i Sverige', Uppsala universitet, Geografiska regionstudier nr 52, Eklundshofs Grafiska, Doctoral dissertation, Uppsala University Sweden.

Aldrich, Howard E. (1999), *Organizations Evolving*, Thousand Oaks, CA, USA and New Delhi, India: SAGE Publications.

Allen, J.C. (1992), *Starting a Technology Business*, London: Pitman.

Alvarez, Shannon and Lowell B. Busenitz (2001), 'The entrepreneurship of resource-based theory', *Journal of Management*, **27**, 755–75.

Ardichivili, A., R. Cardozo and R. Sourav (2003), 'A theory of entrepreneurial opportunity identification and development', *Journal of Business Venturing*, **18**, 105–23.

Barney, Jay B. (1991), 'Firm resources and sustained competitive advantage', *Journal of Management*, **17**(1), 99–120.

Bateman, T.S. and J.M. Crant (1993), 'The proactive component of organizational behavior: a measure and correlates', *Journal of Organizational Behavior*, **14**, 103–18.

Becherer, R.C. and J.G. Maurer (1999), 'The proactive personality disposition and entrepreneurial behavior among small company presidents', *Journal of Small Business Management*, **37**(1), 28–36.

Bozkaya, Ant, Astrid Romain and Bruno van Pottelsberghe de la Potterie (2003), 'Surveying technology-based small firms: a perspective from Belgium', Region de Bruxelles-Capitale, Working Paper nr 23, http://www.iir.hit-u.ac.jp/file/WP03-23bruno.pdf, extracted on 1 May 2004.

Brush, Candida G., Patricia G. Greene, Myra M. Hart and Linda F. Edelman (1997), 'Resource configurations over the life of ventures', *Frontiers of Entrepreneurship Research 1997*. http://www.babson.edu/entrep/fer/papers97/brush/bru1.htm, extracted on 1 May 2004.

Chaganti, Radha and Patricia C. Greene (2002), 'Who are ethnic entrepreneurs: a study of entrepreneurs' ethnic involvement and business characteristics', *Journal of Small Business Management*, **40**(2), 126–43.

Dalhammar, Tobias (2004), 'Voices of entrepreneurship and small business

– immigrant enterprises in Kista, Stockholm', Licentiate thesis, Royal Institute of Technology, Stockholm, Sweden.

Davidsson, P. and B. Honig (2003), 'The role of social and human capital among nascent entrepreneurs', *Journal of Business Venturing*, **18**, 301–31.

Fletcher, Denise (2003), 'Framing organizational emergence: discourse, identity and relationship', in Chris Steyaert and Daniel Hjorth (eds), *New Movements in Entrepreneurship*, Cheltenham, UK and Northampton, MA, USA: Edward Elgar, pp. 125–42.

Gartner, William B. (1985), 'A conceptual framework for describing the phenomenon of new venture creation', *Academy of Management Review*, **10**(4), 696–706.

Gartner, W.B., N.M. Carter and G.E. Hills (2003), 'The language of opportunity', in C. Steyaert and D. Hjorth (eds), *New Movements in Entrepreneurship*, Cheltenham, UK and Northampton, MA, USA: Edward Elgar, pp. 103–24.

Greene, Patricia G. and Terrence E. Brown (1997), 'Resource needs and the dynamic capitalism typology', *Journal of Business Venturing*, **12**, 161–73.

Greene, Patricia G., Candida Brush and Terrence E. Brown (1997), 'Resources in small firms: an exploratory study', *Journal of Small Business Strategy*, **8**(2), 25–40.

Holmquist, C. (2003), 'Is the medium really the message? Moving perspective from the entrepreneurial agent to the entrepreneurial action', in Chris Steyaert and Daniel Hjorth (eds.), *New Movements in Entrepreneurship*, Cheltenham, UK and Northampton, MA, USA: Edward Elgar, pp. 86–102.

Hytti, Ulla (2003), 'Stories of entrepreneurs – narrative construction of identities', Doctoral thesis, Turku School of Economics and Business Administration.

Institutet för tillväxtpolitiska studier (ITPS) (2002), 'Nyföretagandet i Sverige 2000 och 2001', http://www.itps.se/pdf/s2002_008.pdf, extracted on 1 September 2002.

Johannisson, Bengt (2000), 'Modernising the industrial district: rejuvenation or managerial colonisation', in Michael Taylor and Eirik Vatne (eds), *The Networked Firm in Global World: Small Firms in New Environments*, Aldershot: Ashgate Publishing, pp. 283–308.

Johannisson, Bengt (2001), 'Såsom i en spegel – invandrarföretagande att lära av', in NUTEK (ed.), *Marginalisering eller integration – Invandrares företagande i svensk retorik och praktik*, Stockholm: ADEBE Miljötryck, pp. 265–81.

Katz, Jerome and William B. Gartner (1988), 'Properties of emerging organizations', *Academy of Management Review*, **13**(3), 429–41.

Keeble, David and Frank Wilkinson (2000), 'High-technology SMEs, regional clustering and collective learning: an overview', in D. Keeble and F. Wilkinson (eds), *High-Technology Clusters, Networking and Collective Learning in Europe*, Aldershot: Ashgate Publishing, pp. 1–20.

Kirzner, Israel (1973), *Competition and Entrepreneurship*, Chicago, IL, USA and London, UK: University of Chicago Press.

Light, Ivan (1973), *Ethnic Enterprise in America*, Berkeley and Los Angeles, CA: University of California Press.

Light, Ivan and Steven J. Gold (2000), *Ethnic Economies*, San Diego, CA: Academic Press.

Mitchell, Bruce (2003), 'Ethnic entrepreneurship: preliminary findings from a South African study', *Journal of Small Business an Entrepreneurship*, **17**(1), 47–62.

Najib, Ali B. (1999), *Myten om Invandrarföretaget – En jämförelse mellan invandrarföretagande och övrigt företagande i Sverige.* (*The Myth of Immigrant Business – a comparison of immigrant and native entrepreneurs*). NUTEK och Svenska ELL Programkontoret, Rådet för arbetslivsforskning, Stockholm.
NUTEK (2001a), *Invandrares företagande i Sverige: Kartläggning och analys*, Sundbyberg: Alfa Print.
NUTEK (2001b), *Marginalisering eller integration – Invandrares företagande i svensk retorik och praktik*, Stockholm: ADEBE Miljötryck.
Penrose, E. (1959 [1985]), *The Theory of the Growth of the Firm*, New York: John Wiley & Sons.
Pitelis, C. (ed.) (2002), *The Growth of the Firm: The Legacy of Edith Penrose*, Oxford: Oxford University Press.
Pripp, Oscar (2001), *Företagande i minoritet – Om etnicitet, strategier och resurser bland assyrier och syrianer i Södertälje*, Stockholm: Tumba Mångkulturellt Centrum 2001:5.
Ram, M. and D. Smallbone (2001), 'Ethnic minority enterprise: policy in practice', UK DTI Small Business Service Research Report, http://www.sbs.gov.uk/SBS_Gov_files/embf/Ethnic_Minority_Enterprise_Policy_In_Practice.pdf, extracted on 3 November 2005.
Samuelsson, M. (2001), 'Modeling the nascent venture opportunity exploitation process across time', *Frontiers of Entrepreneurship Research 2001*, http://www.babson.edu/entrep/fer/Babson2001/I/IF/IF.htm, extracted on 30 November 2003.
Saxenian, A. (2001), 'The role of immigrant entrepreneurs in new venture creation', in C. Schoonhoven and E. Romanelli (eds), *The Entrepreneurship Dynamic in Industry Evolution: Origins of Entrepreneurship and the Evolution of Industries*, Stanford, CA: Stanford University Press, pp. 68–108.
Statens offentliga utredningar (SOU) (1999), 'Invandrare som företagare', Rapport 1999:49, Novum Grafiska AB, Stockholm.
Stinchcombe, A.L. (1965), 'Social structure and organizations', in J.G. March (ed.), *Handbook of Organizations*, Chicago, IL: Rand McNally & Company, pp.142–93.
Swedberg, Richard (2000), *Entrepreneurship: The Social Science View*, Oxford: Oxford University Press.
Van de Ven, A.H. (1993), 'The development of an infrastructure for entrepreneurship', *Journal of Business Venturing*, **8**(3), pp. 211–30.
Waldinger, Roger, Howard Aldrich and Robin Ward (1990), *Ethnic Entrepreneurs. Immigrant Business in Industrial Societies*, Newbury Park, CA: Sage Publications.
Waldinger, Roger, Howard Aldrich and Robin Ward (2000), 'Ethnic entrepreneurs', in Richard Swedberg (ed.), *Entrepreneurship: The Social Science View*, Oxford: Oxford University Press, pp. 356–88.

12. The entrepreneurial environment: business incubation in the Charlotte metropolitan region

Peter M. Frank

12.1 INTRODUCTION

A focus on regional economic development and policy has grown in earnest since the early 1990s. Regions in the US and around the world have grown considerably during the vast economic transformation that has occurred during this time period. Whether considering the rise of the 'new economy' or the 'knowledge economy', or whatever moniker is used to label the global shift toward economies dominated by information technology, the unit of analysis garnering significant attention is the region. While regions have always played an important role in national economic growth and development, they have more recently usurped the nation as the most significant piece on the global economic map (Ohmae, 1993). Juxtaposed with the rise of regional economic development and the technological transformation of economies throughout the world is the birth of what has been labeled the entrepreneurial society (Florida, 2001).

These two economic transformations, the ascension of the region and the entrepreneurial society, have brought about significant efforts by researchers and policy-makers to explain how regions can grow and develop. Regions throughout the world are seeking to develop and maintain an entrepreneurial environment that will help them participate in the economic growth enjoyed by many. As the economy shifts toward technology-intensive knowledge-based economic activity, there are more opportunities for entrepreneurs to create new businesses and discover unique products or production methods. This change toward a knowledge-based economy is credited for creating an increase in small businesses and entrepreneurial activity (Wennekers and Thurik, 1999). Additionally, Porter (1990) offers insight into the link between entrepreneurship and economic growth with his analysis of how regions establish a competitive advantage. He notes that invention and entrepreneurship are at the heart of this advantage. Thus, one pressing question regions are faced with is how to establish an environment that fosters growth via entrepreneurship.

One strand of research, pioneered by Richard Florida (2002), has catalyzed extensive efforts by regions to attract those responsible for initiating entrepreneurial ventures and subsequent regional growth. Florida's work on the 'creative class' has led regional leaders and policy-makers throughout the world to shift their focus from developing capital inputs to attracting young, creative entrepreneurial workers. Thus, efforts in Charlotte, in North Carolina, USA are focused on establishing the region as a premium location for creative workers to reside and practice their innovative talents. The Charlotte City Committee is a group of about 200 young professionals within the Charlotte region focused on attracting this creative class in order to enhance the region's economic survival. This committee commissioned Next Generation Consulting of Madison, Wisconsin to analyze the Charlotte region and make subsequent recommendations on how to attract young, talented creative class workers.

A component of the report generated by the analysis of Next Generation Consulting pointed to a particular area of weakness within the Charlotte region: the entrepreneurial environment (Ryan, 2005). According to this report, Charlotte ranks low in entrepreneurialism and scores near the bottom on the innovation index.[1] One solution proposed by Next Generation Consulting, to attract and retain creative workers, is to boost the region's entrepreneurial climate by making room for growing companies and start-ups through business incubators.

The purpose of this chapter is to initiate a larger project examining the entrepreneurial environment in the Charlotte region, while also analyzing the policy options emphasized by the aforementioned report. Questions that arise from the efforts of Charlotte leaders to position the region for future growth and development are: (1) In what ways can the entrepreneurial climate develop? (2) How does business incubation fit into this development? (3) What is the current status of business incubation in Charlotte and the state of North Carolina? and (4) How does the incubation process facilitate the development of growth companies or start-ups (that is, do incubators enhance a region's entrepreneurial climate)? What follows is an examination of two business incubators in North Carolina, attempting to answer the fourth question posed above and to establish a model for understanding how the incubation process facilitates incubatee development.

12.2 WHY FOCUS ON THE ENTREPRENEURIAL ENVIRONMENT?

Entrepreneurship is an essential feature of economic growth in a regional context. Entrepreneurs drive economic growth, and an environment conducive to entrepreneurial activity is necessary to attract those that are creative and innovative. This process is so important because: 'by noticing and acting on previously unnoticed ways to combine assets, individuals and firms acting as entrepreneurs direct assets into uses where their value is increased . . . this increase in value is economic growth' (Steele, 1998, p. 64). Research and development (R&D) are important for growth to occur, but they cannot account for the entire story. Once research is completed, the results must be applied to decrease the cost of production or to produce new goods and services, which is the role of entrepreneurship (Holcombe, 1998). In terms of technological innovation, equilibrium models depict R&D as inputs in the production function, yet problems exist with viewing technological progress as a function of R&D (Pack, 1994; Steele, 1998). Technological change is more than the result of applying effort and human capital because gaps in knowledge exist. One does not fully know the outcome of R&D efforts, nor does one fully know where to look. When new technology is discovered it does not automatically follow that the knowledge of how to implement this breakthrough is immediately known; as a result: 'the discovery and implementation of new, value-creating production projects or practices is not a technological issue but an economic issue, one which is solved by entrepreneurship' (Steele, 1998, p. 70).

Empirical work to support this theoretical understanding has been used to analyze the role that entrepreneurship plays in economic growth. Evidence indicates the importance of competition for economic growth in terms of new firms and new ideas, and this is a ripe area for future research (Friis et al., 2002; Geroski, 1994). Small and new firm start-ups have been the subject of empirical investigation as well, and the research shows their importance for economic growth (Acs et al., 1999b; Carree and Thurik, 2002). This research enhances the case for an environment that encourages economic growth via entrepreneurship.

Some economists note industrial changes that enhance entrepreneurship and subsequently economic growth (Acs et al., 1999a). As indicated above, the economy is continually shifting toward technology-intensive knowledge-based economic activity, and there are more opportunities for entrepreneurs to create new businesses and discover unique products or production methods. It is argued that after the (institutional) conditions are met to provide incentives for entrepreneurs, there is not a direct link to economic growth. The intermediate linkages of innovation and competition are a result of entrepreneurship, and after these linkages are in place then economic growth occurs (Wennekers and Thurik, 1999). For economic growth to occur, entrepreneurs must use technological innovations to channel resources to their highest-valued uses. This is exactly why 'technology' as an input cannot by itself lead to economic growth; thus, regions are paying close attention to ensure that they attract young, talented professionals who will yield entrepreneurial endeavors.

Generating an environment for entrepreneurs to carry out their innovative ideas is attributed to institution-building especially in a cross-national context (North, 1990). Providing incentives for entrepreneurs to act and to create innovative products or methods of production is the key element for a vibrant entrepreneurial environment. Yet, on a regional scale formal governmental institution-building has limits and regions must seek unique ways to enhance their entrepreneurial climate. In the US context, as workers are continually gaining power due to the changing demographics such as retiring baby boomers, creative methods of attracting entrepreneurs will increasingly grow in importance.

Entrepreneurs are attracted to regions where innovation and creativity are prominent components of the economic landscape. In addition, talented young workers are increasingly choosing a region to live in (that is, where to live) before they chose a specific firm or industry (that is, where to work) (Florida, 2002). Providing an environment for these creative workers to 'scratch their entrepreneurial itch' is thus at the forefront of the regional economic policy agenda (Ryan, 2005). What follows is an analysis of the business incubation process focusing particularly on North Carolina and the Charlotte region. Due to the vital importance of generating entrepreneurial activity for regional survival, policy-makers in Charlotte have been directed to enhance the environment for new business activity partly through incubation.

12.3 THE ENTREPRENEURIAL ENVIRONMENT IN THE CHARLOTTE REGION

Charlotte ranks 42nd on an Entrepreneurialism scale according to the recent analysis by Next Generation Consulting.[2] This ranking was determined by number of patents, Bureau of Labor Statistics (BLS) data, and several secondary sources including Florida's Creativity Index (Ryan, 2005). In this report on attracting creative workers to Charlotte, the weak entrepreneurial environment is said to be one of the region's flaws. Fewer entrepreneurs per capita compared with other regions in the country (Hall,

2005) could hinder economic growth and development in the future. In addition, Charlotte scores 124 on the Innovation Index (1 = Best) in the same report by Next Generation Consulting. Together, these factors imply that the Charlotte region needs to focus on enhancing its entrepreneurial environment in order to attract the coveted creative class worker.

Charlotte's unique economy, which is dominant in banking and financial services (the second-largest banking region in the US), contributes to its lack of entrepreneurialism. The large number of banking and financial services firms 'skews professional options' and creates a more conservative environment (Ryan, 2005, p. 25). The implication being that the banking and financial environment fails to generate the risk-taking needed for entrepreneurial activity.[3] Thus, one method of improving the environment for entrepreneurial activity is to establish more business incubators that foster new business start-ups and thus economic growth (or reduce the risk for entrepreneurs who also want to run a business).

12.4 BUSINESS INCUBATION

Business incubation is an economic development strategy which is intended to establish and grow businesses in a region. In addition, incubators provide a shared facility for young firms, and they provide business services such as marketing plans, sales consulting and assisting with obtaining capital. Start-up or growth-stage businesses enter an incubator where they typically become tenants in the incubator building. Business incubators provide significant tangible and intangible benefits, including reduced operating costs, access to services, moral support and advice, and access to information from other firms within the incubator (Markley and McNamara, 1995). New firms enter an incubator for a period of time while they establish their business, and then they graduate, existing on their own, to remain viable in their region.

The number of incubators in the US in 1985 was only 40, and that number increased to over 600 by 1995 (Sherman and Chappell, 1998). Incubator numbers continued to explode during the late 1990s and, while it may be tempting to dismiss the value of these facilities, 1100 remained open in 2005 (Dahl, 2005). Incubator facilities are often large warehouse-style buildings that offer extensive working space for various businesses at the same time, and they are typically funded by state or regional governments, or private sources such as foundations. For example, some areas use public monies for land and equipment purchases, tenant financing and management assistance, while others use funds for operating expenses (Allen and Weinberg, 1988). Often business incubators are established with both private and public funding as economic development projects, while others are started through universities or non-profit organizations (Ressler, 1995).

The importance of business incubators is that they are not intended to burden the government with the role of being a highly perceptive market player. Eisinger suggests that an economic development approach such as business incubation reduces the burden of entrepreneurs to perceive all potential market opportunities, yet this does not necessarily imply that the government must then attain such foresight. A business incubator simply uses public resources to remove some of the barriers to 'encourage and focus' a potential entrepreneur (Eisinger, 1988, p. 229). Eisinger does not speak directly about business incubators, but his language expresses the intention for the overall purpose of these types of economic development policies.

Business incubators are important agents in the local and regional economic development process for several reasons. Primarily, incubators are focused toward stimulating demand for local goods and encouraging an environment for indigenous entrepreneurs to operate in (Reese, 1993). Entrepreneurs who desire to bring their ideas to the market are sometimes reluctant because of the lack of infrastructure or business knowledge, yet if they are able to start a new business it can have a significant impact on their region. In 1993, over half of all employment in the United States was in firms with fewer than 500 employees, and small businesses are responsible for 55 percent of all innovations (Sherman and Chappell, 1998). The importance of business incubators is that they help to facilitate the growth of these small businesses, while providing an impetus for success. Small businesses often struggle to survive (over half of all firms have dropped out of the economy within their first four years of operation), and incubators can increase the chances of survival.

Another benefit of business incubators is their ability to focus economic development toward the economic strengths of a region. Incubators are not responsible for creating entrepreneurs, but rather for simply providing a means for them to establish their businesses in a certain location. Research conducted on incubators all over the nation found that 84 percent of firms that graduate from incubator programs remain in their communities (NBIA, 2001).

Two studies on the impact of business incubators reveal some important information regarding their ability to spur economic development in a region and enhance the entrepreneurial environment. One study, by Markley and McNamara (1995), examined an incubator in a small metropolitan area with a population of 117206; and the other study, by Sherman and Chappell (1998), analyzed a sample of 126 firms around the country that had been through an incubator program or were currently in an incubator. These studies were analyzed because they are independent of the National Business Incubator Association (NBIA), which performs extensive analysis of incubators, yet some of their results have been criticized.

The first study examined an incubator in Milltown (fictitious name) that was started with a $2.1 million dollar public investment as part of the regional development policy, and the analysis was conducted over a six-year period (Markley and McNamara, 1995). The data of 23 tenant and graduate firms show that during the six-year period, total salaries and wages were $22.5 million while sales were $127 million. Additionally, an estimate of state tax revenue from these firms during the time period was a little over $2.5 million. Also, for the Milltown incubator the cost per job during the six-year period was $6580, while costs per job for two manufacturing plants, Nissan in Tennessee and Subaru-Isuzu in Indiana, were $11 000 and $50 588 respectively.

In the second study of 126 businesses, Regional Economic Models Inc. (REMI) and surveys were used to analyze the impact of the firms on their region (Sherman and Chappell, 1998). Again during a six-year period (1990–96), the firms' sales grew an average of $239 247 annually, and full-time employment grew from three to ten people on average, according to the surveys. Also, the REMI model sampled 23 firms and revealed that these firms employed 278 people and created 467 jobs including spin-offs, while adding $10.1 million to local personal income in 1996 and $402 000 in local tax revenue to four communities.

These results are not intended to indicate that business incubators are solely responsible for economic development in these communities. In addition, it is not clear that the entrepreneurial activities undertaken by firms in these communities would not have occurred in the absence of the business incubator. Yet, the data above do reflect a positive economic change in communities where policy-makers were searching for viable economic development programs. Business owners in the Milltown study expressed that the reduced operating costs were a primary incentive to locate in the incubator, and in the larger study, 66 percent of firms said the incubation process was important or very important in their success (Sherman and Chappell, 1998). It is clear in these examples that the existence of a business incubator not only improved the chances of success for its client businesses, but also resulted in a positive economic impact on the region.

These studies demonstrate that incubators provide benefits to a region beyond employment and income growth. First, they provide an incentive for entrepreneurs to start businesses that may otherwise go unrealized.

The improved environment for entrepreneurship provided by an incubator goes beyond the financial inducements, but it includes support from other clients, networking and counseling by the incubator manager (Markley and McNamara, 1995). Research also indicates that incubators are an important contributor to a region-wide 'system' conducive for entrepreneurial activity especially in the technology industry (Neck et al., 2004). On the other hand, a firm that simply decides to locate in one region as opposed to another provides jobs (which some view as a marginal impact: see Dewar, 1998; Krumholz, 1999), but little else in terms of institutional development.

Another important way in which business incubators facilitate economic development is by providing a potential outlet for entrepreneurs within universities (many incubators are partnered with universities). Incubators are responsible for encouraging technology transfer in starting new businesses, as well as technological innovation (Allen and Weinberg, 1988; Ressler, 1995). A California-based business incubator is a good example of this activity through a partnership with the University of California. Mary Ferguson, co-founder of the Technology Development Center, said, 'Our focus is on technology transfer from the University of California at Davis, where there are many ideas and patents that have not been commercialized' (Ressler, 1995, p. 153). Hence, this ability to move technology from ideas to the marketplace is an economic development strategy which can impact regions allowing them to keep and attract creative workers and researchers.

The above examples of incubators that release successful companies reflect growth in the tax base of communities, and the public monies that are sometimes used to develop incubators usually do not compare to the massive incentives passed along to large firms as subsidies with locational policies. Often previous regional development policies that focused on firms instead of workers were more costly than some of the later policies used to lure the creative class. If public funds are used in the development of incubators, these funds typically result in a substantially lower cost per job figure than other policies (see the figures above). Consequently, the tax revenue paid by incubator firms can add, over a short period of time, to the overall tax base of a region.

Not all the research on business incubators reflects the positive results revealed above. There are some difficulties in evaluating the impact of incubators which, in some cases, is said to taint the perceived effect. In evaluating incubators it is difficult to measure truly their impact on start-up businesses. They offer a wide variety of services and each business has different needs, so it is not easy to determine how the incubator actually provides for the new business. Secondly, business incubators can be extremely specialized to meet the needs of the local or regional economy; therefore, it is hard to compare them across regions (Sherman and Chappell, 1998). These two evaluation difficulties make analyzing incubators challenging for policy-makers and researchers alike.

In addition, Bearse (1998), a frequent critic of the NBIA's assessment of business incubators, emphasizes additional difficulties in evaluating the impact of incubators on local and regional economies. He claims that the NBIA typically measures incubator performance in terms of sales and jobs (which are principally economic growth measures), and not in terms of economic development criteria. There is no question that it is more difficult to measure economic development variables (Brinkman, 1995), yet Bearse sees no attempt by the NBIA to do so even though they claimed it should be done. In addition, the NBIA continues to make suggestions on how better to evaluate the economic outcomes of incubators, yet in its new reports it fails to take heed of its suggestions (Bearse, 1998). There seems to be little desire by the NBIA to measure the less easily quantifiable components of business incubators that may have an economic development implication.

The research presented here intends to help address a gap in the current research on incubation by providing the first stage of an incubation process model to answer the question of how incubators facilitate the development of start-up and growth-stage businesses. In a recent meta analysis of incubation research, Hackett and Dilts (2004) point to this gap in the existing research. How does the incubation process facilitate incubatee development? Additionally, future questions arise from the current policy focus on business incubation that are part of a larger research agenda than what is presented here, but as regions focus on fostering an entrepreneurial environment to attract creative workers incubators may resurface as an essential policy tool.

12.5 NORTH CAROLINA BUSINESS INCUBATORS

North Carolina has a somewhat unique economy in that it has three metro regions that are within the top 50 regions in the US, and these three regions are all very close in size. Charlotte is the largest metro region in the state with approximately 1.4 million residents, while the Greensboro–Winston Salem metropolitan statistical area (MSA) has approximately 1.2 million residents and the Raleigh–Durham MSA has approximately 1.1 million residents (Atkinson and Gottlieb, 2001). Despite this relative size equality, there is a significant difference in the number of incubators within each metro region. The Raleigh–Durham MSA, which is home to the state capital and three of the nation's leading universities, contains eight incubators. The Greensboro–Winston Salem MSA contains two incubators, and the Charlotte MSA contains one growth-stage incubator (SBTDC, 2004). While the purpose of this research is to focus on the incubation process, it is important to note that the strong presence of leading universities in the Raleigh/Durham region help explain the increased number of incubators compared to the other two regions.

A question that arises from the distribution of incubators within North Carolina is: are incubators viable only in regions with a strong presence of universities? While incubators may be funded wholly or in part through universities, what drives the success of an incubator is the existence of successful start-ups that enter the facility and exit as growing firms. The presence of a university, while it provides certain components for entrepreneurs such as access to research, does not necessarily provide a primary ingredient for incubatee success (Smilor, 1987). Consequently, an effort by regional leaders to enhance the entrepreneurial environment in the Charlotte region and capitalize on luring the talents of creative class workers is possible with the existence of only one major research university. The Charlotte region is well positioned to capitalize on the new economic transformation that continues throughout the US, especially when considering its relative ranking on the Creativity Index. Even though the Raleigh–Durham region leads the state in creativity (ranking sixth nationally), Charlotte ranks 28th nationally (Florida, 2002) and with an improved entrepreneurial environment the Charlotte region can better attract and improve the potential of its creative workforce. What follows is an examination of two business incubators in North Carolina that provide insight into the incubation process, and this analysis is used to build a model to explain how and why this process works.

12.6 THE INCUBATION PROCESS

It is no secret what business incubators intend to accomplish. An effective incubator seeks to add value to a region by providing a facility for tenants to launch and hopefully grow an entrepreneurial idea into a successful business. In addition, the literature on business incubation and the information provided by incubators themselves is clear on what these facilities offer in terms of business advice, shared infrastructure, and so on (Barrow, 2001). Yet what is less clear, as pointed out by Hackett and Dilts (2004), is how and why the incubation process facilitates the development of incubatees. The answer to this question is especially important, as regions such as

Charlotte are trying to enhance their entrepreneurial environment via the establishment of business incubators.

In order to understand the incubation process, with the goal of determining the policy implications of supporting business incubators designed to enhance the entrepreneurial environment, this research examines two incubators in North Carolina. The first is an incubator located in the Raleigh–Durham metro region providing space for start-ups. The second is the only incubator located within the Charlotte metro region, which is designed for growth-stage companies. Within each of these incubators, I surveyed five companies and I spoke with several of the entrepreneurs directly. The formal survey provided data on two very different incubators in terms of tenant base and the requirements for entering the facility. The data were used to establish an incubation process model explaining how a start-up incubator and a growth-stage incubator develop viable firms that eventually leave the facility and remain positive economic contributors in their respective regions.

12.6.1 The First Flight Venture Center

The First Flight Venture Center (FFVC) is a business incubator in the Raleigh–Durham region that operates under the auspices of the North Carolina Technological Development Authority, Inc. (NCTDA). This business incubator is designed to offer entrepreneurs and emerging companies office and laboratory space with flexible leases, shared business services and equipment, technology support services, and assistance in obtaining much-needed financing.[4] Businesses enter the FFVC in the start-up stage of their development. Of the five companies surveyed at the FFVC, two entered at start-up, two entered within a couple of months of start-up, and one entered in its first year. Thus, these are all companies that entered the incubator at a vulnerable stage of their existence, hoping to establish a viable company long-term.

The incubation process for these start-up companies centers around two key elements: business support infrastructure and location. All five of the companies surveyed stressed the importance of needing office space with flexible lease terms, support infrastructure (that is, phones, copiers, laboratory space, meeting rooms, internet access, and so on), and a location close to their clients. Since the FFVC is located in Research Triangle Park, for some of these entrepreneurs the emerging biotech industry within this region is an essential component of their incubation process. The classic real estate adage, 'location, location, location', as one entrepreneur replied in his survey.

The second most important element in the incubation process for

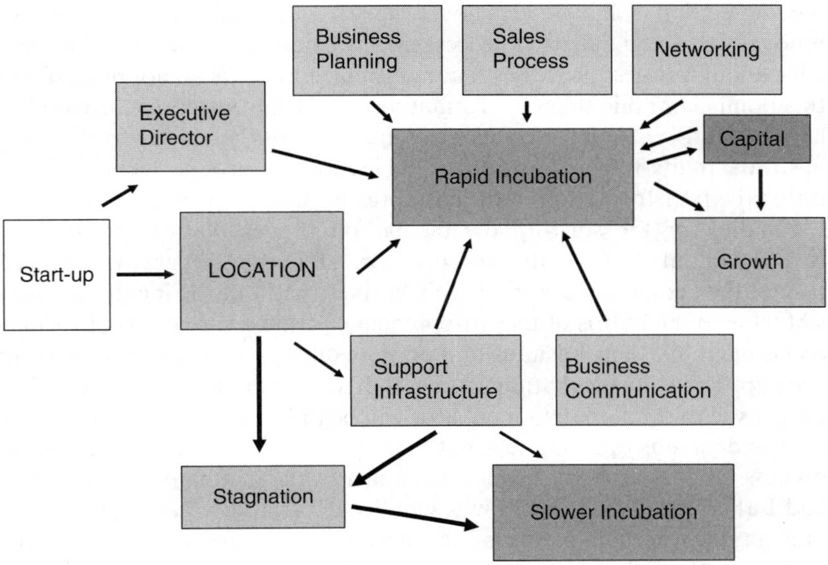

Figure 12.1 Start-up business incubation process

start-up firms is the relationship developed with the incubator director. The tenants of the FFVC who saw their companies grow and develop and who were pleased with their progress, what I refer to as rapid incubation, all spoke with or worked closely with the incubator director 'all the time' or 'almost every day'. The one entrepreneur surveyed that has recently left the incubator and that was not pleased with the development of his firm (as a result of locating at the FFVC) did not have a positive relationship with the incubator director.

Figure 12.1 displays the first iteration of the incubation process for start-up firms. This model graphically depicts how start-ups go from idea to growing firm via business incubation. This model depicts the importance of location and incubator leadership, as well as the support infrastructure. The next several components that improve the process and lead to rapid incubation are business planning, business communication, learning sales processes, networking and capital acquisition. Representatives of each company surveyed that stated they were experiencing successful growth and development, moving from a start-up to a growth-stage business, emphasized the importance of the incubator meeting their needs in a specific area of weakness. Thus, for start-ups the incubation process includes the availability of expertise in areas such as how to interact and communicate with businesspeople. One entrepreneur surveyed, a scientist, mentioned that he had no idea how to speak with businesspeople about his innovation. The incubation process includes developing skills and knowledge about business processes that many entrepreneurs do not possess. On this point economic theory is formative in that the entrepreneur who has an idea, and is able to discover a potential gap in the market, potentially has little ability to run a business. The incubation process includes facilitating the transformation of the entrepreneur into a business manager.

Finally, for the start-up the incubation process varies considerably with the initial ability of the entrepreneur. All five entrepreneurs surveyed believe they could have started their business without the incubator (possibly due to the hubris of the entrepreneur), yet they vary on whether they could maintain their business and on how difficult it would have been to start up. Thus, the incubation process is driven by the start-up's needs. It is unrealistic to think that an incubator will be fully equipped to meet all the diverse demands of a start-up, but tenant selection aids in the incubation process (as well as in the economic impact of the incubator; see Kuratko and LaFollette, 1987). There was significant variability among the entrepreneurs surveyed in terms of the importance of networking with the other tenants in the incubator. An important part of the rapid incubation process appears to be the overlap of tenants facing similar situations and/or tenants with experiences that recent entrants to the incubator can learn from. Though the companies surveyed did not all operate in the same industry, the incubation process appears to be improved where networking is effective. The next subsection examines the incubation process at a growth-stage incubator.

12.6.2 The Ben Craig Center

The Ben Craig Center (BCC) is the only business incubator in the Charlotte region, and it is a facility that focuses on growth-stage companies. The University of North Carolina at Charlotte, along with leading private sector interests, created the BCC in 1986. The purpose of the incubator is to provide state-of-the-art office space to the region's most promising companies in order to accelerate their growth by offering them advisory services, mentoring relationships, sales and marketing expertise, and access to capital.[5] The BCC is referred to here as a growth-stage incubator because the typical tenant enters the facility with a minimum of 3–5 employees and $500 000 in capital on hand. These criteria are in contrast to the FFVC, which requires tenants to possess growth potential but not established capital. As indicated, the BCC is the only incubator in the Charlotte region.

The incubation process differs for companies that have passed the initial

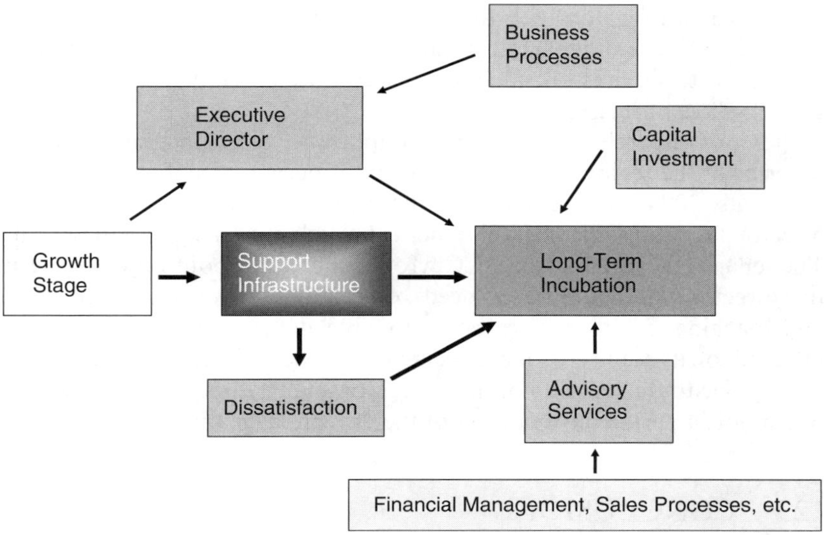

Figure 12.2 Growth stage business incubation process

start-up stage. Each company surveyed at the BCC has existed for at least seven years, while their time spent at the incubator varies from one year to 12 years. The incubation process for growth-stage companies is slower than the process for start-ups. The BCC reports that the average client resides in its facility for 3–4 years, yet four of the five companies surveyed have spent at least seven years at the incubator. In terms of the incubation process, entrepreneurs who enter the BCC are more likely to enter for a specific reason, as opposed to for overall business development. Yet, the two primary components of the incubation process for growth-stage businesses are still support infrastructure and executive leadership at the incubator.

Figure 12.2 displays the first iteration of the growth-stage incubation process. What is unique about this model is that incubation is a slower process and the executive director and/or leadership of the incubator have the potential of playing a significant role in the process. Additionally, support infrastructure is a crucial component in the process. Growth-stage businesses that enter the incubator are initially interested in a facility with reasonable rent, a phone system and the basic services needed to run a business. While location is important for these businesses, the basic services to run a firm take precedence. Since this finding is unique to a growth-stage incubator in the Charlotte region, it would be hard to universalize the idea that location is less important for growth-stage businesses. This finding has a lot to do with the economic differences of the two regions analyzed. On the other hand, location decisions in terms of networking and access to services outside the incubator are possibly less essential for growth-stage businesses.

Previous research has revealed the importance of the incubator director in terms of the regional economic impact of business incubators (Hackett and Dilts, 2004). Yet, in terms of the incubation process, the incubator director facilitates client development through extremely specific means. The tenants surveyed at the BCC wrote concretely about how the executive director met their business needs, especially in terms of sales processes and coaching, or they wrote about 'horrible' deficiencies of the incubator in terms of its failure to meet their needs. The deficiencies revealed are mainly due to the inability of the incubator and its director to meet a need or support a particular weakness of the growth-stage business.

12.7 CONCLUSION

The surveyed data presented above were the results of a project that intends to build a model to explain how and why business incubation facilitates incubatee development. Also, this research will inform the Charlotte region and others as to the role of business incubation in enhancing the environment for entrepreneurship. Does the incubation process reveal an enhanced entrepreneurial environment? Should the Charlotte region heed the recommendation to establish more business incubators? Based on the initial iterations of these models it is too early to tell to what extent the incubation process improves the entrepreneurial environment of a region. Yet, it is clear that incubators do provide an invaluable resource for those entrepreneurs who want to bridge the gap from creator/inventor/discoverer to business manager. While the industrial composition of a region certainly contributes to the environment for entrepreneurial activity (that is, the information technology and biotech concentration in Raleigh–Durham versus the banking and finance concentration in Charlotte), there is evidence from this research that the incubation process does provide an opportunity for entrepreneurs – encouraging them to follow through with their ideas – even in less economically dynamic regions.

It is clear from this research that for start-ups the location of the incubator is an essential component for incubatee success. Thus, the direction of causation must be examined further: that is, does the incubator enhance the entrepreneurial environment of a region or does the dynamic entrepreneurial activity of a region portend incubator successes? There is likely evidence to support both sides of this question, especially when examining regions that have significantly different industrial compositions, yet in the case of the Charlotte region versus the Raleigh–Durham region both areas want to foster dynamic entrepreneurial activity.

By creating a region that is friendly to entrepreneurs and innovative activity, regions can successfully compete for the creative class workers that are coveted, and will increasingly be coveted in the years to come. Regions will have to maintain their economic viability by attracting people instead of firms alone in the decades ahead. The 'knowledge economy' that continues to evolve and change the face of regions throughout the world is defined by entrepreneurs creating and discovering innovative products and production methods, and these entrepreneurs are in high demand. Florida followed up his landmark research on the creative class with this very notion: these innovative and creative workers are going where they are wanted and where the environment is ripe (Florida, 2005).

NOTES

1. This report scores Charlotte in part based on current 2004–05 data. Previous research by Atkinson and Gottlieb (2001) ranks the Charlotte region in the top five nationally for jobs in gazelle companies (new rapidly growing firms) and ranks the region twelfth nationally for economic dynamism (that is, regions epitomized by fast-growing entrepreneurial companies).
2. Ranking is among all cities in the US with population greater than 100 000.
3. The economic literature differentiates the entrepreneur from the risk-taker (the capitalist who funds the entrepreneur) (Kirzner, 1973; Schumpeter, 1961 [1911]), yet in the context of this analysis the Charlotte region could lack the institutional structure necessary to finance entrepreneurial ventures, contributing to the weak environment for entrepreneurial activity (Stough et al., 2004). The existence of venture capital (VC) will not necessarily attract entrepreneurs to a region (the presence of entrepreneurs draws VC) (Kreft and Sobel, 2003), but a more robust funding infrastructure may help encourage indigenous entrepreneurs carry out their ideas.
4. www.nctda.org.
5. www.bencraigcenter.com.

REFERENCES

Acs, Z.J., B. Carlsson and C. Karlsson (1999a), 'The linkages among entrepreneurship, SMEs and the macroeconomy', in Z.J. Acs, B. Carlsson and C. Karlsson (eds), *Entrepreneurship, Small and Medium-Sized Enterprises and the Macroeconomy*, Cambridge: Cambridge University Press, pp. 3–42.

Acs, Z.J., R. Morck and B. Young (1999b), 'Productivity growth and firm size distribution', in Z.J. Acs, B. Carlsson and C. Karlsson (eds), *Entrepreneurship, Small and Medium-Sized Enterprises and the Macroeconomy*, Cambridge: Cambridge University Press, pp. 367–96.

Allen, D.N. and M.L. Weinberg (1988), 'State investment in business incubators', *Public Administration Quarterly*, **12**(2), 196–215.
Atkinson, R.D. and P.D. Gottlieb (2001), *The Metropolitan New Economy Index: Benchmarking Economic Transformation in the Nation's Metropolitan Areas*, Washington, DC: Progressive Policy Institute.
Barrow, C. (2001), *Incubators*, Chichester: John Wiley & Sons.
Bearse, P. (1998), 'A question of evaluation: NBIA's impact assessment of business incubators', *Economic Development Quarterly*, **11**(4), 322–33.
Brinkman, R. (1995), 'Economic growth versus economic development: toward a conceptual clarification', *Journal of Economic Issues*, **29**(4), 1171–88.
Carree, M.A. and A.R. Thurik (2002), 'The impact of entrepreneurship on economic growth', in D.B. Audretsch and Z.J. Acs (eds), *Handbook of Entrepreneurship*, Boston, MA: Kluwer Academic Publishers, pp. 437–71.
Dahl, D. (2005), 'Percolating profits', *Inc.*, February, 38.
Dewar, M.E. (1998), 'Why state and local economic development programs cause so little economic development', *Economic Development Quarterly*, **12**(1), 68–88.
Eisinger, P.K. (1988), *The Rise of the Entrepreneurial State*. Madison, Wisconsin: The University of Wisconsin Press.
Florida, R. (2001), 'The entrepreneurial society', paper presented at the Conference of Entrepreneurship and Public Policy, Kennedy School of Government, Harvard University.
Florida, R. (2002), *The Rise of the Creative Class*, New York: Basic Books.
Florida, R. (2005), *The Flight of the Creative Class: The New Global Competition for Talent*, New York: Harper Business.
Friis, C., Paulsson T. and C. Karlsson (2002), *Entrepreneurship and Economic Growth: A Critical Review of Empirical and Theoretical Research*, Jonkoping, Sweden: Institute for Industrial Analysis, Jonkoping International Business School.
Geroski, P.A. (1994), *Market Structure, Corporate Performance and Innovative Activity*, Oxford: Clarendon Press.
Hackett, S.M. and D.M. Dilts (2004), 'A systematic review of business incubation research', *Journal of Technology Transfer*, **29**(1), 55–82.
Hall, K. (2005), 'We're cool – just ask her', *Charlotte Observer*, 20 April, p. B1.
Holcombe, R.G. (1998), 'Entrepreneurship and economic growth', *Quarterly Journal of Austrian Economics*, **1**(2), 45–62.
Kirzner, I.M. (1973), *Competition and Entrepreneurship*, Chicago, IL: University of Chicago Press.
Kreft, S.F. and R.S. Sobel (2003), 'Public policy, entrepreneurship, and economic growth', unpublished manuscript, West Virginia University, Department of Economics.
Krumholz, N. (1999), 'Equitable approaches to local economic development', *Policy Studies Journal*, **27**(1), 83.
Kuratko, D.F. and W.R. LaFollette (1987), 'Small business incubators for local economic development', *Economic Development Review*, **5**(2), 49–55.
Markley, D.M. and K.T. McNamara (1995), 'Economic and fiscal impacts of a business incubator', *Economic Development Quarterly*, **9**(3), 273–8.
National Business Incubator Association (NBIA) University of Michigan (2001), *Business Incubation Works*, Athens, OH: NBIA Publications.
Neck, H.M., G.D. Meyer B. Cohen and A.C. Corbett (2004), 'An entrepreneurial

system view of new venture creation', *Journal of Small Business Management*, **42**(2), 190–208.
North, D.C. (1990), *Institutions, Institutional Change and Economic Performance*, Cambridge: Cambridge University Press.
Ohmae, K. (1993), 'The rise of the region state', *Foreign Affairs*, **72**(2), 78–87.
Pack, H. (1994), 'Endogenous growth theory: intellectual appeal and empirical shortcomings', *Journal of Economic Perspectives*, **8**(1), 55–72.
Porter, M. (1990), *The Competitive Advantage of Nations*, New York: Free Press.
Reese, L.A. (1993), 'Categories of local economic development techniques: an empirical analysis', *Policy Studies Journal*, **21**(3), 492–506.
Ressler, T. (1995), 'Business incubators', in R.L. Kemp (ed.), *Economic Development in Local Government: A Handbook for Public Officials and Citizens*, Jefferson, NC: McFarland & Company, pp. 149–56.
Ryan, R. (2005), *Attracting and Retaining the Next Generation to Charlotte*, Madison, WI: Next Generation Consulting.
SBTDC (2004), *North Carolina's Business Incubators*, SBTDC Raleigh, NC: North Carolina Small Business & Technology Development Center (SBTDC).
Schumpeter, J.A. (1961 [1911]), *Theory of Economic Development*, Oxford: Galaxy Books.
Sherman, H. and D.S. Chappell (1998), 'Methodological challenges in evaluating business incubator outcomes', *Economic Development Quarterly*, **11**(4), 313–20.
Smilor, R.W. (1987), 'Managing the incubator system: critical success factors to accelerate new company development', *IEEE Transactions on Engineering Management*, **EM-34**(4), 146–56.
Steele, C.N. (1998), 'Entrepreneurship and the economics of growth', *Advances in Austrian Economics*, **5**, 51–84.
Stough, R.R., P.M. Frank, and G.E. Shockley (2004), 'The institutionalization and endogenization of venture capital: a regional analysis of Northern Virginia in the 1990s', in H.L.F. de Groot, P. Nijkamp and R.R. Stough (eds), *Rising Entrepreneurship in a Shrinking World: A Spatial Perspective*, Cheltenham, UK and Northampton, MA, USA: Edward Elgar, pp. 136–51.
Wennekers, S. and R. Thurik (1999), 'Linking entrepreneurship and economic growth', *Small Business Economics*, **13**(1), 27–55.

13. University spin-offs: an exploration of age-patterns of obstacles to growth

Marina van Geenhuizen and Danny P. Soetanto

13.1 THE EUROPEAN PARADOX

Growth of small high-technology firms has become a prominent issue in the past decades as they represent a potentially important opportunity to increase economic growth and innovation in regional and urban economies (for example Acs, 2002; Acs and Audretch, 1990). Small high-technology firms are seen as contributing significantly to the creation of new jobs and to innovation of the (regional) economy through knowledge transfer and linkages with larger firms (for example van Geenhuizen et al., 2004; OECD, 2001). Accordingly, start-up and early growth processes have been the focus of considerable research effort, with the aim to identify factors and conditions that contribute to start-ups' success or act as barriers. However, there is also a debate about the role of small high-technology firms, mainly due to their heterogeneous nature. Some of them have remained oriented locally, use short time horizons in planning and have a limited propensity to grow, while others – including the so-called first-movers – are highly specialized in their innovation and, accordingly, aim at growth in international markets (for example Storey and Tether, 1998; Heirman and Clarysse, 2004).

Many small high-technology firms are spin-offs from universities and research centers. Following Pirnay et al. (2003), academic spin-offs can be defined as a particular type of spin-off, created for the purpose of commercially exploiting knowledge, technology or research results developed within a university. In addition, the company founder(s) must come from the university, and the transfer of knowledge from the university to the company is direct. Accordingly, spin-off firms are connected with the university through three types of relationships: those with the founder (graduates or staff), the knowledge on which the company is built, and the supportive relationship with the university as the mother organization. Fostering academic spin-off firms is today at the core of many national economic policies in Europe. One of the major reasons for this policy attention is what is called the 'European paradox' – the contradictory situation of a high level of publicly financed knowledge production at universities and research institutes and a small economic use of this knowledge in the private sector. In this context, the policy aim in the Netherlands is to improve three constraining conditions: (1) a low level of entrepreneurial skills; (2) a weak entrepreneurial culture; and (3) difficulties in attracting venture capital (MEA, 2003b). Most founders of high-technology firms originate from technical universities or technical faculties of general universities and often lack the necessary entrepreneurial attitudes and skills (Cooper and Hetherington, 2005; van Geenhuizen and Soetanto, 2005). Taking courses in entrepreneurial skills is optional and not a part of the standard curriculum. In addition, the Dutch culture is not really supportive of those wishing to start their own businesses. In particular, policy at universities is mostly geared to risk reduction, and the comfortable labor conditions enjoyed by academic staff do not encourage entrepreneurship; this is strongly in contrast with the situation in the US. The third condition, difficulties in attracting risk capital, is basically caused by reluctance of venture capital providers to invest in the preparation or seed stages of start-ups, and by an overall relatively small focus on innovative start-ups (compared with the US). On the other hand, there is also reluctance among high-tech entrepreneurs to become involved with formal venture capital, because of the strict rules of the game and a fear of losing independence (van Geenhuizen and Soetanto, 2005).

Academic incubation policies are certainly not new but have regained attention in the past few years. Universities have good reasons to develop nurturing policies for their spin-offs aside from just research commercialization, such as strengthening relationships with the local business community, improving the image of the university and fulfilling commitments to society, particularly in economically depressed areas, to support innovation and restructuring of the regional economy (for example Charles, 2003).

The term 'incubator', used in this chapter, refers to the supportive environment created to ensure the survival and growth of new technology-based firms, and is not necessarily equivalent to accommodation providing cheap and flexible space. Incubation policies of universities may include a whole range of actions and supportive measures, for example: a (proactive) screening of the faculties to identify promising candidate firms or business ideas; supplying relatively simple seedbed conditions, such as cheap and flexible workspace shared services (secretarial, cleaning, and so on), and standard courses; and supplying advanced support such as customized courses and mentoring, support in networking, access to research facilities and mediation for financial capital such as 'friendly' types of loans. In recent years, there has been a move beyond support focused on covering needs for physical infrastructure (accommodation, services) to support that also includes improving the entrepreneurial capabilities of the founders through supplying courses, mentoring and, more recently, through the creation of opportunities for internal and external networking by spin-offs (Bøllingtoft and Ulhøi, 2005). It is also increasingly recognized that spin-off firms follow different stages, each with distinct needs and obstacles, and critical junctures; and that the pattern of these stages may differ between spin-offs (Ndonzuau et al., 2002; Reid and Garnsey, 1998; Roberts, 1991; Vohora et al., 2003). Like small high-technology firms in general, spin-offs are heterogeneous to a certain extent. They may be involved only in research and development (R&D), or in manufacturing or services; they may be driven by different entrepreneurial ambitions and strategies concerning innovativeness. All potentially lead to diverse age-patterns of needs for particular resources, capabilities and competences, and to situations that hamper growth. There is, however, little attention in empirical research for such age-patterns and for differentiation between diverse spin-offs, and if there is attention, it is mostly based on case-study research and not on medium-sized and larger samples.

This study strives to understand how different spin-off firms deal with obstacles to growth at different ages. The objective is to explore the age-dimension of obstacles in a systematic way by using a sample of spin-off firms. Since it cannot cover all differences between spin-offs, the study focuses on a major one, that is, the level of innovativeness. The study addresses the following questions: (1) How does the pattern of obstacles change by age and what does this say about changing capabilities of spin-offs to deal with obstacles? (2) What is the nature of obstacles at different ages and which obstacles are most difficult to overcome? (3) To what extent is the decline of obstacles by age different for highly innovative spin-offs compared with other spin-offs? (4) What are the implications of the above outcomes for the kind of support needed?

This chapter builds on a previous study based on cross-section data of age-patterns of obstacles (Soetanto and van Geenhuizen, forthcoming) by adding insights from a longitudinal analysis and curve-fitting attempts. The chapter is structured as follows. Section 13.2 provides a resource-dependence perspective on start-up and early growth of university spin-offs. An introduction to the case study, that is, spin-offs from Delft University of Technology in the Netherlands (section 13.3) is followed by an analysis of the nature of obstacles faced by spin-offs (section 13.4).

Next, the chapter focuses on how obstacles to growth change by age, using both transversal and longitudinal data (section 13.5) and on the differences that occur between highly innovative spin-offs and others, including the best models based on curve-fitting (section 13.6). The final section is a discussion of the findings in a broader context, including policy implications and future research.

13.2 RESOURCE GATHERING

From a resource-based perspective, firms may be conceptualized as heterogeneous bundles of assets or resources tied to the firms' management. Firms acquire or search for resources as an input and convert these into products or services for which revenue can be obtained (Barney, 1991; Barney et al., 2001). Resource-based theory deals with circumstances under which a resource leads to high returns over longer periods of time, for example, those that are characterized by uniqueness and are difficult to imitate; and with circumstances which may block a path to higher returns, such as when entrepreneurs fail to anticipate the need for new resources or fail to access the required resources in time. By their nature, university spin-off firms are short of various resources (Groen et al., 2005; Reid and Garnsey, 1998; Roberts, 1991). The literature most often mentions lack of investment capital and lack of non-technical knowledge and skills. Accordingly, to be able to progress through the early phases, spin-offs must organize access to these resources. The range of growth opportunities, therefore, critically depends on the nature of the environment and on the capability of spin-offs to network with key providers of resources in this environment, such as the mother organization, customers, suppliers and investors (Hoang and Antoncic, 2003; Reid and Garnsey, 1998). Different resource requirements and different capabilities and ways of accessing complementary resources in the environment lead to different growth paths and degrees of success (Figure 13.1), that is, early failure or a steady growth, followed by different outcomes, such as growth reinforcement, stability (eventually oscillation) and growth reversal. In particular high-technology areas, entrepreneurs must be able to assess their resource requirements as accurately as possible because they may gain a disproportionate benefit if they meet critical requirements at the right point in time. In contrast, lack of this capability can cause growth to stop, either by entering a relatively steady phase or by falling back to a previous stage. Indeed, growth paths may be full of iterations (Vohora et al., 2003). For example, failure in the resources generation phase may imply returning to the mobilization of resources. The risk of stagnation or falling-back forces

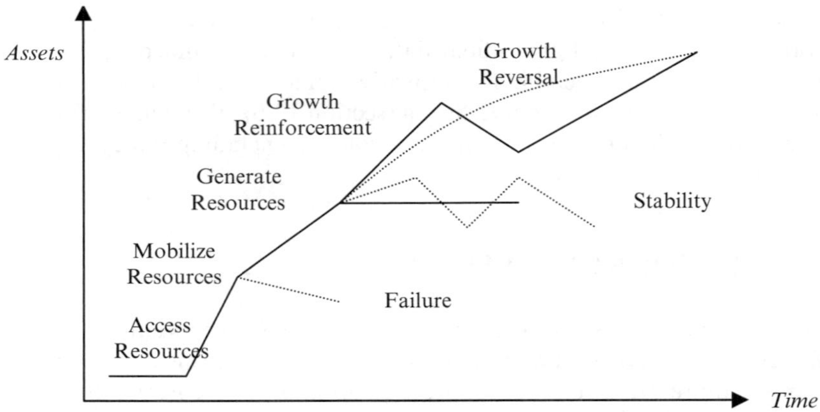

Source: Reid and Garnsey (1998).

Figure 13.1 Growth paths of new high-technology firms

spin-offs continually to evaluate their position and to deal with future uncertainty by developing strategies and scenarios.

A specific position is held by first-movers (or early entrants) in emerging markets. The potential of these firms to acquire superior resources and capabilities is often addressed in the literature on first-mover advantages, but the outcomes of empirical research are ambiguous. Lieberman and Montgomery (1998) found the following superior resources: prime physical locations, a protected technology position (by patents), and monopoly in the market eventually by making a superior brand and establishing product specificities that cause 'shifting costs' for customers. But the two authors equally stress that first-movers may miss the best resources because these are obscured by technological and market uncertainties. Likewise, they mention that first-movers may gain a head start in achieving key capabilities and competencies on the basis of learning curve advantages. However, this may not be typical for a first-mover market position, but may be personal characteristics of entrepreneurs that are attracted by risk-taking in general.

From a resource perspective, incubator organizations play the role of resource gatherer, as an intermediary agent serving spin-off firms. Incubator organizations perform a bridging function by sourcing and 'macro-managing' the innovation process for emerging, weak but promising (nearly) firms, infusing them with resources at different points in time in the incubation process (Hackett and Dilts, 2004). Incubator organizations now often connect spin-offs with actors that supply critical resources instead of having either the incubator organization or the university own the resources themselves. Such 'networked' incubators make increasing use of information and communication technology, thereby reducing the costs of searching for resources such as investment capital, potential partners for collaboration and potential markets.

13.3 INTRODUCTION TO THE CASE STUDY

This empirical study draws on a case study of 43 spin-offs from Delft University of Technology in the Netherlands, based on a detailed survey in 2003. The sample includes selected spin-off firms that were established in the years from 1994 and supported by the university in a standard support program or beyond (prior to) this program. The original sample size was 64 spin-off firms. On the basis of a response rate of 67.2 percent this led to an actual sample of 43 spin-offs. The survey focused on the identification of problematic needs and the point in time at which these occurred and disappeared. In addition, it focused on the innovative level. The survey was followed by five in-depth studies to increase understanding of obstacles to growth.

The analysis of obstacles at different ages of the spin-offs is descriptive in the sense that various development paths are identified and differentiated for types of obstacles and the innovative level of spin-offs. For descriptive purposes, the study defines two indicators: the obstacle incidence rate (OIR) and the obstacle reduction rate (ORR). It uses both cross-sectional data and longitudinal data. Before proceeding with the discussion of the results concerning age-patterns of obstacles, it is necessary to introduce the case study: Delft University of Technology.

Delft University of Technology is in Delft, a small town (about 95 000 inhabitants) in the densely populated western part of the Netherlands. It represents a category of technical universities in Western Europe that became involved in the development of new technology-based firms relatively late. The first official program, named the Techno-starter program, was introduced in 1998, but a similar kind of support had been provided a few years prior to 1998. The Techno-starter program supports firms founded by graduates, students and academic staff. The program does not provide space in a special incubator building or in a science park (both are currently under construction and almost finished). Rather, the spin-offs are housed in faculty buildings, in some old laboratories of the university (temporary), and in various business buildings that host start-ups in the town of Delft. The Techno-starter program provides support in terms of initial investment, entrepreneurial courses, office space and laboratories, with the faculty, and there is a mentoring program.

With regard to the number of spin-offs established in the past few years, the program can be seen as a moderate success when compared with other technical universities in the Netherlands and with the agricultural (life sciences) University of Wageningen. The University of Twente has been most productive of all universities in the Netherlands through the early 2000s, with 7.9 spin-offs per 1000 full-time employees in 1999–2001 (2.1 spin-offs for Delft University of Technology) (MEA, 2003a). Spin-off productivity, however, must be seen in a regional-economic policy perspective to some extent. The University of Twente was established in the 1960s as part of national and European policy to support the restructuring of the regional economy (Twente) following the collapse of the textile industry. This university started to develop an incubation policy beginning in the late 1970s (Karnebeek, 2001). In contrast to Twente, Delft is in the economic core area of the Randstad with relatively large cities, adjacent to The Hague and also close to Rotterdam, with its own university and incubation program. The region of Delft is not eligible for regional development funds (national or European Union).

In terms of characteristics of the sample, the following can be observed. With regard to age, the largest category (39.5 percent) is that of youngest firms (<3 years), whereas older age groups (3–5 years and six years and older) are slightly smaller (32.6 and 27.9 percent). The age structure explains why most spin-offs are relatively small; more than half of the spin-offs employ fewer than five persons (53.5 percent) and almost one-third employs 5–15 persons (30.2 percent). Large firms may be slightly underrepresented in our sample, because some have left the municipality in search of large accommodation. In terms of innovative level, a significant number of the spin-offs can be seen as highly innovative on the basis of their product (service) qualification as 'new for the sector' or 'new as a breakthrough', and on the basis of spending a relatively high share of turnover on R&D (55.8 percent). These spin-offs can be seen as first-movers in their specific market areas (niches).

13.4 NATURE OF OBSTACLES

In this study, obstacles include resources and capabilities that are experienced as problematic because of limited presence or non-availability. Aside from this, there are a few situations that may hinder firms directly in utilizing available resources, for example bureaucratic delays in providing permits. The results of the case study indicate that there are a whole range of such obstacles (Table 13.1). Market-related obstacles are in first place and management obstacles and financial obstacles are in second and third

Table 13.1 Obstacles to growth

Categories	Specification	Abs.	%	Rank
Market-related	Marketing knowledge	20	14.5	1
	Sales skills	17	12.3	4
	Customer base	10	7.2	6
Management	Dealing with uncertainty	19	13.8	2/3
	Management (overload)	14	10.1	5
Finance	Cash flow	19	13.8	2/3
	Investment capital	9	6.5	7/8
	R&D investment (development)	7	5.1	10
Physical	Accommodation	8	5.8	9
	Infrastructure	5	3.6	11
	Distance (to suppliers, markets, etc.)	1	0.7	12
Government	Regulation, bureaucracy	9	6.5	7/8
Totals		138	100	

Source: Adapted from van Geenhuizen and Soetanto (2005).

place, respectively. Lack of marketing knowledge is the most frequently occurring obstacle, followed by a lack of cash flow, lack of capability of dealing with uncertainty in management, lack of sales skills, and management overload. This compares with what is presented in the literature as being the most prominent problems among university spin-offs in general (see section 13.2). It is not surprising that lack of marketing knowledge is one of the main obstacles, since the spin-off firms evolve from an initial idea in a non-commercial environment, to becoming established as a competitive profit-generating firm, a stage in which new and completely different resources (knowledge) and routines are required (Oakey, 2003; Vohora et al., 2003). Despite efforts to prevent the rise of market-related obstacles, for instance by providing courses in marketing knowledge and sales skills, these obstacles are relatively prominent. Maybe marketing knowledge is not something that can be achieved through courses. The results of in-depth interviews indicate that, firstly the markets involved are often niche markets and standard courses are not sufficiently specific to provide the right knowledge. Secondly, sales skills include skills in communication, negotiation and convincing actors in niche markets, and these skills cannot be provided in a standard marketing course. An important additional point needs to be mentioned here: credibility in the market. Some spin-offs are subject to a vicious circle – they fail to acquire a large customer simply because they have not served a large customer previously.

Some of the above high-ranked obstacles effectively influence the growth of spin-offs, as has become evident in the estimation of a regression-model including these obstacles among other factors (van Geenhuizen and Soetanto, 2005). Thus, lack of marketing knowledge has a negative influence on growth, whereas the problem of dealing with uncertainty has a positive influence on growth. The latter result suggests that spin-offs dealing with uncertainty in a conscious manner, for example, using strategic planning or flexible strategies, tend to face better opportunities to grow.

13.5 OBSTACLES BY AGE

The study focuses on the occurrence of obstacles by age using two perspectives, a cross-sectional (transversal) one of spin-offs in different age-categories in the present situation, and a longitudinal one of present spin-offs looking back into their past (retrospective). To measure the occurrence of obstacles over different ages the analysis uses the so-called 'obstacle incidence rate' (OIR), derived by dividing the total number of obstacles per age-category (class or year) by the number of spin-offs in that category, as follows:

$$\textit{Obstacle incidence rate (OIR)} = \frac{\sum_{i=0}^{t} oi}{\sum_{i=0}^{n} xi}$$

O = number of obstacles per age-category
X = number of spin-offs in the age category
t = age category or year
$n = 0, 1, 2, \ldots$

In the first years, different obstacles tend to arise simultaneously, such as problems with cash flow, market demand and management overload, and to a smaller extent, accommodation and infrastructure problems. In the second age category (3–5 years), some of these obstacles still exist but their number has clearly decreased. There is a decline in the average number of obstacles per firm by 26.1 percent between the first and second age-categories. Next, particular problems are almost solved in the second and third age-categories, that is, concerning physical infrastructure and

Table 13.2 Current obstacles per age category (cross-section)

Obstacles	< 3 years (t)	3–5 years (t + 1)	≥ 6 years (t + 2)
Market-related	15	12	7
Finance	17	9	3
Management	13	11	5
Physical (e.g. accommodation)	8	1	0
Remaining (e.g. regulation)	3	1	1
Total obstacles	56	34	16
Total firms	17	14	12
Obstacle incidence rate (*OIR*)	3.29	2.43	1.33
t-test (t) and (t + 1)		0.245	
t-test (t+1) and (t + 2)			0.225
t-test (t) and (t + 2)			0.023*

Note: * Significant at the 0.05 level.

financial problems, while others tend to remain resistant. The reduction of the number of average obstacles between the second and third age-categories amounts to 45.3 percent. Overall, the OIR of the three age-categories (3.29, 2.43 and 1.33 respectively) and the outcomes of the t-tests (Table 13.2) suggest a significant decrease of obstacles between the first and the third age-categories only (by 59.6 percent), indicating a slow but sure increase of the capability of spin-offs to solve (or prevent) problems.

To discover trends, the study employed the 'obstacle reduction rate' or ORR, measured by dividing the difference of OIR in two age categories with the initial OIR:

$$\textit{Obstacle reduction rate (ORR)} = \frac{OIt + n - OIt}{OIt} \times 100\%$$

OIR_t = obstacle incidence rate in the t age category
OIR_{t+n} = obstacle incidence rate in the t+n age category
t = age category or year
n = 0, 1, 2, . . .

The reduction rates (ORR) over the three age-categories are:

- 34.1 percent for market-related obstacles (OIR_t is 0.88 and OIR_{t+2} is 0.58).
- 75.0 percent for financial obstacles (OIR_t is 1.00 and OIR_{t+2} is 0.25).

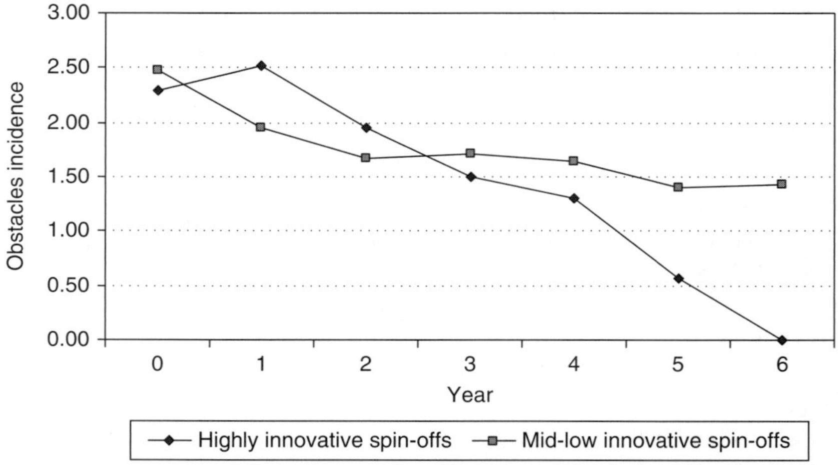

Figure 13.2 Major obstacles per age-category (cross-section)

- 44.7 percent for management obstacles (OIR_t is 0.76 and OIR_{t+2} is 0.42).

The above reduction rates show that market-related obstacles tend to be more resistant to disappearing with age than other obstacles (Figure 13.2).

By contrast, most financial obstacles tend to be resolved fairly easily. This contradicts some other studies that indicate that financial problems increase or culminate after a few years of existence of the spin-offs when the product (service) has proven to be viable and (small) series production facilities are needed, or when additional R&D is necessary following the first seed-stage, such as in research-intensive medical biotechnology (van Geenhuizen, 2003). Probably, the Delft spin-offs solve financial problems partially by means of self-financing. Previous research indicates that a majority of the managers of Delft (72.1 percent) undertake some routine work in the spin-off firm or have part-time jobs elsewhere to enable self-financing (van Geenhuizen and Soetanto, 2005). According to an alternative explanation, older spin-offs facing financial problems would collapse more frequently than older spin-offs facing other problems.

From the longitudinal perspective, the study focuses on obstacles that spin-offs have faced during their lifetime. It uses data covering seven years (year zero to year six) (Table 13.3). Although the impact of a memory gap has caused some bias in the longitudinal data (note a generally lower level of obstacles compared with cross-section data) it is still possible to assume

Table 13.3 Obstacles over time (longitudinal)

Age (N)	Obstacles incidence	Reduction rate
0 (43)	2.37	
1 (42)	2.26	−4.64
2 (38)	1.82	−19.47
3 (26)	1.62	−10.99
4 (21)	1.48	−8.64
5 (17)	1.06	−28.38
6 +(12)	0.83	−21.70
Obstacle reduction rate age 0 to age 6+		−64.98

a sufficient reliability of the longitudinal results if these broadly confirm patterns found on the basis of cross-sectional data.

Table 13.3 indicates that obstacles experienced by firms during their lifetime decline significantly at age two and at later ages (five and six plus). Overall, the reduction rate is 64.98 percent, meaning that in six years' time there is a significant decrease of obstacles to growth. This broadly compares with the reduction rate based on the cross-section data (59.6 percent). The reduction tends to fall back at the age of three and four which may point to a critical situation in terms of resource-gathering and access to markets.

13.6 HOW DIFFERENT ARE INNOVATIVE SPIN-OFFS IN DEALING WITH OBSTACLES?

This section focuses on highly innovative spin-offs and compares them with medium- to high-tech spin-offs. Highly innovative spin-offs as defined in this study (section 13.3) are often market leaders facing few or no competitors, but who most probably deal with technological problems such as the need for costly improvements of first versions of a new product. It is plausible that these spin-offs, due to willingness to undertake greater risks, are more vulnerable to problems at the start than other spin-offs. The cross-sectional results on OIR in Table 13.4 indeed suggest that highly innovative spin-offs face a relatively high incidence rate in the first years (3.92 versus 1.80). However, in the next two age-categories, highly innovative spin-offs tend to overcome (or prevent) obstacles to a strong degree, whereas medium- to low-innovative spin-offs first face a lesser capability to overcome (prevent) obstacles. Overall, highly innovative spin-offs tend to face more problems than medium- to low-innovative spin-offs but show

Table 13.4 Incidence (OIR) of all obstacles (a)

Age category	Highly innovative spin-offs (HIS)	Med-low innovative spin-offs (MLIS)	t-test HIS and MLIS
< 3 years (t)	3.92	1.80	0.111
3–5 years (t+1)	2.43	3.40	0.875
⩾ 6 years (t+2)	1.20	2.00	0.008**
Total OIR	2.92	1.89	
Number of firms	24	19	
Number of obstacles	70	36	
t-test (t) and (t + 1)	0.179	0.663	
t-test (t + 1) and (t + 2)	0.113	0.504	
t-test (t) and (t + 2)	0.036 *	0.897	

Note: * significant at the 0.05 level; ** significant at the 0.01 level.

a much stronger capability to resolve them in later years, demonstrated by an OIR of 1.20 (versus 2.00) in the third age-category. The latter results are supported by the outcomes of the t-test (Table 13.4); the difference in the obstacle incidence rate between the first and third age-category is only significant for highly innovative spin-offs and, in a comparison of the two types of spin-offs for each age-category, the difference is significant only for spin-offs in the third age-category.

The study also explores trends by age on the basis of longitudinal data (Table 13.5). Note that the small numbers of spin-offs per age on a yearly basis only permits identifying broad patterns. The number of obstacles among highly innovative firms tends to increase right after start-up but then decreases at higher rates than among medium- to low-innovative spin-offs (for example obstacle reduction rates of +10.04 versus –21.05 for the first year, and –22.62 and –14.36 for the second year) (see also Figure 13.3). At age six, all obstacles are solved among highly innovative spin-offs, whereas medium- to low-innovative spin-offs still suffer from a few obstacles (an OIR of 1.43). The age-pattern of the latter type of spin-offs suggests some stagnation in removing (prevention) of obstacles at age three and four, which is similar to the pattern seen in the entire sample of spin-offs.

The results of the above longitudinal analysis broadly comply with those of the cross-sectional analysis. However, the results of the cross-sectional analysis suggest a higher problem incidence among highly innovative

Table 13.5 Obstacles over time (longitudinal)

Age	Highly innovative spin-offs		Medium-low innovative spin-offs	
	Obstacles incidence	Reduction rate	Obstacles incidence	Reduction rate
0	2.29		2.47	
1	2.52	10.04	1.95	−21.05
2	1.95	−22.62	1.67	−14.36
3	1.50	−23.08	1.71	2.40
4	1.30	−13.33	1.64	−4.09
5	0.57	−56.15	1.40	−14.63
6+	0.00	−100.00	1.43	2.14
Obstacle reduction rate 0 to 6+		−100.00		−42.11

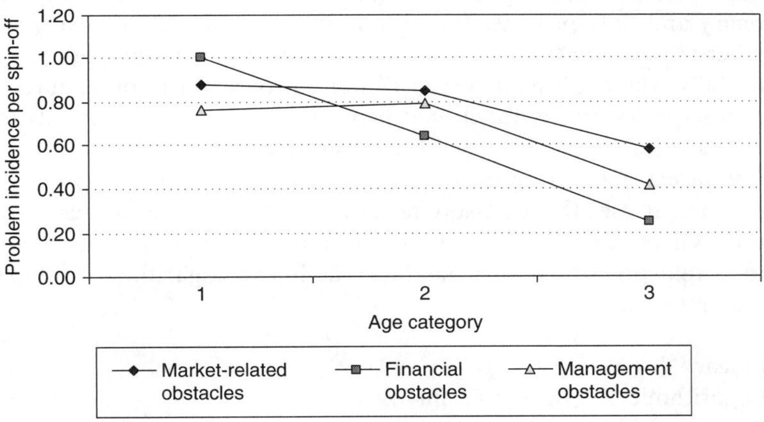

Figure 13.3 Obstacle incidence (OIR)

spin-offs that are young than the longitudinal analysis (for young medium- to low-innovative spin-offs it is the other way around). One possible explanation is this: young and highly innovative spin-offs (in 2003) tend to be more vulnerable than those that were young in the 1990s, under more favorable macroeconomic conditions. For the remaining, the previously indicated higher obstacle incidence rate in cross-sectional data is true for both highly innovative and medium- to low-innovative spin-offs.

Given the limitations of the data, it is possible to understand the development of highly innovative spin-offs as apparent from their histories as follows. Highly innovative spin-offs enjoy the advantage of being first-movers into new markets and consequently face no competitors or only a few of them. Their high problem incidence (as compared with medium- to low-innovative spin-offs) after the start may be caused by problems linked with technological uncertainty. A strong market position tends to smooth the growth path in the subsequent years. The relatively high reduction rates by age may also be explained by a process of positive selection: undertaking highly innovative activities is seen as a challenge primarily by those persons who have high capabilities in preventing and solving problems, for example through networking with key suppliers of resources.

The final step was conducting a curve-fitting procedure to find the best model for representing the data characteristics of highly innovative spin-offs and medium- to low-innovative spin-offs. The purpose of the curve-fitting procedure is to identify the central tendency of the *Y* variable's distribution (obstacle incidence) at different positions within the *X* variable's distribution (age). Note that our curve-fitting procedure is preliminary and only provides broad indications, given the relatively small number of points in time (seven) and the relatively small sample.

Initially, the analysis involved running a parametric procedure that requires specifying the functional form of the relationship in advance. The algorithm then optimizes the fit between the specified form and the empirical data. Regression analysis is the best-known parametric procedure. It uses the least-squares criterion to fit a line to a set of data points. Given the plotted curves, the analysis then considered three models that possibly match the data: the linear, logarithmic and exponential models:

Linear (Y = b0 + (b1 * t))
Logarithmic Y = b0 + (b1 * ln(t)).
Exponential Y = b0 * (e**(b1 * t)) or ln(Y) = ln(b0) + (b1 * t).

Note: the series values are modeled as a function of time (age), therefore t = time, b*x* = constant.

Table 13.6 and Figure 13.4 show the results of the curve-fitting procedure. These results suggest that for highly innovative spin-offs, the best model is the linear model (Goodness of fit R^2: 0.932); for medium- to low-innovative spin-offs it is the logarithmic model (Goodness of fit R^2: 0.938). This preliminary result indeed suggests an essentially different development for the two categories of spin-offs, leading to different vulnerability at early and later ages.

Table 13.6 Results of curve fitting

	Linear	Logarithmic	Exponential
Highly innovative spin-offs	y=-.407X+3.076 $R^2 = 0.932$	y=-1.154X+2.854 $R^2 = 0.754$	y=-.703X+12.359 $R^2 = 0.598$
Medium-low innovative spin-offs	y =-.152X+2.350 $R^2 = 0.803$	y =-.517X+2.383001 $R^2 = 0.938$	y =-.083X+2.400 $R^2 = 0.849$

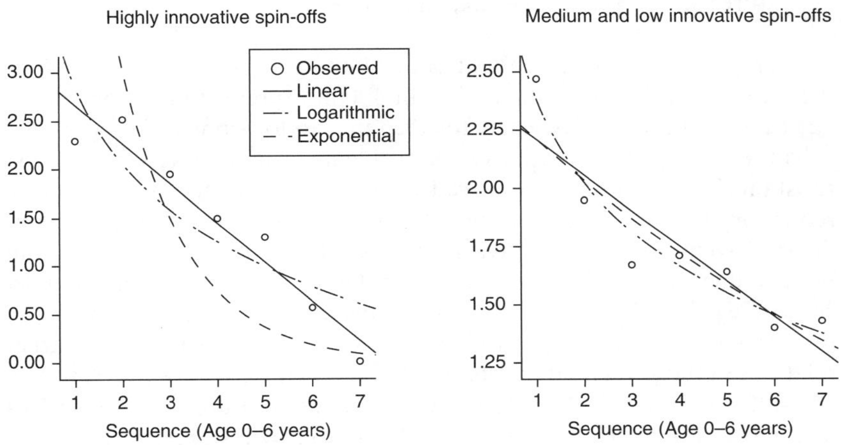

Figure 13.4 Results of curve-fitting

13.7 SUMMARY AND CONCLUSION

This chapter explores how patterns of obstacles faced by spin-offs change by age, using Delft University of Technology in the Netherlands as an example. Taking into account a small potential bias towards well-performing spin-offs and towards smaller ones, we believe that the sample is sufficiently representative to guide technical universities in North-Western Europe that have adopted a 'low selective' incubation strategy, meaning that spin-offs employing divergent levels of innovativeness may enter the program (Clarysse et al., 2003). The analysis was able to identify various trends of age-patterns of obstacles to growth, based on cross-sectional data and longitudinal data. These can be summarized as follows:

- Overall, the capability to solve (prevent) obstacles is initially low, but improves later on; a stagnation in this capability at age three and four suggests a reinforcing of market access problems.
- Market-related problems tend to be most resistant to resolution, followed by management problems. Surprisingly, financial problems tend to be resolved in a timely manner.
- Highly innovative spin-offs tend to face a relatively high obstacles incidence at a very young age, but they have a strong capability to remove obstacles in later years. By contrast, medium- to low-innovative spin-offs tend to face a stagnation in this capability at age three and four (stronger than all spin-offs).

There are several research and policy implications of the study's findings. First, the trend of stagnation in solving (preventing) problems at age three and four (particularly for medium- to low-innovative spin-offs) calls for policy attention. Although problems of market access are most resistant, it is not known what causes this particular decline in obstacle reduction. Knowledge about critical ages (turning points) in the development of spin-offs is still limited and calls for future studies to underpin better a fine-tuning of support measures. These may include, for example, continuing eligibility for incubation support in critical years and intensifying support in networking with key actors to solve bottlenecks in market relations in those years. If market-related problems are not solved in time, spin-offs tend to lack the credibility to generate resources by themselves and may never be able to progress to the next growth stages.

Second, the observed trend among highly innovative spin-offs – that they are relatively vulnerable to obstacles in early years but are relieved by a relatively sharp decrease of obstacles in later years – is interesting from a theoretical point of view. A positive selection mechanism may play a role in causing highly innovative spin-offs to be relatively successful in developing and utilizing networks later on through which they can access external key resources. Whether such a selection mechanism holds true needs to be studied on the basis of a larger sample. In addition, there are many related questions, such as: how does such independent selection unfold and through which criteria can such selection be imitated in the practice of granting access to incubation programs? Also, the role of market dynamics and the strategies of first-mover spin-offs in response to these dynamics call for attention in future research. Additional in-depth research of the development of highly innovative spin-offs is also most relevant in the context of the emerging new incubation policy in the Netherlands that attempts to increase the number of highly innovative spin-offs as offspring of universities (Three TUs, 2004). There is another argument in favor of more research on selective strategies for giving access to incubation programs and increasing the number of highly innovative spin-offs, which is that the knowledge accumulated in universities and research institutes will be better utilized, thus contributing to relieving the European paradox.

Third, the methodological basis of the measurement of problems among spin-offs must be improved. This study suggests the influence of a memory gap, based on higher levels of obstacles incidence in cross-sectional data compared with longitudinal data. However, it is not only a matter of memory gap: there is also the potential impact of different macroeconomic settings, for example between companies that were young in the 1990s (longitudinal data) and those that were young at the time of the study (2003) (cross-sectional data). The construction of a panel of spin-offs in which the data are semi-annually (or monthly) updated seems an adequate solution.

ACKNOWLEDGEMENT

This study is part of the Delft University of Technology Center of Sustainable Urban Areas.

REFERENCES

Acs, Z.J. (2002), *Innovation and the Growth of Cities*, Cheltenham, UK and Northampton, MA, USA: Edward Elgar.

Acs, Z.J. and D.B. Audretsch (1990), *The Economics of Small Firms, A European Challenge*, Dordrecht: Kluwer Academic Publishers.

Barney, J. (1991), 'Firm resources and sustained competitive advantage', *Journal of Management*, **17**(1), 99–120.

Barney, J., M. Wright and D. Ketchen (2001), 'The resource-based view: ten years after 1991', *Journal of Management*, **27**(6), 625–42.

Bøllingtoft, A. and J.P. Ulhøi (2005), 'The networked business incubator: leveraging entrepreneurial agency?' *Journal of Business Venturing*, **20**, 265–90.

Charles, D. (2003), 'Universities and territorial development: reshaping the regional role of English universities', *Local Economy*, **18**(1), 7–20.

Clarysse, B., A. Heirman and J. Degroof (2003), 'Growth paths of technology-based companies in life sciences and information technology', Innovation Policy Studies series, European Commission Enterprise Directorate-General, Report No. 32. 2003.

Cooper, S. and L. Hetherington (2005), 'Developing entrepreneurial capability to facilitate academic entrepreneurship and technology commercialisation', in W. During, R. Oakey and S. Kauser (eds), *New Technology-Based Firms in the New Millennium, Volume IV*, Amsterdam: Elsevier, pp. 23–40.

van Geenhuizen, M. (2003), 'How can we reap the fruits of academic research in

biotechnology? In search of critical success factors in policies for new firm formation', *Environment and Planning C*, **21**, 139–55.
van Geenhuizen, M., D. Gibson and M.V. Heitor (eds) (2004), *Regional Development and Conditions for Innovation in the Network Society*, West Lafayette, IN: Purdue University Press.
van Geenhuizen, M. and D. Soetanto (2005), 'Fostering academic entrepreneurship: an evolutionary perspective', in H. Groot, P. Nijkamp and R. Stough (eds), *Entrepreneurship in the Modern Space-Economy: Evolutionary and Policy Perspectives*, Cheltenham, UK and Northampton, MA, USA: Edward Elgar, pp. 252–68.
Groen, A., I. Jenniskens and P. van der Sijde (2005), 'Needs of start-up technology-driven enterprises: starting points for government policy', in W. During, R. Oakey and S. Kauser (eds), *New Technology-Based Firms in the New Millennium, Volume IV*, Amsterdam: Elsevier, pp. 219–34.
Hackett, S.M. and D.M. Dilts (2004), 'A real option-driven theory of business incubation', *Journal of Technology Transfer*, **29**, 41–54.
Heirman, A. and B. Clarysse (2004), 'How and why do research-based start-ups differ at founding? A resource-based configurational perspective', *Journal of Technology Transfer*, **29**, 247–68.
Hoang, H. and B. Antoncic (2003), 'Network-based research in entrepreneurship: a critical review', *Journal of Business Venturing*, **17**, 1–23.
Karnebeek, A.J. (2001), *Spin-offs and the University of Twente*, Enschede: Twente University Press.
Lieberman, M.B. and D.B. Montgomery (1998), 'First-mover (dis)advantages: retrospective and link with the resource-based view', *Strategic Management Journal*, **19**, pp. 1111–25.
Ministry of Economic Affairs (MEA) (2003a), 'Technology-based start-up survey 2003', The Hague: Ministry of Economic Affairs.
Ministry of Economic Affairs (MEA) (2003b), *TechnoPartner Action Program. From Knowledge to Prosperity*, The Hague: Ministry of Economic Affairs.
Ndonzuau, F.N., F. Pirnay and B. Surlemont (2002), 'A stage model of academic spin-off creation', *Technovation*, **22**(5), 281–9.
Oakey, R.P. (2003), 'Technical entrepreneurship in high technology small firms: some observations on the implications for management', *Technovation*, **23**, 679–88.
Organisation for Economic Co-operation and Development (OECD) (2001), *Fostering High-Tech Spin-offs: A Public Strategy for Innovation, STI Review*, **26**, Special Issue.
Pirnay, F., B. Surlemont and F. Nlemvo (2003), 'Toward a typology of university spin-offs', *Small Business Economics*, **21**(4), 355–69.
Reid, S. and E. Garnsey (1998), 'Incubation policy and resource provision: meeting the needs of young, innovative firms', in R. Oakey and W. During (eds), *New Technology Based Firms in the 1990s*, Volume V, London: Paul Chapman, pp. 67–80.
Roberts, E.B. (1991), *Entrepreneurs in High Technology. Lessons from MIT and Beyond*, New York: Oxford University Press.
Soetanto, D.P. and M. van Geenhuizen (forthcoming), 'University spin-offs at different ages: in search of obstacles to better match support', in R. Oakey and A. Groen (eds), *New Technology Based Firms in the New Millennium*, Volume VI, Amsterdam: Elsevier (forthcoming).

Storey, D.J. and B.S. Tether (1998), Public policy measures to support new technology-based firms in the European Union', *Research Policy*, **26**, 1037–57.
Three TUs (Delft University of Technology, Eindhoven University of Technology and University of Twente) (2004), 'Alertness in innovation!', (internal paper, in Dutch).
Vohora, A., M. Wright and A. Lockett (2003), 'Critical junctures in the development of university high-tech spinout companies', *Research Policy*, **33**, 147–75.

14. FDI inflows to Sweden: consequences for innovation and renewal

Börje Johansson and Hans Lööf

14.1 INTRODUCTION

Why should a firm decide to have several establishments located in different regions and countries? We may also ask why the number and expansion of multinational firms have increased for several decades. Antras and Helpman (2003) argue that the expansion of foreign direct investment (FDI) flows reflects a growing specialization of production. The main mechanism for FDI is mergers and acquisition (M&A), and since the late 1980s the cross-border share of total M&A has been relatively constant (UNCTAD, 2000). Hence, the tendency of multi-location solutions is as strong within countries as it is between countries.

Dunning (1977) suggests that a multi-location firm has specific assets that give it an advantage over potential competitors in a given region. In addition, the location of a subsidiary in a given region must also provide some advantage that is not obtained if the firm were exporting from some 'home location'. Extending this argument, the assumption is that a lack of markets for firm-specific assets, including various forms of knowledge, provides the individual firm with incentives to internalize production and other supply activities in owned subsidiaries abroad (Caves, 1982; Braunerhjelm, 1999). Because of this, and with reference to Coase (1937), a firm may decide to penetrate a foreign market by means of direct investments instead of forming agreements to cooperate with firms in the foreign market, including licensing arrangements.

When a multinational firm makes a direct investment in a foreign market it establishes an FDI firm in that market. In view of the discussion above, how will an FDI firm influence the knowledge flows, the research and development (R&D) intensity and R&D collaboration in the local economy where the FDI firm is located? In what other ways may it influence the host-country and host-region economy? In general we refer to the consequences for a regional as well as national economy as 'local economy effects'.

A basic observation has stimulated the research efforts in this chapter. The observation is that multinational firms are network organizations. As such a multinational firm has geographically (globally) spread information and knowledge sources. An individual FDI firm can draw on all this information, and hence it has the potential of introducing more novelties than a non-multinational domestic firm. Even when a new FDI firm is established through a merger with or acquisition of a domestic multinational firm, the new network would be enlarged. In this latter case the counteracting force is that headquarters decisions move out of the host country.

The network in which an FDI firm is an integral part could also make the firm more productive and innovative, with sales that to a large extent are based on product innovations. When the latter is the case, novelties will penetrate the local economy.

It has been conjectured that the establishment of an FDI firm in an economic environment brings novelties to the local economy (Aitken et al., 1996). These novelties can be in the form of new production techniques, new products and new market networks, and the novelties may as a consequence improve productivity and profitability in the local economy (Keller, 2004). The FDI firms may be more productive than the existing average firm. In addition, they may influence the environment in several other ways, such as delivering inputs with better quality and higher performance characteristics to local firms. They may also stimulate product development among local firms when they act as input customers. In addition they may, in a less direct way, diffuse technology to the local milieu of firms.

There are clear reasons to contemplate the influence that FDI firms can have in their local economic environment. Normally they belong to large multinational concerns with extensive R&D programmes. In recent times a lot of their innovation activities have become decentralized to subsidiaries abroad, that is, to FDI firms. Kuemmerle (1999) reports for five Organisation for Economic Co-operation and Development (OECD) countries how the share of R&D carried out outside the firm's home country increased from 6.2 percent in 1965 to almost 26 percent in 1995. Similar observations can be found in Zander (1994) and Cantwell (1998).

Obviously, FDI firms are gradually becoming more R&D-intensive in their own right. The effect of this can be an impulse to innovations and economic renewal in the region where an FDI firm locates and in the pertinent country. In a previous paper the authors examine how multinational firms influence innovation activities in a set of Swedish geographical areas (Johansson et al., 2005). In that study a careful distinction is made between effects on the innovation behavior that are associated with: (1) different attributes of a firm; and (2) any additional region-specific characteristic. The outcome is that there are certain additional regional effects (see also Ebersberger and Lööf, 2005).

The present study employs basically the same data set (2086 firms) for Sweden as in Johansson et al. (2005), but now with a specific focus on FDI firms. Sweden is divided into three geographical areas: Stockholm, West Sweden and the rest of Sweden. The difference in sample sizes is explained by a merger of Community Innovation Survey (CIS) data and register data in Johansson et al., which had the negative consequence that 170 observations had no matching observations in the register data. The first of these geographical areas can be classified as a proper functional (metropolitan) region with proximity externalities; the second contains a metropolitan region but comprises also other functional regions; and the third area (rest of Sweden) provides a base for reference. The chapter contributes to existing knowledge by systematically comparing FDI firms with other corporate structure classifications. It should be observed that the study comprises firms in both manufacturing and service industries.

In the empirical analysis and econometric models we investigate the R&D and knowledge intensity, sector and size distribution, and a series of innovation characteristics of FDI firms, while controlling for location. Moreover, the interaction of FDI firms with local innovation systems is investigated as well as the relative importance of FDI inflows for the establishment of new firms. Especially, we compare FDI firms with other categories of firms with regard to innovation results, type of innovation and methods to privatize the knowledge assets that FDI firms build up. In the analysis of the regional economic milieu and how FDI firms affect this, we primarily employ descriptive statistics to compare the Stockholm metropolitan region with the other two geographical areas.

Section 14.2 presents an overview of how FDI flows have developed internationally and for Sweden. It reviews existing theories of FDI incentives and the effects of FDI decisions. The section also provides a discussion of the role that FDI firms can play with regard to technology transfers and knowledge flows.

Section 14.3 presents the data source of the study and specifies the different variables that are used in the analyses. On the basis of descriptive statistics, the section continues by examining how FDI firm characteristics vary across regions and how FDI firms in general differ from other firms in the Swedish economy.

In section 14.4 we carry out a series of regression analyses. The tool is a two-step probit model, with results that allow for more precise conclusions than in section 14.3. The econometric analysis is followed up by a

Table 14.1 Development of FDI-firm activities in Sweden 1995 and 2001

FDI firms' role in Sweden	1995	2001
FDI firms' share of manufacturing output	20.7%	33.9%
FDI firms' share of total R&D investments	20.7%	40.7%
FDI firms' share R&D man-years	20.1%	40.3%
Number of FDI firms	3300	7800

Source: ITPS (2005a).

matching approach in section 14.5, where FDI firms are systematically compared with non-affiliate, uninational and domestic multinational firms. Section 14.6 contains concluding remarks, including a discussion of Swedish innovation policy in view of FDI inflows.

14.2 POTENTIAL ECONOMIC IMPACTS OF FDI

14.2.1 FDI, Globalization and the Swedish Economy

Since 1990 the worldwide production in firms located outside the owner's country of residence has increased from 6 to 11 percent of world output (UNCTAD, 2002). The increase in Sweden has also been large, as recorded in Table 14.1.

In 2001 a considerable share of manufacturing output in Sweden had FDI firms as a source, and more than 40 percent of all R&D efforts in Sweden took place in FDI firms. The growth in the number of FDI firms between 1995 and 2001 was also considerable, and signals that the domestic economy of Sweden is strongly integrated in the global economy. The latter is accentuated if we add that more than 50 percent of the private employment in Sweden can be found in foreign and domestic multinationals. Data for 2003 show that around half of the export from Sweden originated from FDI firms and the corresponding figure for imports to Sweden was 59 percent (ITPS, 2005b). This latter observation implies that on average FDI firms have a higher export and import intensity than domestic firms.

FDI in OECD countries like Sweden have primarily the form of acquisitions, where foreign multinationals expand their network of production, sales and R&D units and locate them as FDI firms across a set of countries (Lipsey, 2002). In Sweden the globalization of multinational enterprise (MNE) networks is reflected by a change from 3300 foreign-owned firms in the middle of the 1990s to 7800 in the beginning of the 2000s.

The described development is not particular for Sweden. Around 90 percent of the global FDI stock in 2003 was owned by OECD multinationals, and more than 70 percent of the FDI flows were directed towards OECD countries (UNCTAD, 2004). All this reflects a global network formation for business decisions and knowledge flows. Obviously, this will have an impact on how the international economy will function and develop. But what is the impact on technology diffusion and development in the Swedish economy and its different regions?

14.2.2 FDI Incentives and Consequences

What are the motives of a firm that decides to make a foreign direct investment? An answer to this question is provided in the ownership, location and internalization (OLI) framework, as suggested by Dunning (1977). In this framework an FDI firm tries to exploit three advantages simultaneously, namely ownership, location and internalization advantages. An ownership advantage is based on firm-specific assets that may spring from innovations in the form of successful products and superior production techniques, but also knowledge and skill assets of the firm.

Internalization of a firm's proprietary assets is essential, since it represents a way to increase the potential returns to the firm-specific assets. Internalization means that the firm keeps control of the use of its assets by establishing firm units in many locations, thereby capturing a larger economic rent based on its assets. When such locations are in other countries, the firm is multinational.

In addition there should be something to gain from establishing a facility in a specific location – in another country. In the OLI context the facility may be a production unit or a subsidiary firm that organizes the contact with the local market (market motive). The incentive to locate a production unit could be that the selected location can offer superior or cheaper resources (resource motive).

The above framework is often interpreted in a static and narrow way, disregarding that a firm is not only a supplier and producer, buying inputs, producing and selling its output. Potentially a firm is also carrying out development and innovation activities, which may lead to changes in output attributes, new routines of production and distribution and design of interaction patterns with new customers (Johansson, 2005).

In the recent literature on FDI firms the perspective is different from the focus in the OLI model. The shift in perspective is an increased interest in technology transfer associated with the establishment of FDI firms, as well as the knowledge base and productivity of these firms. Elements of this new focus go all the way back to Dosi (1988), Porter (1990) and

Nelson (1992), and in this context the conjecture is that FDI firms can be an important part of the local innovation systems of a region, and that they can enrich the regional innovation processes through a local diffusion of knowledge flows that spring from their own global networks. These aspects are emphasized in Jaffe et al. (1993), Audretsch and Feldman (1996), Kuemmerle (1999) and Cantwell and Janne (1999).

We have seen in Table 14.1 that FDI firms in Sweden carry out a fair amount of the R&D investments in Sweden. Still, there are clear empirical indications saying that multinational firms are reluctant to reallocate their R&D operations to their FDI firms. The latter are more often used in production, sales activities and marketing. The majority of R&D seems to stay in the home country of each multinational firm (Narula, 2002). Contributions by Freeman (1992), Ehrnberg and Jacobsson (1997) and Narula (2002) argue that this can be explained by each firm's embeddedness in innovation systems at home.

14.2.3 FDI, Technology Transfers and Knowledge Flows

This study aims at examining whether the location of an FDI firm in an urban region adds new features to the region. We must then ask: what features are particular to an FDI firm? As an instrument for this discussion we will make use of the distinction between proximity externalities, and network (or link) externalities (Johansson, 2005). In view of this we observe that urban proximity means that firms can benefit from mutual proximity and that makes the costs of distance-sensitive transactions lower and reduces costs of all sorts of interaction. Hence, it affects how firms can interact via the market and how they can influence each other outside the market with regard to non-pecuniary information and knowledge flows.

The proximity-based reduction of transaction costs generates an externality that affects both the input and output sides of a firm. In the absence of proximity, two interacting firms can make a joint link investment that can help to reduce transaction and other interaction costs also over long distances (Johansson and Quigley, 2004). Such link investments are in general economically sound only when a transaction link is used frequently. At the same time we observe that economic links between firms are easier (less costly) to establish between firms that are located in the same functional region, again due to lower interaction costs.

A multinational firm is different from other firms, because it consists of a mother firm and a set of interlinked FDI firms. At the same time, the location of each FDI firm is based on a decision to make use of proximity externalities in the regional milieu where it is placed. This feature of combining proximity and link externalities has implications for the supply activities of the FDI firm. However, there should also be consequences with regard to the firm's development activities.

The foreign multinational firm decides to place an FDI firm in a particular location, because it expects to gain something by being in that region. The performance of supply activities may improve due to interaction with input suppliers and customers in the local context. In addition, such interaction may generate pure knowledge spillovers but also stimulate joint R&D efforts.

In view of the last observation, the FDI firm may also gain advantages related to its development activities. The firm may gain from information about: (1) preferences and technology of local customers; (2) technology of competitors as well as input suppliers; and (3) R&D efforts of competitors, input suppliers and customers. An FDI firm may also benefit from pure knowledge spillovers from the innovation systems in the regional milieu (Johansson, 2005). One may conjecture that these flows of information and knowledge that occur in a regional context may cover information with relevance for the entire country to which the region belongs.

Having made all these observations, there are additional and important questions. Do the firms in a region benefit from getting an FDI firm as a neighbor? Are there positive feedbacks from the FDI firm to the innovation and development processes of the existing firms in the region (and country)? What are the reasons for asking this kind of question? First, an FDI firm may get involved in knowledge transactions with actors in its location. Second, in the course of its interaction with suppliers, customers and knowledge providers, the firm could benefit from (non-pecuniary or pure) knowledge spillovers. Third, the FDI firm can bring novelties into the local economy by bringing demand for new product attributes into the local market place as well as supplying equipment and services with new attributes.

In this study the first two aspects will be elucidated by examining a set of FDI firm characteristics and comparing them with the characteristics of three different categories of host-country firms: non-affiliate firms (single-establishment firms), uninational firms (multi-establishment firms that are not multinational) and domestic multinationals. By matching the FDI firms against these three categories of firms, it becomes possible to reveal to what extent the FDI firms bring novelties into the economy. The matching analysis will comprise comparisons of the following set of innovation activity attributes:

- Introduction of new firms (newly established).
- Scientific collaboration within the innovation system.
- Vertical collaboration within the innovation system.

- Horizontal collaboration within the innovation system.
- Collaboration in global innovation networks.
- Orientation towards product innovation.
- Orientation towards process innovation.
- Innovation that is novel (non-imitation) in nature.
- R&D intensity.
- Innovation sales, that is, sales of new products.

14.3 THE ROLE OF FDI FIRMS IN THE SWEDISH ECONOMY

14.3.1 Data Sources for the Empirical Analysis

This study uses data from the Community Innovation Survey (CIS) III for Sweden. The survey was conducted in 2001 and it covers the period 1998–2000. The observations cover both the manufacturing and business services sector. The sample contains 2086 firms, of which half are identified as innovative firms.

The CIS allows for broad comparisons across firms and countries. However, its usefulness in analyses of regional aspects is somewhat limited. Firms are for instance not asked to report on the proximity of their domestic collaboration on innovation with external partners. The reporting units are firms, whose geographical locations are known, but R&D and production activities in establishments located in other geographical areas will also be included in the data that refer to the reporting unit. In order to reduce – but not eliminate – these problems, we have disaggregated the Swedish economy into three large regional areas. In addition, we have assumed that the firms' establishments as well as their collaboration in innovation processes mostly are limited to the same geographical areas as the reporting firm.

14.3.2 Variable Description

In the analysis we employ the selection variable 'innovative firms' which refers to firms that report one or several of the following events during the most recent three-year period: product innovation, process innovation and innovation efforts. The study considers five different categories of innovation characteristics. For each category, the study explores its relationships to a set of determinants. The five categories of characteristics are defined as follows: (1) innovation input measures the firms' expenditures on R&D and other innovation activities per employee; (2) embeddedness in the domestic science base is a composite dummy variable indicating if the firm is collaborating with universities, and private and public R&D laboratories; (3) embeddedness in the domestic vertical innovation system is a composite variable indicating whether the firms collaborate on innovation with customers and suppliers; and (4) embeddedness in the domestic horizontal innovation system is supposed to capture a firm's collaboration on innovation with competitors or consultancies. The fifth category, (5) global innovation network, refers to innovation collaboration with actors outside Sweden.

The study makes use of two different measures of the firms' output performance. The first is non-imitation innovations, which is a dummy variable that indicates whether a firm has introduced a product which is partly or completely new to the market. The second measure is innovation sales, that is, sales revenue from new products. The innovation sales variable is expressed in intensity terms (per employee).

Findings by Kuemmerle (1999), Criscuolo et al. (2002), Ebersberger and Lööf (2005) and others indicate that corporate structure has an influence on innovative activities and location. In our study FDI firms are separated from firms with other corporate structure and compared with non-affiliate enterprises (firms not belonging to a group), uninational enterprises (firms belonging to a group with only domestic affiliates) and domestic multinationals.

The main firm characteristics in the study are firm size, human capital (university educated/total employment), physical capital, knowledge capital (current and recurrent R&D), product and process innovation. In addition a firm can be newly established, but also the result of a merger or an acquisition. In order to control for industry-specific factors, six sector dummies are included in the analysis, as well as information about the firm's most significant market (local, national or global). The variable list is presented in the Appendix (Table A14.1).

In the empirical analysis we examine the role of FDI firms across corporate structure and across geographical areas. The spatial decomposition of the Swedish territory is described in Table 14.2. This specification allows us to control for firm location and to detect whether the Stockholm region affects innovativeness in any particular way.

The first region corresponds to the Stockholm metropolitan region, whereas West Sweden includes both the Gothenburg metropolitan region and three other medium-sized urban regions. The area 'Rest of Sweden' is used as a reference area for comparisons.

In the matching processes we employ additional information that is not included in Table A14.1. The new information classifies protection methods that each firm uses as means to keep its intellectual property

Table 14.2 The three geographical areas in the study

Region	Definition
Stockholm	Stockholm county
West Sweden	Västra Götaland and Halland counties
Rest of Sweden	All remaining counties

Table 14.3 Distribution of corporate structures in the sample of the study (number of firms)

Corporate structure	Stockholm	West Sweden	Rest of Sweden	Total
Non-affiliate	194	197	498	889
Uninational	179	138	335	752
Domestic MNE	21	13	28	62
FDI firms	194	197	498	889
All firms	523	416	1148	2086

secret or private. These protection methods include: (1) patent applications; (2) patent possessions; (3) registration of patented design; (4) copyright; (5) secrecy; (6) complexity of design; and (7) lead-time advantage.

As a final overview information we present in Table 14.3 the distribution of corporate structures across regions. The table shows how the firms in the sample are distributed, and we may conclude that the sample has a fairly proportional distribution with regard to corporate structure. The only exception is the overrepresentation of domestic MNEs in the Stockholm region.

14.3.3 Spatial Distribution of Technology Groups and Knowledge Intensity

The main objective of this subsection is to examine how the Stockholm region differs from the other two geographical areas in Sweden. We will investigate the distribution across the three areas with regard to the size of firms, the number of firms in different sectors, knowledge and R&D intensity of firms, the frequency of newly established firms, and the intensity of innovation-system collaboration.

This type of examination will partly reveal to what extent the Stockholm region offers FDI firms and firms in general another type of economic milieu than the other parts of Sweden. In simple terms: can FDI firms benefit more from a location in Stockholm and, reciprocally, can the

Table 14.4 Share of firms in different sectors and firm entry across regions in the sample

Sector groups and entry	Stockholm	West Sweden	Rest of Sweden	Total
High-tech manufacturing	32.5	15.9	51.6	100
High–medium-tech manuf.	11.8	22.7	65.5	100
Low–medium-tech manuf.	9.4	16.9	73.7	100
Low-tech manufacturing	14.9	23.9	61.2	100
Knowl.-intense services	51.7	14.7	33.6	100
Other services	29.2	22.1	48.7	100
Newly established firms	43.5	18.4	38.1	100
All firms	25.0	19.9	55.1	100

Stockholm region benefit more than other regions from FDI inflows? Inspecting these descriptive statistics generates information about the need to control for firm location when we proceed to the econometric analyses in subsequent sections.

As regards the size of firms, there is only one spatial characteristic. Measuring the number of persons employed, Swedish multinationals in the Stockholm region are larger than elsewhere in the country. The distribution of industry sectors is on the other hand quite particular in Stockholm, with a composition that reveals higher knowledge intensity than elsewhere. This is illustrated in Table 14.4, where we can detect a disproportionately high share of high-tech manufacturing and knowledge-intensive services. In addition, the firm entry is much higher in the Stockholm region, measured as the share of newly established firms.

The analysis indicates strongly that the Stockholm region is a more knowledge-oriented economic milieu than other parts of Sweden. This feature can be further demonstrated by examining the set of innovative firms across regions. These firms have positive R&D expenditures, have introduced new products or carried out process innovations.

Table 14.5 shows that the Stockholm region has a high share of the employment with university education (human capital), a comparatively high R&D intensity (R&D expenditures per employee), and a high ratio of innovation sales to total sales.

Table 14.5 Characteristics of innovative firms in the sample across regions

	Stockholm	West Sweden	Rest of Sweden
Human capital	29.5	18.5	15.0
R&D staff	8.9	7.2	6.0
R&D intensity	11.5	7.4	7.9

Table 14.6 Share of firms in different sectors across corporate structure in the sample

Sector groups	Non-affiliate	Uni-national	Swedish MNEs	FDI firms	Total
High-tech manufacturing	38.1	34.1	7.1	20.6	100
High–medium-tech manuf.	30.7	34.5	6.6	28.2	100
Low–medium-tech manuf.	43.8	35.7	2.6	17.9	100
Low-tech manufacturing	49.6	36.9	1.3	10.1	100
Knowl.-intense services	46.6	33.3	3.0	17.0	100
Other services	41.1	40.1	0.7	18.0	100
All firms	42.6	36.0	3.0	18.4	100

An examination of how firms collaborate in the innovation systems shows that the distribution is roughly the same across regions. In summary we have seen that compared with other parts of Sweden, Stockholm is more knowledge-intensive, has a higher R&D intensity and has a higher entry rate of new firms. All this tells us that it is important to control for location in the econometric work in subsequent sections.

14.3.4 Comparison of FDI Firms with Other Firms

In this section we start to compare FDI firms with other types of firms with regard to a technology classification of sectors and with regard to firm entry for all firms, including those classified as non-innovative. Thereafter the comparison is between innovative firms, classified with regard to corporate structure.

Table 14.6 shows that FDI firms have a disproportionately high

Table 14.7 Entry and innovativeness across corporate structure in the sample (share of firms)

	Non-affiliate	Uni-national	Swedish MNEs	FDI firms	Total
Newly established	32.7	40.1	4.1	23.1	100
M&A	28.8	46.6	2.4	22.1	100
Innovative firms	35.5	35.9	5.8	23.2	100
All firms	42.6	36.0	3.0	18.4	100

Table 14.8 Knowledge and R&D intensity and innovation sales across innovative firms

	Non-affiliate	Uni-national	Swedish MNEs	FDI firms
Human capital	21.2	19.1	21.1	18.0
R&D staff	6.5	6.1	18.1	6.5
R&D intensity	9.8	8.4	15.0	6.2
Share of innovative sales	17.4	15.2	23.9	18.7

representation of high-medium-technology manufacturing and a contrasting low share of low-technology manufacturing. Hence, they differ from Swedish multinationals, which in particular are characterized by a high share of high-technology manufacturing. Hence, the observations in Table 14.6 imply that our subsequent econometric exercises should control for sector. We also observe that non-affiliate firms have a disproportionately high share of knowledge-intensive producer services.

The second type of questions asked relate to how firms are established and whether they are classified as innovative. Table 14.7 shows that FDI firms are characterized by a larger than proportional entry rate. They are also established through merger and acquisition more often than proportionately. Finally, they are classified as innovative at a higher than proportional rate.

If we limit the description to the subset of innovative firms, we can conclude that FDI firms are slightly less knowledge-intensive than other firms, have a lower R&D intensity than other firms, but have a slightly higher share of innovation sales than non-affiliate and uninational firms. All this is illustrated in Table 14.8.

Having described the knowledge and R&D intensity of FDI firms, we

Table 14.9 Collaboration within the innovation systems, across types of innovative firms

	Non-affiliate	Uni-national	Swe. MNEs	FDI firms
Scientific IS	17.5	17.9	63.3	29.8
Vertical IS	25.4	23.4	82.2	34.6
Horizontal IS	17.7	18.4	54.8	24.5
Global IS	16.1	16.1	82.2	35.9

Table 14.10 Type of innovation and knowledge protection measures across innovative firms

	Non-affiliate	Uni-national	Swe. MNE	FDI firms	Total
Product innovation	34.9	31.9	7.9	25.3	100
Process innovation	35.9	34.1	7.0	23.1	100
Non-imitation innov.	37.8	28.5	9.8	24.0	100
Patent application	21.3	30.9	13.4	34.4	100
Patent possession	20.9	30.8	11.3	36.6	100
Trade mark	26.0	32.5	9.4	32.1	100
Secrecy	26.1	31.6	12.9	29.4	100
Lead-time advantage	29.3	33.2	10.0	27.5	100
All firms	35.2	35.9	5.8	23.2	100

may consider their collaboration with actors in the scientific, vertical, horizontal and global innovation systems (IS). Descriptive statistics in this case indicate that FDI firms collaborate more intensively than non-affiliate and uninational firms, but less than domestic multinationals. Swedish multinationals are characterized by having a much higher collaboration share than all other categories. This conclusion is especially clear with regard to vertical and global innovation interaction (Table 14.9).

Table 14.10 reveals that there is no bias among FDI firms with regard to the share of product and process innovations, and non-imitation innovations. However, among FDI firms there is a higher degree of knowledge protection than among non-affiliate and uninational firms. The highest share of firms with knowledge protection is found for Swedish MNEs.

14.4 ECONOMETRIC ANALYSES OF INNOVATIVE FDI FIRMS

14.4.1 Estimation Model

Section 14.4 analyzes how the innovation behavior of firms is affected by their corporate structure, which provides a comparison between FDI firms and other categories of firms. We use an econometric model as a means to control for region, sector and the distinction between firms that are innovation active and those that are not. The additional determinants are corporate structure and firm characteristics. As a tool we apply a two-step estimation procedure, with a generalized Tobit model, comprising the selection equation (14.1) and a performance equation (14.2). This model is consistently estimated by means of full maximum likelihood techniques, using observations on both innovative and non-innovative firms.

The estimation procedure aims to solve the econometric problem of selection bias. Our approach takes into account that not all firms are engaged in innovative activities. When only the innovation sample is used in some part of the model, the firms are not randomly drawn from the larger population, and selection bias may arise. The two-step model used in the analyses accounts for this possible problem by formulating the following choice structure. In the first step firms decide whether to engage in innovation activities or not (selection equation). Given that a firm has decided to invest in innovation projects, the eight different performance variables are estimated. More specifically, we are using the following model:

$$y_{0i} = \begin{cases} 1 & \text{if} \quad y_{0i}^* = X_{0i}\beta_0 + \varepsilon_{0i} > 0 \\ 0 & \text{if} \quad y_{0i}^* = X_{0i}\beta_0 + \varepsilon_{0i} \leq 0 \end{cases} \tag{14.1}$$

$$y_{1i} = y_{1i}^* = X_{1i}\beta_1 + \varepsilon_{1i} \ \text{if} \ y_{0i} = 1 \tag{14.2}$$

where y_{0i}^* is a latent innovation decision variable measuring the propensity to innovate, y_{0i} is the corresponding observed binary variable, being 1 for innovative firms and zero for others. y_{1i} signifies the eight performance variables. X_{0i} and X_{1i} are vectors of various variables explaining innovation decision and innovation performance. The β-vectors contain the unknown parameters for each equation. ε_{0i} and ε_{1i} are independent and identically distributed drawings from a normal distribution with zero mean, jointly correlated.

In the next two subsections we present results based on eight regression equations. For all these cases, the selection equation shows that the probability of being an innovative firm is positively influenced in a clearly significant way (1 percent) by: (1) firm size; (2) sales per employee; (3) merger and acquisition; (4) knowledge intensity; (5) national and global market extension. All together, the selection equation has 14 determinants.

14.4.2 Innovation Behavior

In this subsection we analyze variables that affect an individual firm with regard to R&D intensity and collaboration in the scientific, vertical and horizontal information systems. Results from these regressions are specified in Table 14.11.

The R&D intensity may be considered as the most important indicator here, since we want to know if FDI firms add to the local R&D intensity. Most of the results are straightforward. The sector classification has a significant impact. Moreover, the R&D intensity is positively influenced by persistent R&D and process innovation, and negatively by firm size. There is no region-specific effect. Finally, corporate structure has an effect: all other things equal, Swedish multinationals have a higher R&D intensity and FDI firms do not.

Another way that FDI firms can fuel the innovation processes in the local economy is by participating actively in the various innovation systems. Our reference is the innovation system participation of uninational firms. Everything else being equal, Swedish multinationals interact with higher frequency with actors in all three innovation systems (scientific, vertical and horizontal). With regard to the vertical innovation system, the parameter for FDI firms is positive and significant. So is the parameter for non-affiliate firms.

The conclusion is that our regression model cannot detect any strong indication of specific effects from FDI inflows on R&D intensity and on innovation system activities, except for vertical innovation collaboration, where FDI firms are more likely to collaborate than uninational firms.

14.4.3 Type of Innovation and Returns to Innovation Efforts

So far we have seen that FDI firms do not seem to intensify the interaction within the scientific and horizontal innovations networks in Sweden. And FDI firms are not more FDI-intensive than non-affiliate and uninational firms. FDI firms might influence innovation processes by having more product innovations or more process innovations than other firms. Regression equations (14.5) and (14.6) in Table 14.12 provide answers to this latter question.

Table 14.11 R&D and innovation activities of firms, regression results

Equation Description	(1)		(2)		(3)		(4)	
	R&D intensity, log		Collaboration within scientific IS		Collaboration within vertical IS		Collaboration in horizontal IS	
	Coeff	St. err.	Coeff	St. err.	Coeff	St. err.	Coeff	St. err.
Corp Struct.								
Swedish MNE	0.852***	0.231	0.915***	0.200	1.298***	0.208	0.620***	0.184
FDI firms	0.120	0.132	0.190	0.126	0.229**	0.116	0.097	0.118
Non-affiliate	−0.122	0.117	0.239**	0.121	0.215**	0.109	0.153	0.112
Uninational	Ref		Ref		Ref		Ref	
Regions								
Stockholm	0.082	0.122	−0.392**	0.126	−0.250**	0.113	−0.129	0.114
West Sweden	−0.064	0.128	0.074	0.124	−0.037	0.116	0.048	0.116
Rest of Sweden	Ref		Ref		Ref		Ref	
Firm attributes								
Newly establ.	−0.149	0.206	−0.089	0.194	0.151	0.169	0.017	0.175
Merger & acq.	−0.254	0.164	−0.333**	0.148	0.039	0.134	0.261	0.129
R&D inv /empl.			0.129***	0.033	0.114***	0.028	0.119***	0.028
Persistent R&D	1.132***	0.108	0.736***	0.127	0.636***	0.101	0.608***	0.105
Process innov.	0.214**	0.097	0.204**	0.096	0.244***	0.088	0.193**	0.090
Employm log	−0.409***	0.040	0.203***	0.050	0.111***	0.040	0.180***	0.036

Sector dumm.								
High-tech	0.555**	0.224	0.235	0.206	0.169	0.190	0.029	0.198
High–medium	0.336**	0.170	−0.175	0.159	−0.103	0.148	−0.093	0.151
Medium–low	0.213	0.178	0.092	0.165	−0.015	0.149	0.022	0.154
Knowl. services	1.083***	0.168	0.248	0.162	0.159	0.144	0.140	0.147
Other services	1.007***	0.186	−0.021	0.204	−0.015	0.175	0.011	0.179
Low-tech	Ref		Ref		Ref		Ref	
Intercept	2.658***	0.266	−2.281***	0.477	1.949***	0.340	−2.630***	0.266
Log likelihood	3253		1692		1808		1740	
Wald chi-square	277		94		161		168	

Notes:
Significant at the <1% (***), <5%(**) and (*) <10% level of significance.
Six sector dummies are included, where low-technology manufacturing is used as reference.
Number of observations is 2086, with 1015 censored observations.

Table 14.12 Type of innovation and innovation output, regression results

Equation Description	(14.5) Product innovation		(14.6) Process innovation		(14.7) Non-imitation innovation		(14.8) Innovation sales	
	Coeff	St. err.	Coeff	St. err.	Coeff	St. err.	Coeff	St. err.
Corp Struct.								
Swedish MNE	0.970***	0.247	0.220	0.185	0.683***	0.184	0.650**	0.270
FDI firms	0.325***	0.112	0.044	0.106	0.215*	0.110	0.530***	0.147
Non-affiliate	0.252***	0.097	0.199**	0.095	0.325***	0.100	0.252**	0.127
Uninational	Ref		Ref		Ref		Ref	
Regions								
Stockholm	0.240**	0.105	0.121	0.099	0.095	0.102	0.489***	0.130
West Sweden	0.149	0.108	−0.053	0.104	0.154	0.107	0.237*	0.137
Rest of Sweden	Ref		Ref		Ref		Ref	
Firm attributes								
Newly establ.	−0.153	0.155	0.072	0.152	0.243	0.154	−0.254	0.257
Merger & acq.	0.100	0.130	0.333***	0.122	−0.002	0.127	0.120	0.211
R&D inv /empl.	0.027	0.026	0.057**	0.025	0.064**	0.026	0.140***	0.033
Persistent R&D	0.399***	0.098	−0.072	0.092	0.461	0.098	0.176	0.131
Process innov.	−0.115	0.081			0.239***	0.082	0.053	0.104
Employm. log	−0.044	0.038	0.131***	0.036	−0.074	0.037	−0.360***	0.055

Sector dumm.								
High-tech	0.069	0.187	−0.240	0.177	0.297	0.181	−0.588**	0.289
High–medium	−0.006	0.132	−0.116	0.128	−0.107	0.133	−0.144	0.211
Medium–low	0.045	0.136	0.039	0.132	0.161	0.137	−0.359	0.220
Knowl. services	0.090	0.132	−0.017	0.128	0.078	0.134	−0.319	0.209
Other services	0.040	0.152	−0.039	0.151	0.021	0.158	0.795***	0.234
Low-tech	Ref		Ref		Ref		Ref	
Intercept	0.329	0.322	−0.791**	0.311	−0.655*	0.337	4.578***	0.417
Log likelihood	1890		1980		1909		3380	
Wald chi-square	55		38		84		156	

Notes:
Significant at the <1% (***), <5%(**) and (*) <10% level of significance.
Six sector dummies are included, where low technology manufacturing is used as reference.
Number of observations is 2086, with 1015 censored observations.

With regard to product innovations we find that FDI firms, Swedish multinationals and non-affiliate firms all have more frequent product innovations than uninational firms, as indicated by equation (14.5). In addition, the probability of product innovations is higher in the Stockholm region than elsewhere in Sweden.

Turning to process innovations, FDI firms are not associated with a higher innovation probability. Instead, non-affiliate firms represent the only corporate structure with a positive and significant parameter, as shown in equation (14.6).

A third issue is the probability of generating non-imitation innovations. Equation (14.7) in Table 14.12 shows the regression result for non-imitation innovations (radical innovations). High and very significant parameters are found for Swedish multinationals and non-affiliate firms. For FDI firms the parameter is significant at the 10 percent level, which indicates that they are more likely to have non-imitation innovations than uninational firms.

The last equation (14.8) in Table 14.12 reflects how innovation sales are determined by our explanatory variables. In this case we find that FDI firms come out with a positive result. For FDI firms, the parameter estimate indicates that innovation sales are significantly larger than for uninational firms at a 1 percent level. At a 5 percent level Swedish multinationals and non-affiliate firms also appear to be superior to the uninational firms. We may also note that the parameter values are higher for FDI firms and domestic multinationals, and this may reflect that these two categories can base their sales success on innovation efforts in their entire multi-country network.

14.5 A MATCHING ANALYSIS OF FDI FIRMS

14.5.1 Nearest Neighbor Matching Method

Section 14.4 presents results based on parametric selection equations. In order to investigate the robustness of the results from these selection equations, we apply in section 14.5 a semi-parametric matching approach. For each FDI firm, our matching estimators find a similar uninational, non-affiliate and Swedish MNE firm, respectively. In this way three sets of pairs are formed, where each FDI firm has a comparison 'partner'. When this is obtained we interpret the difference in their outcomes (attributes) as the effect of FDI ownership.

Methodologically, we rely on the Rosenbaum and Rubin (1983) 'propensity-score' matching. The matching estimation procedure that is employed can be described as follows. Initially a probit model is applied in order to estimate the propensity score for each observation. The dependent variable expresses whether the firm is an FDI firm or not. The vector of determinant variables contains the same set of characteristics as were employed in the selection equations in the previous section. After the determinants are identified and the probit model is estimated, a mono-dimensional propensity score is calculated for every observation. This measure is used to find counterfactuals for each FDI-firm.

In the next step we conduct a non-parametric matching approach based on the propensity score. Here the procedure is as follows. Firstly, the observations are separated with respect to their corporate ownership: that is, FDI firm or not. Secondly, an FDI firm *i* is selected. Thirdly, we utilize the propensity score and calculate a correct measure of distance to find the nearest neighbors or matched firms for each FDI firm. Finally, the impact of FDI firms is evaluated by comparing the average outcomes between the groups of FDI firms and non-FDI firms.

The literature (for example Smith, 2000) points out that nearest neighbor matching can be operated with more than one nearest neighbor and with or without replacements. The latter means that a given non-participant observation can form the counterfactual for more than one participant. In the subsequent analysis we use the two nearest neighbors. The main advantage of a large number of neighbors, compared to pair-wise matching, is a reduction in the variance of the estimators (Smith and Todd, 2004). Moreover, this method admits that observations without a sufficiently close neighbor are ignored.[1]

14.5.2 Matching FDI Firms against Other Corporate Structure

In section 14.3 we could see indications that FDI firms might bring novelties to the local economy in Sweden. The approach in section 14.4 represents a more controlled way of detecting such signs. However, the regression results in that section do not convince us that FDI firms bring new features into the innovation process in the local economy. In the subsequent analysis we compare FDI firms systematically with uninational firms, non-affiliate firms and Swedish multinationals, using the matching approach described in subsection 14.5.1 above.

Table 14.13 compares FDI firms and uninational firms with regard to mean values before and after matching. There is a set of significant differences between the two sets of firms. FDI firms collaborate more frequently in innovation networks with regard to all four innovation systems. In addition, they have larger innovation sales per employee. With lower significance value, FDI firms also are more R&D-intensive. Thus,

Table 14.13 Two sample t-test results. FDI-firms versus uninational firms

Variables	Before matching			Nearest neighbor matching		
	UNI	FDI	t-test value	UNI	FDI	t-test value
Observations	322	220		440	220	
Target variables						
Newly established	0.077	0.081	−0.175	0.050	0.081	−1.497
Human capital intensity	0.197	0.163	1.159	0.149	0.163	−0.712
Collaboration SIS	0.183	0.327***	−3.755	0.204	0.327***	−3.308
Collaboration VIS	0.238	0.368***	−3.197	0.252	0.368***	−3.000
Collaboration HIS	0.177	0.263**	−2.366	0.190	0.263**	−2.066
Global collaboration	0.164	0.381***	−5.592	0.220	0.381***	−4.209
Product innovation	0.624	0.722**	−2.428	0.609	0.722***	−2.976
Process innovation	0.484	0.518	−0.769	0.531	0.518	0.330
Non-imitation innov.	0.322	0.377	−1.296	0.325	0.377	−1.318
R&D intensity	1.212	1.409	−1.322	1.172	1.409*	−1.650
Innovation sales	1.519	2.418***	−3.553	1.990	2.418***	−2.680

Note: Significance is marked as *** for the 1% level, ** for the 5% level and * for the 10% level.

compared with uninational firms, FDI firms should be expected to enrich the local innovation processes. In particular, we observe that the product innovation value is higher in a significant way for FDI firms. At the same time, the matched uninational firms do not have a lower value for process innovations.

Table 14.14 compares FDI firms with non-affiliate firms. The set of FDI firms contains both small and large firms, whereas small firms dominate the group of non-affiliate firms. This may affect the matching result. At the same time, we recall that the comparison is made only across innovative firms.

For the matched sets, we observe that the FDI firms have a higher mean value than non-affiliate firms in two regards: FDI firms have a higher

Table 14.14 Two sample t-test results. Non-affiliate firms versus FDI firms

Variables	Before matching			Nearest neighbor matching		
	Non-affil.	FDI	t-test value	Non-affil.	FDI	t-test value
Observations	322	220		440	210	
Target variables						
Newly established	0.062	0.081	−0.860	0.033	0.085**	−2.464
Human capital intensity	0.212	0.163**	2.207	0.251	0.167***	4.050
Collaboration SIS	0.192	0.327***	−3.490	0.307	0.309	−0.060
Collaboration VIS	0.263	0.368**	−2.551	0.300	0.362	−1.544
Collaboration HIS	0.186	0.263**	−2.091	0.290	0.257	0.889
Global collaboration	0.180	0.381***	−5.143	0.290	0.380**	−2.247
Product innovation	0.670	0.722	−1.296	0.807	0.714**	2.529
Process innovation	0.521	0.518	0.081	0.580	0.500*	1.920
Non-imitation innov.	0.406	0.377	0.692	0.530	0.376***	3.734
R&D intensity	1.148	1.409*	−1.894	1.211	1.352	−1.024
Innovation sales	2.019	2.418**	−2.495	2.927	2.355***	3.659

Note: Significance is marked as *** for the 1% level, ** for the 5% level and * for the 10% level.

proportion of newly established firms and they interact more frequently in global innovation networks. However, there are five characteristics for which we may think of non-affiliate firms as 'superior'. The latter have a higher score with regard to knowledge intensity, product innovation, process innovation, non-imitation innovation and innovation sales. These five observations imply that non-affiliate firms must be considered as an important component in a region's innovation milieu. We may also recall from Table 14.6 that non-affiliate firms comprise a high proportion of knowledge-intensive service suppliers and a high proportion of low-tech manufacturing. Firms in the latter group are to large extent non-innovative firms. Thus, the subset of innovative non-affiliate firms displays

Table 14.15 Two sample t-test results. Swedish multinationals versus FDI firms

Variables	Before matching			Nearest neighbor matching		
	FDI	SWE MNE	t-test value	FDI	SWE MNE	t-test value
Observations	220	59		114	57	
Target variables						
Newly established	0.081	0.101	−0.453	0.052	0.105	−1.142
Human capital intensity	0.163	0.222	−1.426	0.290	0.222	1.352
Collaboration SIS	0.327	0.694***	−5.385	0.473	0.684***	−2.703
Collaboration VIS	0.368	0.830***	−7.826	0.464	0.824***	−5.199
Collaboration HIS	0.263	0.542***	−3.878	0.412	0.526	−1.404
Global collaboration	0.263	0.542***	−3.878	0.508	0.842***	−4.492
Product innovation	0.722	0.915***	−4.056	0.824	0.912*	−1.685
Process innovation	0.518	0.610	−1.270	0.543	0.596	−0.653
Non-imitation innov.	0.377	0.627***	−3.497	0.570	0.631	−0.771
R&D intensity	1.409	2.282***	−3.618	1.663	2.215**	−2.061
Innovation sales	2.418	3.054**	−2.345	2.561	2.991	−1.535

features that correspond to an innovation profile that is superior to that of innovative FDI firms.

Overall these observations show that innovative non-affiliate firms form a group of knowledge- and technology-intensive firms. As can be seen from the table, several of these latter results are not present when comparing the two populations before matching.

Our final exercise is to compare Swedish multinational with FDI firms. The result of this comparison is presented in Table 14.15. We may first observe that before the two populations have been matched, the difference is greater than after matching. For example, after matching the statistical difference with regard to innovation sales per employees disappears.

After completed matching we can observe that FDI firms have a lower frequency than domestic multinationals with regard to innovation collaboration in scientific, vertical and global networks, and with regard to product innovations. In addition, FDI firms have lower R&D intensity. At a lower significance level, we may also observe a higher frequency of product innovations among the Swedish multinationals.

14.6 CONCLUSIONS

In the previous sections we have compared the FDI firms in Sweden with other firms with the help of parametric and non-parametric methods. What can we learn from these comparisons? First, our two methods do generate consistent results. In particular, both methods reveal that the group of uninational firms is different from the other three categories of corporate structures. Uninational firms are clearly less integrated than all other firms in all types of innovation collaboration. They are less active in generating both product and process innovation, and their frequency of non-imitation innovations is lower. This is the most robust finding from the statistical analyses.

What does the literature say about the effects that FDI firms have on the local economy in which they are integrated? According to the review in Lipsey (2002) and Ebersberger and Lööf (2004), a large number of studies report on empirical regularities that are relevant for this question. First, there is robust evidence that within countries, foreign-owned firms almost always pay higher wages than domestically owned firms. Second, foreign-owned firms generally have higher productivity than local firms. Third, the literature does not present any strong evidence of positive impacts from FDI firms on innovation activities and output. At best, we may say that the empirical information is mixed. Fourth, there is no unambiguous support for the idea that FDI firms should affect the growth rate positively in the local economy.

This study adds a small but important piece of information to the current knowledge by making the distinction between domestic multinationals, uninationals and non-affiliates in the analyses. In this way the existing statements in the literature can be qualified. Our result suggests that FDI firms may bring new elements into the innovation systems of the local economy through acquisitions of uninational firms.

Another finding, which should not be surprising, is that FDI firms are more active in global innovation networks than uninationals and non-affiliates. One should also observe that we have not included in our study the indirect effects that FDI firms may have by adding new patterns of demand for inputs of services and components, and by supplying new types of services and products as inputs into the production of domestic firms. We would need quite different data and methods to be able to illuminate this issue.

Finally, the study has an important by-product. The matching of non-affiliate firms against FDI firms reveals that the former have higher knowledge intensity; more product, process and non-imitation innovations; and larger innovation sales per employee. This result comes out in the matching process, but not if we just compare average values that are affected by the large share of low-tech industries among non-affiliate firms.

It seems worthwhile to investigate the non-affiliate firms further and let them be matched against all corporate structures. In such a study we may also consider how innovative non-affiliate firms are linked to multinationals, to what extent they are the result of spin-offs and similar dynamic processes, and in which industries their innovation performance is above average.

NOTE

1. For a more detailed description of the general methodology, see Heshmati and Lööf (2005).

REFERENCES

Aitken, B., and A. Harrison and R.E. Lipsey (1996), 'Wages and foreign ownership, a comparative study of Mexico, Venezuela and the United States', *Journal of International Economics*, **40**, 345–71.

Antras, P. and E. Helpman (2003), 'Global sourcing', NBER Working Paper No 10082.

Audretsch, D.B. and M.P. Feldman (1996), 'Knowledge spillovers and the geography of innovation and production', *American Economic Review*, **86**, 630–40.

Braunerhjelm, P. (1999), 'Knowledge capital, firm performance and network production', JIBS Dissertation Series No 004, Jönköping International Business School.

Cantwell, J. (1998), 'The globalisation of technology: what remains of the product-cycle model?' in A. Chandler, P. Hagström and Ö. Sölvell (eds), *The Dynamic Firm*, New York: Oxford University Press, pp. 263–88.

Cantwell, J. and O. Janne (1999), 'Technological globalisation and innovative centres: the role of corporate technological leadership and location hierarchy', *Research Policy*, **28**, 119–44.

Caves, R.E. (1982), *Multinational Enterprises and Economic Analysis*, Cambridge: Cambridge University Press.

Coase, R.H. (1937), 'The nature of the firm', *Economica*, **4**, 386–405.

Criscuolo, P., R. Narula and B. Verspagen (2002), 'The relative importance of home and host innovation systems in the internationalisation of MNE R&D: a patent citation analysis', Eindhoven Center for Innovation Studies (ECIS) Working Paper Series 02.20.

Dosi, G. (1988), 'The nature of the innovation process', in G. Dosi, C. Freeman, R. Nelson, G. Silverberg and C. Soete (eds), *Technical Change and Economic Theory*, London: Frances Piter Publishers, pp. 221–338.

Dunning, J. (1977), 'Trade, location of economic activity and the MNE: a search for an eclectic approach', in P.-O. Hesselborne, P.-M. Wijkman and B. Ohlin (eds), *The International Allocation of Economic Activity*, London: Macmillan, pp. 395–418.
Ebersberger, B. and H. Lööf (2004), 'Multinational enterprises, spillovers, innovation and productivity', CESIS Working Paper Series No 22.
Ebersberger, B. and H. Lööf (2005), 'Innovative behaviour and productivity performance in the Nordic region. Does ownership matter?' CESIS Working Paper Series No 27.
Ehrnberg, E. and S. Jacobsson (1997), 'Technological discontinuities and incumbents' performance: an analytical framework', in C. Edquist (ed.), *Systems of Innovation Technologies and Organisations*, London: Pinter Publishers, pp. 320–26.
Freeman, C. (1992), 'Formal scientific and technical institutions in the national system of innovation', in B. Lundvall (ed.), *National Systems of Innovation. Towards a Theory of Innovation and Interactive Learning*, London: Pinter Publishers, pp. 169–90.
Heshmati, Almas and Hans Lööf (2005), 'The impact of public funds on private R&D investment: new evidence from a firm level innovation study', Discussion Papers 11862, Jokioinen Finland: MTT Agrifood Research Finland.
ITPS (2005a), 'Utländska företag – ekonomiska uppgifter 2003' [Foreign-owned firms – Economic Data 2003], Swedish Institute for Growth Policy Analysis (ITPS), Stockholm.
ITPS (2005b), 'Den växande utlandskontrollen av ekonomierna I Norden' [The growing foreign control of the economies in the Nordic area], Swedish Institute for Growth Policy Analysis (ITPS), Stockholm.
Jaffe, A., M. Tratjenberg and R. Henderson (1993), 'Geographical localisation of knowledge spillovers as evidence by patent citations', *Quarterly Journal of Economics*, **108**, 577–99.
Johansson, B. (2005), 'Parsing the menagerie of agglomeration and network externalities', in C. Karlsson, B. Johansson and R.R. Stough (eds), *Industrial Cluster and Inter-Firm Networks*, Cheltenham, UK and Northampton, MA, USA: Edward Elgar.
Johansson, B., H. Lööf and A. Rader-Olsson (2005), 'Firm location, corporate structure, R&D investment, innovation and productivity', CESIS Working Paper Series, No 31.
Johansson, B. and J. Quigley (2004), 'Agglomeration and networks in spatial economies', *Papers of Regional Science*, **83**, 165–76.
Keller, W. (2004), 'International technology diffusing', *Journal of Economic Literature*, **42**, 752–82.
Kuemmerle, W. (1999), 'Foreign direct investment in industrial research in the pharmaceutical and electronic industries – results from a survey of multinational firms', *Research Policy*, **28**, 179–93.
Lipsey, R.E. (2002), 'Home and host country effects of FDI', NBER Working Paper No 9293.
Narula, R. (2002), 'Innovation systems and inertia in R&D location: Norwegian firms and the role of systemic lock-in', *Research Policy*, **31**, 795–816.
Nelson, R. (ed.) (1992), *National Innovation Systems: A Comparative Analysis*, Oxford: Oxford University Press.
Porter, M. (1990), *The Competitive Advantage of Nations*, London: McMillan.

Rosenbaum, P. and D. Rubin (1983), 'The central role of the propensity score in observational studies for causal effects', *Biometrica*, **70**, 41–55.
Smith, J. (2000), 'A critical survey of empirical methods for evaluating active labor market policies', *Zeitschrift für Volkswirtschaft und Statistik*, **136**, 1–22.
Smith, J. and P. Todd (2004), 'Does Matching Overcome Lalonde's Critique on Nonexperimental Estimators?' *Journal of Econometrics*, **125**(1–2), 305–53.
United Nations Conference on Trade and Development (UNCTAD) (2000), *World Investment Report, 2000*, New York, Geneva, USA and Switzerland: United Nations.
United Nations Conference on Trade and Development (UNCTAD) (2002), *World Investment Report 2002*, http://www.unctad.org.
United Nations Conference on Trade and Development (UNCTAD) (2004), *World Investment Report 2004*, http://www.unctad.org.
Zander, I. (1994), *The Tortoise Evolution of the Multinational Corporation-Foreign Technological Activity in Swedish Multinational Firms 1890–1990*, Stockholm: Institute of International Business.

APPENDIX

Table A14.1 Primary variables for the empirical analyses

Explanatory variables	Definition
Firm structure	
Non-affiliated enterprises	Domestically owned firms without affiliates
Uninational enterprises	Domestically owned firms belonging to a group with only Swedish affiliates
Domestic multinational enterprises	Domestically owned firms belonging to a group with foreign affiliates
FDI enterprises	Foreign-owned firms (belonging to a group) with foreign affiliates
Firm characteristics	
Size	Number of employees
Productivity	Turnover per employee
Human capital	Share of the employment with a university degree
Physical capital	Gross investment
Innovation input	Innovation expenditures (R&D intensity)
Persistent R&D	Dummy for continuous R&D engagement
Process innovation	Dummy variable indicating that a firm has introduced a new or significantly improved process
Non-imitation innovation	Dummy indicating that new products have been introduced
Newly established	The enterprise has been established during the last three years

Table A14.1 (continued)

Explanatory variables	Definition
Recent history of merging and acquisition	The enterprise has been involved in M&A during the last three years
Collaboration on innovation	
Embeddedness in the regional science base	Dummy indicating collaboration with universities and R&D laboratories
Embeddedness in the regional vertical innovation system	Dummy indicating innovation collaboration with customers or suppliers
Embeddedness in the regional horizontal innovation system	Dummy indicating innovation collaboration with competitors and consultants
Embeddedness in global innovation systems	Dummy indicating innovation collaboration in a cross-border network
Market	
Significant market area – local	The firms' most significant market
Significant market area – national	The firms' most significant market
Significant market area – global	The firms' most significant market
Sector	
High-technology manufacturing sector	Nace 353, Nace 2423, Nace, 30, Nace 32, Nace 33
Medium–high-technology manuf. sectors	Nace 24 excl Nace 2423, Nace 29, Nace 31, Nace 34, Nace 352, Nace 359
Medium–low-technology manuf. sectors	Nace 23, Nace 25, Nace 26, Nace 37, Nace 28, Nace 351, Nace 354
Low-technology manufacturing sectors	Nace 15, Nace 16, Nace 17, Nace 18, Nace 19, Nace 20, Nace 21, Nace 36, Nace 37
Knowledge-intensive services	Nace 64, Nace 65, Nace 66, Nace 67, Nace 71, Nace 72–74
Other services	Other services than knowledge-intensive services

Index